D0908264

UNCOVERING LIVES

UNCOVERING LIVES

The Uneasy Alliance of
Biography and Psychology

ALAN C. ELMS

OXFORD UNIVERSITY PRESS

New York   Oxford

1994

Oxford University Press

Oxford   New York   Toronto
Delhi   Bombay   Calcutta   Madras   Karachi
Kuala Lumpur   Singapore   Hong Kong   Tokyo
Nairobi   Dar es Salaam   Cape Town
Melbourne   Auckland   Madrid

and associated companies in
Berlin   Ibadan

Library of Congress Cataloging-in-Publication Data
Elms, Alan C., 1938–
Uncovering lives : the uneasy alliance of biography and psychology
/ Alan C. Elms.
p. cm.   Includes bibliographical references and index.
ISBN 0-19-508287-7
1. Psychology—Biographical methods.   2. Biography as a literary form.
3. Psychologists—Psychology—Case studies.
4. Politicians—Psychology—Case studies.
5. Authors—Psychology—Case studies.
I. Title.
BF39.4.E46   1994
920'.001'9—dc20   94-16699

2 4 6 8 9 7 5 3 1
Printed in the United States of America
on acid-free paper

Permissions

For Dee

ACKNOWLEDGMENTS

Many people helped me during the preparation of this book. Some are acknowledged in the appropriate chapters or in the endnotes. I want to give special thanks to those who read and commented on portions of the draft manuscript: Irving Alexander, James W. Anderson III, Deanna Evans-Schilling, Robert Hogan, Heather Kaiser, Lilah Koski, Karol Maybury, William McGuire, Gita Morena, Michael Robinson, Mary Rose, Eva Schepeler, William (Todd) Schultz, Sonu Shamdasani, Karen Sutton, plus members of the Bay Area Psychobiography Study Group, including Daniel Benveniste, James Breslin, Marilyn Fabe, Bruce Heller, Peter Ostwald, and Stephen Wallrod, and members of the Davis Writers' Group, including Karen Joy Fowler, Don Kochis, Debbie Smith, Kevin Mims, Nina Vasiliev, Sara Streich, Adam Bridge, Darcy Smith, Clinton Lawrence, and Cy. William McKinley ("Mac") Runyan read the entire manuscript and gave detailed feedback when it was most needed. My editor, Joan Bossert, strongly supported the entire project, turning an especially keen eye on the Nabokov chapter. My daughters, Heather and Laurel, provided significant input during the prehistory of several chapters. Most important, Dee and Josh gave me a study to work in and a home to share.

Davis, California   A.C.E.
July 1994

CONTENTS

PART ONE

Why Psychobiography?

1

The Psychologist as Biographer

H omo sapiens is the biographical animal. Humans differ from other creatures not only in anticipating their group and individual future but in reviewing and recounting their personal past—and in being fascinated by the personal pasts of other humans. Even in cultures where formal biography has remained undeveloped, details of individual life history are shared and spread by gossip, rumor, and personal confession.

In our culture, the biographical impulse still operates much of the time at this informal level. But a tradition of formal biography has evolved as well, beginning with Plutarch's *Parallel Lives*. In this tradition, the biographer studies an individual's life and prepares an orderly account of it. Factual accuracy is balanced with an attempt to tell a good story. The biographer not only lists the surface events of the life but seeks to identify the subject's primary motives, goals, or ambitions. Lessons for the reader may be pointed out, or left for the reader to discover.

Over the centuries, biography has shifted in style and emphasis. Its formal tone has increasingly yielded to a casual or even racy voice. For much of its history it was largely hagiographic, recording the saintly qualities of genuine or putative saints. Then it developed at least a pretense of being "objective"—a pretense that often served as pretext for the latest compilation of malicious gossip. Perhaps the most dramatic changes in the very essence of biography took place when broad theories of personality, developed by psychiatrists and psychologists, began to be adopted by biographers. Psychological approaches to biography flowered in the 1920s and 1930s, languished for several decades, then flourished anew in the 1970s and 1980s. Early on, these approaches acquired a generic name: psychobiography.

The word *psychobiography* looks innocent enough. It's a syllable or two too long to come trippingly off the tongue, but it gets easier with practice. It has good Greek roots, which separately entered the English language a long time ago. And it means pretty much what it says: biography that makes substantial use of psychological theory and knowledge.

But even as the approaches it describes have gained rapidly in numbers of practitioners and readers, *psychobiography* has become a dirty word. Critics now apply it with a sneer to any biography whose inferences strike them as dubious. George Will's definition is representative:

> In "psychobiography" the large deeds of great individuals are "explained" with reference to some hitherto unsuspected sexual inclination or incapacity, which in turn is "explained" by some slight the individual suffered at a tender age—say, 7, when his mother took away a lollipop.[1]

Entire books have been written to denounce psychobiography and its sibling psychohistory as conceived in sin.[2] Even scholars who conduct careful psychobiographical research often prefer more innocuous labels for their work: *Life history. Narratology. Psychological biography.*

Some of those who denounce psychobiography would still reject it no matter what it's called or how carefully it's done. They yearn for a bygone world of genteel biographers and unblemished heroes. But psychobiography has not been an innocent spectator at the sharp decline of its own reputation. Its biggest problem is obvious: Bad psychobiography is easier to write than good psychobiography. Psychobiography may be written for the wrong reasons or for no good reason. It may rely on shoddy data or misguided methods or inappropriate theories, or all of those together. Writers have used psychobiography to grind axes from the right (for example, Nancy Clinch on the Kennedy family[3]) and from the left (for example, Fawn Brodie on Richard Nixon[4]). Writers have claimed to augment their biographies with serious psychological analysis, when all they've done is to shove famous people into pathological pigeonholes (for example, Albert Goldman's diagnosis of Elvis Presley as a "split personality" and a "delusional paranoid"[5]). I've never encountered a real psychobiographical explanation quite as silly as George Will's fictional Lollipop Hypothesis. But reductions of an adult personality to the child's earliest and crudest motives happen often enough for Erik Erikson to have given the process a gently sarcastic label: "originology."[6]

The first originologist was Sigmund Freud, who practiced his trade on such complex geniuses as Leonardo and Goethe. Freud usually displayed at least a modicum of restraint in his applications of originology to genius. Many later psychoanalysts and pseudoanalysts have applied Freud to biography with such abandon that the term "Freudian biography" is now an even more derogatory term than "psychobiography."

Ironically, Freud himself has become a prime target of such Freudian excesses. One writer has built an elaborate analysis of Freud's personality and theories on the teetering foundation of the punchline to one of Freud's jokes. According to this writer, the punchline contains a concealed reference to the secret sins of

Freud's father, which were somehow sensed and then repressed by Sigmund the child.[7] Another writer continues to argue that Freud's major theories must have derived from a hypothesized affair between Freud and his wife's sister, which led to a supposed attempt by Freud to procure an alleged abortion of the postulated child his sister-in-law had presumably conceived.[8] Still another writer has interpreted various remarks in Freud's letters and books to mean that Freud was an "obsessed murderer" with a "necrophiliac passion" for his victims.[9] Little wonder that in order to avoid being lumped with biographers as imaginative as these, more data-bound researchers run for cover.

But running for cover is not the best response to bad psychobiography. The best response is good psychobiography. The best response to traditionalists' demands for less psychology in biography is more and better psychology. The best response to the gradual takeover of psychobiography by people who don't know what they're doing is a takeover by people who do know what they're doing.

Eighty-five years ago, Freud told Jung it was time for psychoanalysts to "take hold of biography."[10] Freud produced the first psychobiography less than a year later, and biography has not been the same since. Now it's time to issue a similar call to psychologists: "Take hold of psychobiography!"

Psychobiography is not only a way of doing biography; it's a way of doing psychology. Most psychologists have been trained to stay as far as they can from looking at one whole human being or one life at a time. But they can learn a lot about psychology by taking such a look, and by doing it over and over again. At the same time, they can bring a great deal to the field of psychobiography.

The domination of psychobiography by psychoanalysts has produced a modest number of capable works, a few masterpieces, and some genuine disasters. Good psychobiographies have been written by psychoanalytically-inspired political scientists, historians, and literary scholars. The personal qualities needed to become a decent psychobiographer can be found in any field: a controlled empathy for the subject and a devotion to collecting solid biographical data. Nonetheless, leaving psychobiography largely to psychoanalysts and their disciples has not yielded a coherent, cumulative, consistently responsible discipline of individual life history. Psychoanalytic contributions may have been a necessary part of the development of psychobiography, but they are not a sufficient base for its continued development. An infusion of research-trained psychologists, skilled in diverse approaches to the study of human behavior, can remake and reinvigorate the field.

Imagine where psychobiography would be now if it had developed as a recognized part of research psychology, starting seven or eight decades ago. Imagine that in the mid-1920s a few eager young psychologists began to make psychobiography the center of their theoretical and methodological attention. The field might still have detractors in our time—as any area of psychology does—but by now it would be a field that could comfortably tolerate such detractors. In my alternate-world fantasy, I see dozens of experienced psychobiographers expertly plying their trade, while book reviewers bitterly criticize any biography that fails to ground its efforts in sound psychological thinking. I see rows of library shelves weighed down with thoughtful research monographs that examine the psychological histories of every major creative artist, scientific theorist, and political leader of the past century. In the next row over are shelves of critiques of these studies, adjacent to shelves of methodological handbooks designed to refine and strengthen the psychobiographies of the next century. It could have happened that way. Perhaps it almost did.

In 1925, a brilliant young scientist named Henry Murray began to write a biography of Herman Melville. This was Murray's first effort at psychological analysis. Indeed, as he told me some 50 years later, it was the first professional research he had ever attempted, "outside of chemistry and embryology and things like that."[11] His scientific training had been in medicine and physiology; he became a psychologist on-the-job, first as Assistant Director and then as Director of the Harvard Psychological Clinic. Off the job, he continued to explore the psychology of Melville. After working on the biography for several years, Murray asked a newfound literary friend, Conrad Aiken, to look at the first hundred pages. According to Murray, Aiken "spent a day over it and then he said, Oh, it was just terrible. . . . He said, 'Start again, throw it away, no good, can't do anything with it.'"[12] Murray may have exaggerated Aiken's negative response, but he took it to heart. Though his interest in Melville remained, he left the manuscript largely untouched until the late 1930s. When Murray showed Aiken a revised draft in 1939, Aiken's response was even more devastating. The book was never completed.[13]

Murray did eventually publish something on Melville. But it was neither a full-scale psychobiography nor an incisive psychological journal article. Instead it was a 90-page introduction to one of Melville's least-read novels, *Pierre, or, the Ambiguities*.[14] His introduction to *Pierre*, together with an essay on *Moby-Dick* that appeared in a literary quarterly two years later,[15] represented only a fraction of Murray's thinking and writing about Melville across a quarter-century. Nonetheless, the psychological insights contained in those two publications "transformed Melville scholarship," according to a later scholar.[16]

Had Murray published his full-scale study of Melville in the 1920s or 1930s, in a form readily accessible to other psychologists, he might have transformed scholarship in biographical psychology as well. Indeed, he might have *created* a scientific discipline of biographical psychology through his bold and brilliant example. But although Murray was one of the most courageous figures in twentieth-century psychology, a leader in the struggle against both physiological and behavioristic reductionisms, he feared to make a fool of himself concerning Melville. He was afraid his biographical conclusions, as thoroughly researched and innovatively conceptualized as they were, would be ridiculed by other psychologists, by literary critics, and especially by other Melville scholars. He also feared that his book on Melville might reveal too much about his own private affairs, so intertwined had Murray's personal passions become with his thinking about *Pierre* and *Moby Dick*.[17] For strongly psychobiographical reasons, then, Murray's Melville studies failed to establish psychobiography as a legitimate area of psychological research.

Murray's own career did not end there. He moved on to provide a solid and expansive foundation for a psychology of the whole personality. He pioneered a wide-ranging eclecticism in personality theory, borrowing openly and skillfully from the narrower formulations of a variety of theorists. He invented, refined, or incorporated into his studies of personality an impressive array of personality assessment techniques, ranging from the collection and comparison of semi-standardized autobiographies to the motivational analysis of imaginative story sequences (the Thematic Apperception Test, or TAT). Murray published few case histories and made only one or two limited excursions into psychobiography beyond his Melville work.[18] But throughout his long life he remained firm in his insistence that psychology must attend not only to its usual bits of behavioral data but to the entire life history:

> [T]he life cycle of a single individual should be taken as a unit, the *long unit* for psychology. . . . The history of the organism *is* the organism. . . . [W]ith the perishing of each moment the organism is left a different creature, never to repeat itself exactly. No moment nor epoch is typical of the whole. Life is an irreversible sequence of non-identical events. Some of these changes, however, occur in a predictable lawful manner . . . . These phenomena make [psychological] biography imperative.[19]

Perhaps another psychologist could have taken up the psychobiographical torch that Murray never quite ignited. Indeed, several soon-to-be-prominent psychologists turned to individual biography for a time in the 1920s and 1930s. One of Gordon Allport's earliest efforts at personality theory was an analysis of a bizarre autobiographical volume called *The Locomotive God*.[20] Abraham Maslow's ideas about self-actualization grew out of his fascination with the lives and personalities of two exemplary individuals, anthropologist Ruth Benedict and psychologist Max Wertheimer.[21] Even B. F. Skinner, early in his career, taught and wrote about the psychological development of such writers as Lewis Carroll, D. H. Lawrence, and Fyodor Dostoyevsky.[22]

But Maslow abandoned his early biographical studies for more theoretical enterprises. Gordon Allport, always a champion of individual psychological uniqueness in the abstract, apparently found the messy individuality of *The Locomotive God*—and later the *Letters from Jenny*[23]—so distressing that he declined to pursue other examples in greater detail. Skinner soon concluded that science has no place for human individuality—or for personality, consciousness, or the Freudian unconscious.

Without strong scientific role models, psychobiography went on to develop in haphazard fashion at best. Sages such as Erik Erikson and Leon Edel have occasionally issued pronouncements on proper methodology, with the hope of improving the field.[24] An occasional psychologist has added his or her methodological voice.[25] But most psychologists have not been listening. Leave psychobiography alone, they seem to feel, and it'll go away. Call it by another name without the "psycho-" prefix, and psychologists needn't even feel guilty about ignoring it. What can psychologists really offer biography, anyway? And when did biography ever do anything for psychology?

What Psychologists Can Do for Psychobiography

Good biographies, even exceptional biographies, can still be written with little formal use of psychological concepts. A recent example is David McCullough's *Truman*.[26] McCullough is a careful researcher and a sensitive writer, who sets Truman firmly within his time, his family, and his culture. Truman's character is depicted largely through uninterpreted quotations from his diaries and letters, and through descriptions of his behavior as seen by others. McCullough doesn't probe more deeply. He mentions Freud only to say that Truman never mentioned him. Even so, we come away from the biography feeling we know Truman well—a good deal better than we know most of our friends and neighbors.

And yet, and yet . . . I suspect that even as fine a traditional biography as *Truman* will leave many readers vaguely dissatisfied. They may wonder about Truman's strongly conflicted relationship with his father, who seems to have been his model for uncomplaining hard work and for his intense political interests—but also his model for gambling repeatedly on the "main chance," the big but risky decision that might bring either bankruptcy or wealth. They may wonder about Truman's years of passive devotion to Bess Wallace, and about how he dealt internally with the frustrations he must have often felt before she finally agreed to marry him. They may wonder whether the emotional patterns of Truman's youth later contributed to his decision to bomb Hiroshima—a "main chance" if ever there was one.

If you're writing a biography of Nixon—any sort of Nixon biography—you're virtually obligated to do a certain amount of psychological analysis. Truman biographers face a wider array of options. David McCullough appears to have made a deliberate decision to go with his own strengths as a researcher and writer, leaving the deeper psychological probing to others. But McCullough's superb example of traditional biography may be one of the last of its breed. Psychobiography, for all its failings, is now an essential approach to the study of lives—famous lives, well-known lives, obscure lives. It cannot and will not be abandoned in order to satisfy certain critics' continuing desire for unanalytic books of polite admiration. But it can be improved, and psychologists can do much to improve it. Indeed, they are strategically positioned to deal with the most frequently heard criticisms of psychobiography. They can help psychobiography move from theoretical narrowness to a range of theoretical choices; from methodological looseness to methodological restraint; from a passion for pathography to examinations of psychological health; and from explanatory reductionism to explanatory complexity.

From theoretical narrowness to theoretical choice   Perhaps the most frequent criticism of psychobiography concerns its heavy dependence on psychoanalytic theory. Freudian interpretations are a pervasive feature of psychobiography, whether they involve identifying the sort of "hitherto unsuspected sexual inclination or incapacity" that so distresses George Will, or a more serious version of his Lollipop Theory of childhood trauma, or a developmental chronology of the continuing battle among an individual's unconscious armies of the night. There are good reasons for that pervasiveness; analytic theory directly addresses an array of powerful emotional issues that define the course of many lives. But the basic elements of psychoanalytic explanation have been overused and under-elaborated. Down through the years we've been given a lot of Oedipal explanations of famous writers—so many that ownership of an Oedipus complex seldom seems to explain much any more, unless it comes with an elaborate package of optional accessories.

Psychoanalytic theory has continued to develop beyond Oedipus, and certain of those developments have found a place in psychobiography: Erikson's psychosocial development stages (identity crisis and all),[27] Kohut's or Kernberg's versions of self and object-relations (especially the narcissistic varieties),[28] Winnicott's emphasis on transitional objects.[29] But psychologists who don't cloister themselves within one or another psychoanalytic camp can offer a much broader array of potentially applicable theories. Psychobiographers should be able to make effective use, for instance, of Henry Murray's inventory of psychological needs, plus the psychosexual stages he added to Freud's list;[30] David McClelland's and David Winter's extensions of Murray, especially in terms of power motive patterns;[31] Theodore Millon's classifications of character problems, already incorporated into standard diagnostic manuals;[32] and Silvan Tomkins' script theory with its "nuclear conflicts,"[33] especially as explicated by Rae Carlson.[34] And there's much else out there.[35]

Henry Murray's great contribution to personality theory was not any specific idea about the need for achievement or the claustral stage of pre-birth personality development; it was his eclecticism. He began with the basic psychoanalytic concepts, but he concluded that understanding either personality-in-general or personality-in-particular requires an openness to theoretical ideas from all over. Contemporary research psychologists may favor one or two pet theories, but they've usually been trained eclectically, to seek out and to use whatever is useful from the known universe of psychological theories. No one psychological theory can effectively elucidate every personality we want to understand. Therefore psychobiography needs to incorporate as much eclectic diversity as it can find.

From methodological looseness to methodological restraint   Too many psychobiographers have become true believers not only in psychoanalytic theory but in psychoanalytic method. Freud and his followers made several valuable contributions to research methodology—free association, close examination of slips of the tongue or pen, symbolic interpretation of dreams and other imaginative productions. But in many psychoanalytic psychobiographies, "method" seems to refer mainly to reliance on the analyst's intuitive ability to divide the wheat of clinical insights from the chaff of ordinary verbal conventions. This self-confidence in one's own interpretive skills, little restrained by clear judgmental criteria or procedural rules of thumb, often yields interpretations of biographical data that strike the unconverted as far-fetched at best.

The standard training of research psychologists rarely touches upon single-case research methods, even in the most psychobiographically relevant areas: personality, developmental, social, and clinical psychology. But most research psychologists do learn to be eclectic in their methods as well as in their theories. If they're trained well, they also learn restraint in their application of any particular research method. Are my conclusions closely tied to my data? What alternative interpretations are available, and how do I decide among them? Can the data be grouped into different patterns, and if so, why is one pattern superior to the others—more meaningful, more elegantly explanatory? Will my method of analyzing the data yield the same results if someone else tries it, and if not, what's wrong with it or with my explanation of it? Would another method work better, be more clearly communicable, yield a more persuasive analysis of the data? These kinds of questions arise constantly in other kinds of psychological research; all are applicable to psychobiography. Psychobiographers should have been asking them often, of themselves and of others in the field. Most have not.

From pathography to psychological health   In the first paragraph of his first psychobiography, Freud insisted that he was not writing a pathography, an account of the psychological failings of a great man.[36] Few people believed him then, and few believe his followers' similar disclaimers now, for good reason: psychoanalytic biographies are still much more often pathographic than eugraphic. (If you've never heard the latter term, neither have I—a strong indication that psychobiographies rarely map out how their subjects became psychologically healthy.) Erik Erikson made a point of de-emphasizing not only originology but pathography in his own work. But even Erikson, in books like *Young Man Luther* and *Gandhi's Truth*, had a hard time staying away from the clinical-diagnostic mode.

Clinical psychologists are almost as likely as psychoanalytic psychiatrists to approach biography with pathography on their minds. But many other psychologists are trained to deal not with patients *in extremis* but with fairly normal people: school kids, college students, average citizens who just happen to be included in a research sample. Whenever these psychologists take up psychobiography, they may expect to find a few abnormalities in their chosen subject; after all, totally "normal" people don't get famous enough to be chosen as subjects, except perhaps for Harry Truman. But such psychologists will probably also be more attentive than most clinicians to how their subject responds creatively to the demands of ordinary life and to the challenges of a career. In their previous studies—of children-as-survivors, of highly intelligent women and men in the prime of life, of psychological adaptations to old age—these psychologists have accumulated useful comparison data for individual studies. At the same time, and maybe more significantly for the long run, they've been training themselves to do those individual studies from a nonpathographic point of view.

From reductionism to complexity   As psychobiographers look for the pattern in the weave, for the keys to a padlocked personality, for the clues that will solve a psychological mystery, they seek to reduce complexity to simplicity. Their aim is reasonable, but it's often pursued with too much enthusiasm and too little subtlety. As published critiques of such works often run, "This biographer claims to explain So-and-so's political career/literary oeuvre/theoretical system/life history entirely in terms of _____." (Fill in the blank with your favorite explanatory variable.) Typically, the critic has further simplified the biographer's simplifications, by ignoring the reservations and qualifications that surround the central hypothesis. Nonetheless, the critic is often largely on target.

Psychology is itself, by and large, a reductive field. Large portions of contemporary psychology are busily concerned with reducing human complexities of thought and emotion to simplicities of cognition and neurology. Therefore, bringing a randomly assembled cadre of psychologists into psychobiography will not automatically cure its endemic reductionism.

However, a substantial number of psychologists do deal in their daily research with whole human beings—with people who talk and behave as people, not as bundles of nerve fibers or as simplified sensory systems. Sooner or later, many of those psychologists realize that reductionism as an overriding research strategy doesn't work. The more research they do in human development, personality, and social psychology, the more complicated their findings get and the more complicated their explanations must become. A Theory of Everything may be near enough in physics to keep a lot of physicists awake at night, but in psychology it's not even a believable dream. In the middle decades of this century, psychologists often seemed to assume that the basic secrets of human behavior were nearly within their grasp. Today that kind of illusory confidence is reserved mainly for psychologists whose research focus permits them to ignore human complexity. Psychologists who are familiar with such complexity among humans *en masse* should be able to recognize it even more clearly when they study a human *en solo*.

What Can Psychobiography Do for Psychology?

If you know anything about the current state of psychology, you may find it peculiar that I'm calling on psychologists to save—or at least to improve—the field of psychobiography. Psychology has its own serious problems as a scientific enterprise and especially as a source of wisdom about the human condition. Research psychology as a whole, including my favorite sub-fields of personality, developmental, and social psychology, continues to suffer from a heavy emphasis on the statistical analysis of data as the ultimate criterion of "truth." That means it also suffers from emphases on easily testable hypotheses and on studying the general rather than the specific. The one area of psychology that could be regarded as an exception, clinical psychology, has its own problems from a research standpoint. Special difficulties arise from its dependence on essentially private data, which have been collected from patients and which are therefore ethically unavailable for public study. Fortunately, at the same time that psychology goes about remedying psychobiography's problems, an infusion of psychobiography could substantially remedy some of the problems faced by psychology, at least in the following ways:

Testing the statistically significant against the personally significant   As a college freshman, I was taught John B. Watson's dictum that the scientific goal of psychology is "the prediction and control of behavior." That wasn't *my* goal in becoming a psychologist, and it wasn't the initial goal of most of the psychologists I know or have studied. But we all did want to be scientists, and scientists do often predict things, and scientific prediction often involves numbers, and because humans aren't precisely predictable, the numbers usually involve calculations of statistical probability. To get data that can be statistically analyzed, it helps to have some control over the organisms you're studying, through experiments or short-answer questionnaires. You can't let your "subjects" behave any old way they please, or you'll end up with a statistical garbage heap. Science is clean, science is abstract, or so we were taught. Psychology can be a science only by controlling its frisky data-sources while the data are being collected, and then controlling the data even more tightly through statistical data analysis.

However, lives are not lived in the laboratory (except for the lives of a few thousand researchers). In the real world, personalities are not divided into statistically analyzable compartments. Experiments and correlational studies, and statistical analyses of the data they generate, may identify significant variables in the lives of people-in-general. But I haven't encountered a psychologist yet who could put together a whole person from those statistical body-parts and honestly cry out, "IT'S ALIVE!" As Gordon Allport often suggested, the final test of a psychological hypothesis comes not when it passes a cut-off level for statistical significance, but when it makes sense within this life here, or that one there, or another over there. Statistical analysis has become sophisticated enough to detect amazingly subtle experimental effects and very complex correlations. In the end, though, we need to know whether these statistically significant effects and correlations display any personal significance when we look at one life at a time. Psychobiography is one good way to look.

Making comparative analyses of an individual case through use of public data One kind of psychologist already has a substantial history of studying one life at a time: the clinical psychologist. However, the data collected by clinical psychologists are problematic in more ways than one. First, they're basically pathographic in orientation: concerned with individual lives, true, but most often with lives being lived at far less than an optimal level of functioning. Second, the data themselves are bounded by various legal and ethical constraints. The clinician may draw conclusions about his or her clients, and may under certain circumstances share those conclusions with the rest of us. But the clinician is rarely free to share with us the full range of data on which those conclusions were based. Instead, we must trust that the clinician has drawn reasonable conclusions from an unseen body of data—data whose full dimensions are unspecified and which are represented to us only by the clinician's chosen examples. Furthermore, this mostly unseen body of data was initially generated by questions and suggestions put to the patient by the clinician, in a process largely unobserved by anyone else. The possibilities for unchecked bias are obvious. Even on those occasions when an extensively detailed clinical case history is published—a rare event among the large number of clinical cases actually treated—the client's identity must be carefully concealed. The clinician must not only omit any readily recognizable details of the client's life, but in many cases must actually misrepresent some significant aspects of the life, in order to mislead readers who might otherwise be able to identify the client.

The further development of personality psychology requires, as in other sciences, that competing hypotheses be tested on publicly available bodies of data.[37] Several critics of clinically based personality theories have argued that case-history data on personality are inherently unscientific, because they're so strongly contaminated by the private biases inherent in the therapeutic relationship.[38] But psychobiographical data are in most cases fully public—drawn from published biographical data and accessible archives. The psychobiographer doesn't need to disguise the identity of the subject, as in clinical cases; the main point of most psychobiographical research is to provide a clearer understanding of the psychology of a public figure. So psychobiographical data can make such criticisms moot. When a psychobiographical study is published, other researchers can examine the same data and evaluate the first researcher's interpretations, or even offer their alternative versions of the subject's life. In the process, the study of that life moves from case history to science.

Gaining ideas for new theories, new hypotheses, or new groupings of data   This is perhaps the most readily accepted use of individual case-history research in psychology. Even psychologists who sternly insist on the most rigorous forms of empirical research are usually willing to admit that a good theory can come from anywhere—even from a psychobiography. Indeed, the comprehensive study of a single human life is likely to generate so many theoretical questions that the overwhelmed researcher may return eagerly to studies of maze-running in rats or five-interval attitude scales. Theory generation may be better served by narrowing the research focus to the features that are most strongly represented in a particular life.

Ordinarily I leave theory-building to other people. But a few years ago I tried to use a construct I had already identified among 1960s activists, a process I called "superego-tripping," in a psychobiographical study of the statesman and moralist John Foster Dulles. I had originally conceptualized superego-tripping as a kind of moral self-aggrandizement, expressed in a person's firm belief that the external world will always fall into congruence with his or her most strongly felt superego concerns. The world doesn't always work that way, of course, as Charlie Brown lamented in *Peanuts*: "How can we lose when we're so sincere?"[39] But the superego-tripper goes on expecting sincerity and morality to triumph, and denying their frequent failures.

As Eisenhower's Secretary of State, Foster Dulles was well known for his endless moralizing about the sacred mission of the United States and the inevitable downfall of the godless Communists. But try as I might, my superego-tripping construct didn't seem to describe much of Dulles's experience or thinking. Eventually I was forced to distinguish superego-tripping from a related construction that I called *ego-idealism*: judging external events and behavior principally in terms of how well they measure up to one's standards of moral perfection, rather than in terms of their pragmatic effects. When you're superego-tripping, you expect reality to fall into line with your moral certitudes; as a practicing ego-idealist, you feel your moral certitudes are always more important than any other considerations, and reality be damned if it doesn't square with those certitudes. (See Chapter 14.) Ego-idealism worked much better than superego-tripping in analyzing Dulles. I suspect it will do the same for similar biographical subjects as I encounter them in the future.

Sometimes a psychobiographer chooses a specific biographical subject with the idea that this subject may be especially useful in teasing out the strands of a new theoretical understanding. Freud seems to have chosen Leonardo as a subject partly so he could work on his theories about homosexuality. Freud may also have felt ready to make his initial formulation of the Oedipus complex more complex. Leonardo was useful there too, since he (perhaps) didn't live in a patriarchal family during his early childhood. (See Chapter 3.) But in many other instances of life-history research, the choice of subject is not so deliberate. New theoretical constructs rise unbidden, perhaps not even closely related to the subject at hand. The specific biographical subject in such instances serves mainly to keep the theoretical pot bubbling, not to provide the clay for a specific theoretical brick. I don't know of a single major theoretical construct that grew out of Henry Murray's six-decades-long study of Melville. But Murray felt *challenged* by Melville until the end of his own life—challenged to understand more, to conceptualize personality in new ways, to keep revising the hypotheses he had already formulated. Melville was a large enough subject to maintain such a challenge; indeed, he proved to be the giant white whale that Murray never successfully harpooned. Though Murray expended much of his explanatory effort on smaller fish, his career as a personality theorist gained a great deal from the Melvillean challenge.

Understanding important single cases   In their continuing struggle for scientific respectability, most psychologists steer away from pronouncements about any specific case. Instead, they relentlessly pursue the general. They tend to dismiss individual variation as statistical "error." They ignore the work of scientists in other fields who celebrate detail, diversity, or contingency. One of those scientists is the brilliant physicist Freeman Dyson:

> [W]e have two kinds of scientists, the unifiers looking inward and backward into the past, the diversifiers looking outward and forward into the future. Unifiers are people whose driving passion is to find general principles which will explain everything. They are happy if they can leave the universe looking a little simpler than they found it. Diversifiers are people whose passion is to explore details. They are in love with the heterogeneity of nature and they agree with the saying, "Le bon Dieu aime les details." They are happy if they leave the universe a little more complicated than they found it.[40]

In psychology, Dyson's distinction between unifiers and diversifiers is described by the terms *nomothetic* and *idiographic*. Gordon Allport introduced the nomothetic-versus-idiographic distinction into American psychology as a way to advocate the increased study of the individual.[41] Allport's intentions were good, but he initially defined the idiographic approach with language as extreme in one direction as any of the positivists or statisticians had used in the other. Idiographic personality research was to be a science of the totally unique—altogether distinct from the generalizing nomothetic approach prevalent in psychological science then and now.

Allport preached his idiographic gospel for 25 years. Then one of his former students, Robert Holt, published such a devastating criticism of it that few psychologists remained willing to attempt individual case-history research of any sort, except as an idle exercise in "artistic" psychology.[42] Holt repeatedly drew the line: idiographic equals art, nomothetic equals science. For example, "On this particular point, I shall try to show, the artist in [Allport] has probably dimmed the vision of the scientist." "[T]he feeling of understanding [rather than prediction and control] is a subjective effect aimed at by artists, not scientists." "There is a legitimate art of personality, literary biography. An artist like Andrè Maurois is not hindered by not being a scientist of any kind."[43] And so on.

Allport quickly realized that he had made a strategic error in trying to draw so sharp a contrast between idiographic and nomothetic approaches. He thereafter tried to replace "idiographic" with a less extreme term, "morphogenic," which refers to studying individualized patterning processes in personality rather than totally unique personalities.[44] As Allport recognized, a personality researcher can find ways to capture the processes that *create* a subject's individuality, while remaining a serious scientist who abides by all the unartistic "hindrances" involved in responsible treatment of data. But the word "morphogenic" never really caught on. The word "idiographic" remains a term of opprobrium among psychologists who want to think of themselves as scientists and not artists. In fact, it's right up there with that bad word "psychobiography."

But it's time for psychologists to sniff a rose or two, instead of merely measuring the mean attitudes of a thousand-person random sample toward red roses versus white. It's time for psychologists to hold that rosy scent in their own nostrils long enough to appreciate its distinct rosiness, instead of struggling to identify the basic sensory processes that make us prefer the scent of roses to the stink of sewer sludge. At least some psychologists, some of the time, need to subdue their urge toward the nomothetic, to relax their hold on an outdated scientific puritanism, to look at a real life because of the sheer interest and individual value of that life.

Surely the understanding of a single life can be an important goal in itself, with no necessity to justify it by reference to other ends. That's especially true when the life being studied is of one of the greats among humanity: Melville or Gandhi, Einstein or Freud, Florence Nightingale or Thomas Jefferson. Leon Edel didn't set out to write a five-volume biography of Henry James in order to see how well a Freudian interpretation would fit *Daisy Miller*. Rather, he felt that James was "a Shakespeare of the novel" who demanded close attention.[45] And if James was a Shakespeare of the novel, who is the Shakespeare of rock 'n' roll singers? That's why clinical psychologist Bruce Heller and I have been working on a psychobiography of Elvis Presley for the past decade.[46] We aren't seeking to test a particular brand of psychological theory or to develop a nomothetic typology of rock musicians. We just want to gain a better grasp of the personal psychology and charismatic appeal of one of the key figures of contemporary culture. After all, Elvis was The King. For many people, he still is. What greater justification do we need?

Lesser figures demand attention as well. The sheer particularity of personality should provide sufficient grounds for us to say, "Sometimes let's look not only at what is found in everybody or in most people, but in a few or in one." The old woman whom Gordon Allport called Jenny contributed little to our culture. In her final years she probably caused more hurt than help to a variety of people. She might well have died unknown and unlamented. But she wrote a stack of letters to Allport and his wife. In those letters she emerged as a distinct individual, not easily pinned down or pigeonholed by any single theory, but worth looking at for her own singularity.[47] Obviously that's a statement of value. But what value is worth defending more vigorously in these times than the value of the individual human life? And won't psychology as a field be the better—the more responsible, the more inclusive—for recognizing and acting upon that value?

The Rest of the Book

The next fourteen chapters show a psychologist doing psychobiography. I hope these chapters will interest readers who have no intention of ever doing a psychobiography themselves, will instruct non-psychologists who want to do something psychobiographical but aren't sure how to go about it, and will inspire psychologists who already know how to do it but just need a little push. Two chapters are mainly methodological, but they refer to specific cases as well. Twelve chapters are mainly discussions of specific cases, but they also illustrate and explain my psychobiographical methods. The case-history chapters are grouped into three content areas, which happen to be three of the major areas of psychobiography in general: studies of *theorists* (mine are all psychological theorists); studies of *creative artists* (mine are all writers of the fantastic); and studies of *politicians* (mine are all Americans, except for one anti-American).

In these remaining fourteen chapters, will I practice what I've preached in Chapter 1? Most of the time, but perhaps not always. Psychobiography is a tricky business and it's hard to keep all the balls in the air all the time. The range of theories I've used isn't as wide as it might be, though I've tried in each case to choose the theory that best explains the person I'm studying. My methods are often whatever will work at the time, rather than a carefully-planned-in-advance strategy of data collection and analysis. Sometimes I had a careful strategy and it didn't pay off, so I dumped it and took advantage of a fortuitous combination of circumstances. I do usually try to look for evidence of psychological strengths in the people who most interest me, though I may not have done that quite enough for Henry Kissinger and Alexander Haig in Chapter 14. I may be more reductive than some readers would like when I discuss their favorite author or theorist— but I'm not offering my conclusions as full or final answers to anybody's life mysteries.

Do I really expect other psychologists to answer my call to get involved in psychobiography? A few already have. A few others had begun to work the field before I ever gave a thought to proselytizing. There are still too few of us to have made a strong impact yet, either on psychology or on psychobiography, but we're gaining strength.[48] Biography is one of the most popular genres in publishing today. Psychobiography, whether it's called that or something else, is an increasingly popular approach to biography. Psychobiography and psychologists need each other. I don't expect a flood of applicants to my so-far-imaginary Institute of Psychobiography, or a mountain of manuscripts to my so-far-fantasy *Journal of Biographical Psychology.* But the seeds are there. As Thoreau said, "Convince me that you have a seed there, and I am prepared to expect wonders."[49]

2

Starting from Scratch

IN ONE OF MY previous lives I was an experimental social psychologist. I learned that when you change people's attitudes in the laboratory, the change often fails to influence their later behavior, *unless* you give your audience a detailed and practical plan of action to carry into real life.[1] I don't work on experimental research subjects' attitudes any more, but I suspect that what I learned then applies to what I'm doing now. To promote the cause of psychobiographical progress most effectively, I need to go beyond inspirational homilies. So this chapter will offer a variety of specific, basic suggestions about how to get started as a psychobiographer—especially about how to collect the data you'll need when you try to understand a life. Even if you're absolutely sure you're never going to write a psychobiography, I suggest you give the chapter a try. It will take you Behind the Scenes, and in the process it should transform you into a more perceptive reader of psychobiographies.

Choosing Your Subject

My first word of advice on this necessarily first topic is: Let your subject choose you. Any psychobiographical study will make substantial demands on your time and energy—maybe years and years of your time and energy. So you'd best begin to work on a subject you'll be willing to live with (in your head) for a long time. And subjects *will* choose you, if you let them. I've never had to look for a psychobiographical subject; they're lurking all about, in my childhood and adolescent enthusiasms, among my professional role models and *bêtes noires*, in the politicians who have ruled or now rule or will rule large areas of my life, in the creative artists who continue to delight and challenge me. You needn't commit yourself to one psychobiographical subject till death do you part, as in the case of Henry Murray and Herman Melville; a year or two of intense involvement may be quite sufficient. But you need to start with a level of intensity similar to Murray's, or your project is likely to drift into limbo.

However, the intensity of your enthusiasm for a subject shouldn't be your sole guide. As Freud cautioned us at the field's beginning, you should stay away from subjects you already totally idolize or totally detest—the most extreme of your role models and *bêtes noires*.[2] (Freud ignored his own advice, as we'll see in Chapter 3. But you shouldn't ignore it.) Historian Fawn Brodie, for instance, was good at accumulating biographical information about Richard Nixon, and she knew quite a bit about psychoanalytic theory.[3] But she should never have attempted a psychobiography of Nixon; she started off hating him too much to be even remotely fair. In the other direction, Ernest Jones could and did draw some very well-informed psychobiographical conclusions about Sigmund Freud's personality when he wrote his classic three-volume biography.[4] But Jones pulled his punches so often, out of friendship and admiration for Freud, that he provided a rationale for a whole industry of Freud-bashing "psychobiographies." Most of them say they're just correcting Jones's omissions and exaggerations.

Subjects you *largely* admire or *largely* dislike are fair game. But you need to be open to doubts about the admired figure's perfection as you become more familiar with his or her imperfections. Likewise, you should be willing to accept clear evidence for the human worth of a previously disliked figure. Either of those positions may be most easily attained by choosing a subject about whom you feel considerable ambivalence—strongly positive *and* strongly negative feelings, roughly equal in intensity. Such figures have never been in short supply for me: Elvis, whose personal life I found as dismaying as his music was fascinating; C. G. Jung, whose ideas came in equal parts nutty and sane; Vladimir Nabokov, who was a literary genius of the first rank and who insisted on repeatedly proving to his readers that they were not.

Several biographers and psychoanalysts have argued that you should be fully psychoanalyzed before you dare begin a psychobiography, or at least that you should check in with an analyst periodically as you work on your project, to keep your ambivalences under control.[5] Under ideal circumstances of unlimited time and full funding, those sound to me like nice ideas. However, the field of Freud studies is littered with the work of psychoanalysts who presumably have been thoroughly analyzed themselves, but who (like Ernest Jones) remain unable to control *their* strong positive or negative transferences toward the Old Man. Psychoanalysis is not a cure-all, either as theory or as therapy. Other strategies can be used to improve and maintain your intellectual honesty while you're doing a psychobiography. One is simply to keep in mind the prospect that you'll eventually have to submit your work for inspection by your more critical colleagues.

Practically speaking, it's a good idea to make an initial choice not only of a biographical subject, the *person* you'll be working on, but also of a delimited *topic*—a specific, psychologically interesting question or set of questions you'll be trying to answer about the subject. That's for your own protection, to keep you from committing yourself at the beginning to an open-ended and essentially unendable research project. Psychobiographical projects rarely if ever grow smaller in scope over time. Mostly they expand. Even if you decide at first not to cover a whole life history but to look at one specific achievement, or at one six-month period of your subject's life, or at one puzzling aspect of his or her personality, you may soon find yourself looking at the whole life again.

When I began to study Nabokov, I was pursuing what seemed to me a very specific question: Why was Nabokov so hostile to Freud? What I first thought of as a single journal article soon expanded to the scope of a small book, then to a large book, which would necessarily cover much of Nabokov's life and most of his published work. I didn't have the time or the expertise or the chutzpah to write such a book then, so I deliberately re-narrowed my focus to one Nabokov short story and several closely related life events. Chapter 11 presents my narrow-focus study, plus some of the broader context. But enough questions and enough data remain to fill that big book about Nabokov. I haven't written it yet, but it continues to tempt me. To keep your psychobiographical projects at manageable size, you must ruthlessly chop away the outlying runners and creepers. I'm not the best person to dispense advice on how to do that.

One final piece of advice about choosing a subject: To keep your readers interested, you need to have a mystery. Serviceable but boring psychological studies can be written about anyone. A fascinating study is one that examines puzzles, contradictions, previously unexplained leaps and twists in a person's psychological development. For many years I thought of Woody Allen as a prime candidate for a psychobiography—except that drawing the connections between his life and his work looked too simple. His neurotic characteristics and their sources in his family history were all up there on the screen. But once he translated his long-standing fantasies into an unanticipated reality (middle-aged but wise intellectual falls in love with middle-aged lover's teenage daughter), Woody Allen began to appear rather less simple than before. Or maybe he's *so* simple that his sudden simplemindedness itself requires an explanation. Psychobiographers, let the hunt begin!

Using Published Data

After the questions "Who really interests you?" and "What mysteries remain?" your next question should be, "What data are already available?" The first specific question under that broad one should be, "Has my potential subject already been written up in at least one full-scale biography?" If the answer is yes, you may think, "Too bad; I'll just have to find another subject." But my response to finding a published biography of a potential subject is more likely to be, "Hooray! Somebody has already done the grub-work for me!" Maybe it wasn't done very thoroughly or accurately (here almost any published biography of Elvis will serve as an example), and most likely I'll have to make corrections as I go along. But even a minimally competent biography will have organized substantial blocks of the subject's life history. After reading it, I can move on to more interesting questions.

Perhaps a previous biographer has done the basic biography very well indeed. Peter Gay's biography of Sigmund Freud is one such example; Elisabeth Young-Bruehl's biography of Anna Freud is another.[6] Perhaps, in addition, this published biography has dealt with several interesting psychobiographical questions along the way. So *now* you'll have to choose another subject, right? That's how people often react when I mention that I'm working on Presley or Freud: How can I possibly say anything on the subject that hasn't been said already? But Elvis and Sigmund were complicated people who led complicated lives. Much remains to be resolved about both of them. As long as you think you can find an interested audience for your fresh contributions, the amount of previously published research on a biographical subject shouldn't deter you. It could even be argued that the only interested audience you really need is *you*, though in the practical world the demands of editors and tenure committees also need to be kept in mind.

While locating the available biographies (if any) of your potential subject, you should also make a quick canvass of additional published data: letters, diaries, autobiographies, memoirs, the subject's other writings. In a number of prominent instances—Freud, Darwin, Byron, Lewis Carroll, for starters—vast amounts of such primary biographical materials have already been published under careful scholarly editorship. The more such material in print, the better for you. To the passionate psychobiographer, the phrase "Too much data" is an oxymoron. You should worry mainly at the other end of the scale, where your potential subject's life may have left virtually no trace of primary biographical data. Freud really should *not* have ventured to write, at least in the detail he did, about Leonardo's developmental history. Freud's later willingness to speculate about Moses' life and work is simply astonishing.[7] In neither case did Freud have anywhere near the amount of data he needed, nor did he have any practical way to add to the limited array of previously published records.

Gathering Unpublished Data

But you do have ways to come up with more data, if you've chosen wisely. Let's say you've picked a nineteenth- or twentieth-century figure of some public note, a politician or writer or artist or scientist. You've scoured the university libraries and the biggest bookstores around for published works by and about your subject. You've checked the Chicago Psychoanalytic Index and other bibliographic aids to see whether anyone else has done a psychobiographical study that you can contradict, incorporate, or at least cite. You could stop your data collection right there and start writing your psychobiography. A considerable number of psycho-biographers do stop there, some to very good effect.[8] Or you can move on to where much of the work and most of the fun of biographical research really begin: unpublished data sources. Depending on how recently your subject was still active, these unpublished sources may be entirely archival, or they may involve your getting in touch with live people.

Even if you think you can get by with the published sources on your subject, I urge you to give archival research a try. It will probably broaden and deepen your perspectives more than you anticipate. The published versions of primary sources often inadvertently omit just those small clues that a psychobiographer may find most useful.[9] Even worse, the editors of such material may (perhaps uncon-sciously) distort the published record so that it better supports a particular interpretive viewpoint—and does so in ways undetected unless you go beyond the public record to the raw archives.

Many archival collections include not only the original manuscripts of pub-lished primary sources, but also large amounts of biographical material that have never been published and that may bear importantly on your own hypotheses. Sometimes this material will have remained not only unpublished but virtually unread by anyone before you. At other times you can almost see the eye-tracks of dozens of previous scholars crisscrossing every page—on the Freud papers in the Library of Congress, for example. But even then, it's worth taking a look at the real thing. The simple act of handling your subject's own letters and manuscript drafts can give you a renewed appreciation for his or her humanity *and* genius.

Archival research is a world unknown to most psychologists. It takes place mainly in quiet rooms with heavy furniture, thick drapes, and limited access. Fees are rarely charged for access to archival collections; it helps to have an institution-al affiliation, but your main credential will be some indication of serious research intent. You may be able to obtain small amounts of archival data in response to phone or mail inquiries, but more substantial research questions will usually require your physical presence at the archival location. For a while the National Endowment for the Humanities operated an efficient small-grants program for travel to archival collections. In return for minimal paperwork that did *not* go through the usual overhead-burdened university channels, a researcher could get a flat $750 grant that would cover modest costs of a one-week trip to nearly any archive in this country. That low-budget source of funds seems to have been gobbled up by other NEH programs; I hope it will come back. But even when it was available, it wasn't nearly enough to pay for all the research travel that psychobiographical projects often require. People who do much archival work learn to piggy-back their research expeditions onto trips for other purposes. I rarely attend a professional conference or visit friends and relatives without spending at least a couple of extra days at a nearby archival site.

The professional archivists, the people in charge of the archives, are paid decent salaries to deal with researchers like us. But they are also paid to protect their archival collections, and the two roles regularly clash. Photocopying of archival materials, for instance, may be forbidden or severely restricted, because documents could be damaged while being copied. Note-taking by hand may be limited to pencil use only, for fear of permanent damage from ball-point pen impressions or fountain pen ink. Taking notes with a pencil for seven to nine hours a day, five or six days a week, may permanently damage the researcher's physical and mental health, but the manuscripts will survive.

In the early 1980s I began to lug a "portable" (26-pound) personal computer to archival sites. At first the computer made archivists nervous. They seemed to feel I wasn't playing fair by trading in my #2 pencil for a KayPro II. But most archival locations now permit small computers, though you'd better carry your own extension cord. The next time I go archiving, I'd like to bring along a hand-held scanner that will read archival documents line by line and feed the words directly into my computer. The scanning software I've tried doesn't read more than a few typefaces with high accuracy, and I doubt that any software will ever be able to read Freud's Gothic scribbling, but the technology is improving rapidly. Even when the software gets good enough to read any typescript without significant error, however, the archivists may forbid contact between scanning devices and valuable manuscripts.

Most archivists I know are pleasant people as well as responsible professionals, interested in my projects and more helpful than I've had any right to expect. But archives are not like the main part of the library, where every item is clearly labeled, cross-indexed, and conveniently browsable. Archival materials are usually hidden away in regions to which only the archivists have direct access. Often the indexing is inadequate or nonexistent, because the archives are understaffed and underfunded. The archivists move at their own pace and by their own rules, which may include ambiguities that permit them considerable discretion to make your research life either very difficult or very rewarding. Elena Danielson, Associate Archivist of the Hoover Institution, has written an inside account of such archival decision-making, which gives a good idea of the contending pressures faced by the professional archivist as well as the "key role [the archivist plays] in mediating these conflicting interests."[10] Dr. Danielson has been extremely helpful during my occasional visits to the Hoover Institution, and I hope she will be again. But even if I were planning never to return to the Hoover, I'd recommend her paper with enthusiasm.

You may be lucky enough—or in some circumstances unlucky enough—to locate biographical materials held by your subject's family, before those materials come to rest in a formal archive. I say "lucky enough" because the family may grant you first or exclusive rights to the material, may let you use a pen while you take notes, may even let you photocopy everything you want to use. I say "unlucky enough" because family members are likely to be much more biased about your subject than most professional archivists will be. To gain or maintain access to the data under their control, you may have to establish your credentials not just as a researcher but as a researcher with the correct attitudes toward your subject. You may even be asked to sign a contract that will require you to express those correct attitudes in print, if you want to quote from any unpublished biographical documents.

Current laws and court decisions give an individual's legal heirs complete control over the publication of any previously unpublished documents written by that individual. Even if you physically own a letter by Sigmund Freud—even if you paid a lot of money for it, or got it as a gift from Anna Freud—you can't legally publish it without obtaining the written permission of Sigmund Freud Copyrights, Ltd. The same laws apply to material still in the family's hands, and to most unpublished material held in formal archives. But archivists can be helpful with those laws at times, by negotiating a blanket agreement that covers any responsible use of previously unpublished items in a collection, rather than leaving every researcher to work out publication arrangements individually with the heirs. On the other hand, archivists and heirs sometimes work together in a kind of polite collusion, where each publicly blames the other for denying you access, or at least for greatly slowing down the process of granting access.

Interviews and Other Contacts

Those heirs may also play important roles with regard to your main remaining source of data: direct contact. If your subject is still alive, the most productive direct contacts will probably be with him or her—whether by letter, by phone, or in person. But most psychobiographies are written about dead people. That leaves you corresponding or talking with the heirs again, as well as with other surviving relatives, friends, and colleagues of the deceased. Friendly heirs and surviving friends can help you a lot; unfriendly ones can make your job hell. (For evidence of the latter, see the biographical literature on Sylvia Plath.[11])

The legal status of oral communications is less problematic than that of archival documents. Without his heirs' permission, you can't publish a letter from Freud even if he wrote it in direct reply to your very specific questions. But if you had been able to interview Freud or get analyzed by him, and actually heard the pearls of wisdom flowing from his mouth, you could quote any of those pearls in print to your heart's content. A number of Freud's colleagues and ex-patients have done so. Whether other people will accept the accuracy of your quotations is another matter.

I interview psychobiographical subjects in person whenever that's practical. I also try to interview an array of other people who've known a subject well enough to answer interesting questions about his or her life. At times I've managed to obtain useful information through mailed inquiries, and I've done a few good interviews by long-distance phone, but in-person interviews are likely to be the most productive. For one thing, they enable the respondent to evaluate You the Interviewer. If you look honest and behave decently, the respondent may open up much more readily than if you're just a voice on the phone. At the same time, You the Interviewer can obtain useful information by observing the respondent's nonverbal behavior. If the interview is conducted on the respondent's own territory, as I usually request, the surroundings may convey further information. That's especially true when you can interview your primary psychobiographical subject at home. I learned a lot about Henry Murray by being allowed to interview him several times in his living room. Crystal whales and stained-glass whales and woven whales and sculptured whales were distributed all about. Oil portraits of Murray's New England ancestors loomed large on the walls. His current scientific, literary, and philosophical reading matter lay arrayed on the nearest coffee table.

Interviewing a subject's relatives in their homes may also pay off in unanticipated ways. Several years ago I was working on a study of Cordwainer Smith, a science fiction writer (among other interesting things) who had died in 1966. (See Chapter 7.) His widow told me that one of his most important stories, "Alpha Ralpha Boulevard," had been inspired partly by his first wife's attraction to another man and partly by a French painting called *The Storm*. I knew from other evidence that the widow's recollections were sometimes unreliable, so I wasn't sure how much to make of her information in this instance. "Alpha Ralpha Boulevard" does depict the male protagonist's female lover as being tempted by another man, and the story does end with a storm. But when I finally located the painting in question, stored away in the Metropolitan Museum in New York, it simply showed a young man and a young woman trotting along together in a high wind. Why did Cordwainer Smith bring Wife Number One and this romantic nineteenth-century French painting together in a science fiction story? I couldn't guess.

Then I went to interview Smith's 94-year-old Aunt Alma in a small Missouri town. Aunt Alma was living by herself, in the house that Smith had often visited for days or weeks at a time during his childhood and adolescence. Aunt Alma couldn't remember much of interest about her nephew. But on her living room wall—she said it had been hanging there for decades—was a tapestry reproduction of the French painting *The Storm*. On the adjacent wall hung a lithograph that had been there just as long; it showed Mephistopheles tempting Margaret, from the legend of Faust. Cordwainer Smith's first wife had been named Margaret. I felt as though I had suddenly walked into a chamber of Smith's brain, where his free associations were stored away like stage props.

When I do interviews, whether of live subjects or of dead ones' friends and relatives, I observe several rules of thumb. I usually write a letter first, explaining my overall objectives and why I think an interview would be valuable. If the person is willing to talk with me (an exchange of several letters and phone calls may be necessary to establish this), I ask for a meeting at a time and place where I can be largely alone with the subject for an hour or two. (I've tried doing joint interviews with a husband and wife. Sometimes they work, but more often they reduce the frankness of both respondents.) I then do my homework prior to the interview, by reading everything I can find by and about the subject. That tells me which questions are likely to be most productive in terms of adding to the published record. If the respondent has already answered a question clearly and at length in print or in previous interviews, why ask it again? (Harry Murray complained to me about an earlier interviewer's unoriginal questions: "Stale beer!") If, on the other hand, I know enough to ask questions that go beyond the public record, the respondent may be impressed by this demonstration of my genuine interest in the subject. As a result, the respondent's answers may break out of the mold established by previous interviewers. Such preparation for an interview also enables you, the interviewer, to organize your questions in advance to make the most efficient use of the limited time a typical busy respondent can give you.

I no longer ask interviewees to sign an informed-consent statement of the kind now required in most psychological research on humans. Whenever I've tried to obtain informed consent, the interviewees reacted either with annoyance at the form's bureaucratic tone, or with inappropriate anxiety at its standard descriptions of the worst possible outcomes imaginable. When I don't provide such a form, nobody seems to miss it. My interviewees are not in court, after all, and they can easily avoid answering any question I ask. (My university's Institutional Review Board has usually tolerated this omission, given the kinds of interviews I conduct and the kinds of people I interview.) I do state at the beginning of each interview that before I quote or closely paraphrase the respondent's statements in print, I'll provide a draft of the work in which the quotation is to be used, and the respondent will be given the option of clarifying or retracting any statement at that time. I don't give respondents the option to insist on changes in my interpretations or conclusions, but I tell them I'll gladly consider suggestions that will improve the accuracy of my work—and I mean it.

When I conduct interviews of the psychobiographical subjects themselves, I prefer to tape-record the interviews, with the subject's advance knowledge and permission. Such recordings not only enable me to verify the respondent's exact words; they may someday be of archival interest to other researchers. When I interview a person who knows (or knew) my subject, I usually don't tape unless I've already established a congenial relationship with the respondent, or unless I anticipate a lengthy and detailed interview about noncontroversial matters. Relatives and friends of a prominent individual are often hesitant to put their unvarnished recollections on tape, even when the subject is dead; they're thinking of other relatives and friends whose feelings might be hurt. Instead, I take notes as the interview proceeds, then remedy any gaps in the notes with my own tape-recorded recollection of the interview soon afterward. I don't use my recollections as the basis for "exact" quotations, but only for general background.

This latter procedure—the recorded post-interview wrap-up—is a good idea even if you've recorded the entire interview. You may not have been able to record quite everything—for instance, during the half-minute or so when you're changing tapes. The recording process itself may leave occasional words or phrases incomprehensible, though they sounded quite comprehensible when you were listening to the interviewee "live." I once went through extended negotiations to get Erik Erikson to agree to an interview. When he finally consented, after several rounds of correspondence and some deep thought on both sides concerning what we would talk about, I went out to his summer home on Cape Cod and confidently positioned my fancy portable tape recorder in the middle of his dining room table. Erikson seemed a bit dismayed at the prospect of being recorded, though he had already agreed to it. He was quite reserved in his answers at the beginning, but he gradually warmed up, and by the end of the session both he and I expressed pleasure at how well the interview had gone. I drove happily off toward Boston with my tape recorder and my precious tape. When I got home I found that I hadn't pushed quite the right combination of buttons on my complicated recorder. Erik Erikson was there on the tape, but he was faint at best. At times, his soft German/Danish accent grew indecipherable, and I had to rely on my fading memory of exactly what he had said to fill in the transcript. Nowadays I check my recorder settings more carefully, but no machine is absolutely failsafe or foolproof. Recording your own recollections soon afterward, whether you've taped the whole interview or have only written notes, is a convenient safeguard that easily outlasts your unrecorded memories of the event.[12]

How easy is it to set up interviews with a potential subject, or with the subject's friends and relatives? You'll have to find them first. If they're not on a university faculty or in a professional directory, that can be a problem. However, if you know an approximate geographical location, standard city telephone directories may be more useful than you'd expect.[13] A process akin to what sociologists call "snowball sampling" may be even more helpful: start with the interviewees you can readily locate, then ask each one for information on the whereabouts of others, and so on down the line. Being able to say you were referred by a familiar name may also improve the cooperation of the next interviewee.

Prominent individuals in almost any field are, in my experience, reasonably responsive to requests for interviews. You just have to get up enough nerve to ask them, and present yourself as a serious scholar. They may cooperate even if they have grave doubts about psychobiography in general or about your line of questioning in particular. If they realize you're going to go ahead and write about them anyway, they may give you an interview in sheer self-defense, to get their preferred responses on the record.

When the great behaviorist B. F. Skinner hesitantly agreed to my request for an

interview, he made it clear that he remained totally unreceptive to psychodynamic explanations of his behavior or anyone else's. But he politely responded
to my questions anyway, politely argued with me later about some of my conclusions, and politely asked for half a dozen reprints of my paper about him when it
was published. (Chapter 6 is based on that paper. I have no idea what Skinner did
with the reprints.)

Isaac Asimov likewise answered a series of increasingly impertinent questions
from me, in his case always by return mail. Again, Asimov had no use for
psychological explanations of his acrophobia and agoraphobia. But he was willing
to write to me at length about how completely happy and totally unconflicted he
was, and how he spent up to fourteen hours a day, seven days a week, turning out
page after nonstop page of fiction and nonfiction, just because he liked to write.
Asimov later complained that I had led him into a no-win situation, where
anything he said could be used to support my predetermined conclusions. But
that hadn't been my intent, and he had readily given me permission to quote in
print everything he had written to me. (See Chapter 9.) People may change their
self-images, as well as their impressions of others, over time—so if you've obtained a particularly interesting set of responses from a willing psychobiographical subject, you'd better get the material into print as soon as you can, before the
subject decides he's told you too much or hasn't said it right.

I must confess that I never requested interviews with Henry Kissinger and
Alexander Haig, two of my other subjects, or even asked them to respond to
mailed inquiries before I published psychobiographical studies of them. (See
Chapter 14.) Both had already written long and revealing memoirs, but that's not
the only reason I didn't seek them out. I assumed that prominent political figures
in general, and especially those as controversial as Kissinger and Haig, would be
unlikely to answer my kinds of questions with any degree of honesty. But perhaps
that assumption only reflects my personal biases. Next time I do a similar study,
I'll at least write a letter of inquiry.

The superstars of the entertainment world can also be a problem. I never
requested an interview with Elvis Presley, but I did address a series of questions to
him and his managers fairly early in his career (and very early in mine). I got
answers, too, from Colonel Tom Parker's top assistant, Tom Diskin. Diskin was
more responsive to my inquiries than I had anticipated, but his protectiveness
toward Elvis was already quite clear. The staff of Elvis Presley Enterprises continues that protectiveness to this day, maintaining tight control of all the biographical records that might in other cases have been deposited in scholarly archives by
now. (In the years since Elvis's death, I've dreamed several times that I'm interviewing him at length. Alas, I'm never able to remember his answers when I wake
up.)

The protectiveness of Elvis's managers, both when he was alive and after his
death, is unusual in its intensity. But similar attitudes can be found among the

survivors of deceased individuals in any field. Biographers and psychobiographers have come to recognize a role often played by one or more relatives or friends of the deceased: Defender of the Faith. I used to think of it as the Surviving Spouse Syndrome, but not all spouses show it, as Nina Murray (Harry's widow) once pointed out to me. The Defender of the Faith may instead be one of the subject's children, or a daughter-in-law, or a grandson, or a former graduate student. The Defender assumes the special task of protecting the departed subject's preferred public image—protecting that image not only from casual gossip but also from serious biographical inquiry. The personal papers left behind may be destroyed in one big bonfire, or items may be removed selectively before an archival collection is opened to researchers. Certain items may be locked away from researchers for decades, as designated in the terms of deposit, which the archivists must then obey faithfully. Those same items may sometimes be doled out early and informally by the relatives to selected advocates of the subject.

A resourceful Defender of the Faith can be virtually impossible to get around, if you're not on the "Approved" list. If you're relatively young, you can simply try to outwait the Defender, in hopes that he or she will die before you do. That's how Sigmund Freud scholars finally overcame the obstacle of Anna Freud, his superprotective (and self-protective) daughter. Or you can appeal to a more tolerant friend or relative of the deceased, either to help you change the Defender's mind or to cooperate with you in other strategies to make the forbidden papers available.

Calling Sherlock Holmes

I should warn you, finally, that pursuing primary data for a psychobiographical study can become addictive. Discovering previously unknown evidence about a well-known subject's life generates an excitement that you won't feel when you're dealing with already published biographical data. As you do primary research, you're never quite sure what the next stack of personal papers may reveal, or which of your hypotheses may be strengthened or flattened by the next batch of snapshots or the newly identified deathbed tape-recording. Once you've gotten heavily involved in researching a person's life history, you'll soon begin to feel that no set of biographical data will ever be quite enough. Whatever you find, you'll still have at least one more question to answer, then another, and yet another.

Being a psychobiographical researcher is the closest most of us will ever come to being a private detective. Sigmund Freud had good reason to compare himself to Sherlock Holmes. There's a resonant passage in Sue Grafton's novel *B Is for Burglar*, told first-person by private eye Kinsey Millhone:

> Most of my investigations proceed just like this. Endless notes, endless
> sources checked and rechecked, pursuing leads that sometimes go no

place. . . . plodding along methodically, never knowing at first what might be significant. It's all detail; facts accumulated painstakingly.[14]

That sounds like psychobiographical research to me. It may sound boring to you, and it often is. But Kinsey Millhone, who became a private investigator without quite realizing what she was getting into, now feels she can't give it up. I feel the same way about psychobiography, especially when it involves research into unpublished primary life-history data. I don't carry a nickel-plated, ivory-handled, semi-automatic .32-caliber pistol when I work. But I do love the feel of those clues piling up, certain that a solution to some dark biographical mystery waits just beyond the next page in that dull gray archives box.

PART TWO

The Heart of the Theorist

3

Freud as Leonardo

IN ONE OF MY first public appearances as a psychobiographer, I filled in for Erik Erikson. A Freud scholar named Herbert Lehmann was scheduled to speak at the San Francisco Psychoanalytic Institute on one of Freud's dreams. Erikson had reanalyzed Freud's most thoroughly analyzed dream in a classic paper,[1] so he had been asked to serve as the official discussant following Lehmann's talk. When Erikson canceled because of illness, the search began for a substitute. I wasn't an analyst and had visited the Institute only once or twice, but I had written about the same Freud dream that Erikson had reanalyzed. A friend who's a training analyst at the Institute proposed that I take Erikson's place. I felt like a member of the chorus who goes on for the ailing diva.

Lehmann's talk concerned a dream Freud had in 1910. In the dream's central image, Freud's three daughters are showing him several small curios, including an object that bears a profile of the Florentine religious fanatic Savonarola. Lehmann discussed the dream mainly in terms of Freud's fear that Jung would soon become his successor and would then turn psychoanalysis into a religion. When my turn came to comment, I observed that Freud was especially worried that Jung, as the new leader of the psychoanalytic movement, would abandon Freud's sexual theories. Then I went on to note various ways in which the 1910 dream reflected Freud's sustained resentment about the early termination of his own sex life. He and his wife had decided to stop having intercourse as of 1895, because of his wife's poor health during pregnancy, the rapid growth of his large family, and the lack of effective contraceptives. Those three daughters in the dream, as well as his three sons, had by their very existence turned Freud's sexual parts into nothing more than "small curios." If anyone's dreams could be interpreted through Freudian sexual symbolism, it seemed to me, Freud's dreams were the place to start.

I felt uneasy about how my interpretations were being received by all those august Freudians in the audience. I wasn't bashing Freud, but I wasn't visibly venerating him either. The formal meeting ended, as I recall, with mild applause —no standing ovation for my brilliant insights. I began to feel rather isolated as the analysts milled around, catching up on each other's latest gossip. (Psychoanalysts as a group must rank among the world's great gossips.) But soon one analyst, then another and another, came up to tell me in more or less the same words, "We don't feel free to discuss Freud's sex life in public, but thank you so much for doing it for us. It needed to be done."

By now the dam that blocked public discussions of Freud's private life has not only been broken but swept away. At that time it was still massively in place. Henry Murray once told me that Erik Erikson had visited him soon after Erikson finished writing that classic paper on Freud's dream. Erikson had been greatly agitated during the visit, because Anna Freud was insisting that the psychoanalytic journals refuse to publish his paper until an offending passage about her father's sex life was deleted. Several years after I heard the story from Murray, Erikson told me he couldn't remember any such incident. In its published form, his paper deals mainly with Freud's midlife identity problems and contains only vague allusions to Freud's sexuality.

Just as I feel that Freud's own dreams are the most likely target for a Freudian sexual interpretation, so I assume that any comprehensive psychobiographical study of Freud should discuss how his sex life influenced his analysis of the sexuality of others. There's no call for sensationalism in such a discussion; Freud's sex life was sensational only in its absence. But when he fathered the field of psychobiography, he began with an application of his sexual theories. To understand why he began there, it makes sense to look psychobiographically at the history of Freud's own sexual patterns.

Freud founded psychobiography by analyzing Leonardo da Vinci.[2] Though other writers had already begun to concern themselves with the psychology of "great men," they were mainly engaged in diagnosing each Great Man's psychopathology. In *Leonardo da Vinci and a Memory of His Childhood*, Freud went much further. He applied his systematic theory of personality to the entire span of one creative individual's life, and he sought psychological explanations for Leonardo's achievements as well as his failures.

More than 80 years later, Freud's book remains in certain regards a model psychobiography. Through a close reading of small as well as large clues about Leonardo's life and work, Freud analyzed aspects of Leonardo's character that had long puzzled art historians. Even Leonardo scholars who are not psychoanalytically inclined have acknowledged Freud's insights. In his classic work on Leonardo, Kenneth Clark praises Freud's study for its "passages of fine intuition" and for its "beautiful, and I believe profound, interpretation" of Leonardo's *Virgin and St. Anne*.[3] One major collection of art-historical studies of Leonardo begins with Freud's description of him: "He was like a man who awoke too early in the darkness, while the others were all still asleep."[4] According to the most recent full-scale biography of Leonardo, "Freud was the first to bring into the open the crucial problem of Leonardo's illegitimacy and his parents' separation."[5]

Yet Freud's psychobiography of Leonardo has also been much criticized. It has been attacked not only for dragging the great Leonardo in the mud, but for serious factual errors and lapses in logic. The book has been cited as the prime example of all that's wrong with the whole field of psychobiography—most insistently by David Stannard. Stannard describes Freud's book as "among the finest indicators of the potentials . . . of psychohistory," containing "some of the brightest examples of what makes the best psychohistory so stimulating."[6] But Stannard's praise is merely a device to turn the Leonardo book into a straw man, which Stannard can then pummel in order to discredit not only psychohistory and psychobiography, but all of Freudian theory and practice.

Freud's *Leonardo* offers much to criticize. But it is by no means the best work of which psychobiography is capable. Indeed, its errors leave it far from the best work of which Freud himself was capable. By using the book to present a number of sound guidelines for writing psychobiographies, Freud showed that he knew better. Then why did he violate virtually every one of those guidelines, in the very book in which they appear? That's where his sex life comes in. But before we get to the sexy parts, we need to look at other aspects of the book's origins.

Why Did Freud Write the Book?

First let's consider why Freud wrote the *Leonardo* book at all. He was already quite busy in the fall of 1909, when he began to work on the manuscript. He certainly didn't need anything new to occupy his time. He was treating a heavy load of psychoanalytic patients for at least eight or nine hours a day. He was writing down for publication the set of basic lectures on psychoanalysis that he had delivered without notes at Clark University in September. He was overseeing publication of the third edition of *The Psychopathology of Everyday Life* and planning a second edition of *Three Essays on the Theory of Sexuality*, two of his major works. He was giving free training analyses to at least two colleagues; presenting regular seminars; playing an active role in the Wednesday evening meetings of the Vienna Psychoanalytic Society; working to expand the international psychoanalytic movement; editing books and journals of psychoanalytic writings by others; and carrying on a voluminous correspondence, in longhand, with many colleagues and disciples, especially C. G. Jung and Sandor Ferenczi. Freud wrote to Jung that October, in the same long letter that first mentioned the Leonardo project, "My week's work leaves me numb. I would invent the seventh day if the Lord hadn't done so long ago. . . . Quite against my will I must live like an American: no time for the libido."[7]

So when Freud took on the Leonardo project as well, he must have had compelling reasons to do so, even though he didn't plan it as a major work at first.[8] He mentioned several reasons to Jung. He said he had recently come across a "neurotic" who resembled Leonardo physically and psychologically, but "without his genius." This gave Freud an inspiration about "the riddle of Leonardo da Vinci's character," involving the great man's sexual development. He feared he couldn't find enough useful data, but he hoped his insight into Leonardo's character would provide "a first step in the realm of biography."[9]

Freud may have had other reasons for undertaking the project at that time, which he didn't mention to Jung. He had become increasingly annoyed at the efforts of a budding psychoanalyst named Isidor Sadger, a contentious man who was turning out pathographies of distinguished writers.[10] Sadger relied on speculative hereditary constructs to arrive at pathological diagnoses of his subjects. Freud sternly told Sadger at a meeting of the Wednesday evening group in late 1907, "This is not the correct way to write pathographies. . . . [T]here is altogether no need to write such pathographies. The [psychoanalytic] theories can only be harmed and not one iota is gained for the understanding of the subject."[11]

A year later, Karl Abraham began telling Freud of his plans to write "a psychoanalytic study of Giovanni Segantini [a nineteenth-century Swiss painter], whose personality and works can be understood only with the help of the theory of sexuality."[12] Freud encouraged him, perhaps seeing the trusted Abraham's work as a corrective to Sadger's pathographies. But Abraham was slow to proceed. Toward the end of 1909, Freud announced that he was working on a paper about Leonardo and told Abraham he'd like to see the Segantini paper published in the same volume. "Then there would be two advances into biography writing as we see it."[13] Freud may well have been inspired by Abraham's example to write a psychobiography of an artist. He may also have come to feel that a study of a minor Swiss painter would not be the most impressive way to replace pathography with psychobiography. There may even have been an element of competition with the considerably younger Abraham, though that is not explicit in the correspondence between them.

None of these reasons account for the way the Leonardo project soon became Freud's "obsession," as he described it to Jung in December 1909.[14] Nor do they account for his pushing ahead so vigorously with the Leonardo book over the next four months, in spite of unexpected difficulties and his heavy workload. In February 1910, he reported to Jung, "Nothing is changed. I work every day to the point of exhaustion and then I write a few lines on the Leonardo."[15] In early March, he told another friend, "I am currently in the midst of a writing fit (a study of Leonardo)."[16] Later that month, after reviewing plans for a major psychoanalytic congress, Freud wrote to Jung, "Otherwise I am all Leonardo."[17] Finally, Freud's reasons for writing the book fail to account for the errors he committed in the process, in spite of his own best advice to himself.

Why Did Freud Go Astray?

Freud's errors have been explained in various ways. No one has dared to suggest that Freud was stupid, but a number of commentators on his *Leonardo* book have assumed he was ignorant. A thorough and accurate psychobiography of Leonardo would have required comprehensive knowledge not only of psychoanalytic theory, which of course Freud above all others possessed, but also of art history, Italian culture in the fifteenth and sixteenth centuries, Roman Catholic religious history and tradition, the Italian language, paint chemistry, European Renaissance politics, and several other fields. Freud certainly didn't possess full command of all those areas. So why shouldn't he make errors?

Actually, Freud was remarkably accurate in presenting solid factual information about Leonardo—more accurate, indeed, than some of his later critics.[18] He didn't try to address every aspect of Leonardo's life and work. But with regard to those psychologically interesting aspects that he chose to examine, Freud knew what contemporary scholarship had to say about Leonardo and his times. On the whole he used that knowledge judiciously.

Freud was flatly wrong on one important point. As we now know, he used an erroneous German translation of Leonardo's childhood memory or fantasy or dream about a bird repeatedly thrusting its tail into Leonardo's mouth. In the faulty translation of the Italian word *nibbio*, a European bird of prey (the kite) became an Egyptian bird of prey (the vulture), and that caused major problems. In retrospect, we can say that Freud should have been unusually cautious about verifying the translation's accuracy, since he placed such great emphasis on Leonardo's *nibbio* memory in his book. He didn't exercise such care, and the consequences of that failure will be discussed later in this chapter. But Freud made very few simple, ignorant errors of this kind.

If ordinary ignorance didn't lead Freud into most of his errors, what did? Several critics have suggested that it was a matter of projective identification: Freud identified with Leonardo, and he increased his sense of identification by endowing Leonardo erroneously with some of Freud's own characteristics. Indeed, Freud's errors and weak arguments do remarkably often touch on a supposed characteristic of Leonardo's that we know to have been shared by Freud. Freud himself never publicly acknowledged that he identified with Leonardo, though he admitted to identifications with Hannibal and several other important historical figures. But his identification with Leonardo is evident in the *Leonardo* book and elsewhere. According to Ernest Jones, who knew Freud well, "much of what Freud said when he penetrated into Leonardo's personality was at the same time a self-description; there was surely an extensive identification between Leonardo and himself."[19] And in her unpublished account of her analysis with Freud, Marie Bonaparte reports having confessed to an identification with Leonardo, whereupon Freud said that he too felt such an identification.[20]

But explaining Freud's book in terms of identification and projection is a rather static approach, if all it involves is listing points of identification. Why did Freud feel such a powerful need to identify with Leonardo, or to endow Leonardo with his own qualities? Why did he develop this identification so strongly at that particular time? Why did he stress certain ways in which he identified with Leonardo and not other ways? Why did this become such an important book for Freud at a personal level? Here we begin to delve into some really Freudian motives for Freud's behavior.

Freud's Violations of His Own Guidelines

In the *Leonardo* book Freud sets forth a number of guidelines for psychobiography. He offers some through *prescriptive* example and others by *proscriptive* statement. The prescriptive examples mainly illustrate procedures that a good psychobiographer should follow. Freud demonstrates how to amass various kinds of psychologically interesting data, how to examine the internal as well as the external validity of biographical anecdotes, how to compare the biographical subject's behavior with that of contemporaries in order to evaluate its relative normality or deviancy. The proscriptive statements are explicit pronouncements by Freud about what the good psychobiographer should avoid. These proscriptions are the guidelines that Freud sooner or later violated—at times within the same paragraph. Each substantial violation of a proscriptive guideline appears to have been what Freud himself would have called a *motivated* violation, not just an accident or oversight. Each time, an important aspect of Freud's identification of Leonardo was involved. I'll point out four such proscriptive guidelines, along with Freud's most likely motives for violating each one in the Leonardo book.

Avoid arguments built upon a single clue   As Freud says, "[I]t is unsatisfactory when a peculiar feature is found singly."[21] Or as David Hackett Fischer says in his book *Historians' Fallacies* (without reference to Freud), "If the argument is a single chain, and one link fails, then the chain itself fails with it. But most historians' arguments are not single chains. They are rather like a kind of chain mail which can fail in some part and still retain its shape and function."[22]

Freud's arguments in the *Leonardo* book are sometimes of the chain-mail variety, as with his multiple lines of evidence for Leonardo's homosexual tendencies. But his most spectacular chain of arguments—which he picks up again just after he has paused to warn against arguing from "a peculiar feature . . . found singly"—consists of one single link after another, with only the first link coming from Leonardo himself. That link happens to consist of the mistranslated word *nibbio*, which Freud assumed to mean "vulture."

Freud's full statement is: "Remembering that it is unsatisfactory when a peculiar feature is found singly, let us hasten to add another to it which is even more striking." He then resumes the sequence of arguments already begun, which amounts to no more than a sequence of Freud's own learned associations to the word "vulture." Among other matters, he discusses Egyptian and medieval legends about vultures as mother goddesses and as virgin mothers—a discussion Freud uses as evidence that Leonardo must have spent his first several years alone with his unmarried mother before going to live with his father and stepmother. Freud also notes that the Egyptian vulture mother goddess was believed to possess both male and female sex organs; he speculates that Leonardo assumed the same about his mother; then Freud concludes that all this has something to do with Leonardo's version of homosexuality. Freud even manages to relate the vulture to Leonardo's paintings of women with mysterious smiles, including the Mona Lisa.[23] This astonishing assortment of inferences grows from that single illusory clue of the "vulture" in Leonardo's childhood memory.

Why did Freud so quickly and extravagantly violate his own guideline in this instance? He must have had a compelling reason to do so—and indeed he did. When he wrote *The Interpretation of Dreams* in 1899, the earliest childhood dream that Freud could remember involved Egyptian bird-headed figures, which little Sigmund had associated with gods. Freud reports the dream thus: "I saw *my beloved mother, with a peculiarly peaceful, sleeping expression on her features, being carried into the room by two (or three) people with birds' beaks and laid upon the bed. I awoke in tears and screaming, and interrupted my parents' sleep.*"[24] In Freud's incomplete interpretation of this dream, he suggests that his anxiety upon awakening did not reflect a concern about his mother dying as he first assumed, but instead expressed "an obscure and evidently sexual craving."[25] Ten years after *The Interpretation of Dreams*, Freud interprets Leonardo's childhood dream/fantasy/memory also as involving sexual yearnings between son and mother. Then he associates this imagery with Egyptian bird-gods, much as he had free-associated to his own dream.

Freud describes Leonardo's actual relationship with his mother (rather than the relationship in Leonardo's "vulture" story) as involving an early idyllic period of total love, which is then disrupted by figures from outside. Elsewhere Freud paints a similar picture of his own early relationship with his mother. But in both cases, even before the idyll is disrupted by external forces, disturbing forces develop internally. In Leonardo's case, the mother proves to be too loving: "So, like all unsatisfied mothers, she took her little son in place of her husband, and by the too early maturing of his erotism robbed him of a part of his masculinity."[26] Thirteen years earlier Freud had told his friend Fliess how his own libido had first been aroused at about age three by seeing his mother naked when they spent a night together on a train. In the same letter he described how his nursemaid had been "my teacher in sexual matters and complained because I was clumsy and unable to do anything. (Neurotic impotence always comes about in this way.)"[27] Here as elsewhere, Freud tends to divide his images of his early maternal contacts into a good mother and a bad mother.[28] What his two mothers (his real mother and his nursemaid) did to him sexually in early childhood can be seen as equivalent to what, in Freud's speculative version, the child Leonardo's mother did to Leonardo.

But why did the Freud of late 1909 or early 1910, hard at work on the Leonardo manuscript, suddenly become so interested again in issues that related to a childhood dream of his mother's apparent death, or to his mother's arousal of his libido circa 1859? His mother was still relatively healthy in 1909–1910; she lived for another 20 years. His father had been dead for 13 years. We know of no major external events in Freud's life at this time that would have provoked a renewed concern with his mother's role in the development of his sex life. However, certain more subtle events were at work to stimulate this concern. We'll see them emerge along with Freud's remaining proscriptive guidelines for psychobiography.

Avoid pathographizing the psychobiographical subject and avoid idealizing the psychobiographical subject   Freud placed these opposing guidelines at the beginning and the end of the *Leonardo* book. The book's first sentences are:

> When psychiatric research . . . approaches one who is among the greatest of the human race, it is not doing so for the reasons so frequently ascribed to it by laymen. "To blacken the radiant and drag the sublime into the dust" is no part of its purpose, and there is no satisfaction for it in narrowing the gulf which separates the perfection of the great from the inadequacy of the objects that are its usual concern.[29]

So much for Isidor Sadger and his mean-spirited pathographies! Freud warns against the other side of this coin in the first paragraph of the book's final chapter:

> . . . [B]iographers are fixated on their heroes in a quite special way. In many cases they have chosen their hero as the subject of their studies because—for reasons of their personal emotional life—they have felt a special affection for him from the very first. They then devote their energies to a task of idealization, aimed at enrolling the great man among the class of their infantile models—at reviving in him, perhaps, the child's idea of his father. . . . That they should do this is regrettable, for they thereby sacrifice truth to an illusion, and for the sake of their infantile phantasies abandon the opportunity of penetrating the most fascinating secrets of human nature.[30]

These two guidelines are sound precepts, valuable for every psychobiographer. But from what we've already seen of Freud's strong identification with Leonardo, we know he violated the proscription against idealization as soon as he chose to write about Leonardo. At the least, he "felt a special affection" for Leonardo "from the very first." Freud began to violate the proscription against pathography almost as soon as he started to discuss Leonardo's character. He intensified this violation when he approached Leonardo's early relationship with his mother Caterina.

Again, Freud said that Caterina did two bad things to little Leonardo: She initiated "the too early maturing of his erotism," and she "robbed him of a part of his masculinity."[31] That is, Caterina aroused Leonardo's sexual interest at a time when he couldn't really do anything about it, and she then forced him into becoming an abstinent homosexual. She did the latter by loving little Leonardo so hard that in self-defense he identified with her. When he reached adulthood, this identification left Leonardo able to love only little boys who were much like himself as a child—little boys who were as sexually unattainable as he had been to his mother.

Freud held a relatively tolerant view of homosexuality, but he knew that the general reading public of his day did not. (He warned one correspondent that the *Leonardo* book "is not likely to be to your taste. It takes for granted that the reader is not shocked by homosexual topics."[32]) So when he firmly affixed a label of homosexuality to Leonardo, he realized he would be seen as "blackening the radiant and dragging the sublime into the dust," at least by much of that reading public. In the course of the book Freud also cited a number of neurotic symptoms displayed by Leonardo, and he repeatedly discussed the frustrations and failures of the man he otherwise referred to as a "universal genius."[33]

However, shortly after he blackened Leonardo's name by identifying his core psychological problems, Freud resumed the opposite process of idealization. He did so by adopting several positions that rarely if ever appeared in Freud's writings on other individuals. Did Leonardo have an excessively strong "craving for knowledge"? Yes, says Freud, but it was not neurotic in origin; it was probably inborn, organic, "already active in the subject's earliest childhood," and was only reinforced by the attentions of Leonardo's love-starved mother.[34] Indeed, Leonardo's "instinct for research" was "the rarest and most perfect" type, escaping "both inhibition of thought and neurotic compulsive thinking."[35] Was Leonardo homosexual? Yes, but his homosexuality "was restricted to what is called ideal homosexuality . . . sublimating the greater part of his libido into an urge for research."[36] Was Leonardo neurotic? Well, says Freud, "we should be inclined to place him *close* to the type of neurotic that we describe as 'obsessional,' and we may *compare* his researches to the 'obsessive brooding' of neurotics, and his inhibitions to what are known as their 'abulias.'"[37] So Leonardo *resembled* a neurotic in a number of ways, but Freud was reluctant to *call* him a neurotic.

Why this protectiveness about Leonardo's intense instinct for research, about his presumably unexpressed homosexuality, about his not quite neurotic symptoms? In part, Freud was simply trying to avoid sounding pathographic as he proceeded to identify ways in which Leonardo diverged markedly from typical developmental patterns. But he also appears to have felt reluctant to give deviant or pathological labels to characteristics in Leonardo that he recognized in himself.

Once more the question arises: Why were such matters so salient to Freud at this time that he needed to give voice to them, and simultaneously to defend himself from their negative implications, through his identification with Leonardo? That "why" question will finally be answered in the course of dealing with Freud's fourth proscriptive guideline for psychobiography.

Avoid drawing strong conclusions from inadequate data   Near the end of his book, Freud says that when a psychobiographical "undertaking does not provide any certain results—and this is perhaps so in Leonardo's case"—psychoanalytic theory should not be blamed. "It is . . . only the author who is to be held responsible for the failure, by having forced psycho-analysis to pronounce an expert opinion on the basis of such insufficient material."[38] But here is Sigmund Freud, the founder and leader of the psychoanalytic movement, two pages away from concluding a manuscript full of "expert opinions" based on clearly "insufficient material," and eager to publish it as soon as he can. What's going on? Why is he driven to finish this study and get it into print a mere six months after he began to work on it seriously?

In the fall of 1909, Freud's inner life was deeply troubled in two major psychological domains—the ones that he's said to have identified politely as "love and work,"[39] but that he often described less politely as sex and ambition.[40] When we look at what was particularly troubling him in these areas, we may better appreciate why Freud strove so hard at that time to show how the great Leonardo da Vinci suffered similar difficulties in precisely the same areas, and how Leonardo triumphed over them. I'll examine Freud's problems with love and sex in some detail. His difficulties with work and ambition were also important, but in keeping with Freud's own theoretical emphases, I'll give them only a brief glance.

In the area of love and sex, Freud's personal history had been largely one of inhibition, overcome by passion, followed by frustration. He had held great hopes for marriage during his abstinent four-year courtship of Martha Bernays. But when it came, the marriage proved to be a profound disappointment both sexually and emotionally. The sexual aspect appears to have been largely terminated at an early age for both parties, when Freud was 39 and Martha was 34. Freud alluded guardedly to this early termination of his marital sexuality in comments to his friends. In an essay written two years before the Leonardo book, he was much more explicit about married sex in general:

> This brings us to the question whether sexual intercourse in legal
> marriage can offer full compensation for the restrictions imposed before

marriage. . . . [O]ur cultural sexual morality restricts sexual intercourse even in marriage itself, since it imposes on married couples the necessity of contenting themselves, as a rule, with a very few procreative acts. As a consequence of this consideration, satisfying sexual intercourse in marriage takes place only for a few years; and we must subtract from this, of course, the intervals of abstention necessitated by regard for the wife's health. After these three, four or five years, the marriage becomes a failure in so far as it has promised the satisfaction of sexual needs. For all the devices hitherto invented for preventing conception impair sexual enjoyment, hurt the fine susceptibilities of both partners and even actually cause illness. Fear of the consequences of sexual intercourse first brings the married couple's physical affection to an end; and then, as a remoter result, it usually puts a stop as well to the mental sympathy between them, which should have been the successor to their original passionate love. The spiritual disillusionment and bodily deprivation to which most marriages are thus doomed puts both partners back in the state they were in before their marriage, except for being the poorer by the loss of an illusion, and they must once more have recourse to their fortitude in mastering and deflecting their sexual instinct.[41]

We don't know how many marital relationships Freud had observed closely enough to support such a dismal view of love and sex in marriage. But this passage describes the Freuds' marriage almost exactly, at least from Sigmund Freud's perspective. Several writers have concluded, from the early cessation of Freud's sexual relationship with his wife, that he must have possessed a low or heavily inhibited sex drive throughout his life.[42] But the passage just quoted, including such phrases as "original passionate love," "bodily deprivation," and "fortitude in mastering and deflecting their sexual instinct," does not sound as though Freud easily accepted the halt in his marital sexuality. Other evidence suggests that he struggled for several years with the question of abstinence before finally acceding to the pressures of a too-rapidly-growing family and his wife Martha's health problems.[43] Freud's subsequent dreams, over a period of ten or more years, often appear to express strong resentment toward Martha.[44] He felt resentful because she became pregnant so easily, because she often became ill during her pregnancies, and because she refused to engage in any kind of sexual activity beyond what he refers to in the passage above as "a very few procreative acts." Freud himself sometimes experienced partial impotence,[45] which added to their sexual problems. His impotence probably derived in part from his anxiety lest he should make Martha pregnant again, and partly from the crude contraceptive devices available at the time. But Sigmund mainly blamed Martha for forcing the almost complete termination of his sexual activity—or rather, he blamed

Martha plus the mother and the nursemaid who had warped his sexual development in infancy.

Beginning at about the time his active sexual life came to a halt, circa 1895, Freud entered a hugely creative period of theoretical development. One concept that began to emerge during this period was *sublimation*, the transformation of sexual energy into culturally creative acts. Freud's incorporation of sublimation into psychoanalytic theory was probably inspired to some degree by his personal observation that when he stopped being sexually active, his creativity increased substantially. Furthermore, he may have been able to temper his bitterness concerning his diminished sex life by concluding that his libido was now being transformed into brilliant ideas.[46]

Over the decade following his first references to sublimation,[47] Freud saw himself as growing old and felt his creative powers subsiding. Initially, these self-perceptions did not influence his ideas about sublimation. As late as 1905, he wrote that "powerful components are acquired for every kind of cultural achievement by this diversion of sexual instinctual forces from sexual aims and their direction to new ones—a process which deserves the name of 'sublimation.'"[48] But he continued to worry about the aging process, and when in 1907 he wrote to Jung about his "entry into the climacteric years,"[49] he was referring at least in part to a fading of his sexual capacities. By the time Freud next discussed sublimation at any length, he no longer perceived a direct link between sexual abstinence and genuine creativity. In the same 1908 essay where he characterized marital sex so dismally, he observed that abstinence might be useful for the "young *savant*," who "can, by his self-restraint, liberate forces for his studies." But, said Freud, "An abstinent artist is hardly conceivable. . . . [He] probably finds his artistic achievements powerfully stimulated by his sexual experience. In general I have not gained the impression that sexual abstinence helps to bring about energetic and self-reliant men of action or original thinkers or bold emancipators and reformers."[50] Far from being a young *savant*, Freud would surely have included himself in one of the latter categories, for which he no longer saw sexual sublimation as having strong generative power.

Interestingly, this devaluation of sexual abstinence was followed by the temporary return of Freud's sexual vigor. Nearly all we know of this is from a letter to Jung in February 1910, when Freud refers to a discussion that took place during their trip to America the previous September: "My Indian summer of eroticism that we spoke of on our trip has withered lamentably under the pressure of work. I am resigned to being old and no longer even think continually of growing old."[51]

That official English translation of the passage is fairly loose. Freud's German word *Johannistrieb* is not exactly equivalent to the English term "Indian summer"; it refers instead to a second blossoming or a late love. Whatever Freud's second blossoming of eroticism involved, it seems to have lasted from sometime before the American trip until at least the end of the year or a little longer, several months in all. It was surely not an affair with his sister-in-law Minna or with another woman. As an old man, Jung gossiped about remarks he said Minna had made to him during his first visit to the Freud home in 1907, suggesting an "intimate" relationship between her and Sigmund. He would surely have gossiped a lot more if Sigmund had told him, two years later, of an Indian summer of love with Minna.[52] Most likely the second blossoming that Freud described to Jung was a temporary resumption of sexual relations between Sigmund and Martha, after she had indisputably passed the upper limit of childbearing age. It need not even have gone that far. Freud may simply have experienced renewed feelings of sexual potency that were not carried into any active sexual relationship.

Whatever his *Johannistrieb* was, it occurred in close conjunction with another shift in Freud's views about sublimation. He began to work on the Leonardo book shortly after he returned from the American trip. Freud mentioned sublimation in his first description of the work to Jung,[53] but at that point the concept was not prominent in his consideration of Leonardo's adult achievements. When Freud presented a preliminary version of his work to the Vienna Psychoanalytic Society in December 1909, he described Leonardo's sublimation largely as a process occurring "in earliest childhood," when Leonardo "translated his libido into the drive to investigate, and so it remained. With this, the greatest part of his sexual activity was exhausted for all time to come."[54] There Freud was at least back to sublimation as a basis for some kind of important creative activity (Leonardo's scientific investigations), but it seemed to remain unimportant to Leonardo's artistic creativity.[55]

However, by the time Freud finished the *Leonardo* manuscript at the beginning of April 1910—after his "Indian summer of eroticism" had subsided—one of his major focal points had become sublimation as an essential foundation for both scientific and artistic creativity. Moreover, Freud had added a great deal about Leonardo's renewal of artistic creativity in middle age, including the book's most striking passage:

> At the summit of his [Leonardo's] life, when he was in his early
> fifties—a time when in women the sexual characters have already under-
> gone involution and when in men the libido not infrequently makes a
> further energetic advance—a new transformation came over him. Still
> deeper layers of the contents of his mind became active once more; but
> this further regression was to the benefit of his art, which was in the
> process of becoming stunted. He met the woman who awakened his
> memory of his mother's happy smile of sensual rapture; and, influenced
> by this revived memory, he recovered the stimulus that guided him at
> the beginning of his artistic endeavours. . . . He painted the Mona Lisa,
> the "St. Anne with Two Others" and the series of mysterious pictures

which are characterized by the enigmatic smile. With the help of the oldest of all his erotic impulses he enjoyed the triumph of once more conquering the inhibition in his art. This final development is obscured from our eyes in the shadows of approaching age. Before this his intellect had soared upwards to the highest realizations of a conception of the world that left his epoch far behind it.[56]

That passage is remarkable for more than its rhetorical flourishes. First, Freud refers to a "further energetic advance" in the libidos of many middle-aged men. That proposition is considerably more emphatic than any other statement Freud ever published about midlife sexual development.[57] Second, he implies that Leonardo himself experienced just such an energetic libidinal advance, which overcame long-standing inhibitions and stimulated a regression to "the oldest of all his erotic impulses," presumably Leonardo's sexual yearnings for his sensually rapturous mother. Now, there is no biographical evidence at all that Leonardo underwent any kind of libidinal advance in his early fifties, or that Leonardo's early erotic impulses toward his mother were ever rearoused. But Freud had recently described his own second blossoming of eroticism in his early fifties. One can also read the results of the self-described "obsession" which Freud developed toward Leonardo at that time—a book in which the weakest arguments and the most prominent errors involve the assertion of an ambivalent infantile erotic relationship between Leonardo and his mother. That assertion recapitulates Freud's memories of his own infantile feelings much more accurately than it describes anything known about Leonardo.

Here, finally, we can see why Freud felt compelled to write a book at this particular time in his life which dealt with the maternal arousal of a child's libido. It need not have had anything to do with his mother's behavior in 1909 or 1910. It need not have involved his meeting some woman who reminded him of his mother's ambivalent sensuality during his childhood, as he says was the case with Leonardo and Mona Lisa. It required no more than what we know from Freud's own words: that his feelings of eroticism were aroused again for a time, and that he entertained renewed hopes that middle-aged eroticism could be sublimated into a resurgence of creativity. The case of Leonardo, read in that way—or projected onto in that way—would have reassured Freud in 1910 much as he had been reassured by his initial elaboration of the sublimation concept, after his sex life came to a halt in 1895. It can be a good thing to give up your practice of sex, he was telling himself repeatedly, if it makes you a better theorist of sex.

And what of Freud's insistence that Leonardo was a homosexual, but an "idealized" homosexual? As his marital sexuality had begun to founder in the 1890s, Freud developed an increasingly intense intellectual and emotional relationship with his friend Wilhelm Fliess. There was never anything overtly physical about the relationship, but Freud later admitted that strong homosexual emotions were involved. In October 1910, he told a male friend that he was working through those homosexual feelings toward Fliess again, even though he had broken off the friendship with Fliess eight years earlier.[58] His correspondence of the time suggests that in 1909–1910 Freud was also experiencing what he considered to be homosexual feelings toward Jung, Ferenczi, and perhaps others among his younger male disciples. Finding himself again frustrated in expressing his erotic urges heterosexually when the "Indian summer of eroticism" ended, Freud may have experienced both an intensification of homosexual feelings and an increased need to justify them. He justified them first by seeing in Leonardo a model of the great creative figure who is homosexual, but only psychologically and not behaviorally so. He justified them second by postulating that Leonardo's homosexual *and* heterosexual impulses were effectively sublimated into creative activity, as Freud's own impulses could be too.

Then there were Freud's feelings about "work or ambition." Those feelings added to his sense of identification with Leonardo in 1909–1910, reinforced his obsession with getting the book written, and led him into further psycho-biographical fallacies. A major line of argument in the book, which leads to several pronounced exaggerations if not downright errors, involves these inter-connected elements: (1) Leonardo's emotional and intellectual isolation; (2) his rejection of religious and traditional authority in favor of empirical observation; and (3) the inability of Leonardo's contemporaries to understand his genius, which was fully recognized only by posterity. This line of argument may be linked to Freud's growing anxieties about Jung's religious mysticism and about the inadequacy of Jung or any other psychoanalyst to become Freud's successor. Freud was further disappointed with the general public's failure to give psycho-analysis its due, and he was becoming increasingly worried about how his age, ill health, and death would affect the psychoanalytic movement, beyond the issue of finding a successor. Several of these concerns became much more explicit in his only other psychobiographical book, *Moses and Monotheism*, written over 25 years later.[59] Freud again had personal reasons for writing that book at that particular time,[60] and he fell into some of the same kinds of errors because of those personal reasons.

Two final points should be made about the earlier book. First, Freud's *Leonardo* is not representative of psychobiography in general, because its crucial errors derive from idiosyncratic factors bound up in Freud's personal conflicts. Those specific errors need not be repeated by other psychobiographers. Second, Freud's *Leonardo* still offers valuable lessons to practicing psychobiographers and to readers of their work. Not only does it present a number of valid guidelines for doing psychobiography well; it also tells us a kind of cautionary tale, showing what can happen if we ignore Freud's guidelines as he did. The moral of this tale can be expressed in one last proscriptive guideline for all psychobiographers everywhere: *Avoid assuming that you are less susceptible to psychobiographical error than Freud was.* Freud knew what to avoid doing, but for his own personal reasons he did it anyway. You may know what to avoid, but you can easily fall into the same kinds of traps if you don't watch out.

4

The Auntification of C. G. Jung

Henry Murray often said that all theory is autobiography. André Maurois observed that biography is sometimes disguised autobiography.[1] I'd almost be willing to add a dictum of my own: "No psychobiography without autobiography." It's frustrating if not impossible to do a psychobiographical analysis when your data deal only with the externals of an individual's life. A few autobiographers have striven to remain entirely in the realm of observable behavior,[2] but most blend descriptions of their subjective experiences with accounts of external events. Rarely is the inner life given as large a role as in C. G. Jung's *Memories, Dreams, Reflections*.[3]

Memories, Dreams, Reflections (henceforth cited as MDR) has become one of the most widely read autobiographies of our time. Initial reviews and later assessments of the book emphasized both Jung's honesty and the autobiography's unusually inward orientation: its focus on Jung's dreams and visions throughout his life, rather than on people, places, or public events. In so characterizing the autobiography, others have followed the lead of Jung himself. He is quoted in the introduction as complaining about the "self-deceptions and downright lies" of "too many autobiographies." He says that in order to consider "the very first beginnings of my life . . . in an objective fashion," "in order to assure for myself the necessary detachment and calm," he has had to promise himself "that the results would not be published in my lifetime." He continues:

> Only what is interior has proved to have substance and a determining value. As a result, all memory of outer events has faded, and perhaps these "outer" experiences were never so very essential anyhow, or were so only in that they coincided with phases of my inner development. An enormous part of these "outer" manifestations of my life has vanished

from my memory. . . . On the other hand, my recollection of "inner"
experiences has grown all the more vivid and colorful.[4]

This autobiography is the principal or sole source of information on key
periods in Jung's life, especially his early childhood and the period of profound
psychological distress following his breakup with Freud. *MDR* has therefore
served as a foundation for all subsequent biographies of Jung.[5]

But the conditions under which *MDR* emerged were no guarantee of its accuracy or its comprehensiveness. A close examination of the autobiography and its
evolution shows it to be less factually honest than has usually been assumed.
Furthermore, preliminary drafts show Jung to have been a good deal more concerned with external events and personages in his life than we have been led to
believe. In addition, the published versions of *MDR* completely omit or barely
mention certain events and relationships highly important to Jung's inner life.

Reshaping one's life history to fit a final self-image is not unusual in autobiographical writing. Early in his prologue Jung acknowledges that he is doing
just that: "I have now undertaken . . . to tell my personal myth. . . . Whether or
not the stories are 'true' is not the problem. The only question is whether what I
tell is *my* fable, *my* truth."[6] Actually that's not the only question, especially when
the reader is asked to accept Jung's stories as true accounts of the behavior of
other individuals (e.g., Sigmund Freud) whose lives were significant beyond their
role in Jung's personal myth. But Jung's statement does convey an important
aspect of the autobiographical impulse, one that carries a degree of personal
privilege: any autobiography is written at least in part to get down on paper how
the world looks from one uniquely idiosyncratic perspective. Unfortunately, Jung
was not fully permitted to exercise that privilege. He *tried* to tell his own personal
myth, but his autobiography was then tampered with by others, who remodeled it
in ways with which he did not altogether agree.

The history of Jung's autobiography has received little public discussion. Jung's
inner circle in Switzerland (and faithful Jungians everywhere) have been far more
protective of his public image than even Freudians have been of Freud. The major
collections of Jung's personal papers in Switzerland and elsewhere have not been
easily accessible, though the situation is improving. I've pieced together the
following information over more than a decade from several unpublished sources,
in addition to the published autobiography in its variant editions and a growing
library of books and articles about Jung's life. A resourceful private eye with an
ample expense account might have added everything up a lot faster, but spending
a decade of intermittent research on a psychobiographical subject isn't that unusual. As in this case, the subject's papers may be distributed over several archival
locations, some of which restrict access longer or more severely than others.
Certain sources of information may remain unknown until you stumble over
them, or until somebody better informed takes pity on you and points the way.

Certain pieces of the psychobiographical puzzle may make no sense until other pieces turn up—accidentally or after a concentrated search. A brief tour through the unpublished sources I've consulted on Jung (in chronological order of my access to them) will give a representative picture of the typically meandering course of such long-term archival investigation.

My search began with an oral history of Jung, called the C. G. Jung Biographical Archive, housed at Harvard Medical School's Countway Library in Boston. This oral history was assembled in the late 1960s and early 1970s by Gene Nameche, a young scholar who was supported financially by a Jung-oriented private foundation.[7] Nameche interviewed everyone he could find who had known Jung well enough to possess significant firsthand memories of the man. To encourage openness, Nameche promised the mostly elderly interviewees that none of their recollections would be made available to scholars for at least ten years. Most of the files had only recently been opened when I began to look at them in the early 1980s. (Certain sensitive interviews or portions of interviews will remain closed for years to come. Some interviews appear to have been altogether erased from the record.)

At the Countway Library, I also came upon a heavily copyedited manuscript of the initial English-language version of the autobiography. This was not quite the legendary Urtext, the original German-language manuscript prepared in close collaboration by Jung and his secretary. But the Countway manuscript *was* the document that several translators, editors, and copyeditors worked on at Pantheon Books to establish the basic form of the autobiography's first published edition. (For both personal and legal reasons, Jung insisted on the book's publication initially in English translation rather than in the original German.) The Countway manuscript was used to establish the specific phrasing of many passages, which were then translated back into German for the autobiography's subsequent publication in Europe. I had not known of the manuscript's existence when I began doing research on Jung. A friendly fellow researcher pointed it out to me after I had rummaged through the Jung oral history off and on for over a year.[8]

Several years and several hundred miles away, I happened upon the correspondence files of the Bollingen Foundation, which had been deposited in the Library of Congress. The Bollingen Foundation (founded and funded by Paul and Mary Mellon, who had been analyzed by Jung) has financially supported many projects connected with Jungian psychology, especially the publication of Jung's *Collected Works* in an authoritative English translation. In the late 1980s, while I was doing research on Freud in the Library of Congress's Manuscript Reading Room, I noticed the Bollingen Foundation papers on a list of the Library's archives. I thought the papers might include a few items dealing with the translation of the *Collected Works,* but I didn't expect to find anything on Jung's memoirs, since the Bollingen Foundation had not been officially involved in the translation or publication of *MDR*. I soon found, however, that several of the people involved in translating, editing, and publishing the *Collected Works* also played a significant informal role in the evolution of the autobiography, and often corresponded with others in Jungian circles about how it was coming along.

By this time, I had heard from various sources that Jung's own personal papers were sitting in an archive in Zürich. But nobody I talked to knew what was there or how to get into it. I tried to obtain the autobiographical components of the archive by mail, or at least to learn whether any parts of the autobiography were included, but my inquiries met with little success. The Jung papers were not well organized, I was told, and the Jung family was not eager to grant access.

I finally flew to Zürich in 1991 and took a local train to Jung's house in the suburb of Küsnacht. There I spent a remarkable three hours in Jung's study, much of the time in friendly argument with C. G.'s 82-year-old son Franz Jung about whether anyone outside the family could have any valid reason to look at any of C. G.'s unpublished papers.

Franz Jung was a gracious host, and he told delightful stories about his father's architectural ineptitude. (Franz is a professional architect; C. G. was an eager amateur.) But I left the house feeling discouraged about the prospect of ever getting into the archives. When I went to the ETH-Bibliothek two days later, the archivist (Dr. Beat Glaus) said that Franz Jung had sent word to let me look at all the manuscripts I had asked for. I wouldn't be allowed to photocopy them, but I could take as many notes as I wanted. So for a week my fiancée and I ignored the touristic temptations of Zürich and copied out in longhand various fragments of *MDR*'s German-language manuscript. The ETH-Bibliothek didn't have as much of the manuscript as I'd hoped to see, but it was the real thing. Portions were written in Jung's hand; the rest had been typed by his secretary and collaborator, Aniela Jaffé. We're talking Urtext here, folks!

On the same day that I got my first taste of the Urtext, I interviewed Aniela Jaffé at her Zürich apartment. In her mid-eighties, Frau Jaffé was frail and nearly blind, but she remained sharp of mind and tongue. She dwelt at some length on her troubles with the Jung family. She told me they had repeatedly tried to deprive her of the title-page credit and the royalties she deserved for co-authoring the autobiography. She also said she couldn't understand why I'd want to write anything about the history of *MDR*, since she had already written everything that needed to be said about it. But she answered my questions anyway.

When I had looked through the Bollingen Foundation papers at the Library of Congress, I noticed references to a set of Jung "protocols" that had been tucked away there for a decade but were still off-limits to scholars. At first I thought these "protocols" were records of Jung's dreams and visions, perhaps transcribed from his personal diaries—potentially interesting but not what I was looking for. However, through an exchange of letters with William McGuire (executive editor of Jung's *Collected Works* and the most reliable scholar in the Jungian camp), I came to realize that the "protocols" contained many additional parts of the German Urtext of *MDR*. More precisely, they were a sort of proto-Urtext, including large and small chunks of the materials from which Aniela Jaffé had assembled the Urtext itself. On another visit to the Library of Congress in the summer of 1992, I learned from staff members that McGuire had the authority to give me permission to look at the "protocols" well in advance of their scheduled declassification. So I went to a pay phone in the hallway outside the Manuscript Reading Room, called McGuire in Princeton, and asked for permission. He gave it, and I went back in to feast on the "protocols." I eventually determined that substantial portions of *MDR*'s original manuscript are neither at the Library of Congress nor at the ETH-Bibliothek. But between those two depositories of Jungian texts, there was quite enough Ur to make one researcher happy for many weeks.

History of the Autobiography

As early as 1925, Jung described significant portions of his life history to a group of his students. He then pointed out, in good psychobiographical fashion, how his life had influenced his theories.[9] Jung was less forthcoming about his personal history after 1925, except for occasional individual disclosures to personal friends and patients. He showed no inclination to write an autobiography, and he was reluctant to cooperate with biographers—refusing, for instance, to make available his correspondence with Freud, and indeed denying that it was of serious interest to anyone. As Jung grew older and more famous, individuals friendly to the Jung cause repeatedly tried to develop an official or semi-official biography with his help, before his priceless memories passed away forever. Every such attempt failed, up to 1956.

In that year, the brilliant German/American publisher Kurt Wolff began to sound out several people close to Jung who might be more successful at obtaining the Old Man's cooperation. (By this time Jung was 81.) Wolff first approached Jolande Jacobi, a Jungian analyst from Vienna who had written a basic introduction to Jungian theory that Jung himself had blessed with a foreword. Wolff proposed that Jacobi interview Jung at length and write a biography based largely on those interviews. Jacobi later stated:

> I refused, because I was afraid there would be difficulties with Jung. I knew that he was very moody and difficult to handle. And I also had no time. I wanted to do my own things. I suggested that Mrs. Jaffé should do it with him. She was his secretary and she saw him every day anyway. I went to Jung and told him about Kurt Wolff's wish for the biography, and was able to convince him. It was difficult to do so, and [to get him] to accept Mrs. Jaffé to collaborate.[10]

Aniela Jaffé was not an obvious choice to become the authorized biographer of a world-renowned intellectual figure. She had done some writing for Jungian publications, but she was neither a professional scholar nor a prominent member of Jung's inner circle. She had, however, been analyzed by Jung; she had practiced a modest amount of Jungian therapy; and she had answered enough of his correspondence, with Jung's feedback about the appropriateness of her answers, to be able to write with some confidence in his voice.[11] There were also practical aspects to letting her write the authorized biography rather than assigning it to someone else. Jaffé had been working for the Jung-Institut and then for Jung himself over many years, at only a modest salary. According to people familiar with the circumstances, Jung accepted the idea of Jaffé's doing the authorized biography and receiving the royalties as a way of providing an informal pension for her after he died. (As the book developed in unexpected ways, the pension arrangement was somewhat curtailed; Jung's final written agreement with Jaffé divided the royalties between her and the Jung estate 50-50.[12] Nonetheless, over the years she must have done well financially by the arrangement.)

Initially, Frau Jaffé was supposed to develop a biography that combined interview responses from Jung with various unpublished autobiographical materials he had already written. The latter included his seminars of 1925, his descriptions of his major trips abroad, and the private volumes he kept of his dreams and visions, both the "Red Book" and the even more personal "Black Book." By May 1957, Jaffé had already collected a substantial amount of interview material, which she recorded in shorthand. However, as Frau Jaffé notes in her introduction to the published work, Jung himself became increasingly intrigued with the project. In late 1957, he began to write out in longhand his own account of his early life. By the time he stopped, three or four months later, he had written roughly 150 pages of manuscript, which would form most of the first one-third of the published book.

Frau Jaffé supplemented what Jung had written about his childhood and youth with related material from their interviews. She pieced together large portions of the remaining chapters from his earlier unpublished writings. Jung himself subsequently wrote part or all of at least two additional chapters, and edited Jaffé's manuscript of the chapters that he had not written especially for the autobiography.

As I've noted, Jung decided to have the autobiography published first in English translation by an American press rather than in the original German. He did so partly because this particular project had been initiated and strongly encouraged by Kurt Wolff, who was at that time head of Pantheon Books in New York. There was a legal angle as well. Jung had a long-standing contract with a Swiss publishing house that applied to any of his works first published in the German language. Jung was not altogether happy with that publisher or with its subsidiary arrangements for publication of his work in other countries. He reportedly entertained hopes that the autobiography might gain a wider audience through another publisher. So the first-edition American publication of *Memories, Dreams, Reflections* was a means of getting around the restrictive Swiss contract.

Jung wanted to have the autobiography translated into English by the official translator of his *Collected Works*, Richard F. C. Hull. Hull was an Englishman, a professional translator who had known little about Jung or Jungian theory before he was hired to begin translating the *Collected Works*. In short order Hull became an expert on Jungian concepts. He was willing and eager to translate the autobiography, but he was at that time in the midst of translating a major volume of the *Collected Works*, the formidably obscure *Mysterium Coniunctionis*. Hull was also regarded by Kurt Wolff and others as possessing too formal a writing style for an appropriate translation of the relatively informal autobiography.[13] Wolff instead hired Richard and Clara Winston, who were experienced at translating German literary works, to do a sample translation of Jung's first three chapters. Wolff quietly held in reserve the possibility that if the Winstons did not work out, Hull could be brought in to translate the entire autobiography.[14]

At this point, early in 1960, C. G. Jung himself abruptly stepped back into the autobiographical process. Jung was nearly 85, easily tired and increasingly frail. (He would die a year and a half later.) He had finished his major written contributions to the manuscript by the summer of 1959, and others may have thought or hoped he was finished with the project forever. But on one of his recreational drives into the Swiss countryside with his housekeeper and an old friend, he took a side trip to visit R.F.C. Hull, who was hard at work on the *Mysterium Coniunctionis* in the town of Ascona. Five months later, Hull wrote a detailed and dramatic account of Jung's visit, which has not previously been published. Before quoting at length from Hull's account, I should explain a key term in it. This is the German word *Tantifizierung*, apparently invented by Jung on the basis of the word *Tante* or aunt, and literally translated by Hull as "auntification"—that is, the process of turning a person into a stereotypical maiden aunt. Jung wanted to present himself in the autobiography as blunt, fiercely honest, intimately self-revealing—the opposite of that stereotypical aunt on all counts. The verb form *tantifiziert*, literally "auntified," was also used by Jung. Here is Hull's account:

> The old man turned up on leap-day with Mr McCormick and Miss Bailey, said he wanted to talk, and talked solidly with me alone for over an hour about the autobiography. I gathered that there was some controversy going on as to the "authentic" text. (At this time I had seen no texts at all.) He impressed upon me, with the utmost emphasis, that he had said what he wanted to say in his own way—"a bit blunt and crude sometimes"—and that he did not want his work to be "tantifiziert" ("auntified" or, in Jack [Barrett]'s felicitous phrase, "old-maidified.") "You will see what I mean when you get the text," he said. As he spoke at

some length about the practice of "ghost-writing" by American publishers, I inferred that any "Tantifizierung" would be done by Kurt
[Wolff]. I thereupon asked Jung whether I would have the authority to
"de-old-maidify" the text supplied to me by Kurt. "In those cases," he
said, "the big guns will go into action," pointing to himself. I found all
this rather puzzling, because Kurt had said earlier that, especially in the
first three chapters, the impact lay precisely in the highly personal tone
and unorthodox outspokenness, which should at all costs be preserved.

Early in March, Kurt brought me the German text of the first three
chapters, together with a translation of them by [Richard] Winston. . . .
I noted, on reading the German text through, that it contained numerous alterations, and quite a few deletions, as well as a few additions on
separate sheets. Remembering my talk with Jung, and not knowing
whether these alterations were Kurt's, or [Aniela] Jaffé's, or Jung's own
revisions, I sent the text to Jaffé, asking whether the alterations were
"authentic." It came back with more changes and deletions, and with the
statement that this was the authentic text.

. . . I began the translation, or rather, the revision of Winston's translation, which I found to be quite brilliant. . . . It soon became apparent
that the alterations in the German text were all of a kind which toned
down and "old-maidified" Jung's original written words. Further, Winston's translation had been made from an earlier text, parts of which were
not represented in Jaffé's "authorized version" at all. As some of the deleted passages seemed to me extremely important for a proper understanding of the subsequent narrative, I restored them from Winston's
version, together with a number of critical references to Jung's family,
and some remarks which couldn't shock anyone except the Swiss bourgeoisie, including a highly dramatic use of the word "shit." I suspected
that the "auntie" was to be found not at the Hotel Esplanade in Locarno
[i.e., Kurt Wolff], but nearer home in Küsnacht, and that it was Aniela
Jaffé. . . . [In early May] I . . . wrote to Kurt giving him a detailed account of the emasculation of Jung's Urtext by Aniela Jaffé, which had
since been unwittingly confirmed by her in her answers to my queries
regarding the restoration of the deleted passages and toned-down
phrases. Kurt replied that my findings were of the utmost importance,
and that he would discuss the matter fully with me a few days later.

At this interview Kurt seemed to be in a very agitated state . . . and
had to be repeatedly calmed down by Helen [his wife]. It came out that
there had been friction all along between him and Aniela Jaffé, that he
had consistently opposed the bowdlerizations and interpolations made by
her, and that, as a last straw, Jung had recently stated in a letter to him
that the book was to be regarded not as an autobiography but as a vol-

ume of memoirs edited by Jaffé or even as her biography of him. Kurt asked me if I had any suggestions to offer. As it was clear that he set enormous store by publishing a translation of the Urtext in its full Jung-ian flavour, I could only ask, rather helplessly, whether a clean break could be made between the German and the English editions: in other words, let Jaffé bring out her version in German, and Kurt bring out the Urtext in English, not as edited by Jaffé, but as Jung's own autobiogra-phy. I proposed that a translation should be prepared from a careful comparison of the two texts and that, when complete, it should be sub-mitted to Jung for his personal approval. If he okayed it and stood by his express wishes as told to me in February, then the Urtext could appear in English despite any protests from Jaffé. It seemed to me possible that Jung, with his "two personalities" who invariably contradict each other (the book is largely about the lifelong process of their individuation!), might well be satisfied with—or perhaps even be aiming at—a "respect-able" German version and a more personal and idiosyncratic English one.

Kurt's direct appeal to me—which I may have taken a bit too directly—did much to dispel my misgivings regarding the translation, and I assured him that I would collaborate wholeheartedly with him in the work of comparing the texts and trying to establish the "authentic version." I said I would still like to collaborate with Winston if that were possible. . . . Kurt said he was going to discuss matters further at the end of June with Jaffé and [Walther] Niehus [Jung's son-in-law], who had now been appointed Jung's literary executor.[15]

Thus began a series of arguments among C. G. Jung, Aniela Jaffé, the Wins-tons, Hull, Wolff, several of Jung's adult children and their spouses, plus various editors and copy editors at Pantheon Books. They argued intensely about what should go into or be taken out of or somehow get changed in Jung's autobiogra-phy. Each person who proposed to make substantial modifications in the central copyedited manuscript of the English translation used a different-colored pen or pencil: Red ink for changes by Frau Jaffé, transmitted through Richard Winston; black ink for changes by Winston as translator; purple ink for R.F.C. Hull; dark pencil for Wolfgang Sauerlander, a copy editor; occasional notes in whatever color, initialed G. G., for the senior editor at Pantheon, Gerald Gross; and a few notes in red initialed CGJ, not written directly by C. G. Jung but presumably relayed from him. The margins of the manuscript are sprinkled with little discus-sions in which one or more individuals recommend a change or deletion and others concur or disagree, adding exclamation marks when they feel strongly about the issue. Some of these revisions were merely matters of standard copy-editing or slight changes in translation. Others were more substantive.

The substantive arguments had already begun to fly before the German-language manuscript was effectively completed in April 1960. The arguments continued through and beyond the Winstons' completion of the English-language translation in February 1961; they continued past the first American edition's publication in 1963; they continued on beyond the first German-language edition which appeared in Switzerland soon after, and through several subsequent British and American editions. The persistence of these editorial arguments is indicated by an obscure statement on the copyright page of the current U.S. version of *MDR*: "Final revised edition in hardcover published by Pantheon Books, February 1973"—that is, a decade after the first edition came out. Indeed, some of those arguments remain unresolved 30 years after the book's first publication, though they've been attenuated by the deaths of most of the principal figures in the controversy.

Before I review various instances of attempted and successful deletions from the autobiography, let's consider who is most likely to have contributed to the "auntification" process and why. There were several suspects, not all of whom Hull identified in his summary of the situation:

Kurt Wolff.   As overall editor of the project, he came under Hull's immediate suspicion. Hull absolved him after seeing Wolff become so upset at hearing of the discrepancies between the initial German and English texts. I suspect that Wolff actually did make a number of innocuous deletions from the original manuscript, to tighten the narrative and keep the volume at a reasonable length. On the other hand, he asked Aniela Jaffé to stimulate Jung's memory further with additional questions about certain issues, and he directly asked Jung to write more about his theories for inclusion in *MDR*. Jung turned down his request, on the grounds that he'd already said enough about his theories elsewhere.[16]

The translators, Richard and Clara Winston.   They seem to have played a role in editing as well as translating the book, but there's no evidence that they had any specific axes to grind in suggesting minor deletions. They do appear to have willingly accepted requests from Aniela Jaffé, and perhaps from others in Switzerland, to make changes in the original text.

Aniela Jaffé.   She transmitted the major moves toward auntification, but she probably didn't originate many of them. Indeed, without making a big issue of censorship as R.F.C. Hull had done, she offset some of the losses from the American edition of *MDR* by restoring certain deleted passages to the German-language editions, or by slipping them into her coffee-table book *C. G. Jung: Word and Image* and her other writings about Jung.[17] Jaffé appears to have felt herself caught between two contending sides, especially after Jung's death in June 1961. One side was represented most vociferously by Hull but also included Kurt Wolff and others in the United States, who wanted Jung's words preserved largely intact. The other side consisted mainly of our final group of suspects:

Jung's adult children and their spouses, especially his daughter Marianne, her husband Walther Niehus, and Jung's only son Franz. As R.F.C. Hull eventually determined to his satisfaction, and as several other sources have attested, these were the major auntifiers, both before and after Jung's death.[18] Why? To some degree, the Defender-of-the-Faith phenomenon was at work: surviving children of famous individuals often attempt to protect the dead parent's public image from criticism. The unusual aspect of the Jung situation was the children's insistence on censoring the parent's autobiographical self-presentation even while the parent was alive and in full command of his faculties. The Jung children appear to have had two major motives for doing so: a concern for the reputation of their mother, Emma Jung, who had died several years earlier, and a concern for their own reputation in Zürich and its vicinity as members of the Jung family.

Emma Jung had been a good deal more directly involved than C. G. in the children's upbringing, and on the whole they felt closer to her. They also shared her traditional Swiss values regarding family privacy. As the autobiography proceeded, they managed among other things to delete parts or all of several letters from C. G. to Emma that had been included in the early draft. According to Hull, the children argued that "One doesn't publish one's father's love letters."[19] They also were victorious in obtaining the deletion of an appendix about the Jung family's history, which included C. G.'s charming but (to them) impermissibly intimate description of his first meeting with Emma, when he was 21 and she was 14. He says that at that meeting, "I knew immediately, and with absolute certainty, that she would be my wife." (This material was included in the German-language edition of *MDR*, and an English translation appeared 21 years later in the Jungian journal *Spring*,[20] but it's still omitted from English-language editions of the autobiography.)

As for the children's concern about their reputation as Jung family members, Hull described them as being "with all due respect . . . bourgeois to the backbone and . . . all absolutely terrified of what that man [their father] was going to say next."[21] They were especially worried, according to Hull and others, about public exposure of Jung's unorthodox religious views. At one point during the controversy Hull commented, "Experiences with the Vita [Hull's nickname for the autobiography] have shown that there were pressures from Zürich which sought to exercise what I can only call an 'ideological censorship' of Jung's statements." Hull then referred to various expressions of what he called "sectarian sensibility" prevalent in the family.[22] Soon after Jung's death, Hull protested the son-in-law's decision to make a "wholesale cutting" of a lengthy section on Jung's adolescent religious concerns. Here Hull used the term "family falsifications."[23] Jung himself had remained circumspect about the role of the children in the whole business. Others felt that as his health became increasingly delicate, he was afraid to criticize directly the family members upon whom he would have to depend during his final months.

Varieties of Auntification

Exactly what was the nature of those efforts at auntifying Jung? First, I'll note some efforts that failed—in effect, arguments about the book's content that R.F.C. Hull won, thus enabling Jung to overcome auntification at least to a degree. Then I'll note other auntification efforts that R.F.C. Hull tried to combat but was unable to prevent. Finally, I'll point out certain kinds of deletions or omissions that Hull seems not to have protested, and that perhaps Jung himself either approved or actually imposed upon the autobiography.

R.F.C. Hull's Victories

1. On page 15 of the published American editions of *MDR*, Jung describes how as a child he was "fascinated to watch a pig being slaughtered." Somebody crossed that out of the translated manuscript; Hull got it back in. On page 24, Jung says that when he started attending the Gymnasium (high school) in Zürich, "I became aware how poor we were, that my father was a poor country parson and I a still poorer parson's son who had holes in his shoes and had to sit for six hours in school with wet socks." The relatives tried to delete this and other references to the Jung family's poverty; Hull persuaded Jaffé to restore such references.

2. On pages 39, 40, and 47 of the American editions, Jung describes an adolescent religious vision that distressed him a great deal. In the key paragraph he says, "I saw before me the [Basel] cathedral, the blue sky. God sits on His golden throne, high above the world—and from under the throne an enormous turd falls upon the sparkling new roof, shatters it, and breaks the walls of the cathedral asunder."[24] In the original unpublished translation, Jung describes God's activity even more bluntly than that. On four different occasions in his account, Jung uses the word "shits" or "shitting"—or rather, the translation takes those words directly from Jung's German, which employed various forms of the verb *scheissen*. I assume that Jung used such words not simply to be blunt but to emphasize how horrified he felt as a teenager to see God do this awful thing to the cathedral. The relatives were horrified too, and they apparently demanded deletion of the whole passage. Hull got the passage back in, minus the words "shit" and "shitting."

3. On page 55 of the American editions, Jung describes the extreme disappointment he felt at his first communion, which he says was "a total loss." He reports that he thought to himself then, "Why, that is not religion at all. It is an absence of God; the church is a place I should not go to. It is not life which is there, but death." Hull says these thoughts were reduced to "The church is a place where I should not go." When Hull complained, the full passage was restored. "Small things, but very significant," Hull said about this and similar passages.[25]

4. Not so small a thing, but still on religious issues, is a long passage on Jung's

adolescent religious doubts (pages 66–78). I won't quote it, but it appears important to an understanding of Jung's psychological development. Several months
after Jung's death, Aniela Jaffé sent a telegram to Pantheon Books, relaying Walther Niehus's order to delete the entire section, nearly twenty pages of manuscript. Hull's response was a lengthy letter to Jaffé, in which he said, "Mr. Gross
[the editor at Pantheon] was *appalled* by your telegram—he felt thoroughly
'beschitsen' (in fact he used the English equivalent when he read it!), because
there had been no mention in Zürich that the whole of this passage might be cut.
I have no idea what steps he is going to take; he didn't know himself until he
consulted his colleagues. I can only say that, when he left here, he did not
consider himself in any way bound by Mr. Niehus's decision." Hull then described
to Jaffé, apparently for the first time, the visit during which Jung urged Hull to
resist the forces of auntification. Hull continued to Jaffé:

> I mention this visit now because Jung expressed these very emphatic
> views at a time when he was in the fullest possession of his faculties and
> keenly interested in the fate of the book. As we have seen, it is not al-
> ways easy to establish what the "authentic text" is: No. 1 and No. 2 [per-
> sonalities] wrote different things at different times. But in the case of
> this long section [of the manuscript], there was never any disagreement
> between them. No. 1 and No. 2 appear to have been in remarkably good
> harmony. The passage is, as it were, a joint statement by both of them, a
> statement of such importance that it constitutes the emotional and intel-
> lectual backbone of the book.[26]

I'm not sure I'd agree with Hull as to the passage's central importance, but
fortunately it was left in the book, except for a few lines.

R.F.C. Hull's (and C. G. Jung's) Defeats

1. Deletion or revision of several critical comments about Jung's parents. One
comment that Marianne, Jung's daughter, objected to particularly strongly would
have appeared on page 8 of the American editions. The passage as published
reads, "My mother spent several months in a hospital in Basel, and presumably
her illness had something to do with the difficulty in the marriage." In the
unpublished version Jung diagnosed her illness as neurotic hysteria, and specu-
lated that it came from her disappointment with Jung's father—whose "days of
glory had ended with his final examination," Jung said in a phrase that got
relocated to page 91 of the book. R.F.C. Hull reluctantly yielded to the softening
of this passage, feeling that other arguments were more worth pursuing. Another
portion of the same paragraph in the original English translation, about Jung's
father becoming a country parson and lapsing "into sentimentalism and reminis-
cences of his student days," also got transferred to page 91. The end of that

sentence, a simple remark about the father's problems with a domineering wife, got changed to say he "discovered that his marriage was not all he had imagined it to be." Other negative comments about the parents suffered similar fates.

2. Deletion of all but a few references to Emma Jung. I've already mentioned some of these; other references were present in the preliminary manuscripts but did not survive even as far as the initial English translation. Emma Jung was surely important enough to Carl Jung for him to discuss her seriously in his autobiography. The children thought it was improper for him to do so, but they may have had a strategic reason as well for deleting most references to her. Only by omitting Emma could they also justify deleting every overt reference to an almost equally important woman in C. G. Jung's life: his mistress, Toni Wolff. I'll say more about Toni Wolff shortly.

3. Deletion of a number of Jung's more mystical or superstitious statements. Several of these are quite brief—for example, at the bottom of page 30, where the published version says, "Similar caricatures sometimes appear to me before falling asleep to this day, grinning masks that constantly move and change, among them familiar faces of people who soon afterward died." The final phrase there originally stated that these visions at times actually foresaw the deaths of those familiar faces. Someone evidently thought Jung's foreboding language was a little too strange, so out it went.

A much more extensive omission in this category was the deletion from *MDR*'s first English-language editions of Jung's *Septem Sermones ad Mortuos* (Seven Sermons to the Dead), a strange pseudo-biblical work written during his midlife period of schizoid visions. Jung had intended from early in the autobiography project to include at least portions of *Septem Sermones*, which he regarded as a very personal composition that did not belong in his official *Collected Works*. I don't know who knocked it out of the first American and British editions of *MDR*. It was included in the first German edition, and it later appeared in the American paperback reprints. I suspect, again, that a religiously orthodox member of the Jung family saw the *Sermones* as either too sacrilegious or just too weird.

4. A minor but interesting deletion from page 107 of the book, where Jung refers to the teenage medium about whom he wrote his doctoral dissertation. In *MDR* as we now have it, Jung describes his study of this "young girl" in rather unemotional terms, then says, "After about two years of experimentation we all became rather weary of it. I caught the medium trying to produce phenomena by trickery, and this made me break off the experiments." In the original manuscript translation, Jung continued the sentence by saying he broke off his relationship with the girl as well. That phrase seems hardly worth deleting, unless the family felt particularly sensitive about what sort of relationship it may have been. William Goodheart has written in detail about the circumstances of Jung's research on this medium, who was Jung's first cousin on his mother's side. Jung began his "experimentation" with the girl when he was 19 and she was 13. According to

Goodheart, "What was going on [between Jung and the medium during the early seances] was in reality intimate, erotic and highly charged emotionally."[27] Good reason, perhaps, for the relatives later to delete references to their having had any sort of relationship.

These examples, both of deletions restored and of deletions that stayed deleted, are characteristic of what both Jung and Hull saw as auntifications. Two other instances are more ambiguous, one involving some apparently neutral deletions and the other involving a significant addition to the text. But both, I think, do misrepresent aspects of Jung's life.

The apparently neutral deletions involve the omission of several character sketches of men important to Jung. As the American editions stand, there is a chapter on Sigmund Freud and a five-page appendix on Richard Wilhelm, but Jung rarely mentions any other mentors, colleagues, or friends by name. That may seem unsurprising, since Jung is quoted in Jaffé's introduction as saying that his meetings with most people "were without portent; they soon faded away and bore no deeper consequences."[28] However, the original draft translation of *MDR* also contained several pages each on Albert Oeri (a close friend in college), Theodore Flournoy, William James, and Heinrich Zimmer. In addition, R.F.C. Hull describes the Urtext as having contained "many amusing and sometimes malicious little thumb[nail] sketches of personalities, for instance, H. G. Wells, Thomas Mann, Bernard Shaw. All came out."[29] Some of the longer sketches have reappeared in the German edition, so perhaps they were deleted only to streamline the American edition for an American audience. But their absence gives a false impression of the number and quality of Jung's important social and professional relationships.

The significant addition to *MDR* is on pages 260–261 of the published American versions. Jung is describing his visit to East Africa, at age 50, with two unnamed male friends. They reach the foot of Mount Elgon, on the border between Kenya and Uganda. The next three paragraphs were inserted into the already completed English translation by unidentified hands, in different type than the adjacent manuscript:

> There a letter awaited us from the governor of Uganda, requesting us to take under our protection an English lady who was on her way back to Egypt via the Sudan. The governor was aware that we were following the same itinerary, and since we had already met the lady in Nairobi we knew that she would be a congenial companion. Moreover, we were under considerable obligation to the governor for his having helped us in all sorts of ways. . . . I mention this episode to suggest the subtle modes by which an archetype influences our actions. We were three men; that was a matter of pure chance. . . . That sufficed to produce an unconscious or fated constellation: the archetype of the triad, which calls for

the fourth to complete it, as we have seen again and again in the history of this archetype. Since I am inclined to accept chance when it comes my way, I welcomed the lady to our group of three men.

I assume that Jung really did write this passage, or that Aniela Jaffé wrote it on the basis of information supplied by Jung. Whoever wrote it, however, it is to an unfortunate degree false. The English lady who joined Jung's African party, a 30-year-old single woman named Ruth Bailey, gave a very detailed account of the circumstances to the Jung oral history interviewer many years later. Her account was based on her diary of the African trip, which she was holding in her hand as she talked. She was not "on her way back to Egypt via the Sudan" when she joined the Jung party; she was visiting a sister in Kenya and was planning to return to England by ship from Mombasa at the end of the visit. Nor did she join the Jung party at the request of the Governor of Uganda. Rather, she was enthusi-astically recruited by Jung himself after she had sailed on the same ship as his party from England to Africa, became better acquainted with him in Nairobi, and then spent several weeks camping with him and his friends on Mount Elgon. She remained friends with Jung and his family for the rest of their lives. In Jung's old age, after Emma Jung died, Ruth Bailey moved into Jung's home at his insistence, to become his companion and housekeeper.

Why was this oddly distorted passage added to the manuscript? Perhaps the elderly Jung felt so indebted to Ruth Bailey that he wanted to give her a bit of acknowledgment, indeed more than survived for Toni Wolff. But if he did that as an afterthought to the main manuscript, he apparently didn't get the new passage all the way through the family censors before they forced its revision, thereby eliminating any likelihood that others might suspect an improper relationship. (There is no evidence that the relationship was in any sense improper.) By falsifying the relationship that actually had existed in Africa, however, Jung or whoever did the writing or rewriting also falsified his evidence for the uncon-scious effects of an archetypal triad.

Uncontested Omissions

1. The published version contains almost no mention of the woman who was Jung's mistress, co-therapist, and *femme inspiratrice* for much of his adult life: Antonia Wolff. Arguments have continued to rage about how much Jung may have written about Toni Wolff in his contributions to the original manuscript. At times, Aniela Jaffé said he wrote nothing about her.[30] But in her interview with me she gleefully announced that there was a whole chapter about Toni, which she was planning to publish over the Jung family's strenuous objections. (Alas, Frau Jaffé died before she could see that chapter into print.)

The proto-Urtext material at the Library of Congress does not contain an entire chapter on Toni Wolff, but there is enough material scattered throughout for Aniela Jaffé to have assembled such a chapter. In this unpublished material Jung discusses his early emotional involvement with Toni when she was his patient, his termination of her analysis, and his decision to begin a more personal relationship with her a year later. He describes some of her fantasies and their congruence with his own fantasies. He tells of Toni's reappearance as a robin who hovers near him on the anniversary of her death. He reports with sadness that the only dreams he has had of his wife since her death show her at a distance, whereas in his dreams of Toni she sometimes seems so close that she might be able to re-enter his three-dimensional reality. Often his lines about Toni are so intermingled with his lines about Emma that they would be impossible to separate editorially.

The deletion of this material from MDR has deprived readers of much more than just gossipy tidbits. Toni Wolff became a close collaborator in Jung's therapeutic practice, especially in helping patients with the procedure he called "active imagination." Even more important, she served willingly as a sympathetic companion during his long period of emotional distress while he was wrestling with the inner gods or demons that he later called archetypes. Jung was powerfully attracted to Toni Wolff, and felt that she provided something essential in his life that his wife could not. He refused to divorce Emma, but he also refused to give up Toni. For many years he spent Wednesday evenings and frequent vacations with her. She regularly came to the Jung home for Sunday dinners with C. G., Emma, and their children. Mrs. Jung tolerated this arrangement, but her intense unhappiness with it has been reported by various friends. As children, Jung's son and daughters hated Toni Wolff. It's no surprise that as adults, they insisted on erasing her from the manuscript of MDR.

2. Everyone in the inner Jungian circle knew about Toni Wolff. The official oral history of Jung is full of recollections about her. She was often referred to by others as Jung's anima, and there's little doubt that *he* came to regard her as the human focus of his anima archetype, his unconscious inner feminine. What none of Jung's disciples seems to have realized is that Jung had experienced an intense extramarital relationship even before Toni Wolff, and that the earlier woman had probably been the *original* inspiration for Jung's concept of the anima. When Jung writes in MDR about how his anima first spoke to him in the voice of one of his patients, "a talented psychopath who had a strong transference to me,"[31] he is not referring to Toni Wolff but very likely to his earlier lover, Sabina Spielrein. The same patient is mentioned once more in the published volume, when Jung says he "broke with the woman" sometime in 1918–1919.[32] But the kind of relationship he broke is not explained, and Spielrein's name is never mentioned in MDR. Jung's children knew virtually nothing about her, so they could not have made the decision to omit from MDR any substantial discussion of her role in Jung's life. Jung must have made that decision himself.[33]

If you don't already know the story of Sabina Spielrein, you can find most of it in Aldo Carotenuto's book, *A Secret Symmetry*.[34] I'll just quote from one of Jung's last letters to her, in which he simultaneously excuses his failure to keep his promises to her *and* gives her credit for her influence on his ideas:

> *The love of S. for J.* made the latter aware of something he had previously only vaguely suspected, that is, of a power in the unconscious that shapes one's destiny, a power which later led him to things of the greatest importance. The relationship had to be "sublimated" because otherwise it would have led him to delusion and madness (the concretization of the unconscious). Occasionally one must be unworthy, simply in order to be able to continue living.[35]

Carotenuto, a Jungian therapist, comments, "Anima and shadow emerge from this letter in a striking way."

By the time that letter was written, in 1919, Jung had gone through his major period of psychological distress, had formulated most of his central psychological theories including the concepts of archetype and anima, and had had a decade to think about what his relationship with Sabina Spielrein had meant to him psychologically. He had also experienced several years of conversations with his anima, who in his words "communicate[d] the images of the unconscious to the conscious mind."[36] His anima continued to speak in the voice of the "talented psychopath," his female patient, whom he described as having "become a living figure in my mind."[37] Few other psychological theories appear so directly derived from the theorist's own personal experience with a living person. I think Jung owed Sabina Spielrein something more in his autobiography than an anonymous and derogatory reference to her as "a talented psychopath."

3. One other significant and even more thorough omission from Jung's autobiography involved not a woman but a man. In 1907 Jung wrote to Freud, "[M]y veneration for you has something of the character of a 'religious' crush. Though it does not really bother me, I still feel it is disgusting and ridiculous because of its undeniable erotic undertone. This abominable feeling comes from the fact that as a boy I was the victim of a sexual assault by a man I once worshipped."[38] Jung gave Freud no details about this homosexual "assault," and it is not mentioned in *MDR*. Jolande Jacobi provided more information to the Jung oral history project:

> He [Jung] told me one day that when he was 18 years old one of the best friends of his family was also his best friend—a man of about forty to fifty. He was very proud of this friendship and had the feeling that he had . . . in this man a fatherly friend with whom he could discuss everything until one day this fatherly friend tried a homosexual approach towards him. He [Jung] was so disgusted and afraid that he immediately broke the relationship. . . . [H]e . . . explained to me, when Freud wanted to make him his son and his successor, he had the same feeling,

"No, no, no, I don't want to belong to anybody. I don't want to be embraced."[39]

This episode may have been one of the major undiscussed reasons why Jung ultimately broke away from Freud personally and then from the psychoanalytic movement. Jung says in *MDR* that the break developed primarily because of Freud's insistence on being an authority figure. But it appears also that Freud wanted to share a closer emotional relationship than Jung personally could tolerate. This may also be one of the reasons, though surely not the only one, why Jung rejected Freud's *sexual* theories in particular. Jung seems to have been rather open in discussing his sexual feelings toward women, but he is reported to have been quite upset when male patients expressed sexual feelings toward him. His close friendships with women were many; with men, very few.

I've been rather hard on Jung's children in this chapter. They do deserve criticism for trying to "auntify" one of the autobiographical masterpieces of the twentieth century. But they were Jung's children, and their emphasis on bourgeois respectability did not come entirely from Emma Jung. One of C. G. Jung's two distinct personalities was conventional even by his account. He often preferred to emphasize the other side of himself, the unconventional and society-be-damned side. But his conventional side is reflected in his strong tendency to reject the more controversial aspects of Freud's theories.

Freud rather consistently chose reductionistic explanations of psychological phenomena, as Jung often complained. Freud happily reduced even the spiritual to matters of sex and aggression. Jung, on the contrary, tended to elevate and even to spiritualize sexual and aggressive urges, whether in his own life or in his theories. It was Jung, after all, who at age three dreamed of a huge tree-trunk-shaped object "made of skin and naked flesh," with a faceless, hairless, rounded head that had a single eye on the very top—and it was Jung who later interpreted this image not as some manifestation of sexual anxieties but as symbolizing a "subterranean God," a dark counterpart of Jesus Christ.[40] It was Jung who as an adolescent fantasized that he owned a castle in which a secret device sucked spiritual food from the air, digested it in a complex system of copper tubing reminiscent of an alimentary canal, then produced at the bottom not shit but a kind of sacred gold. It was Jung who, according to George Atwood and Robert Stolorow, managed to translate the basic symptoms of his own profound narcissistic disturbance into the living representatives of a new psychological religion.[41]

I don't mean to imply that Freud was necessarily more correct in his reductionistic approach than Jung was in his spiritualizing approach to psychological phenomena. But I would suggest that when Jung accused others of trying to "auntify" his autobiography, it was an issue to which he was particularly sensitive because he had felt certain inclinations in the same direction. Perhaps someday, when all the Jung archives are opened to scholarly researchers, someone will finally piece the Urtext together and we'll get *Memories, Dreams, Reflections* as Jung (in both of his personalities) meant it to be. Parts of it will still be censored, bowdlerized, auntified versions of episodes in Jung's life; his honesty had its limits as everyone's does. We'll need to keep those limitations in mind as we read the Revised Standard Autobiography. But it will finally and fully be Jung's own myth, and that's well worth having.

5

Allport Meets Freud and the Clean Little Boy

I N GORDON ALLPORT'S brief autobiography, written a year before he died, he asked this question repeatedly about his own life: "How shall a psychological life history be written?" It was a question he had asked recently about another life, as he prepared to publish a book of letters from an elderly woman friend along with an array of theories that might explain her peculiar personality. It was a question he had asked more broadly a quarter-century earlier, when he wrote a monograph on *The Use of Personal Documents in Psychological Science.* It was a question he had asked quite early in his career, in his study of a confessional work as odd as its title: *The Locomotive God.* Indeed, Allport said that even his 1922 doctoral dissertation, *An Experimental Study of the Traits of Personality,* "was an early formulation of the riddle: How shall a psychological life history be written?"[1]

My own first published attempt to answer that riddle was a five-page paper on Gordon Allport, which appeared five years after he died.[2] I felt rather more nervous than usual about the publication of that paper. It suggested an interpretation of Allport's personality, and a set of connections between his life and his work, for which I had uncovered little hard evidence. I had never met Allport. I had never discussed him in detail with anyone who had known him well. To top everything off, I was advancing a psychoanalytically tinged account of the core theoretical concepts of a man who for three decades had been a prominent critic of psychoanalysis.

Fortunately for my budding career as a psychobiographer, reactions to my paper—at any rate the reactions I heard about—were generally favorable. Several of Allport's friends and colleagues told me I had done a pretty good job, at least in so brief a space and for someone who didn't know the man. One person after another offered additional information to support my hypotheses. I felt encouraged enough by these reactions to move on to psychobiographical studies of other theorists whose fame was greater or whose personal lives were more spectacular. But I wasn't completely satisfied with that brief initial attempt at answering the question, "How shall a psychological life history be written?" So I continued to read Allport's work and occasionally to collect new information about him, through interviews and archival research. I haven't yet found all the answers I want, but I think I now understand a good deal more about Allport than I did at the beginning. In some sense a psychobiographer's work is never finished: no life can be known or understood fully, and no set of biographical data is ever truly complete. My research on Allport is an example of how one perspective on a life, as revealing as it may appear at the moment, can over time be broadened, deepened, and redrawn with new data and fresh interpretations.

Allport's Encounter with Freud

My 1972 paper on Allport centered upon his one and only meeting with Sigmund Freud. It was a story that Allport told often—so often that the several written or recorded or filmed versions of it are almost identical, sentence for sentence. It was the sole personal anecdote included in his *New York Times* obituary.[3] The version below remained unpublished for thirty years, but it will sound familiar to the many people who heard the story from Allport himself:

> So, in my callow youth—this story is very much at my own expense—in my callow youth, I wrote Freud a note, announcing that I was in Vienna and no doubt he would be glad to see me. I received a reply in his own handwriting inviting me to come to his office, at a certain time and place. I went there, to the famous red burlap room with pictures of dreams on the wall. He opened the door and invited me into the inner sanctum, and sat there silent. You may not believe this possible, but I was not prepared for silence. It occurred to me it was up to me to say something, so I fished around in my mind and I told him about an episode on the tram car coming out. I had seen a little boy about four years old and the little boy obviously was developing a real dirt phobia. His mother was with him. She was a starched Hausfrau, terribly clean and purposive looking. And the little boy was saying: "I don't want to sit *there*! Don't let *him* sit near me, *he's* dirty." He kept this up all the time, and I thought it might interest Freud how early a phobia of dirt can get set. He listened, and fixed his therapeutic eye upon me and said "Was that little boy you?" Honestly, it wasn't, but I felt guilty.[4]

Allport's adjectives describing the boy's mother vary slightly from version to version: "excessively clean and well starched . . . domineering in manner" (1958, p. 2); "a well-starched *Hausfrau*, so dominant and purposive looking that I thought the cause and effect apparent" (1967, p. 8); "well starched and very prim" (1970, p. 4). The little boy is described in 1958 as looking "excessively clean and well starched" like his mother; in the 1967 account Allport says that to the little boy "everything was *schmutzig*" (dirty; p. 8); otherwise the little boy's description remains the same in each telling. The story's punch line ("Was that little boy you?" or "And was that little boy you?") is always followed by Allport's denial: "It wasn't. (But I felt almost guilty!)" (1958, p. 2); "It was not, honestly, but I felt guilty" (1964 filmed interview, slightly reworded in 1970 print version, p. 4); "Flabbergasted and feeling a bit guilty, I contrived to change the subject. While Freud's misunderstanding of my motivation was amusing . . ." (1967, p. 8).[5]

As Allport indicates here, he told his story both as a kind of joke on Freud and as a joke on the young Gordon Allport. But he also made clear that the incident was ultimately no joke for him. He referred to it as "profoundly revealing" about Freud in ways he had thought back upon "many times since becoming a professional psychologist myself" (1958, p. 2). He said it was "a very important experience to me" (1962, p. 2), "an event of pungent significance . . . . [having] the character of a traumatic developmental episode" (1967, p. 7). Allport described his reaction following the meeting in this way:

> But thinking that little episode over, it grew in importance to me, because the fact is that Freud, with his tendency to see pathological trains, and most of his people who came to see him were patients, of course, it was natural he should break through my defenses and get down to business, you see. But actually, he mistook my motives. If he had said, "Well, here is a brassy young American youth, a tourist who is imposing on my good nature and time," he would have been somewhere near correct, I think. But to ascribe my motivation to the unconscious in this case was definitely wrong.[6]

In his autobiography, Allport summarized the Freud incident's longer-term professional effects: "This experience taught me that depth psychology, for all its merits, may plunge too deep, and that psychologists would do well to give full recognition to manifest motives before probing the unconscious. Although I never regarded myself as anti-Freudian, I have been critical of psychoanalytic excesses. A later paper entitled 'The Trend in Motivational Theory' (1953) is a direct reflection of this episode and has been reprinted, I believe, more frequently than any other of my articles."[7]

Allport's Theory of the Clean Personality

Allport's vigorous and repeated denial that he was the little boy with the dirt phobia intrigued me as it has intrigued others.[8] I try not to be a compulsive originologist, rushing to expose every adult behavior pattern's most infantile sources. But it seemed to me that if Allport insisted so strenuously on denying his resemblance to the clean little boy on the tram-car, we should at least find out what sort of little boy Allport himself had been.

In looking for such information, I quickly struck pay dirt. In his autobiography Allport described his childhood in just one cautiously phrased paragraph. That paragraph, however, appeared to explain a great deal about his reaction to the Freud encounter. It's worth quoting in full:

> Our home life was marked by plain Protestant piety and hard work. My mother had been a school teacher and brought to her sons an eager sense of philosophical questing and the importance of searching for ultimate religious answers. Since my father [a physician] lacked adequate hospital facilities for his patients, our household for several years included both patients and nurses. Tending office, washing bottles, and dealing with patients were important aspects of my early training. Along with his general practice my father engaged in many enterprises: founding a cooperative drug company, building and renting apartments, and finally developing a new specialty of building and supervising hospitals. I mention his versatility simply to underscore the fact that his four sons were trained in the practical urgencies of life as well as in a broad humanitarian outlook. Dad was no believer in vacations. He followed rather his own rule of life, which he expressed as follows: "If every person worked as hard as he could and took only the minimum financial return required by his family's needs, then there would be just enough wealth to go around." Thus it was hard work tempered by trust and affection that marked the home environment.[9]

Largely on the basis of that passage, I drew several connections between Allport's early history and his later career. The key paragraphs in my 1972 paper were these:

> We may now wonder whether Freud's question was received so traumatically . . . because unconsciously he [Allport] was still carrying within him the super-clean little boy whose schoolteacher mother stressed to her children the importance of "plain Protestant piety," philosophical questions, and "ultimate religious answers"; whose physician father had no time for play but transmitted to the children his concern with hard work and tight money; and who himself spent much of his childhood living in the abnormally clean environment of a home-hospital, washing bottles and coping with patients who must either be kept from infection . . . or be avoided as infectious. . . .
>
> Not only might such an early history have made the adult Allport peculiarly sensitive to small boys with dirt phobias; it may also have been

translated into Allport's expressive movements, into a "prim" and "well starched" pattern of gesture, dress, and speech . . . that would have been Freud's only other clue besides the story itself to Allport's presence. Allport later in his life proposed . . . that the "*style of execution*" of a person's behavior "is always guided directly and without interference by deep and lasting personal dispositions."[10] Freud is reported to have been particularly adept at reading such nonverbal cues. . . .

If our inferences are reasonably accurate, then the apparent force of this brief encounter with Freud becomes more understandable. It was [not merely] one misguided comment by Freud . . . that set Allport upon a career of discounting unconscious forces. Allport's reaction can instead be viewed as compatible with his developmental history. The high-minded and clean little boy had become a high-minded and clean young man, unwilling to examine any "dirty" foundations for his choice of conversational gambit, for his "flabbergasted" reaction to Freud's question, or for his behavior in general. This high-minded young man eventually became an important psychological theorist who promulgated a view perhaps appropriately described as [a theory of] "The Clean Personality." He argued against digging into the unconscious except in unusual cases. . . . He rarely discussed sexual motivation except to protest Freud's emphasis upon it. . . . He rejected psychological data on such unsavory creatures as rats, children, and neurotics as being largely irrelevant to an understanding of the mature personality. His key motivational concept was *functional autonomy*, the proposition that most adult motives become somehow totally independent of their baser origins. He saw the ultimate criterion of the mature personality as a unifying philosophy of life, perhaps ideally a religious one. Allport appears to have recognized a certain degree of continuity between his [positive] adult theory-building activities and his parents' "plain Protestant piety"; but it may have been precisely [the same] early training in piety, cleanliness, and order that led him to reject the importance of unconscious and infantile motives to the normal adult personality.[11]

At the end of my paper I cautiously noted, "Our knowledge of Allport's childhood is so slight that we must not push our speculations further." I also pointed out that "Allport's theoretical formulations are clearly the immediate product of much intellectual effort of the highest quality."[12] Nonetheless, it seemed clear to me that Allport's early training in cleanliness and virtue had left him with an unusual sensitivity to certain aspects of personality that other people, including Freud, tended to overlook. The same training had given Allport a distinct insensitivity to (or avoidance of) certain aspects of personality to which Freud was especially sensitive.

I later came across other information that supported this interpretation. For instance, the Allport Papers at Harvard contain a letter from Henry Murray to Allport's widow, describing various aspects of his friendship with Gordon:

> This brings me once more to that old unresolved question . . . Freud's reason for asking: "Was that little boy you?" Gordon (and you) seemed to think that Freud had gained the (mistaken) impression that Gordon was (unconsciously) seeking therapeutic relief in visiting the Master. Is that right? But suppose that Freud made no such mistake (having frequently been visited by similar seer-hunters): he simply noted a certain psychological similarity between i) Gordon's perfect neatness and cleanliness of body and clothes as well as his perfect gentility of speech and ii) the little boy's obsessional determination to keep free from dirt (a similarity which would account for Gordon's special attention to the boy's behavior), and then Freud, not without a touch of malice, asked his question, as if to say: "Were you not, at one time, as intent as that little boy to avoid dirt (dirty words)?"[13]

Dan Ogilvie, at one time a student of Allport's, has recalled an occasion in 1964 on which Allport asked him to retrieve several copies of Allport's first book from a dusty storage space. Allport handed Ogilvie a clean rag so he could wipe the dust from his hands while Allport autographed a copy of the book for him. As Ogilvie recalls, "In the meantime I had removed the dust, but he insisted I use the rag anyway. I did that and seeing that the rag was in no worse shape than when it had been handed to me, I refolded it and placed it on the corner of his desk. With an expression of disgust, he gingerly deposited the rag in a waste basket. Suddenly I was glued to the floor with the realization that in a critical way the little boy [of the Freud anecdote] . . . *did* represent an important aspect of Professor Allport after all."[14] Another of Allport's graduate students has described Allport to me as "extremely orderly," as a man who often referred to "buttoning up things," and who indeed described himself as "buttoning up his life" during the final months of his fatal illness.[15] These images of precise control seem to share a common language with the well-starched Viennese hausfrau of Allport's story.

In my original paper, I avoided speculation on toilet-training history or anal personality traits as sources of Allport's later responses. I had no specific information on such matters and I didn't wish to be so crudely reductionistic. Both Thomas Pettigrew and Allport's son Robert have suggested to me that describing Allport's personality solely in terms of dirt avoidance and orderliness leaves a distorted picture of a complex man.[16] Certainly Allport's heavy smoking habit, which ultimately destroyed his lungs, does not fit the pattern of a compulsively clean and totally self-controlled individual. Nonetheless, the evidence for his strong concerns about cleanliness and for his reluctance to acknowledge them is substantial. Further evidence may be found in Allport's only detailed written description of the rest of his encounter with Freud:

> After this opening episode [which ended with Freud's question,] I realized that my attitude was too much that of a "tourist" and that Dr. Freud had been expecting a professional consultation. I then brought out a more personal idiosyncrasy: my dislike of cooked raisins. I told him I thought it due to the fact that at the age of three, a nurse had told me they were "bugs." Freud asked, "When you recalled this episode, did your dislike vanish?" I said, "No." He replied, "Then you are not at the bottom of it." . . .
>
> I then spoke of a common sexual problem of youthful males of my age. [Here Allport may have been referring to anxieties about masturbation or wet dreams; "self-pollution" was a popular term for such matters at the time.] His [Freud's] reply: "Yes, nature tells a man to marry at 18; and society tells him to marry at 28."
>
> Finally I asked, in general, what analyst he would recommend in America in case I ever wished to undergo analysis. He replied that he would recommend only one man: [A. A.] Brill. (This was in 1920.)
>
> I then departed with a vivid feeling of respect and liking for Freud, even though our short conversation had started at cross purposes.[17]

The Evolution of a Classic Textbook

This last account indicates that, although Allport flatly rejected Freud's equating him with the little boy on the tram-car, his hostility toward Freudian theory in general did not start as quickly or as emphatically as he implied in other accounts. His continuing ambivalence over the next several years was expressed in his correspondence with a friend and former graduate school classmate, William S. Taylor. In July 1922, two years after his Freud encounter, Allport wrote to Taylor that he would soon be returning to Vienna and Berlin, "and hope that we may correspond rather seriously and fully on some of the matters which puzzle us both, and which we might disentangle in writing. I may be able to give first hand the psycho-analytic views, or I may have an opportunity of securing Freud and Jung's answers to our questions."[18] As matters turned out, Allport did not meet Freud again and made no significant contact with other European psychoanalysts. Nor were his questions readily disentangled, as his further letters to Taylor indicate. Five months later he wrote from Berlin:

> The course I have with [Max] Dessoir on "Parapsychologie and Psychoanalyse" is an interesting exposition and destruction of the Freudian formulae. He cannot add much, I believe, to our own criticisms of Freud. Is it not true that some of the fundamental contributions of Freud are as

original and significant as the ideas of any one man can ever be in science? Is it not true also that no psychologist who has balance would hesitate to condemn the silly Freudian superstructure? Freud in Vienna is now the old story of a famous man in his own town. He is hooted and hooted. Everyone here laughs at him, and he has no recognition except in a narrow circle of orthodox admirers. Freud would be far better off should he migrate to America.[19]

After another three months, Allport wrote again on the subject, this time from Hamburg: "I have just finished reading Freud's *Vorlesungen* [Introductory Lectures] —miles of them—and remain no more nor less instructed than before taking up the book. He is totally without respect in his own land. Such is the fate of a prophet or a would-be prophet."[20]

Allport did gain a great deal of new information and new perspectives on psychology in Europe. During the next decade he occupied himself mainly with issues related to these nonpsychoanalytic approaches. But Freud's crucial question to him remained an irritant consciously and perhaps unconsciously, a challenge to his personal and professional identity at several levels. It would be finally addressed—though not addressed finally—as Allport wrote a pioneering textbook in 1936.

The textbook was *Personality: A Psychological Interpretation*, published in 1937. It was the first textbook in personality psychology, but it was more than just first. As Salvatore Maddi and Paul Costa have observed, "The book had a profound impact on the field, virtually defining for many years what was and was not to be considered important in the study of personality."[21]

Allport's official version of how the textbook came to be written deals with rather abstract and intellectual matters:

> My ambition was to give a psychological definition of the field of personality as I saw it. My vision, of course, was influenced by my encounters with social ethics, Anglo-American empiricism and German structural and personalistic theories. I wanted to fashion an experimental science, so far as appropriate, but chiefly I wanted an "image of man" that would allow us to test in full whatever democratic and humane potentialities that he might possess. I did not think of man as innately "good," but I was convinced that by and large American psychology gave man less than his due by depicting him as a bundle of unrelated reaction tendencies. I did not write the book for any particular audience. I wrote it simply because I felt I had to define the new field of the psychology of personality as I saw it.[22]

However, in an informal autobiographical interview, Allport offers a much more personal account of the book's origins. In so doing, he returns to a familiar topic:

That book has a strange feature that I have never mentioned to anyone. I wrote it for no audience. Now, when you're taught to write you're told to have an audience in mind. But, if there was ever a book written because someone had to write it, I think that was it. I didn't think it was a textbook. I didn't think of it as an argumentative treatise. I thought of it as summing up my ideas about human personality. In it, you can see the impact of my encounter with Freud as the origin of my idea that adult motivation is not necessarily a channeling, or conditioning, or overlay of cathected instincts or infantile motivations or fixations.

The result was the concept of functional autonomy. I had no idea at the time that it would be picked up and made an issue of, but it merely seemed to me obvious that motivation was often functionally autonomous of its historical origins in a life. The mainsprings of life get rewound in the course of development. This was a direct answer to Freud, for Freud had thought that I was suffering from an infantile trauma. I wasn't. If he said I was a brassy young American, he would have been right. But, he didn't. He didn't perceive my contemporary motivation. His error impressed me very much, so that I kept working on the problem of motivation from a point of view of the developing adult. I don't deny that there may be traces of infantilism in all of us or traces of neurosis in all of us. I'm not denying or disparaging at all the Freudian contribution. But, Freud's theory to my mind just is not adequate, because some people *do* grow up *sometimes*, in *some* respects. What interested me was what it meant to grow up and be adult and normal in personality function. That is the focus of my concept of functional autonomy and in general of all the 1937 book, as well as much subsequent writing.[23]

That's an interesting statement in several regards. For one thing, it reports in greater detail on something we've already heard about elsewhere: how Freud's question had a powerful effect on Allport's subsequent psychological thinking. Indeed, it emphasizes the magnitude of that effect, by saying that a two-minute exchange with Freud in 1920 led to the writing of a 600-page theoretical-position-paper-cum-textbook 16 years later. Here we have further evidence that Allport was well primed to react to Freud's question, which hit home in ways that Allport never fully acknowledged.

Not a Little Boy

Allport's series of denials, toward the end of the passage just quoted, indicates one of the ways in which Freud's question hit home. According to Allport, "Freud had thought that I was suffering from an infantile trauma. *I wasn't.* If he had said I was a brassy young American, he would have been right. But, *he didn't. . . . I don't deny* that there may be traces of infantilism in all of us or traces of neurosis in all of us" (my italics). But that is just what Allport *had* denied about himself, perhaps silently at first but promptly and vigorously. Then he said it aloud, over and over again, in essentially these words: *I am not that little boy with the dirt phobia.* Keep that sentence in mind—Allport's core response to Freud's interpretation of his behavior—as we examine each element of it.

In my initial analysis of Allport's Freud anecdote, I stressed the denial implicit in the final portion of the core response. "I am *not* someone with a *dirt phobia*," insisted young Gordon Allport, who had been trained by his parents to be clean in mind and body, and who would later develop a theory of the Clean Personality in contrast to dirty psychoanalysis.[24] When Allport later tried to justify giving what he called "so critical and so brief" an account of psychoanalysis in his *Personality* textbook, he offered a similar denial of its theoretical applicability to non-neurotics (and thus non-phobics): "Psychoanalytic concepts are drawn exclusively from neurotic and pathological material . . . and for this reason their applicability to normal personality is in many respects questionable."[25]

But there's more to Allport's reaction, as his 1962 statement on the origins of the *Personality* textbook suggests. He says there, "Freud's theory to my mind just is not adequate, because some people *do* grow up *sometimes*, in *some* respects" (p. 5; his emphases). Now back to our core sentence: "I am *not* that *little boy* . . .."

Regardless of whether any phobic tendencies were involved, it was important for Gordon Allport, at age 22 in Sigmund Freud's office, to deny being a little boy. Allport had always been the baby in his family, five years younger than the youngest of his three brothers. To a considerable degree he had remained in the shadow of his brother Floyd, seven years older than he. Floyd Allport graduated from Harvard before Gordon thought seriously of enrolling there. Floyd was a decorated military hero in World War I while Gordon merely served in the Students' Army Training Corps, performing what Gordon himself called "sophomoric" tasks. Floyd was awarded a Ph.D. degree from Harvard on the day that Gordon got his bachelor's degree. At several points in his short autobiography, Gordon refers either to his "generalized inferiority feeling" as a young man or to specific feelings of inferiority toward Floyd.[26] In an undated description of his "Personal Experience with Racial and Religious Attitudes," Gordon described himself as having been "a youth of great inferiority feeling . . . . I know what it is to be the object of scorn, but for personal and not [group] membership reasons. As I said, this sensitivity gave me a variety of compensatory strivings in myself, and as I overcame my handicaps, I also grew in sympathy with any under-dog."[27] Early in his academic career he told one correspondent, "I have published several articles of no great importance, and am not to be confused with my more eminent brother, F. H. Allport, of Syracuse University."[28]

Gordon Allport did manage after college graduation to go off on his own for a year, to teach in a small English-speaking school in Constantinople, with nobody around who was likely to make him feel inferior. But at the end of the year he headed back to Harvard, ready to become a graduate student in the Psychology Department where brother Floyd was already on the faculty—and at that point Freud had the audacity to tell him he was still a little boy! No wonder so much of the 1937 *Personality* textbook, and of Gordon Allport's later writing about personality development, stresses the *discontinuity* between child and adult, through the development of the functional autonomy of motives and in many other ways.

Allport as Unique Individual

Back to our core sentence again: "I am *not that* little boy . . . ." Allport treated as self-evident the fact that he was not the little boy he had seen on the tram-car. Regardless of any possible similarities that Freud might have hypothesized, Gordon W. Allport was *one* person and the little boy was *another* person. Allport's first sentences in his *Personality* textbook are, "As a rule, science regards the individual as a mere bothersome accident. Psychology, too, ordinarily treats him as something to be brushed aside."[29] Allport was not about to permit his own individuality to be brushed aside. In the book's last paragraph he continues to insist on that point:

> Thus there are many ways to study man psychologically. Yet to study him most fully is to take him as an individual. He is more than a bundle of habits; more than a nexus of abstract dimensions; more too than a representative of his species. He is more than a citizen of the state, and more than a mere incident in the gigantic movements of mankind. He transcends them all. The individual, striving ever for his own integrity, has existed under many forms of social life—forms as varied as the nomadic, feudal, and capitalistic. He struggles on even under oppression, always hoping and planning for a more perfect democracy where the dignity and growth of each personality will be prized above all else.[30]

This stress on the individual was not altogether uncommon in psychology by the 1930s. Gordon's older brother Floyd had already made it a feature of his own influential approach to social psychology—for instance, by attacking the "fallacy" of the "group mind" early in his 1924 textbook, and by arguing instead that the so-called "mental structure" of groups actually consists of "sets of ideals, thoughts, and habits repeated in each individual mind and existing only in those minds."[31] What really distinguished Gordon Allport's position from that of his brother, and from most other psychologists of his day, was Gordon's emphasis on the *uniqueness* of the individual. Early in the final chapter of *Personality*, he states:

> Implicit in the modern point of view is the demand that psychology expand its boundaries, revise its methods, and extend its concepts to ac-

commodate, more hospitably than in the past, the study of the single concrete mental life.

This demand is thoroughly radical. It is directed against the practice in general psychology of drawing the blood and peeling the flesh from human personality, leaving only such a skeleton framework of mind as is acceptable to the sparse canons and methods of nomothetic science. By stripping the person of all his troublesome particularities, general psychology has destroyed his essential nature. The newer point of view reverses the perspective. The person is no longer regarded as a neutral tinted background upon which the all-important design of mind-in-general stands out. Quite the reverse: the uniform design traced by general psychology becomes the ground upon which the integral, three-dimensional, and unique individual emerges as the salient feature.[32]

That's a dramatic declaration of independence from the nomothetic psychoanalysts and behaviorists of Allport's day. Even more, by advocating the study not just of the individual but of the *unique* individual, Allport declared *his* uniqueness in comparison with brother Floyd or with virtually anyone else in psychology at the time. "I am not that little boy," he was saying; "I am nobody but me."

Allport as an Adult

Finally, having dealt with every other element of the core sentence, "I am not *that little boy with the dirt phobia*," we are left with its beginning: "*I am not.*" Erik Erikson, in his psychobiography of Martin Luther, makes much of Luther's so-called "fit in the choir," when Luther is said to have shouted out, "It isn't me!" or "I am *not*!"[33] Declaring what you are not, according to Erikson, is often a way to establish who you are, what your identity is. Gordon Allport, by his testimony, was not a neurotic, not a little boy, not a generic personality interchangeable with other personalities. So what was he? As he suggested in his 1962 "reminiscence" on the origins of the *Personality* textbook ("some people *do* grow up"), he was a grownup, a psychologically healthy adult.

What does that imply? Well, as he said in the book, "There are as many ways of growing up as there are individuals who grow, and in each case the end-product is unique. But," he added, "if general criteria are sought whereby to distinguish a fully developed personality from one that is still unripe, there are three differentiating characteristics that seem both universal and indispensable."[34]

Allport did little to demonstrate the universality or indispensability of the three characteristics that he listed. But they are surely characteristics that he felt he himself possessed in full measure, indeed more than most people—as, on the whole, he did. He identified them as self-extension, self-objectification, and a unifying philosophy of life. *Self-extension* involves having "a variety of autonomous interests," the incorporation into oneself of the many things one loves: "Possessions, friends, one's own children, other children, cultural interests, abstract ideas, politics, hobbies, recreation, and most conspicuously of all, one's *work*."[35] One is reminded here of the busy Allport, who even as an undergraduate devoted himself enthusiastically to volunteer work with boys' clubs, social service agencies, the Humane Society, etc., while joyfully discovering the new intellectual world of Harvard, Cambridge, and Boston—a far cry from the Freud anecdote's narrowly focused dirt-phobic boy and his well-starched mother.

Self-objectification includes the development of self-insight and of that highly correlated quality, a sense of humor. The latter involves, according to Allport, "the ability to laugh at the things one loves (including of course oneself and all that pertains to oneself), and still to love them."[36] We might wonder about Allport's degree of self-insight, as he resolutely insisted that the little Viennese boy had no relevance to himself. But Allport certainly did display a sense of humor about the matter, and he was *very* self-aware regarding the only level of personality he thought important for normal adults—the conscious level.

Allport's final criterion for a fully developed personality is a *unifying philosophy of life*, one that represents to a person "his place in the scheme of things."[37] Allport acknowledged that "there are many . . . unifying philosophies," but he insisted, "Religion is the search for a value underlying *all* things, and as such is the most comprehensive of all the possible philosophies of life."[38] Here the very religious Gordon Allport could feel superior even to his older brother Floyd, who had publicly given up on the idea of a "transcendental, monistic god."[39] On this point Gordon could also feel superior to Sigmund Freud. He observed that in the recently published *New Introductory Lectures*, "Freud declares himself 'perfectly certain' that this particular class of 'illusions' [i.e., religion] springs from infantilism of the mind."[40] Allport thought he knew better; and in knowing better, he recognized himself as the true adult among this company. While discussing his criteria for personal maturity, Allport listed the major limitations of other approaches to the psychology of personality, and here he made one simple complaint about psychoanalysis: "*Freudian psychology* never regards an adult as truly adult."[41] Like every personality theorist before and after him, Allport clearly knew of at least one adult who was truly adult in terms of his own theory: the theorist himself.

I realize that in focusing on the personal sources of his 1937 personality textbook, I am selling Gordon Allport short. I wish he were still around to rally the forces of idiographic psychology; the rest of us need someone of his vigor and eloquence. I've been greatly impressed by the wise and pithy editorial correspondence he sent out during his many years as editor of the *Journal of Abnormal and Social Psychology*. If Allport's editorial suggestions had been heeded more carefully by Abraham Maslow, for example, the third-force humanistic psychology movement might have been built upon firmer ground. I've seen much evidence of

Allport's private kindness to individuals as different from him and from each other as Jenny Masterson (the pseudonymous correspondent of *Letters from Jenny*) and Harry Murray.

I agree with Allport that "In biographies . . . an inevitable exaggeration of consistency occurs. 'Irrelevant' activities and traits are discarded, and the act of discarding makes for over-simplification . . . . The writer wishes to extract the 'essence' or meaning of the life. In so doing remarkable unity emerges, more than was ever present in the animate person."[42] Surely there was much more to Gordon Allport than the clean little boy of his Freud encounter. But Allport himself kept telling that story, telling it much more often than any other story about himself, and tying it directly to his life's work.

A year after Allport's personality textbook was published, another milestone in personality psychology appeared: Henry Murray's *Explorations in Personality*. Murray dedicated his book in part "To Sigmund Freud, whose genius contributed the most fruitful working hypotheses . . . and to Carl G. Jung, whose writings were a hive of great suggestiveness." Allport had properly dedicated the *Personality* text to his mother, whose virtues and teachings had left their strong mark upon his book. But he might well have added to his dedication these words: "And to Sigmund Freud, whose question stung me to make this belated (but thoroughly adult) reply."

6

Skinner's Dark Year and Walden Two

Aᶠᵀᴱᴿ I ᴡʀᴏᴛᴇ my first psychobiographical studies of Freud and Allport, I decided to begin research on living theorists. Most psychobiographical research is done on dead people, for ethical and other reasons (some of which I'll discuss in Chapter 15). In choosing subjects who were elderly but alive, I wasn't trying to be methodologically innovative. I just wanted to get their side of their story while they were still around to give it.

So I made appointments to interview B. F. Skinner and Henry A. Murray on a sweltering August day in 1977. Murray lived two blocks from William James Hall, Harvard University's high-rise behavioral science building where Skinner had a seventh-floor office. I went to see Murray first, at 11:00 A.M. He greeted me at his front door like a long-lost friend. He explained that the upstairs study where we'd be talking was not as cool as it might be, and offered me a drink from his well-stocked bar. Eleven in the morning was a good deal earlier than I was accustomed to drinking anything alcoholic, so I settled for orange juice. We had a delightful conversation, which I taped on my portable recorder.

At 2:00 that afternoon, B. F. Skinner's secretary showed me into his inner office. The office was cool and so was Skinner. He had already made it clear on the phone that he was not eager to do this interview. As I sat down, however, Skinner asked, "Do you want some juice?" I hesitated. Was this a sign that he was already mellowing, or was offering interviewers a preliminary drink some kind of Harvard faculty ritual? Then Skinner gestured toward my tape recorder and said, "For your machine—do you want to plug it in?"

Perhaps I'm overdoing my analysis of small clues, but the contrast seemed revealing. Murray offered juice for me, Skinner offered juice for my machine. Murray was eager to talk about the personal, life-historical context of his ideas; Skinner was reluctant to do the same. He eventually warmed up a bit, though, when we began to discuss the gadgets he had invented to make his research and his life easier.

Long before his death in 1990, B. F. Skinner had become the preeminent behaviorist of our era—indeed, to many people, the preeminent psychologist.[1] Though his empirical findings came almost entirely from observations of white rats and pigeons, the larger part of his published work deals with human beings. To a psychobiographer, the personal sources of his ideas on human psychology appear at first glance elusive. In writing about human behavior—including his own behavior—Skinner tried wherever possible to avoid subjective accounts or figurative speech. But one book, unique among Skinner's many publications, employs figurative language from beginning to end as it describes personality and social interaction from a behaviorist perspective. That book is Skinner's utopian novel *Walden Two*.[2]

Walden Two is Skinner's best-known book, with over 2 million copies in print. It describes a society founded upon principles of operant conditioning, but it is by no means just a mechanical dramatization of Skinner's scientific ideas. Nor was its writing merely an intellectual exercise. According to Skinner, "*Walden Two* was not planned at all."[3] He described himself as caught by surprise when what began as "a description of a feasible design for community living" turned into a novel: "The characters soon took over. In general I write very slowly and in longhand. . . . *Walden Two* was an entirely different experience. I wrote it on the typewriter in seven weeks."[4] Parts of it were written "with an emotional intensity that I have never experienced at any other time."[5] One crucial section was typed out "in white heat."[6] "I would dash off a fair version of a short chapter in a single morning. . . . I revised sparingly. Except for a bout of dramaturgy during my junior year at Hamilton [College], when I wrote a three-act play in one morning, I had never experienced anything like it."[7]

Skinner published several accounts of the novel's origins, advancing at least three distinct kinds of reasons for writing it:

1. *To provide a model of life for returning World War II veterans.* In talking to a friend whose son and son-in-law were on active duty during the war's closing months, Skinner expressed regret that at war's end they and other young people would "abandon their crusading spirit and come back only to fall into the old lockstep of American life."[8] He suggested that, with the aid of "an experimental attitude toward life,"[9] young people could improve upon previously attempted utopian communities and "could build a culture that would come closer to satisfying human needs than the American way of life."[10] The friend encouraged Skinner to put his ideas in writing. Though Skinner said he "gave the matter no further thought"[11] as he completed an already promised scientific paper, he began to write *Walden Two* the day after the paper was finished.

2. *To apply a "science of behavior" to the resolution of dissatisfactions that were*

external but personal.   Some of these dissatisfactions involved family life; others were avocational or professional. Skinner wrote:

> I had seen my wife and her friends struggling to save themselves from domesticity. . . . Our older daughter had just finished first grade, and there is nothing like a child's first year in school to turn one's thoughts to education. We were soon to leave Minnesota and move to Indiana and I had been in search of housing. I would be leaving a group of talented young string players who had put up with my inadequacies at the piano and I was not sure I could ever replace them. I had just finished a productive year on a Guggenheim Fellowship, but I had accepted the chairmanship of a department at Indiana and was not sure when I would again have time for science or scholarship. Was there not something to be done about problems of that sort?[12]

3. *To provide "self-therapy."*   Skinner has described the book as "pretty obviously a venture in self-therapy, in which I was struggling to reconcile two aspects of my own behavior represented by Burris and Frazier," the novel's central characters.[13] Without referring again to self-therapy or to a psychological struggle, Skinner later clarified what he meant by the two aspects:

> I did not know until I had finished the book that I was both Burris and Frazier. Burris, the narrator, is a pedestrian college teacher, particularly unhappy with his lot because he has just returned from an exciting wartime experience. . . . Frazier, the founder of Walden Two, is a self-proclaimed genius who has deserted academic psychology for behavioral engineering, the new discipline upon which the community is based.[14]

Skinner's description of his personal dissatisfactions and of his "venture in self-therapy" suggested to me that *Walden Two* had been Skinner's response to a major midlife crisis. For male professionals in our culture, such crises typically begin at around age 40 or 41.[15] Skinner was 41 when he wrote the book. Evidence of crisis is visible in many aspects of his life at the time, as well as in the feelings reported by Burris—who is not only the novel's narrator but (Burrhus F.) Skinner's namesake. As often happens in men's lives,[16] certain earlier conflicts were reactivated when Skinner's midlife crisis emerged. Those earlier conflicts left their mark on *Walden Two* as well. A crucial set of events had occurred during a period Skinner called the "Dark Year"—a time in early adulthood when he experienced what appears to have been a severe identity crisis. Identity crisis and midlife crisis together, then, gained expression and a kind of resolution in his writing of *Walden Two*.

Skinner's Identity Crisis

In his autobiography, Skinner used the term "identity crisis" only once, and then only as a joke. He described an experience at age 14 or 15, when he "woke up one morning and could not find [his] left arm." After a panicky search, he discovered the arm still attached to his body; it had been twisted sharply under his neck with the circulation cut off. He later referred to this incident as "a partial identity crisis."[17] The term does not appear in his much more extensive description of the Dark Year. Yet Skinner's account of that period includes all the major features of a severe identity crisis, as described by the man who invented the term, Erik Erikson.[18]

Erikson cites as a primary aspect of youthful identity crisis "the inability to settle on an occupational identity."[19] During his final undergraduate term, feeling compelled to choose an occupational identity, Skinner decided to become a writer. He had already written extensively for college publications and had participated in the Bread Loaf summer writing school. At the point of making his career choice, he received an encouraging letter about his writing ability from Robert Frost. He subsequently proposed to spend a year at home writing a novel. His father expressed serious reservations about the plan, but offered to support him financially for the year, on the condition that the 22-year-old Skinner would "go to work" if his writing career was not well launched by year's end.

Within three months, Skinner was already telling himself he was a failure. "The results were disastrous. I frittered away my time."[20] "The truth was, I had no reason to write anything. I had nothing to say, and nothing about my life was making any change in that condition."[21] In his notebook Skinner blamed his parents for "unwittingly forcing" him into his "present course" as well as for making fun of his "effeminate" interests and his time-wasting activities.[22] He blamed the city of Scranton, where his family then lived, for being "ready to quench any ideas of my own I may have. . . . I am too sensitive to my surroundings to stand it." [23] He blamed literature itself for being "a mean satisfaction of a mean instinct" and for being unable to express the subtleties of life.[24] But he felt bound by his agreement with his father to give a writing career a one-year trial: "I found myself committed, with no hope of reprieve, to what I came to call the Dark Year."[25]

The Dark Year was dark for several reasons. Not only did Skinner discover that he was unable to write anything important; he was often the object (or fancied himself as the object) of jibes and innuendoes from people who would have seen even a successful writing career as inappropriate for a healthy young man. Skinner writes, "I was desperately hungry for intellectual stimulation."[26] But, he adds, "there was no one with whom I could talk or even correspond seriously. I was confined to the autistic, not to say auto-erotic, satisfactions to be found in a notebook."[27] His family had moved from his boyhood home to Scranton just

before he entered college, and when he returned to Scranton after college graduation, he had no ties to replace the supportive social and intellectual environment
of his college campus. His parents were themselves undergoing personal crises at
the time and could offer him little emotional support. Skinner began to sit in the
family library for extended periods, where he remained "absolutely motionless in
a kind of catatonic stupor" or made stereotyped movements.[28] He proposed
seeing a psychiatrist, but his father's response was negative.

In his notebooks of the time Skinner wrote,

> Cleverness lost its glamour for me. . . . Nothing is worth doing. . . . The
> world considers me lazy because I do not earn bread. The world expects
> of me that I should measure up to its standard of strength, which means
> that if I "got a job" for eight hours of office work . . . I should be a
> man. . . . I see clearly now that the only thing left for me to do in life is
> to justify myself for doing nothing.[29]

He contemplated opening a model-ship-building shop in Greenwich Village,
or perhaps raising chickens, as a way to support himself while renewing his
efforts to write. He considered "deserting writing for several years" in order to
take advantage of an "opportunity . . . to make a great deal of money"; but that
opportunity "vanished as suddenly as it had appeared."[30] Instead, he temporarily
"rescued" himself and his "self-respect" through other sorts of work.[31] First he
became a laborer for a landscape gardener, but he soon developed a grass allergy.
Then he found a new job as a writer: under his father's sponsorship, he would
prepare one-paragraph digests of over a thousand decisions of a federal agency,
the Anthracite Board of Conciliation.[32] His father had been a lawyer for a coal-
mining company; the mine owners needed a compendium of those decisions in
order to fight more effectively against the mine workers' union. Skinner describes
the job as "hack-work . . . dull and monotonous."[33] But he made money at it, he
earned his father's approval, and by the end of the Dark Year he had finished
writing his first book: *A Digest of Decisions of the Anthracite Board of Conciliation.*

The Dark Year clearly involved an identity crisis. Skinner's occupational identity, which had been gradually constructed during college and then confirmed by
Robert Frost's letter, abruptly collapsed. Moreover, Skinner was unable to find in
the reactions of others any clear indication that he was a worthy individual.
Separated from his boyhood and college friends, he could not fall back on the
ready-made identity of a peer group. He had given up his religious beliefs and felt
alienated from the political system. Even his gender identity was not as firmly
established as he would have liked. His sexual experiences in college had been
less than satisfying; the availability of acceptable female companions in Scranton
was quite limited; and being questioned by his mother about his "effeminate"
activities must have been painful.

Skinner's own descriptions of the Dark Year, both then and later, indicate profound distress. At its worst, the crisis appears to have reached a level warranting Erikson's term, *severe identity confusion*. According to Erikson, severe identity confusion is "defined by a certain self-perpetuating propensity, by an increasing waste of defensive energy, and by a deepened psychosocial isolation."[34] Among the symptoms listed by Erikson are "a special form of painful self-consciousness which dwells on discrepancies between one's self-esteem . . . and one's appearance in the eyes of others" (p. 183); "the display of a total commitment to a *role fixation* . . . as against a free *experimentation* with available roles" (p. 184); "extreme *work paralysis*" (p. 184); and a "*time confusion*" that may manifest itself in such forms as "catatonic immobility" or "an intense and even fanatic investment in a future, or [in] a rapid succession in a number of possible futures" (p. 181).[35] All of these symptoms appear in Skinner's self-descriptions of the Dark Year, and they confirm his own diagnosis of the year as "disastrous" for his "self-respect."

The crisis was finally resolved, as such intense identity crises often are, through the wholehearted acceptance of an ideology—indeed, an extreme ideology. In Skinner's case, the ideology was radical behaviorism. But Skinner did not arrive at this resolution immediately upon the conclusion of his Dark Year in Scranton. Still ambivalent about literature and writing, he considered going back to college for a master's degree in English, and he dabbled in Ouspenskian philosophical mysticism. His own account of the latter "digression" suggests that the identity crisis remained at least intermittently acute following the calendar end of the Dark Year: "I was floundering in a stormy sea and perilously close to drowning, but help was on the way."[36]

Help came in the form of his discovery of John B. Watson and Ivan Pavlov, whose ideas gave focus to his previously scattered reading in psychology. Skinner quickly came to think of himself as a behaviorist. He entered Harvard's graduate program in psychology, and at the end of his first year there could write home to his parents:

> I am looked upon as the leader of a certain school of psychological theories. . . . The behaviorists, whom I represent, have acquired a good deal of strength this year. . . . Many of the new men, coming here this year, will come over to our "party," giving us moral and physical support.[37]

By this time, Skinner held very definite ideas concerning his mission in psychology. He was convinced of the rightness of his position versus the error of others' positions, and he had begun to build a social support system among those who agreed with him. At the age of 25 his identity was firmly established. This new identity served Skinner well for many years. Only when it was threatened by a series of professional disappointments and personal frustrations did Skinner again confront a major psychological crisis. His principal response to the later crisis, incorporating many of the concerns of the earlier one, was *Walden Two*.

Skinner's Midlife Crisis

During graduate school and for several years thereafter, Skinner was preoccupied with laboratory research. His identity as a behaviorist not only gave him a clear position in professional discussions, but supplied a general orientation for his research. His positive research findings in turn strengthened his identity. In his late twenties he was able to set down "in a rather expansive mood . . . plans for the second thirty years" of his life. These plans included statements such as "No surrender to the physiology of the central nervous system" and "Support behavioristic methodology throughout."[38] He also began to write a book (never published) titled *A Sketch for an Epistemology*, in which he distinguished between methodological behaviorism and radical behaviorism for the first time, aligning himself solidly with the latter.[39] He told his behaviorist friend Fred Keller, "It will make everybody mad, I'm afraid, if it gets published."[40] Thus he was identifying himself in terms of the professional enemies he made as well as in terms of who his friends were.

Skinner was now able to resolve other identity issues as well. In his early thirties he began to teach at the University of Minnesota, his first full-time and salaried faculty appointment. Almost simultaneously, he got married. Though professional recognition came more slowly than he would have preferred, success followed success in the laboratory, convincing him that he had developed a powerful research strategy. At the end of 1938, with his first child born and his first psychology book completed, he could write, "The last day of my best and happiest year!"[41]

The latter half of his thirties, however, saw more than the usual run of frustrations. When the book (*The Behavior of Organisms*) was published in 1939, reviews and sales were disappointing. Skinner began to think of writing another book, on the psychology of literature. His father volunteered to pay him the equivalent of a summer-school salary if he would bring his family to Scranton for the summer. Thus Skinner began to write that book in the basement of his parents' home—"as far as possible," he notes, "from the attic study in which I had attacked literature in a different way during that dark year."[42] But he soon concluded that "Scranton was not the place for me at any age."[43] Replaying the Dark Year, he tired of the manuscript and eventually abandoned it.

The day after the Japanese attack on Pearl Harbor, Skinner resumed work on a project he had earlier abandoned: the training of pigeons to guide bombs or missiles to their targets. This was to be Skinner's major research activity during World War II. He found the laboratory results gratifying, but government officials repeatedly drew back from making use of the trained pigeons. After two years of research, the project was finally "declared of no value to the defense of the country," Skinner later wrote. "Project Pigeon was discouraging. . . . My verbal behavior with respect to Washington underwent extinction, and the effect generalized. My co-workers told me after it was all over that toward the end of the project I was not finishing my sentences."[44]

The next year was more satisfying in several regards. Skinner's second daughter was born, and he built her a completely enclosed "baby-tender" (later called an Air-Crib or, by others, a baby-box) as an improvement on the standard crib. He began to write a book titled *Verbal Behavior*, which he enjoyed much more than the psychology-of-literature book. And he agreed to chair the psychology department at Indiana University.

Skinner's wife became unhappy over the prospective move, however. As Skinner recalled, "We looked for houses [in Bloomington] and found nothing we liked. When we were alone, Yvonne was often in tears. The professional advantages meant little to her, and she would be giving up a pleasant house and leaving old friends."[45] Skinner himself saw professional advantages to the move. He would have "more professional weight," his own graduate students, the opportunity to build a new laboratory.[46] But he was not eager to assume the position's administrative duties, and his first major proposal to modify department practices at Indiana was rejected even before he arrived. Skinner writes, "I accepted Indiana's offer in part because I was feeling rather out of things. . . . Under wartime restrictions I had attended no professional meetings and had lost contact with my old friends in the East."[47] But moving from Minnesota to Indiana promised little improvement in that regard. Furthermore, *The Behavior of Organisms* was still selling poorly, "and no one seemed to be taking up the study of operant behavior."[48]

This was Skinner's situation as of mid-1946, immediately prior to the writing of *Walden Two*. It is understandable that he would empathize with returning World War II veterans who had to leave behind their "crusading spirit" as they rejoined the "lockstep" of civilian life. He had spent over two years in the wartime excitement of Project Pigeon, only to be forced to abandon it and return to a mundane academic career. It's understandable, too, that he would worry about the uncertainties of moving to Indiana. In another account he says he was concerned that he as well as his wife would have to struggle to find new friends, and that he might not "again have time for science or scholarship."[49] Given the circumstances, it's equally understandable that he would feel the need for self-therapy, to help reconcile the self-image of "a pedestrian college teacher" with the intriguing potential alter ego of a "self-proclaimed genius who has deserted academic psychology for behavioral engineering."[50] Skinner was at the right age to begin a midlife transition, and the conditions were right to turn the initial phase of that transition into a full-blown midlife crisis.

According to Daniel Levinson, a man's midlife transition typically involves a reappraisal of his adult accomplishments to date, followed by attempts "to modify the negative elements of the present [life] structure and to test new choices," as well as by a resolution of "the polarities that are sources of deep division in his life."[51] For most men,

> this period evokes tumultuous struggles within the self and with the external world. . . . A profound reappraisal of this kind cannot be a cool, intellectual process. It must involve emotional turmoil, despair, the sense of not knowing where to turn or of being stagnant and unable to move at all. . . . A man who attempts a radical critique of his life at 40 will be up against the parts of himself that have a strong investment in the present structure. . . . Internal voices that have been muted for years now clamor to be heard. . . . During the Mid-life Transition he must learn to listen more attentively to these voices and decide consciously what part he will give them in life.[52]

In his autobiographical accounts, Skinner only hints at inner turmoil. His descriptions of this period are much cooler emotionally than those of the Dark Year. But in *Walden Two*, Skinner's mouthpiece Burris speaks openly of his midlife distress.

From the book's second page, Burris expresses dissatisfaction with his career as a college teacher. Of his former students he says, "Their pitiful display of erudition was all I had to show for my life as a teacher, and I looked upon that handiwork not only without satisfaction, but with actual dismay" (p. 2). He "had assumed an appropriate sense of social responsibility" during the war, but as he remarks, "my new interest in social problems and my good will appeared to have exactly no effect whatsoever upon society. I could not see that they were of the slightest value to anyone, yet I continued to pay for them day after day with a sustained feeling of frustration and depression" (pp. 3–4). After two days of touring the utopian village of Walden Two, Burris thinks to himself, "Could I ever escape from the world of books? My eyes ached in vivid reminiscence and I was seized with a violent revulsion, almost a retching" (p. 85).

Further touring leaves Burris's mind "a chaotic jumble." But, he says, he "could not shake off the sheer habit of academic life. It seemed as inevitable as it was unsatisfying" (p.266). When Frazier tells Burris that after he spends a month in Walden Two, he "will shake off the pessimism which fills the abysmal depths to which we've sunk" (p. 273), Burris does not protest the metaphor's extreme language. Instead he becomes increasingly anxious about his future, referring to his "sense of personal failure" (p. 291) and to a loss of faith not only in his own teaching ability but in formal education itself:

> Education was completely bewildered as to its place in the world of the future. It could insure no sense of belonging to a movement, no *esprit de corps*. I could get no satisfaction from atavistic or nostalgic attempts to reconstruct a happier era, and so I contented myself with doing the day's work. (p. 293)

Finally Burris resolves his remaining doubts: "I relinquished my hold on my unrewarding past. It was all too clear that nothing could be made of it" (p. 294).

Burris's feelings cannot be taken as an exact representation of Skinner's feelings at the time. Burris's conflicted character seems intended to offer a dramatic contrast to Frazier's certainty, and his expressed dissatisfactions with mundane life are aroused in part by the idyllic qualities of Walden Two. But Skinner has identified Burris as representing himself to a considerable degree, and various details of Burris's life resemble sources of dissatisfaction present in Skinner's own life at the time. It seems reasonable to assume, then, that Burris's emotional experience of crisis is only a modest exaggeration of Skinner's feelings. The sense of occupational despair and the longing for a new life-style, as reported by Burris, were not resolved for Skinner by the decision to move to Indiana. Instead, they were directly and powerfully expressed in his writing of *Walden Two*.

Walden Two as a Means of Coping with Crisis

On literally his first free day between the end of one set of professional obligations and the beginning of another, Skinner embarked upon the writing of *Walden Two*. At one level the book presents a fairly straightforward series of speculations on a planned society, incorporating Skinner's major empirical findings in the guise of a traditional utopian novel. But Skinner's own testimony concerning the process of writing the book—the speed, the emotional intensity, his lack of planning—suggests that powerful psychological forces were at work, in addition to his strictly intellectual concerns.

When I talked with Skinner in 1977, he affirmed his earlier statement that the book had been a kind of self-therapy. At the same time, he tried to play down that aspect of its writing:

> I don't take much stock in the therapeutic value of literature. There are cases of people who came out of psychoses, also neuroses, by writing a book. It wasn't that serious a problem with me. As a matter of fact, I didn't pay much attention to *Walden Two* for a good many years; I didn't even use it in my own courses for a long time.[53]

However, the evidence I've already cited suggests that relatively serious psychological problems *were* involved. Skinner's failure to "pay much attention" to the book after its completion further suggests that writing it helped him to resolve those problems. How did the book's writing achieve this end?

First, the book incorporated fantasied resolutions of several specific elements of Skinner's midlife crisis. Skinner says the book was easy to write partly because it drew upon various aspects of his life at the time he wrote it. But the book usually presents the positive aspects in an exaggerated and idealized form, with the narrator on the verge of attaining them rather than giving them up (as would happen upon Skinner's own imminent departure to Indiana), and with these idealized benefits promising to continue unabated into the distant future. The residents of Walden Two live in a comfortable, efficient, ingeniously designed physical environment, whereas Skinner was soon to leave his "pleasant" house and was having difficulty finding a satisfactory replacement. The residents' daily social relationships are both warm and undemanding, whereas Skinner was abandoning an established social network to live in an unfamiliar city. Walden Two provides its inhabitants with a ready audience for creative work and with tolerant accompanists for amateur musicians; Skinner was leaving similar (though probably less convenient) circumstances and was not sure he could ever regain them.

In addition, Skinner included in the book imaginary solutions for several concerns that he could not resolve satisfactorily either in his former location or in his new one. For instance, Walden Two's children are raised mainly by professionals rather than by their own parents. Skinner himself moved no further in this direction than the invention of the Air-Crib. In the book, the experimental analysis of behavior is no longer a largely ignored byway of psychology; instead, it's embraced by an entire society as the most effective and rewarding means to a good life. Even the minor physical inconveniences of life have been smoothed out by one gadget or procedural innovation after another. Furthermore, in deciding to move to Walden Two, Burris is able to leave the frustrations of academic life behind while he gains academic security, the opportunity to conduct innovative research in an exciting environment, and ample time to read and write. Even Frazier, a key administrator during the early years of Walden Two, has by now turned over most of the job to others and allows the society to function without his supervision—while Skinner, with considerable ambivalence, was just about to become an administrator. Finally, in the grandest fantasy Skinner could imagine with regard to his current professional life, Frazier has been able to experiment for more than a decade with the lives of nearly a thousand human beings, in a totally beneficent way—so beneficent that he sometimes thinks of himself as superior to God. Skinner's own control over a small population of laboratory rats and pigeons, effective as it was, paled by comparison.

Those were the midlife crisis issues that *Walden Two* resolved only in fantasy. The book simultaneously addressed certain issues left over from Skinner's youthful identity crisis, now renewed by his midlife stresses. One of the book's most prominent themes, beyond that of basing a society on the experimental analysis of behavior, is the proper distribution of time between leisure activities (including intellectual and aesthetic pursuits) and responsible labor. Walden Two's adults willingly perform a maximum of four hours' work for the community each day. By doing so, they gain a sense of participation while freeing themselves for their own pursuits the rest of the time. Frazier emphatically justifies the requirement that part of the work be physical:

The really intelligent man doesn't want to feel that his work is being done by anyone else. He's sensitive enough to be disturbed by slight resentments which, multiplied a millionfold, mean his downfall. . . . That's the virtue of Walden Two which pleases me most. I was never happy in being waited on. I could never enjoy the fleshpots for thinking of what might be going on below stairs. . . . Here a man can hold up his head and say, "I've done my share!"   (p. 51)

This passage, and the general theme it represents, is strongly reminiscent of Skinner's distress at being thought a loafer by his parents and neighbors during the first months of the Dark Year. His relief at getting a job as a gardener's helper seems to have been elaborated into a basic principle of the Walden Two social structure 19 years later. When I suggested this interpretation to him, Skinner accepted it:

I was rescued from the doldrums of an intellectual life that wasn't paying off, simply by putting my eight hours a day in digging holes and planting bushes and things like that. That, I think, is why I wanted in *Walden Two* to have everyone do a little work of that kind.[54]

Descriptions of social life in Walden Two broadly reflect Skinner's concerns at the time of writing the book, but they appear more specifically related to his anxieties as a rather unsophisticated young man. His undergraduate years at Hamilton College had introduced him to "an entirely new world" of intellectual conversations and string quartet evenings at faculty homes.[55] During the Dark Year this world was replaced by awkward social encounters at parentally arranged country club dances and Kiwanis Club luncheons. In *Walden Two*, much is made of the sheer ease of socializing, the careful design of teacups to prevent spillage, the sophisticated but unpressured quality of social graces:

These were delightful people. Their conversation had a measure and cadence more often found in well-wrought fiction than in fact. They were pleasant and well-mannered, yet perfectly candid; they were lively, but not boisterous; affectionate, but not effusive. But they were of another world, and I could not even be sure they were speaking a language I knew.   (p. 24)

This might have been "another world" to Skinner in his early twenties, one he longed to enjoy again as he was suffering through the Dark Year. But it surely would not have been an unfamiliar world to the 41-year-old veteran of Harvard Graduate School, the Harvard Society of Fellows, and many years of interaction with a variety of faculty members, business executives, and government officials.

The professionalization of childraising in Walden Two was in part a reaction to the needs of Skinner's own two small children, and especially to the demands they made on his wife's time and energy. But in the novel, Frazier speaks at length about another gain besides childraising expertise and efficiency: "the weakening of the family structure" (p. 126).

> No sensible person will suppose that love or affection has anything to do with blood. . . . Love and affection are psychological and cultural, and blood relationships can be happily forgotten. . . . The hereditary connection will be minimized to the point of being forgotten.   (p. 133)

> In the family, neither [parent] may have characteristics suitable to the child's developing personality. It's a sort of coerced identification, which we are glad to avoid.   (p. 135)

Burris later agrees:

> Aside from the role of physical resemblance, I could not see that hereditary connections could have any real bearing upon relationships between men. . . . The important thing was not that two people were related, but that they had been told they were related. Better not to bring the matter up at all. The family was only a little race, and it had better go. It was no longer an efficient economic or social unit or transmitter of culture—its current failure [in society at large] was increasingly evident.   (p. 291)

Skinner's descriptions of his feelings toward his children at the time of *Walden Two* are generally quite positive. I doubt that he was really worried about his children being "coerced" to identify with him or his wife. Much of the hostility expressed in *Walden Two* toward parental models, blood relationships, and nuclear families is likely to have come instead from Skinner's difficult relationships with his own parents, especially during the Dark Year. When he admitted failure to himself three months into the Dark Year, well over half of the statement he wrote then blamed his parents for his predicament:

> My family ties prevent my living simply alone, "struggling to write." . . .
> My family ties prevent me, not because I have a great deal of devotion
> and respect for my father and mother, but because they have suffered
> very much in the last four years and because my leaving them would in-
> crease their present anxiety to an unbearable degree. Thus they are un-
> wittingly forcing me into my present course.[56]

If only there were no emotional ties to these blood relations with whom he feels so little identification, the young Skinner seems to be telling himself, there would be no need for dark years! And in *Walden Two*, the ties are indeed being systematically eliminated.

Strong emotion, especially strong negative emotion, is an even broader target in *Walden Two*. When Frazier is asked what children get out of the innovative childraising practices in Walden Two, his eyes flash "with a sort of helpless contempt," and he responds:

> What they get is escape from the petty emotions which eat the heart out of the unprepared. They get the satisfaction of pleasant and profitable social relations on a scale almost undreamed of in the world at large. They get immeasurably increased efficiency, because they can stick to a job without suffering the aches and pains which soon beset most of us. They get new horizons, for they are spared the emotions characteristic of frustration and failure.   (p. 102)

In other words, they get much of the emotional ease and satisfaction that Skinner fervently desired but was unable to attain during the Dark Year.

Even one of Skinner's major theoretical tenets, which he had supported by empirical research on nonhuman organisms and then applied fictionally to the populace of Walden Two, can be seen as related to the family frictions of the Dark Year. Skinner's mother had always relied heavily on techniques of aversive control to regulate his behavior, largely through variants of "Tut tut, what will people think?" Such attempts at aversive control, from both mother and father, appear to have reached their height—or at any rate Skinner became excruciatingly sensitive to them—during the Dark Year. In *Walden Two*, such aversive control is repeatedly described as one of the outside society's worst ills. It is linked with the negative emotional states that must be eliminated: "'Most of what I do [said Burris], I do to avoid undesirable consequences, to evade unpleasantnesses, or to reject or attack forces which interfere with my freedom.' 'All the unhappy motives,' said Frazier" (p. 115). Positive reinforcement is discussed less in terms of its effects on behavior (though Skinner emphasizes that it can be a powerful force) than in terms of the feeling of freedom it generates: "We can achieve a sort of control under which the controlled, though they are following a code . . . nevertheless feel free. They are doing what they want to do, not what they are forced to do. . . . There's no restraint and no revolt" (p. 246). As a radical behaviorist, Skinner could admit neither the absence of control nor the existence of true freedom. But in late adolescence and early manhood, he had yearned to feel free to do as he wished. At the onset of middle age he still valued that feeling, though he knew by then that it was illusory.

As a scientist, Skinner assumed that the environment controls behavior, whether it be the social or the natural environment. During the Dark Year, the social environment came to seem so aversively, suffocatingly controlling that an anguished Skinner could write, "I am too sensitive to my surroundings to stand it."[57] In *Walden Two*, the environment continues to control; Skinner saw no way out of that. But it is as benevolent an environment as Skinner could devise. Even during the darkest days of the Dark Year, Skinner never contemplated a total escape from control. (As he says, "I had never learned to protest or revolt."⁵⁸) But he knew it was possible to have parents or parent substitutes who were less traditionally restrictive than his were at the time—and he knew it was possible to have a more rewarding world than Scranton.

Walden Two: The Final Outcome

In addition to all the specific coping processes embodied in *Walden Two*, two broad effects of writing the book were essential to Skinner's continued personal growth. First, the creation of *Walden Two* itself enabled Skinner finally to overcome the key failure of the Dark Year. He had now written a novel, one in which he had something important to say. Indeed, he had written it in even less time than the three months he had devoted to writing at the beginning of the Dark Year. Second, writing the novel enabled Skinner to make the crucial transition from being mainly a laboratory scientist, going where his animals led him and hoping someone else would follow, to becoming an outspoken public advocate for a behavioristic science of human behavior. *Walden Two* was his first major publication on human behavior. It was followed by *Science and Human Behavior* (1953), *Verbal Behavior* (1957), and numerous other books and papers that were low on empirical data but high on explanation and proselytization. This, finally, is what Skinner seems to have meant when he described *Walden Two* as an attempt to reconcile two aspects of his behavior—an attempt that ended less in a reconciliation than in a one-sided victory. As Skinner told me,

> When I wrote the book, I was not really a Frazierian . . . but I convinced myself, because the things that Frazier said did hang together, I thought, very well, and I'm now a thoroughgoing Frazierian as a result and I'm no longer Burris. I think, quite definitely, I did go back to Walden Two.⁵⁹

The proposals Skinner made in *Walden Two* for revising human behavior patterns and social structures are not invalidated by their partial origins in Skinner's own developmental crises. But those origins produced an "ideal" society of peculiar shape, functioning in terms of a peculiar conception of human personality. Walden Two is above all a society designed to avoid unpleasantness—by weakening emotional ties among family members and by minimizing obligatory parent-child contacts; by relieving guilt or shame over doing less practical work than one's fellows; by eliminating adolescent social discomforts and by making sure an amateur artist never lacks audiences or accompanists; by spreading onerous administrative obligations as broadly and thinly as possible. Walden Two's inhabitants do have their pleasures, to be sure. But by stressing the avoidance of unpleasantness as a major goal of the society, Skinner denied his Utopia's residents much of the variety of behavioral choices, the range of emotional responses, and the introspective richness of which human beings are capable. He did so not because of any Fascist leanings, as some of his critics have charged. He did so because of his own midlife needs to survive a contemporary emotional crisis, and to lay an earlier but still troubling crisis finally to rest.

Skinner's original title for his book, abandoned because another book had recently used a similar title, was *The Sun Is But a Morning Star*.[60] It came from the closing lines of Thoreau's *Walden*: "The light which puts out our eyes is darkness to us. Only that day dawns to which we are awake. There is more day to dawn. The sun is but a morning star." Skinner never explained this choice of title, and in *Walden Two* Burris says he "had always thought of [*Walden's*] last paragraph as a blemish. Its apparent mysticism and its obscurity were unlike the rest of the book and quite un-Thoreauvian."[61] But as Burris turns back to Walden Two in the novel's final pages, he reads that passage again "with feverish excitement," apparently seeing in it the new Golden Age promised by Frazier. The original title and Thoreau's words may have had a more personal implication for Skinner as well. A new day was dawning; a new kind of life was beginning; he was able to see his way clearly again. His personality had been reborn from crisis, and the Dark Year was truly over.

PART THREE

Into the Fantastic

7

The Thing from Inner Space:

John W. Campbell, Robert E. Howard,

Cordwainer Smith

In 1938, John W. Campbell, Jr. published a 50-page novella under the pseudonym Don A. Stuart. "Who Goes There?" is now widely regarded as one of the
best science fiction stories ever written.[1] The 1951 film version, "The Thing from
Another World," is often referred to as a classic. John Carpenter's 1982 remake is
nowhere close to classic, but it does feature one of the most disgusting monsters
in all of science fiction film.

Campbell's story describes an Antarctic expedition that finds an alien spaceship deep in the ice. The expedition's scientists speculate that the ship has been
down there since Antarctica froze over. Then they discover the body of a single
alien, who had escaped the spaceship crash only to freeze in a blizzard. The
expedition's biologist wants to thaw the creature so he can examine its structure
in detail. But a fearful physicist urges the rest of the crew to reject this plan:

> That thing may be dead—or, by God, it may not—but I don't like it.
> Damn it, Blair, let them see the monstrosity you are petting over there.
> Let them see the foul thing and decide for themselves whether they want
> that thing thawed out in this camp. . . . They haven't seen those three
> red eyes, and that blue hair like crawling worms. Crawling—damn, it's
> crawling there in the ice right now!
>
> Nothing Earth ever spawned had the unutterable sublimation of deva-
> stating wrath that thing let loose in its face when it looked around this
> frozen desolation twenty million years ago. Mad? It was mad clear
> through—searing, blistering mad!
>
> Hell, I've had bad dreams ever since I looked at those three red eyes.
> Nightmares. Dreaming the thing thawed out and came to life—that it
> wasn't dead, or even wholly unconscious all those twenty million years,
> but just slowed, waiting—waiting. . . . Put it back where it came from

and let it freeze for another twenty million years. I had some swell nightmares—that it wasn't made like we are—which is obvious—but of a different kind of flesh that it can really control. That it can change its shape, and look like a man—and wait to kill and eat.[2]

As the story develops, of course, the Thing does thaw out. It begins to kill humans, and to change into their shape, and to grow and split and change into more humans. The Thing can so closely duplicate anyone's appearance and behavior that soon nobody is sure whether the person sitting beside him is human or alien, friend or monster. The story gets pretty scary before it's over—scary enough to be chosen for a recent anthology of great horror tales.[3] But it's obviously just fiction, created from whole cloth by the vivid imagination of John W. Campbell.

Campbell dominated what is now called the "Golden Age" of science fiction. During the Golden Age and beyond, from the late 1930s into the early 1970s, he edited *Astounding Science Fiction,* eventually renaming it *Analog* and turning it into a magazine of "Science Fiction *and* Fact." Along the way, he strongly influenced many of the field's major writers, including Robert Heinlein and Isaac Asimov. Campbell was a serious man who preferred science fiction with a believable scientific veneer. "Who Goes There?" is a monster story, but it's told in grittily realistic terms. And indeed the story had a realistic basis—in Campbell's childhood memories.

When Campbell wrote "Who Goes There?" he probably didn't realize that the story was in any significant sense autobiographical.[4] When his first readers responded to the story's emotional power, they had no idea that this power drew from Campbell's own intense early experiences. When the Science Fiction Writers of America chose "Who Goes There?" as the best science fiction novella ever written,[5] few had yet learned of its subjective origins. When millions of viewers shook in their seats at the film incarnation of the monstrous Thing, they were given no hint that the monster came from inner space. But John Campbell had been writing about what he knew best. The monster was not a standard-issue escapee from an abstract id. It was not an archetypal messenger from the collective unconscious. It had lived in Campbell's childhood home, in the heart of his family.

Sam Moskowitz, Campbell's first biographer, identified the crucial connection between life history and fiction. "More than is true of most writers," according to Moskowitz, Campbell's "early life and background shaped the direction he would take in specific plot ideas as well as in method."[6] The boy John's relationships with the women in his family were especially important:

His mother had a twin sister who was literally identical. So close were they in appearance that no one, not even John, could tell them apart. The sisters were in psychological conflict because John's mother had married first, and he found himself used as an innocent pawn by his mother who fawned over him at great length as a subtle taunt to her twin.

The result was that John's aunt treated him with such abruptness that he was convinced she thoroughly hated him. This created a bizarre situation. The boy would come running into the house to impart something breathlessly to a woman he thought was his mother. He would be jarred by a curt rebuff from her twin. Every time his aunt visited the home, this situation posed itself until it became a continuing and insoluble nightmare. Was the woman standing in front of him "friend" or "foe?"[7]

Moskowitz then refers to the story John W. Campbell wrote some 20 years later, "Who Goes There?"—the story of an evil alien who is so perfect a mimic that nobody's identity can be trusted without passing the severest tests. Moskowitz emphasizes the story's biographical source:

From the memories of his childhood he [Campbell] drew the most fearsome agony of the past: the doubts, the fears, the shock, and the frustration of repeatedly discovering that the woman who looked so much like his mother was not who she seemed. Who goes there? Friend or foe?[8]

That was as far as Moskowitz ventured into psychobiography. Straight biography was his primary objective, and even there he had to stop short when he was denied further access to Campbell's personal papers.[9] If he had gone on to analyze Campbell in greater depth, he might have looked more closely at the resemblance of the rage-filled Thing not only to the identical aunt but to Campbell's mother. According to Campbell himself, "My mother had a remarkably sudden temper; it turned on violently with no more than about 3 seconds warning. Unless I carefully calculated every action before undertaking it, Hell popped irreversibly."[10] Moskowitz could also have considered the psychological sources of other Campbell works, such as the pair of "Aesir" stories, which depict a race of matriarchal aliens who enslave humanity and the men who use science to rebel against these "Mothers."[11]

Nonetheless, Moskowitz's depiction of the private terrors behind "Who Goes There?" provides an entering wedge for more extensive psychobiographical explorations of that most remarkable writer and editor. I'd disagree with Moskowitz only when he writes that Campbell's direction as a writer was shaped by his early life and background "more than is true of most writers." The connection between life and work may be especially obvious in Campbell's case, once a resourceful biographer points it out. But every imaginative writer of any originality draws heavily upon his or her own psychological history in creating strange creatures and new worlds.

Indeed, if you're an aspiring psychobiographer who's looking for a good literary subject, I'd suggest a simple rule of thumb: The more imaginative the writer, the better a subject he or she is likely to be. Writers of realistic or semirealistic fiction, who have dominated the literary "mainstream" for much of the past century, have also received the lion's share of attention from literary psychobiographers. But dozens of accomplished writers of science fiction and fantasy are out there waiting their turn. They may not be currently fashionable in the halls of academe, but for that reason the psychobiographer who chooses them doesn't need to plow through layers of previous interpretation to get to something new. Furthermore, the work of such writers often appears so remote from "real life"— from *anyone's* real life—that showing how their life and work are related can provide especially dramatic proof that psychobiography has something useful to say about literature.

Paradoxically, the fantastic writer's choice of characters, plots, and themes may be more directly controlled by unconscious motives and unrecognized inner conflicts than the work of writers who deal with mundane reality. The latter, as they try to keep at least one foot in the ordinary world, are necessarily guided a good deal of the time by the conscious ego. Writers whose bailiwick is the future, or the off-Earth universe, or the world of faery, leave more room for the play of less-than-conscious forces. So the psychobiographical study of such writers may be, at least in some regards, more revealing than the study of realists and semirealists.

However, the aspiring psychobiographer of such writers should recognize at the outset that the path will not be wide or easy. Not only are most science fiction and fantasy writers disapproved subjects in the academic world; literary psychobiography in general has become the most scorned of all kinds of psychobiography. (Political psychobiography has almost as bad a reputation, but we won't get to it until Chapter 12.) That's partly because a number of expertly self-protective writers have attacked psychobiography with every weapon in their verbal arsenals. (Vladimir Nabokov was the ultimate expert at this form of warfare; see Chapter 11.) But it's also because psychobiographical connections between an author's life and the author's work have often been drawn mechanically and reductionistically: the life as a "key" to the works, or the works as a "key" to the life. Psychobiographers who want to improve the field need to ask more sophisticated questions as well. How does life feed into art and art into life, to create an organic relationship between the writer and the work? How do the writer's life and work interact to promote psychological coping and growth? How do significant changes in the writer's work correlate with changes in other aspects of the writer's life, and vice versa? Does one sort of change reliably anticipate the other, or do they tend to occur simultaneously?

The questions I ask first when I do literary psychobiography are functional ones. Writing can serve a variety of useful functions for the writer in the outer world: bringing in royalty checks, seducing potential bedmates, making Mom and Dad proud. But I'm more interested in what happens within the writer's own psyche as he or she writes. What are the dominant psychological functions that a writer's literary creations serve for the writer, and how are these functions carried out? I've found it useful to think in terms of three broad categories: an expressive function, a defensive function, and a restitutive function.[12]

The Expressive Function

For a writer with the normal range of psychological tics and quirks, the process of writing may be principally a means of self-expression. This *expressive function* is the one young writers often identify when they're asked why they write: "I want to express myself." Self-expression is a basic human need, according to several psychological theorists.[13] It's closely tied to the development and maintenance of ego identity or self-concept, according to various other theorists.[14] Writing fiction is one of the more potentially visible—as well as potentially remunerative—ways to express one's self-perceived identity to others. In addition, a writer can conveniently develop fictional characters while getting the expressive function served, by distributing his or her own personal attributes and life circumstances among the characters.

We have little specific evidence of which psychological functions were most well-served by John W. Campbell's fiction. But surely the fiction was, at a minimum, expressive. In his nonfiction and in person, Campbell presented himself as self-confident and assertive, eager to thrust his views upon others. His fiction is not usually as dogmatic, but the best of it speaks in a distinctively Campbellian voice—or rather, Campbellian *voices*, for he was a many-sided man. Even when he borrowed elements of theme and plot and character from other writers or from the science fiction tradition, even when the overriding motive behind his writing was to make a few dollars more in the low-budget world of pulp fiction, Campbell's own character left its deep imprint upon his work.

Campbell's shape-shifting Thing borrows from a long history in science fiction, and a much longer one in myth and legend: devils and witches, werewolves and vampires and silkies. In one science fiction classic, Stanley Weinbaum's "A Martian Odyssey," a particularly odious sort of Martian uses telepathy to detect the human protagonist's yearning for a woman back on Earth, then transforms itself to look like that woman. Only when the creature is shot does it appear to the human in its true form, as "one of those writhing, black, rope-armed horrors."[15] As the human thinks about the danger later, he tells his companions, "Do you see how insidious the monster is? We're warned now—but henceforth we can't trust even our eyes. You might see me—I might see one of you—and back of it may be nothing but another of those black horrors!"[16]

Two years after Weinbaum's story was published (but before "Who Goes

There?"), John Campbell published a story that was an attempt to duplicate Weinbaum's success.[17] Campbell's "Brain Stealers of Mars" is not as natural in its language or as inventive in its imagery, but it sounds a lot more like Weinbaum than like anything Campbell had published before. So the *style* didn't express Campbell's personality, at least not as we know him from other sources; but the principal topic did. Weinbaum spent only two of his story's twenty-five pages on the shape-shifters; Campbell devoted most of his story to the shape-shifters and named it after them. Had his recent reading of the Weinbaum story momentarily revived his long-dead childhood anxieties about the mother who wasn't really his mother—or had those anxieties continued to bubble close to the surface, always available for fictional uses? We don't know. But we do know that "The Brain Stealers of Mars" expressed at least one aspect of Campbell's personal history, one part of the mosaic that formed his personality.

The Defensive Function

Sigmund Freud's first published discussion of creative writing compared it to the symptoms of a neurotic, and said it can be similarly interpreted.[18] A few sentences later, Freud added that "all genuinely creative writings are the product of more than a single motive and more than a single impulse in the poet's mind, and are open to more than a single interpretation."[19] But the message many readers seem to have carried away from this brief passage is that poems and plays and prose fiction are all symptoms of a neurotic defensive structure. Creative writing is still most often characterized in the psychobiographical literature as serving a *defensive* function for the writer.

Writing can function as a psychological defense in a variety of ways. A work of fiction may provide the writer with disguised satisfactions of strong unconscious urges—hostile, sexual, or whatever—while the writer continues consciously to deny that he or she has such urges. The writer may be able to tolerate the continued existence of an unconscious conflict by expressing both sides of it in fiction, even though a permanent solution to the conflict remains elusive. Writing can help distance the writer from intense psychological concerns by placing those concerns, at least temporarily, in another place and time—perhaps long long ago in a galaxy far far away. Indeed, that *temporary* quality is the primary criterion for identifying the writer's attempts to deal with inner problems as "defensive." When writing plays a defensive function, the writer must return again and again to the underlying issues, addressing them in new fictions, expending more energy to keep the struggle going, rather than resolving the issues and getting on with the rest of his or her life.

Perhaps "defensive" is the most appropriate functional category for John Campbell's efforts. When he wrote "Brain Stealers of Mars," he dealt quickly and lightly with the question of whether those closest to you might really be dangerous monsters. On the basis of that story alone, we might as well stay with our previous speculations: he was expressing one aspect of his personal history (his childhood anxiety about the identities of his mother and her identical twin) in a way that fit neatly with the traditional theme of the shape-changer. However, when Campbell returned to the same issue less than two years later in "Who Goes There?" his tone was light no longer. The humans in "Who Goes There?" are terrified of the shape-changing Thing, with an intensity usually reserved for childhood terrors. When they detect a shape-changing "human," they destroy it with a ferocity seldom seen outside of childhood fantasies. Perhaps even in "Who Goes There?" Campbell was merely using his memory of outgrown fears and long-dead hostilities in an expressive way. But the story's expressions of terror and murderous wrath are so strong that the underlying emotions seem likely to have been still alive when the story was written. Those emotions may have lain buried in an inner Antarctica for decades, but their power remained intact once they emerged from the ice.

If Campbell's case remains ambiguous, a man whose writing career spanned almost the same period presents a clearer picture of fiction as defense. Robert E. Howard invented Conan the Barbarian and several other massively muscled protagonists, describing them in a series of stories first published in pulp fantasy and science fiction magazines from 1925 to 1936.[20] Conan was a brutal hero who spent most of his life eviscerating evil enemies, ravishing beautiful women, then casually strolling off toward new adventures. A passage from the novella "The Devil in Iron" is typical:

> Conan met [Jehungir] half-way in a blinding whirl of swords. The curved blades ground together, sprang apart, circled in glittering arcs that blurred the sight which tried to follow them. Octavia, watching, did not see the stroke, but she heard its chopping impact, and saw Jehungir fall, blood spurting from his side where the Cimmerian's steel had sundered his mail and bitten to his spine. . . . With a crash of bending boughs Khosatral Khel was upon them. The girl could not flee; a moaning cry escaped her as her knees gave way and pitched her groveling to the sward. . . . Conan's blood was up. He rushed in, slashing with the crescent blade. And it did not splinter. Under its edge the dusky metal of Khosatral's body gave way like common flesh beneath a cleaver. From the deep gash flowed a strange ichor, and Khosatral cried out like the dirging of a great bell. His terrible arms flailed down, but Conan, quicker than the archers who had died beneath those awful flails, avoided their strokes and struck again and yet again. Khosatral reeled and tottered; his cries were awful to hear, as if metal were given a tongue of pain, as if iron shrieked and bellowed under torment. . . .
>
> [Octavia] felt herself snatched off her feet and crushed to [Conan's]

muscular breast. She fought him fiercely, with all the supple strength of her magnificent youth, but he only laughed exuberantly, drunk with the possession of this splendid creature writhing in his arms.

He crushed her struggles easily, drinking the nectar of her lips with all the unrestrained passion that was his, until the arms that strained against him melted and twined convulsively about his massive neck.[21]

Robert E. Howard's own life displayed few visible similarities to that of Conan. Howard grew up in a small Texas town and seldom strayed far from home. Heavily dependent upon his mother, he was anxious to avoid doing anything that might upset her. He was never able to break the apron-strings, never able to put any substantial psychological space between himself and his mother, never able to develop a fully autonomous personality. Conan's primitive lusts were hardly visible in Howard's constrained encounters with the young women of the town. Though he seems to have strongly resented both his mother's control and his father's emotional neglect, he continued to live with his parents for most of his life.[22]

The Conan stories, along with Howard's other hundreds of thousands of words of pulp fiction, had their uses. They provided him with a modest income during the early years of the Great Depression. They brought him a measure of fame among the pulp readership, as well as the friendship-by-correspondence of such fellow writers as H. P. Lovecraft. But in terms of their central psychological function, the stories were basically elaborate pretenses. While he lived the life of Conan in his fiction, Howard could pretend he was independent of his mother, could pretend to live without her. In his fiction he could travel to far lands; he could destroy anyone who crossed him; he could make love to woman after woman without commitment or regret. But the stories did not help Howard to work through his anxieties about abandonment. They did not resolve his excessive dependence on his mother. They did not lead to any direct expression of his repressed hostility toward both parents.

As his mother lay dying in the family home, all the fictions fell apart. Howard suddenly faced the prospect of beginning a new life on his own. He went out to his car, took a borrowed pistol from the glove compartment, and put a bullet through his head. He was buried with his mother three days later. Conan the Barbarian lives on in books, comics, Arnold Schwarzenegger movies, and CD-ROM adventure games. Robert E. Howard died at age 30.

The Restitutive Function

As B. F. Skinner worked on *Walden Two*, a variety of temporary defensive functions were served. The book helped to relieve his anxieties about his impending move to Indiana, and it reassured him that he was on the right track in his research. But writing *Walden Two* did more than that. It changed him. It turned him into a public advocate for behaviorism as applied to human life. Skinner's revised identity stayed with him from then on; he remained self-confident and felt competent to deal with each new challenge that faced him.

Skinner was reluctant to acknowledge these internal changes, because they didn't fit the external-environment emphasis of his behaviorist theory. Indeed he asked me to delete from my draft manuscript on *Walden Two* his remark that "When I wrote the book, I was not really a Frazierian . . . but I convinced myself . . . and I'm now a thoroughgoing Frazierian as a result and I'm no longer Burris." I responded that the remark was only one of several I could have quoted from our taped interview, all pointing to the fact that he himself believed he had changed in major ways through writing the book. I said that I'd refrain from quoting him if he insisted, but that from my theoretical perspective, his statement about having convinced himself was one of the most important things he had said to me. Skinner didn't agree, but he told me I could go ahead and quote him.

Writing the novel served a *restitutive* function for Skinner. That is, it resolved an inner crisis (or two) and it *restored* him to full psychological vigor. Writing is restitutive when it enables an author to work through his or her psychological problems and to come out a better person. Writing can help the writer to explore emotional conflicts. It can increase the writer's understanding, at least at a symbolic level, of the unconscious processes that have been causing personal difficulties. It can improve communications among various aspects of the writer's self. The writer may find ways to bring similar insights to the reader, but if that happens, it's gravy. As a psychobiographer, I'm mainly interested in the writer's own psychological restitution.

Did writing "Who Goes There?" restore John W. Campbell to psychological health? Did it give him a renewed trust in his mother, or a sense that he could deal more confidently with the dangers posed by the uncertain identities of mother and aunt and others like them? We don't know. The biographical data on Campbell remain inadequate, and the fictional record ends with "Who Goes There?" At the height of his writing success, at age 27, Campbell did not kill himself; instead, he became a magazine editor. He wrote little or no fiction after that, unless we count his editorials endorsing Dianetics and telepathy machines and antigravity devices. We do know that fifteen years later, he and his second wife were spending a lot of time on "home [psycho]therapy" with each other[23]— which suggests that writing "Who Goes There?" had not been totally and permanently restitutive. Campbell's published letters don't say what problems he was still trying to address in his own psyche at that time.

Psychological restitution seldom involves a single dramatic resolution of all the writer's major internal problems, as with B. F. Skinner's writing of *Walden Two*. (Even there, we don't know how many other problems remained active in Skinner's psyche—only the ones he discussed in his autobiography.) The process of working through long-standing repressions and motivational conflicts is typically slow and difficult, even in intensive psychotherapy. The writer may have to work through such matters many times in his or her fiction, exploring their ramifications repeatedly in a variety of contexts before a satisfactory resolution is reached. A good example is the case of Cordwainer Smith.

Several decades after they were written, Cordwainer Smith's thirty or so stories remain among the strangest in science fiction.[24] Ursula Le Guin recently described them as "an extraordinary body of work, not yet adequately appreciated by critics."[25] Though most of the stories take place in the far future, they are told as if the narrator were reporting legends from that far future's distant past—a past/future as distant from us as from the narrator. The opening of "The Lady Who Sailed 'The Soul'" is basic Cordwainer Smith:

> The story ran—how did the story run? Everyone knew the reference to Helen America and Mr. Grey-no-more, but no one knew exactly how it happened. Their names were welded to the glittering timeless jewelry of romance. Sometimes they were compared to Heloise and Abelard, whose story had been found among books in a long-buried library. Other ages were to compare their life with the weird, ugly-lovely story of the Go-Captain Taliano and the Lady Dolores Oh.
>
> Out of it all, two things stood forth—their love and the image of the great sails, tissue-metal wings with which the bodies of people finally fluttered out among the stars.[26]

Cordwainer Smith's fiction describes fantastic events, but at the same time it often conveys a sense of intense psychological realism. Before Smith's true identity was made public, Robert Silverberg suggested in reviewing one of his books that perhaps he was a visitor from that far future or those distant planets of which he wrote, and was merely giving us a vivid account of his real life out there. Silverberg's suggestion was presumably tongue-in-cheek, but he was more perceptive than he may have realized. Cordwainer Smith was the pseudonym for a political scientist named Paul Myron Anthony Linebarger. Linebarger never visited another galaxy or traveled backward through time, but as with John Campbell, his science fiction stories drew heavily upon his own peculiar life history. In Linebarger's case, his stories showed a noticeable progression as he gradually became less peculiar and more emotionally healthy. Their changing imagery displays the restitutive process at work—a psychological restructuring that was aided by many years of psychotherapy, but that was achieved in considerable degree through the writing of the stories themselves.

Linebarger's early childhood was an open invitation to psychological disaster. His father was a legal adviser, fund-raiser, and gun-runner for Sun Yat-sen, before and after the Chinese Revolution of 1911. The father was often away from the family or intent upon secret missions. Paul's mother had established her own career but gave it up for marriage. She hated males in general and told Paul so, but she also said she loved her little Paulie. From his earliest memories Paul felt ugly, sickly, and much too smart for his own good. His parents often put him on display—a five-year-old giving speeches about Sun Yat-sen or posing in traditional Chinese dress for American newspapers.

In an accident at age 6, Paul lost one eye and nearly lost the other. After that, he wore a glass eye and feared total blindness. His childhood was spread across Milwaukee, Chicago, rural Mississippi, Shanghai, Baden-Baden, Nanking, and Washington, D.C. He was left homesick for many places, but with no home town he could call his own. He grew increasingly lonely as he grew older. His loneliness was partly relieved by marriage and parenthood, but World War II interrupted his family life and it never quite returned to normal.

Linebarger wrote a letter from India to his year-old daughter in the States when he was about to begin working as a U.S. Army Intelligence officer in wartime China. In the letter he reflected on his strategies for dealing with his several inner selves:

> [E]ven when I was a small boy in Baden, self-scrutiny became intolerable and I would have to say to myself, "I want to want something. I've got to be crazy about something—old coins, a fountain pen, coins, stamps, excursions, a gun, or something!" And sooner or later Living-and-Doing Paul would blot out Watched and Watching Paul, and the paired antagonists would disappear behind a screen on which the real regular world happened. But I would attain or forget the object of my desire, and return to the non-timed desolation of my inward world. Much of my life has consisted in such wild leaps away from my inward and inescapable self. Somehow, writing comes closest to shadowing out the interior, because Living-and-Doing Paul can pretend that he is Watched-and-Watching Pauls, and he can fool himself for long periods of time.[27]

That's an insightful description of how writing can be used for defensive purposes. Linebarger had written a great deal of fiction and poetry since his early teens; most of it was of little value except for its function as psychological defense. But soon after this letter, he began to write fiction that was publishable and that moved beyond defensiveness into restitution.

In 1945, Linebarger wrote his first substantial science fiction story, "Scanners Live in Vain." The story was promptly rejected by every professional science fiction magazine. (John Campbell told him it was "too extreme.") It was eventually published in a semi-professional magazine with a very small circulation, then was anthologized by a perceptive editor. It has since come to be recognized as a pivotal story in the development of modern science fiction.[28]

Two images dominate "Scanners": spaceships filled with passengers held in suspended animation, and the Scanners who watch over them during long voyages to other stars. The passengers are kept asleep because if they were awake they would go mad or die from the "pain of space," an unbearable psychological pain that overwhelms ordinary humans when they venture beyond our solar system. The Scanners are human too, but they can withstand this pain because all their sensory pathways have been severed except for their optic nerves. This literary imagery represents symbolically both Linebarger's intense feelings of isolation (the pain of space) and a major defensive response: his deadening of emotions.

"Scanners" ends unrealistically, even for a science fiction story. A scientist discovers that the pain of space can be prevented by packing the spaceship's outer shell with live oysters. No longer needed to look after sleeping passengers, the Scanners get their sensory nerves restored, get retrained as spaceship pilots, and presumably live happily ever after. Linebarger was ready to examine his problems in fiction, but at that point he couldn't visualize a realistic way to resolve them.

The next story to appear under Cordwainer Smith's name was written nine years later: "The Game of Rat and Dragon."[29] Between the writing of "Scanners" in 1945 and "Game" in 1954, Paul Linebarger had become a Professor of Asiatic Politics at the Johns Hopkins University, had been divorced and remarried, and saw several psychotherapists. Two new images dominate "Game." First, the dragons: Space travelers are being attacked by "something out there *underneath space itself* which was alive, capricious, and malevolent."[30] The "something out there," perceived by human telepaths as giant dragons, can be destroyed by light if detected soon enough. But the dragons develop quicker and more complex evasive maneuvers, until human reflexes are no longer sufficient to follow their moves. Thus the second image: the pinlighters and their partners. The pinlighters are humans who use electronic headsets to boost their telepathic powers so they can detect the dragons far out in space. Their partners are ordinary housecats, each one telepathically linked with a human pinlighter. Whenever a human detects a dragon, his cat partner is sent out in a tiny spaceship armed with photonuclear bombs. The cats' reflexes are much faster than their human partners', so they can chase down the dragons—which the cats perceive telepathically as giant rats—and destroy them with nuclear light.

"The Game of Rat and Dragon" reflects Linebarger's experiences with psychotherapy in the years since "Scanners." He had encountered a succession of therapists who cast light on his repressed desires and conflicts, thus helping him temporarily to disperse his private dragons. The problems returned as his unconscious tried new evasive tactics, necessitating different kinds of therapy. The story also reflects his increasing closeness to his second wife Genevieve, who shared his involvement with foreign intelligence work and his interest in writing.[31] But that closeness had its limits. The protagonist of "Game" is unable to share his thoughts and feelings fully with any human woman; he can do so only with his partner, a female cat. Linebarger had his own cats by this time, including a one-eyed male named Little Paul (with whom he carried on apparently mutual conversations in front of his graduate seminars) and a female named Melanie (whom Genevieve later described to me as "Paul's little love").

Moving forward another nine years, we find Cordwainer Smith at work on the final draft of his only science fiction novel, *Norstrilia*.[32] The two dominant characters in this work are a young man named Rod McBan, who has been rejected on his home planet of Norstrilia because he can't use telepathy well enough to communicate "normally" like everyone else; and C'mell, a stunningly beautiful cat-woman whom he meets on a trip to Old Earth. (C'mell was named after Linebarger's Cat Melanie.) C'mell is an underperson, bred from cat genes but genetically manipulated to look human. She works as a "girlygirl," a sort of geisha who entertains human males but is forbidden to marry them. She has never had problems with that rule before, but it becomes an issue when she and Rod fall in love.

Rod also meets a cat-man, who happens to be Earth's last clinical psychologist. The cat-man helps him resolve his psychological problems so effectively that Rod at last gains full telepathic powers. Rod and C'mell cannot overcome the reality of the rules forbidding them to marry, but they are granted a 30-minute linked dream in which they live together "for a happy subjective time of about a thousand years. You will live through all the happy things that you might have done together if you had stayed here [on Earth]. . . . *Two living, accelerated minds, thinking into each other.* . . ."[33] Having thus satisfied his dream of perfect love— "It was not marriage which they had had, but it was pure romance"[34]—Rod returns to Norstrilia to marry an ordinary human woman who will, at least, be kind to him.

Again, much of the story is true. Paul Linebarger had spent hundreds of hours, if not a thousand years, sharing his mind with the cat-woman C'mell, while he wrote *Norstrilia* and several short stories about her. He had found a certain amount of psychological peace through psychotherapy and through an increasingly religious perspective. And he had settled down to a comfortable and loving relationship with a real woman for the rest of his real life.

By this time, Genevieve Linebarger had been helping her husband with the Cordwainer Smith stories for several years—writing a bit of verse here, a few paragraphs there. Rod McBan's happy marriage to a real woman at the end of *Norstrilia* was Paul's idea, but the details were written partly by Genevieve. Paul Linebarger liked it that way. He had found many satisfactions in imagination while creating the worlds of Cordwainer Smith. But he had also, with the help of those stories, reached a point in his psychological development where he could enjoy a sustained and mutually rewarding relationship with a real human being. He lived only three more years, much of it passed in illness and pain; he died at age 53. Genevieve was herself often unwell during their final years together, and their marriage was by no means perfect. But a man who could give his hero a thousand years with C'mell in half an hour of real time surely managed to find his own measure of happiness in those last difficult years as well.[35]

The case of Cordwainer Smith, even in this much-abbreviated form, suggests the value of tracking the defensive and restitutive functions of creative writing across time. It also illustrates, along with the examples of Skinner and Campbell and Howard, the array of idiosyncrasies that may be packed into the broad classification of "defense" or "restitution" as applied to any particular artist's work.

As a general approach to creative writers, looking at the expressive, defensive, and restitutive functions of writing is a useful way to organize and analyze psychobiographical data. For any one writer, the functional approach may raise some interesting questions and suggest certain answers. But by itself, this approach is too simple to stay interesting for long. The most intriguing questions continue to be the individual ones: How did *this* writer manage to achieve restitution, in ways different from *that* writer? Why did this *other* writer fail to achieve restitution at all? How did his or her defensive structures shape the fiction? At what point did they fail? Which aspects of the writer's work are genuinely expressive of the writer, and which are borrowed without substantial personal resonance from other sources? I'll use the next four chapters to examine such questions about other writers of science fiction and fantasy in somewhat greater depth.

8

Darker Than He Thought:

The Psychoanalysis of Jack Williamson

W HEN I FELL in love with science fiction in my early teens, Jack Williamson
 was one of the first objects of my adulation. Whether he was writing grand
space opera as in *The Legion of Space*, or philosophical explorations of freedom
versus security as in *The Humanoids*, or prescient melodramas of genetic engineering as in *Dragon's Island*, he clearly knew what he was doing, and he did it
without pretension. Though I had no information about Williamson's background or personality, his books and his no-nonsense name led me to imagine
him as a lean and tough Westerner, a fearless and forthright man of thoughtfully
considered action.

When I began to do psychobiographical research on science fiction writers, I
presented several early papers at the annual conferences of the Science Fiction
Research Association. These conferences were mostly populated by other college
professors, but a few of the regulars were genuine science fiction writers. Jack
Williamson was there as both a college professor *and* a writer. He was in his
seventies by then—lean, yes, and taller than anyone else at the conferences, but
bent in a permanent stoop. He was a Westerner, yes, from New Mexico, but shyer
than most of the professors, quiet and modest when he spoke. He was still writing
science fiction—not the trendiest stuff, but good solid work with a lot of serious
thought and up-to-date scientific knowledge built into it.

A few months after I met him, Williamson published his autobiography.[1] It
intrigued me for a couple of reasons. First, his childhood in rural New Mexico
sounded a good deal like my father's childhood in rural Texas. Second, Williamson had been psychoanalyzed as early as 1936—one of the first science fiction
writers, surely, to undergo a full-scale Freudian analysis. At subsequent SFRA
conferences I cornered Williamson in elevators and hallways, asking him to tell
me more about his analysis and its influence on his fiction. He seemed a bit
uncomfortable talking about the analysis—but then, he seemed uncomfortable

talking about almost anything. He was willing, though, to send me a copy of an unpublished article he'd written about his analysis while he was going through it. He was also willing to identify a case history his analyst had published about him; the analyst had applied the thinnest of disguises to Williamson's identity, but apparently no one had ever recognized him. Finally, Williamson was tolerant—more than tolerant, actually *interested*—when I announced my intention to write about his early history and his analysis and how they came together in one of his best novels.

A writer's personal experience of psychotherapy is a distinctively modern source for fiction. Whether it's successful or not, a lengthy analysis becomes a major life event for any writer who undergoes it. It's likely to stimulate renewed struggles to resolve long-established internal conflicts. It may also involve intense personal clashes between patient and therapist. Both the inner battles and the outer ones can provide powerful material for creative work. Moreover, as with Cordwainer Smith, the writer may continue the therapeutic working-through well beyond the actual analysis, by writing fiction that deals with issues raised in the analytic sessions. If the sessions don't go well, the writer can instead gain a measure of revenge against the therapist who has dominated those sessions, by writing a nasty novel about a mad therapist.

In one subgenre of popular fiction, the writer presents a fairly straightforward and positive account of his or her psychotherapeutic treatment. Perhaps the most popular novel in this subgenre is Hannah Green's *I Never Promised You a Rose Garden*. A number of more ambitious mainstream novels also depict a therapeutic interaction, but elaborate upon it creatively—for instance, Philip Roth's *Portnoy's Complaint*, which is structured as several hundred pages of a patient's ramblings on the couch and a two-sentence response by his therapist.[2] In still other instances, the writer's encounters with psychotherapy are transmuted into a fictional form that looks like something else entirely—as in Saul Bellow's *Henderson the Rain King,* where a Reichian therapist is presented in the guise of an African witch-doctor.[3]

Although science fiction writers often work with psychological rather than technological themes, they have rarely fictionalized their own psychotherapeutic experiences. Cordwainer Smith did it a lot; Robert Silverberg has done it a little; but I can think of few other examples. As far as I've been able to determine, the earliest science-fictional transformation of an author's psychotherapy was Jack Williamson's "scientific werewolf " novel, *Darker Than You Think.*[4]

Darker Than You Think has often been judged as Williamson's best novel. One critic characterized it as "an important development for Williamson and for fantasy generally because of its attempts at accounting for supernatural phenomena scientifically."[5] Another described it as "the finest novel of the occult produced by a science fiction writer."[6] Williamson wrote the novel's original version during the second year of his two-year psychoanalysis.[7] He later expanded the novel for book publication without significantly altering its major themes.

In his autobiography, Williamson says that *Darker Than You Think* "can be read as a comment on my own inner conflicts as I discovered and grappled with them under the analysis." He also observes, "It's still one of the books I'm happiest about, perhaps because of what it had enabled me to say about myself and the analysis."[8] But while he was writing the book he had no conscious intention to deal with his psychoanalysis, except in a peripheral way. In response to my questions on this point he said, "I don't know when I began to realize that Barbee's experience in the novel reflected my own change under analysis, but the time is relatively recent; it certainly happened long after the book revision."[9]

What were those inner conflicts, and how did the analysis address them? What sort of "change under analysis" did Williamson experience, and how did all those matters end up in a science-fictional novel of the occult? Let's begin answering those questions at the beginning.

Williamson's Early History

Jack Williamson's boyhood was marked by both material and emotional deprivation. His family lived much of the time in primitive frontier conditions in Arizona, Mexico, and New Mexico. His mother was especially fearful for his safety as a child, often with good reasons: mountain lions, bears, scorpions, fugitive white men, renegade Indians. At age three, Williamson nearly died of a "deadly diarrhea" and had to learn to walk again.[10] Later in childhood he became ill with rheumatic fever; he remembers "staying in a chair that people dragged around the house, because moving hurt so much."[11] Perhaps even more painful, and certainly more long-lasting, was his sense of isolation. His specific experiences were quite different from those of the world-traveling Paul Linebarger, but the pain of isolation was just as intense. Most of the time Williamson's family lived on poor farmland, remote from towns, schools, or neighbors. "We had few close friends— I had none at all that I remember, and not much chance to learn to make them. . . . Struggling all my life in that paralyzing web of isolation, I have never entirely broken free."[12]

In his autobiography, Williamson doesn't strongly criticize either parent. Indeed he notes various warm and supportive behaviors that each directed toward him as a child. But he also describes his father's repeated failure to attain his goals, and the "contempt for physical toilers and physical toil" displayed by his mother's side of the family.[13] He recalls certain members of his mother's family positively: a kindly grandmother, an admired uncle. But he also vividly remembers, from his father's family, his sternly fundamentalist grandmother and uncle, who showed "very little love for anybody" except God. The uncle "was always harshly critical of me and everything I did," and told Jack his science fiction "was a pack of lies."[14] Jack's father regarded the reading of science fiction as "unhealthy for the mind."[15]

Williamson's reactions to his early physical environment were as mixed as those to his social environment. The not-quite-remembered countryside of rural Mexico, as his parents later described it to him, became "a sort of primitive paradise lost," "a dimension of magic reality, a place of escape from the dull familiarity I knew too well. My first world of wonder."[16] But the New Mexico farm to which his family moved by covered wagon when he was seven was no world of wonder:

> From the age of eight or nine I often worked through long days alone, riding a horse behind cows or some farm implement behind a team of mules. In the dry year of 1918 [at age 10], I remember driving the wagon behind our little herd of starving cattle on a long expedition into Texas to search for grass . . . . [I]t's good for a child to know that he's a useful part of a family. But the isolation and monotony of these tasks did help shape the early Williamson.[17]

Williamson's imagination let him escape from this hard reality—first into those earlier times about which his parents told stories, and into books read aloud by his mother or silently by himself, then through stories he told to his younger siblings. Like many other early science fiction fans, he read the first wonder-filled issues of *Amazing Stories;* like a few of them, he soon began to write for the magazine. That still seems an amazing story in itself: A "poor country kid, poorly educated, ill at ease with people and absent-minded at his work, secure enough in his place in the family but unhappy with his whole environment, longing for something else,"[18] decides to become a writer. He sends off his first few stories to Hugo Gernsback, the founding editor of *Amazing.* He gets quick rejection slips for most of his stories; for one story he gets not even that. One day he's walking past a drugstore in the nearest town, sees through the window a bright magazine-cover illustration for that one story—and suddenly he's an *Amazing* author!

That was in 1928, when Jack Williamson was 20 years old. The publication of his first story established the direction of his career, but it hardly solved his problems. Already beginning to move away from his farm background, he enrolled in a small public college while he continued to write. He received intermittent encouragement from editors and other writers, but he was still poor and essentially isolated:

> I had moments of bitter envy for fellow students who had money and cars and affairs with women, and I kept cultivating unrealistic dreams that fiction might win such things for me, but my endless hours at the typewriter were still more escape than goal-directed. I was a solitary

misfit—as science fiction fans in those days often were. . . . I had made no real friends of either sex anywhere.[19]

Over the next eight years, Williamson's life swung from dream world to unpleasant reality and back again, over and over. He published often, but he seemed unable to predict what would sell or how much he could earn from his fiction in any given year. He dropped out of college, later returning for a time to major in psychology. He made several male friends but remained uncomfortable with women. Intrigued but anxious about sex, he was still a virgin. He developed physical ailments that he later guessed were "mostly psychosomatic: eyestrain, sinusitis, indigestion, a general malaise. . . . I was becoming increasingly unsatisfied with myself and my writing career."[20] Finally, in April 1936, almost 28 years old and "wanting more out of life than I had found,"[21] he traveled to the world-famous Menninger Clinic in Topeka, Kansas. There he was given a series of psychiatric examinations and entered psychoanalysis.

Williamson's Psychoanalysis

Two contemporary accounts of Williamson's first year in analysis are available. One is the slightly disguised case history published in the midst of the analysis by his psychiatrist, Dr. Charles Tidd.[22] The other is the article written by Williamson near the end of the analytic year, intended for anonymous publication but rejected by the magazines to which he submitted it.[23] Williamson has also included a retrospective account of the analysis in his autobiography, based in part on his unpublished article.[24]

The two contemporary accounts are clearly about the same patient, but they diverge in interesting ways. Not surprisingly, Dr. Tidd interprets his patient's behavior in pathological terms much more readily than Williamson does. Tidd refers to a distinct point prior to entering therapy at which the patient "broke down."[25] Williamson describes a period of gradually increasing dissatisfaction with his life and himself, rather than an abrupt breakdown of normal functioning: "My coming here, to be psychoanalyzed, was at once a flight from the life that I had never been able to face successfully, and an attempt to meet it again, on another flank, with the aid of this new science."[26]

Tidd describes the patient's physical behavior at the beginning of treatment as

quite bizarre. . . . Most of the time he sat on the couch holding himself rigidly. Very often he moved his arms or some other part of his body in a manneristic gesture and occasionally he suddenly shifted his entire body in a convulsive manner. His facial muscles were usually held in a tense grimace. He spoke slowly and in a very low tone, and at times his voice sank to a whisper. His delivery was stiff and stilted with frequent intervals of tense silence.[27]

Williamson describes much the same behavior as either situationally determined or as part of a long-established personal style, rather than as bizarrely inappropriate:

> Quickly, feeling a self-conscious restraint, I lie supine on the couch. It is difficult to begin speaking. I delay: my hands ball into fists: my body tenses: I make convulsive striking motions. . . . With a convulsive effort, I begin, usually with some remark upon my nervous fear. I try to talk rapidly, because there is much to say; because the time is costly, and I do not wish to waste it; perhaps because I wish to hurry over some painful, shameful thing. . . . My hurried voice is low—all through life I have spoken softly, as I have stooped, to make myself inconspicuous and avoid aggression and danger. Sometimes I become inaudible. The analyst asks me to repeat, and I make a brief effort to speak distinctly. . . . [W]hen I have come to a difficult matter, upon which I feel strongly, my voice checks and stops. To speak each word takes a desperate individual effort. I catch a deep breath or make random body-movements, to delay the need of speech.[28]

Dr. Tidd's emphasis on pathology extends to his initial diagnosis of Williamson: "Anxiety State in a Schizoid Personality." He adds, "The line between such a diagnosis as this and incipient schizophrenia is exceedingly thin, and, as the evidence given below will show, it is possible that the latter was more nearly correct."[29] However, the evidence Tidd presents is not persuasive. On the strength both of his paper and of Williamson's self-description, I think a distinctly different diagnosis would be made today. Williamson's condition as of 1936 would now be termed a personality disorder, indicating that the condition is not as disruptive of normal functioning as a psychotic or prepsychotic state. Instead of "schizoid personality," the specific diagnostic label would most likely be the recently identified syndrome of "avoidant personality."

Both schizoid and avoidant individuals experience "significant difficulty establishing relationships with other people." But whereas the schizoid personality shows a "basic emotional coldness and indifference to others," in the avoidant personality pattern "there is obviously a strong desire for affection and acceptance which is inhibited by anticipation of rejection."[30] In other words, instead of being uninterested in social contact, the individual with an avoidant personality is painfully sensitive to social rejection, and therefore anxiously avoids most close social contacts. Williamson's self-descriptions are echoed by the defining characteristics of the avoidant personality syndrome:

> Excessive social withdrawal. . . . Hypersensitivity to rejection. . . . Contingent personal relationships (e.g., is self-protectively unwilling to enter into relationships unless given unusually strong guarantees of being un-

critically accepted). . . . Low self-esteem. . . . Emotional dysphoria (e.g., experiences a confusing mixture of feeling tense, sad, angry, and lonely).[31]

Most psychotherapists are well aware that a specific diagnostic label does not define an entire personality. Williamson told me that when he first heard the phrase "schizoid personality" applied to him, Dr. Tidd assured him that "there was no very exact relationship between the phrase and the human being."[32] The erroneous diagnosis could have become a problem if it had been rigidly followed in choosing the kind of treatment applied to Williamson. But in actual practice, Dr. Tidd appears to have used an approach much like that now recommended for treatment of an avoidant personality syndrome:

> The therapist should seek, gently and carefully, to build a sense of genuine trust. Gradually, attention may be turned to the patient's positive attributes, addressing these as a means of building confidence and enhancing feelings of self-worth. This is likely to be a slow and arduous process, requiring the reworking of long-standing anxieties and resentments, bringing to consciousness the deep roots of mistrust, and, in time, enabling the patient to reappraise these feelings more objectively.[33]

Another current recommendation for therapy in such cases is "to assist the patient in arranging for a rewarding environment and facilitating the discovery of opportunities that would enhance self-worth."[34] Dr. Tidd sent Williamson to an ophthalmologist for better glasses, and did not discourage him from seeing a prostitute to help diminish his severe sexual frustrations. But otherwise Tidd made no effort to help Williamson find a "rewarding environment" beyond the Menninger Clinic. Tidd was apparently new to therapeutic practice, and he stayed close to the traditional psychoanalytic domain, addressing the patient's problems on the couch but not outside the office.

A further discrepancy between Tidd's and Williamson's accounts of the psychoanalysis may involve only a difference in emphasis, but it's relevant to Williamson's later writing of *Darker Than You Think*. Tidd reports that his patient had experienced childhood fantasies "that his parents were cannibals, raising him to be eaten," as well as fantasies that he was engaging in sadistic acts.[35] During therapy, the patient expressed other masochistic and sadistic fantasies, and also described the plots of stories he was working on. According to Dr. Tidd, these plots included "a theme that was repeated many times: his hatred and rage (originally directed toward the parents) which gradually spread to include all people and things—the whole world!—not excepting the ego of the patient himself."[36] Williamson's own account of his analysis, even though he planned to publish it anonymously, gives little indication of hostile feelings toward his parents. Instead, most of the negative feelings are expressed toward himself: "a blind, savage anger at my own failings, with the guilty need of self-punishment . . . the old false tyranny of self-control"; "a savage, hopeless anger at myself"; "my attitude of passive defeat"; "the guilty sense of supernatural sin"; "a hurt, bitter, passive stoicism"; "the mistaken, unconscious belief that an act of mine had gravely injured my little sister."[37]

Williamson's one mention of negative feelings toward his parents is couched in almost abstract terms: "It has been painful to discover unconscious ideas of hate, violence, and destruction. . . . It was hard to accept the fact that I have desired to destroy persons whom I love."[38] If Williamson had been able to ask himself directly what had provoked such hatred, or who had engendered in him such strong feelings of passivity and self-condemnation, he might have assigned a greater part of the blame to his parents. His strong reluctance even to entertain such questions during his analysis indicated how difficult it would remain for him fully to acknowledge his own emotions. That difficulty would be confronted fictionally in *Darker Than You Think.*

A final discrepancy between Tidd's and Williamson's accounts of the therapy may have been the most important one: their attitudes toward Williamson's writing. For Williamson, writing science fiction was the most important thing in his life. As he said in the article he wrote during his analysis, "I want to write, perhaps more than anything else I could do." When he found himself confronted with writer's block, he wrote, "I think bitterly of giving up writing. But that is my life. Perhaps, I think, if I try something else, some fresh topic not already dark with the shadow of defeat. . . ."[39] He wanted to do more than "bits of hackwork designed to fit a stifling formula,"[40] but he had no intention of abandoning science fiction. He recalls that when he first arrived at the Menninger Clinic for treatment, an examining psychiatrist "commented that writing science fiction was symptomatic of neurosis. His casual promise that I could be cured of that became one more mental problem, because I wanted no remedy for writing."[41]

Though Dr. Tidd was more circumspect, he clearly shared the other psychiatrist's views of science fiction. In the case history, he describes his patient's works of fiction as "horror stories," though most of the plots Tidd summarizes are clearly of a science-fictional nature and lack horror elements. According to Tidd, the themes of the patient's fiction early in the therapy showed that "the value of fantasy was constantly increasing and that in many ways he was ignoring reality in order to maintain this ever-increasing interest in dereistic [unrealistic] thinking."[42] When the patient writes a story but doesn't tell Tidd about it until it's sold, Tidd concludes that "the work was a substitute for masturbation. It was something that had been prohibited by the father; something that gave the patient pleasure and about which he felt guilty. He felt strongly that it was a gesture of defiance toward the analyst."[43] Tidd feels encouraged, later in the therapy, when the patient's work begins to change:

The plots were not so fantastic. . . . He expressed the feeling that he was no longer able to put a series of astounding events together and be satisfied with it; he began to feel it necessary to make the stories more logical and "real." One result was that the stories were much less shocking.[44]

Perhaps all these judgments are appropriate in some therapeutically oriented sense. But there is no indication in the case history that Tidd was able to judge Williamson's science fiction *as science fiction*. Tidd appears to have felt that psychologically, at least, the bipolar continuum ranging from fantastic to realistic could be equated with a continuum ranging from bad to good. On that basis he communicated to his patient a set of judgments much like those pronounced long ago by Williamson's father and uncle.

Here we arrive at a point where the distinction between "schizoid" and "avoidant" personalities becomes crucial. Not only had Williamson established an "avoidant" behavioral style that continued to interfere with his social development; he was also having serious problems because most people he met didn't respond approvingly to his chosen identity as a science fiction writer. He had little else to sustain him; this identity was the principal source of his small income and his modest reputation. But in the world beyond the pulp science fiction magazines, it meant almost nothing. Williamson himself acknowledged the problem by striving to break into more respectable publications, but with little success. For nearly a decade he had been experiencing a prolonged identity crisis—a crisis focused on the failure of social confirmation for the identity he had enthusiastically chosen.[45] Had he been a schizoid personality as diagnosed by Tidd, he might simply have withdrawn while muttering to himself, "Society be damned." But in the characteristic pattern of the avoidant personality, he continued to long for positive responses from others, for respect, for social acceptance of his occupational identity—while as a science fiction writer, he continued to find all those hard to obtain. In this regard, Dr. Tidd was of little help.

Dr. Tidd did see other signs of improvement in his patient besides greater fictional "realism." By the time Tidd wrote his case history, the patient was showing more care in writing and was planning more seriously for the future. He was, Tidd thought, coming to terms with his feelings toward his parents, and he was achieving greater insight into the origins of those feelings. Williamson himself reports, "Slowly, uncertainly, I had begun to find a less divided inner self that I could like, and to accept parts of me that I had always tried to deny."[46] But the analysis was not completely satisfying, and he found it difficult to write successfully while still in analysis—because of "unconscious resistance," Dr. Tidd suggested. Blaming himself as usual, Williamson decided to break off the analysis at the end of a year: "With those old internal feuds not half resolved, I—one part of me—wanted to stay on with Dr. Tidd. I liked him. I wanted more of his sympathetic support. I needed to go on healing that division in myself. But the outlaw part, still spoiling my work, made that impossible."[47]

During the next two years, Williamson regained his productivity as a writer and established or renewed several friendships. But he failed to achieve the "richer way of life" he had hoped to find after analysis.[48] Describing how he had felt at that time, he keeps his identity problems to the fore: "[T]o most of the people I know, science fiction writers are still puzzling freaks. With more sanity and better common sense, I might have looked for a higher-paying occupation, but the drive to write science fiction has never really wavered. I shrink from any entanglements that might get in the way."[49] One new friend was a woman named Jean, an anthropology student in Santa Fe. "I fell far enough in love with Jean to think seriously of marriage, and always thought better of it. Partly, perhaps, because she didn't think much of science fiction, which still meant more to me than anything. A larger reason must have been my growing feeling that I had let the analysis break off too soon."[50]

In 1940, Williamson resumed analysis with Dr. Tidd, who had moved to Beverly Hills. No detailed description of that year of analysis was written by either participant. Williamson says only that it "must have generated less emotion than the first; I don't recall it quite so vividly, but it was still good for me." It was less intensive therapy (two hours a week instead of five), and Williamson's attention was diverted by the Los Angeles science fiction community, an array of new friends who understood the genre and took it seriously. Williamson's writing was also going better, "at least sometimes."[51]

Williamson's major work during this second year of analysis was a novel that legitimized both his earlier feelings of rage and his identity as a person different from most of society. At the same time, in keeping with Dr. Tidd's literary values, the novel provided a more "realistic" basis for its fantastic elements than any of Williamson's previous work. The novel was *Darker Than You Think*.

The Book

Darker Than You Think is the story of a reporter, Will Barbee, who is assigned to cover the return of a team of anthropologists from an Asian research expedition. The leader of the team is Barbee's former anthropology professor. Barbee is still hurt and bitter about having been left out when the professor chose other students, Barbee's best friends, to train for the expedition. (Here and elsewhere we see indications that Barbee himself is an avoidant personality.) The professor dies as he's about to reveal the dark and ancient secrets brought back from the expedition. Another reporter, a beautiful redhead named April Bell, seems implicated in the anthropologist's death, so Barbee pursues her. She tells him she is what humans call a witch, a member of a different species than humans, with "inborn powers greater than are given men" (p. 69).[52] She appears in Barbee's dreams as a white wolf, and tells him he can change form too: "You can run as the wolf runs, trail as the wolf trails, kill as the wolf kills!" He makes an effort to transform himself into a wolf: "And suddenly he was free. Those painful bonds, that he had worn a whole lifetime, were abruptly snapped" (pp. 84–85).

Barbee-as-wolf then joins April in a series of attacks on his anthropologist friends, who have discovered evidence of the witch-people's existence and are planning to destroy them. Will is reluctant to harm his friends, but April insists that he must do so in defense of his shape-shifting species, *Homo lycanthropus*. He is also lured by her physical attractiveness, whether in wolf or in human form. It's probably no accident that all the people Will becomes involved in killing have to some degree rejected him socially.

Through much of the book, Will remains psychologically divided. He's uncertain whether he can trust April, and he's unsure of his racial allegiance: to humans or to witch-people? "He couldn't endure this waking half-life any longer, with its intolerable tangle of horror and grief and pain and bewilderment and fatigue and wild longing and tormenting uncertainty and staggering panic" (p. 153). So he decides to see Dr. Glenn at nearby Glennhaven, a psychiatric hospital. Dr. Glenn is a cool rationalist who insists that Will's strange experiences all have "a perfectly natural explanation" (p. 164). Dr. Glenn speaks of infantile fear and guilt, disguised feelings of jealousy and hatred, and the amoral, "utterly selfish, utterly blind" unconscious (p. 166). Barbee becomes angry at "Glenn's neat little theories of the mind. He didn't want all his own private shames and fears laid out on Glenn's compact diagrams. Fiercely he began to yearn again for the free escape and the splendid power of his dreams" (p. 164).

Barbee agrees to stay at Glennhaven for a few days of treatment, "confused and utterly exhausted from his long struggle to master situations that had finally been too much for him" (p. 172). But April, the "white wolf bitch," calls him back to the war against their enemies. To escape his hospital room, Will becomes a giant snake: "He let his long body flow across the rug and lifted his flat, triangular head to the window. . . . Laughing silently at Glenn's mechanistic philosophy, he poured out silently over the sill" (p. 176). He meets the "white bitch" again, in a scene charged with sexuality and violence. " 'Your old friends must die,' she told him, 'to save the Child of Night' [the coming leader of the witch-clan]. Barbee objected no more. In this glorious awakening from the long nightmare of life, all his values were changed" (p. 177).

Will revisits Dr. Glenn in an attempt to convince him of the existence of *Homo lycanthropus*. Glenn calmly says, "The unconscious mind does sometimes seem a dark cave of horrors, and the same unpleasant facts are often expressed in the symbolism of legend and myth" (p. 249). He returns Will to his room in the psychiatric hospital, where April soon reappears as a white wolf. In a passage of delightful irony, she explains to Will that the rationalistic Dr. Glenn is a witch himself—Will's half-brother, in fact—who could easily have revealed the truth to

Will. She says, "He probably meant to spend a whole year awakening your ancestral powers, the way he did mine—at forty dollars an hour. But the clan can't wait" (250). She says she and Will are "special beings" even among the witch-folk, products of a systematic breeding program to increase their powers, and that Will himself is the Child of Night. He protests, "I'll not be—your Black Messiah! . . . That—that's insanity" (255). But she insists: "You'll be our leader, Will . . . until a stronger one takes your place. You and I are the most powerful in generations, but a child with both our genes will have still less of the human taint" (258).

Barbee then transforms himself into a giant pterosaur. April mounts his back in naked human form, and they fly off to destroy the artifacts from the anthropological expedition, which could have been used to destroy them. Will lets his one remaining anthropologist friend survive, but he says to April:

> Suppose he's fool enough to tell somebody his story? . . . Suppose some unwary publisher should dare to print it—disguised, perhaps, to look like fiction? . . . Suppose it came into the hands of such a distinguished psychiatrist as Dr. Glenn? . . . An interesting case history, he might say. . . . An illuminating picture of reality . . . as seen through the twisted vision of a disintegrating schizoid personality. The autobiography of a mental breakdown . . . a conventional folk expression of unconscious feelings of aggression and guilt. (pp. 265–266)

In the book's final paragraphs, April once again becomes a white wolf and teasingly runs away from Barbee, "up the dark wooded slope where his wings couldn't follow. The change, however, was easy now. Barbee let the saurian's body flow into the shape of a huge gray wolf. He picked up her exciting scent and followed her into the shadows" (p. 266).

Interpretations

It's clear in retrospect why Jack Williamson eventually concluded that this novel "can be read as a comment on [his] own inner conflicts as [he] discovered and grappled with them under the analysis."[53] The scenes with the psychotherapist, which Williamson says "drew a somewhat satiric picture of Tidd,"[54] hardly go beyond the intellectualized argumentation found in therapy at its shallowest level. The real therapy in the book, the depth therapy, comes from April Bell. It is she who urges Will Barbee to break free from ancient restraints, who offers him motives and reasons to do so, and who provides a model of emotional freedom herself. Through her insistent overcoming of his strong ambivalence, Will achieves an emotional freedom not previously available to Williamson, a freedom to acknowledge and express both aggressive and sexual impulses.[55] By the end of the book, Will has happily abandoned all "civilized" constraints and ambivalences—"A conclusion I found oddly satisfying," says Williamson, "though occasional readers have been appalled."[56]

When read in this way, *Darker Than You Think* depicts a triumph of id over superego, of raw desire over social constraints—definitely not what Freud had in mind in proposing as the goal of psychoanalysis, "Where id was, there ego shall be."[57] Nor does it match the conclusion drawn by Williamson's analyst, who saw his patient as getting better at planning his behavior as well as showing "an increased ability to grasp reality."[58] But for Williamson, an important aspect of both the therapy and the book was his "growing willingness to accept bits of myself that I had always feared or hated."[59]

At another level, the novel can be seen as a triumph of ego over superego, in which a thinly disguised Williamson finally asserts his own identity, without concern for social response. Just as Will Barbee finally accepts his true identity as a witch-man, a member of the species *Homo lycanthropus* who cannot be judged by ordinary human values, so Williamson the writer symbolically affirms his essential identity as science fiction writer—an identity that may appear deviant to ordinary society or to the mainstream literary establishment, but that has its own ancient heritage and may by some criteria be superior to the mainstream. Not only the thematic content of the book, but the writing of the book itself, demonstrated that Williamson was no mere pulp writer. He could now deal with serious themes and mythic images in a style effectively combining the "realistic" and the "fantastic." Furthermore, he could hold to this identity in spite of any psychotherapist's efforts to denigrate it. Like Barbee in the novel, his imagination could encompass the therapist's concepts, take what he needed from them, and then move beyond them.

Was the final restitutive scoreboard, then, all pluses? Not quite. Will Barbee's solution to the problems of being a witch-man—learning to accept his animal urges and then assuming the leadership of a struggle against society—worked better in fiction than in real life. Williamson benefited from acknowledging his sexuality and anger, but he had to go on living in human society, and he genuinely wanted its approval. The subculture of science fiction offered him significant support for his newly affirmed identity, but it was never sufficient support. In his major subsequent works, such as *The Humanoids* and *Dragon's Island*,[60] Williamson's heroes either lose to the overwhelming forces of society or adopt totally fantastic means to escape society's clutches. In real life, Williamson experienced further bouts of writer's block, and his literary work has never gained wide recognition from the larger society.

However, Williamson was by no means passive in the face of persisting challenges to his professional identity. He responded to those challenges not only by continuing to write provocative fiction,[61] but by becoming one of the most vigorous early advocates for the study and teaching of science fiction as a part of literature. He eventually earned a Ph.D. in English literature (writing his dissertation on the science fiction of H. G. Wells) and became a faculty member at Eastern New Mexico University. He helped to found and direct a new organization, the Science Fiction Writers of America, which brought at least some increased respectability and contractual clout to the profession that was his first love. He also became one of the few professional writers to take an active role in the Science Fiction Research Association. In so doing, he lent the SFRA some of his prestige in the field at the same time that the SFRA was further improving his field's respectability.

The rest of us who have some connection with science fiction—the readers, the writers, the researchers—may well be better off because Jack Williamson's problems were *not* completely resolved by his writing of *Darker Than You Think*. He didn't need any neurotic hangups in order to keep on writing, as he had worried that he might; he would have sustained his passion for science fiction in any case. He didn't need to remain shy in order to go on being a nice guy; a basic decency seems to have been ingrained in him from his childhood on. But those continuing anxieties about his personal and professional identities *were* needed to motivate him to become a teacher of college students, a member of planning committees, a leader of professional organizations. Though such roles may offer their own modest rewards, they don't ordinarily attract world-famous science fiction writers. Jack Williamson has been willing to take on all those roles and to do them well. If we have a partial failure of the restitutive process to thank for that, let's pause a moment to give our thanks.

9

Asimov as Acrophobe

So John W. Campbell's science fiction was at least expressive, and Robert E. Howard's was definitely defensive. Cordwainer Smith's science fiction was mainly restitutive, and Jack Williamson's gave a good try at being restitutive, even though it didn't go all the way. After I'd lived with that way of looking at fiction-writing for a while, one other possibility seemed worth pursuing: that for some writers, writing serves no distinctive psychological function at all; it's just another way to make a buck or to offer an argument. In science fiction, ideas rather than strong emotions or violent acts often provide the focus for a story. Writers of such stories may ring intellectual changes on previous work in the field, speculate on the long-range impact of recent or potential scientific discoveries, and work along as efficient wordsmiths. Perhaps that's all they aspire to; they may never feel motivated to become self-therapists or even self-expressers.

So I began to look for just such a writer, to contrast with Robert E. Howard and Cordwainer Smith. I wanted an example of a writer whose work displayed no psychological hangups and served no psychological functions but just told good stories. I first considered Robert Heinlein, another hero of my adolescence; but the obsessions of his later novels quickly disqualified him. Then I thought of Isaac Asimov. He had never won any awards for sheer literary quality, but at a quick glance he seemed to be just what I was looking for: Asimov, the creator of simple characters and complicated science fiction mysteries; Asimov, the genial popularizer of science; Asimov, whose work was enjoyed by everybody and disturbed nobody. Surely Asimov was a clear contrast to the tormented Howard and Smith. Having read little of his fiction since my own adolescence, and knowing even less of his personal history, I found it easy to categorize Asimov initially as a writer whose work served no significant psychological functions for him.

My thinking about Asimov, however, soon turned in a very different direction. The initial stimulus was his 1983 best-seller, *The Robots of Dawn*.[1] I had read his first two robot novels, *The Caves of Steel* and *The Naked Sun*, when they were originally published in the 1950s.[2] I remembered them fondly for their cleanly written, intellectually exciting combination of detection and robotics. I couldn't clearly recall either of the protagonists, human detective Elijah Baley or his robot partner Daneel Olivaw, and I didn't expect anything of great psychological interest in the later robot novel. I just hoped it would be as entertaining as the others.

I quickly discovered that much of *The Robots of Dawn* focuses not on the murder mystery or the interplanetary politics with which it's nominally concerned, but on Lije Baley's struggle to conquer his severe neurotic anxieties. Baley is agoraphobic (loosely, afraid of open spaces), acrophobic (afraid of heights), and phobic in several other ways. He can hardly leave his enclosed underground city without being overcome by panic. He experiences even greater stress when taking a routine spaceflight to another planet, as he must occasionally do in the course of his work. Here's a scene in which Baley approaches the planet Aurora in a spaceship:

> The ship was moving. He was moving. He was suddenly aware of his own existence. He was hurtling downward through the clouds. He was falling, unguarded, through thin air toward solid ground.
>
> His throat constricted; it was becoming very hard to breathe. He told himself desperately: You are enclosed. The walls of the ship are around you.
>
> But he sensed no walls.
>
> He thought: Even without considering the walls, you are still enclosed. You are wrapped in skin.
>
> But he sensed no skin.
>
> The sensation was worse than simple nakedness—he was an unaccompanied personality, the essence of identity totally uncovered, a living point, a singularity surrounded by an open and infinite world, and he was falling.[3]

Hmmm, I thought to myself—Isaac Asimov seems to know a lot about agoraphobic panic attacks. Might he have problems along those lines himself? I didn't think much more about the matter until several months later, when I went to my first Science Fiction Research Association convention. Somebody there told me that both Ray Bradbury and Isaac Asimov had recently taken airplane rides, apparently for the first time in their lives. I already knew about Bradbury's fear of flying, and I'd heard that Andre Norton and several other science fiction writers shared similar fears. I'd been amused by the apparent inconsistency of people who spend their creative lives writing about space travel and intergalactic wars but who fear boarding a plane for a hundred-mile trip. My amusement was tempered by my own uneasiness about flying—an uneasiness with which I often deal by marching onto a plane and quickly losing myself in a science fiction novel.

Now I began to consider *The Robots of Dawn* in the light of Asimov's reported airplane ride. Suppose Isaac Asimov himself suffered from really intense agoraphobia or acrophobia or both. (Clinically they're not far apart, and one person can be afflicted with both, as in the case of Lije Baley.) Suppose Asimov had been struggling to overcome these phobias for many years, just like his hero Baley. Suppose Asimov had been using his writing of science fiction to work through his severe emotional problems, perhaps with a psychotherapist's help, just like Cordwainer Smith. Suppose he'd finally conquered his phobias, boarded a plane, and took off. Another triumph for the psychological restitutive power of writing science fiction!

On the basis of that hopeful hypothesis, I began to gather data on Asimov. First I reread his earlier robot novels. Lije Baley's agoraphobia, I found, was not only named and described in both books but was specifically identified by Asimov with a fear of flying.[4] I also checked several of Asimov's short stories written at about the same time. I found a whole series of stories about another interplanetary detective, Dr. Wendell Urth, whose travel anxieties were so extreme that he "had never in his adult life been more than an hour's-walk from his home on the University campus."[5]

Then I moved on to even earlier works, especially Asimov's first major short story, "Nightfall," published in 1941 and now often named as the best science fiction short story ever written.[6] "Nightfall" is an ironic answer to Ralph Waldo Emerson's rhetorical question, "If the stars should appear one night in a thousand years, how would men believe and adore, and preserve for many generations the remembrance of the city of God?" Asimov's story describes the inhabitants of the planet Lagash, whose six suns give them perpetual sunlight—except for once every 2,049 years, when all the suns simultaneously set or go into eclipse. When that happens, all the Lagashians promptly go stark raving mad. Their madness, according to the story, comes from intense claustrophobia, the exact opposite of Asimov's apparent problems. But as the story ends, claustrophobic and agoraphobic anxieties appear to mix: the Lagashians react with terror not only to seeing the entire sky get as dark as a cave (claustrophobia), but also to experiencing the vastness of the universe for the first time as the stars emerge (agoraphobia). This odd mixture suggested to me that in trying to depict the claustrophobic craziness of the Lagashians, Asimov had drawn upon his own agoraphobic anxieties to get a feel for what it must be like to go mad.

Next I looked at Asimov's massive autobiography. There he refers several times to what he calls his "severe acrophobia." He says, for example, "I was afraid of heights and went out of my mind at the sensation of falling."[7] He describes his negative experiences with roller coasters, his two uncomfortable rides in military planes during World War II (never repeated), and his strong preference for en-closed spaces. Asimov didn't use the technical term for that preference in his autobiography, but he knew it. In *The Robots of Dawn*, a character from a distant planet refers scornfully to "the claustrophilia of you Earthmen, your dislike of leaving your walls."[8] The author is describing his own claustrophilia there. As Asimov puts it in his autobiography, "Why it should be, I don't know, and psychiatrists may make what they like of it (for I will not ask them, and I will not listen if they try to tell me), but I have always liked enclosed places."[9]

Actually Asimov did know something about "why it should be." His auto-biography supplies the beginnings of an explanation at least for his fear of flying, and by inference for his pleasure in enclosed spaces. He says he had to "bear the brunt of his parents' neuroses," and continues:

> My parents—my mother, especially—trembled over my well-being so ex-tremely, especially after my babyhood experience with pneumonia, that I couldn't help but absorb the fear and gain an exaggerated caution for myself. (That may be why I won't fly, for instance, and why I do very little else that would involve my knowingly putting myself into peril.)[10]

I went from Asimov's autobiography to James Gunn's very thoughtful mono-graph on him. (Gunn is, like Jack Williamson, a long-established science fiction writer who's also a college professor.) I found that Gunn had dealt specifically with the intertwined themes of "claustrophilia and agoraphobia" in the first two robot novels.[11] He characterized *The Naked Sun* as being about "Elijah Baley and his battle against agoraphobia." On the basis of extensive interviews with Asimov, Gunn added that Asimov "would say that it doesn't matter how the past has shaped him. He is satisfied to be what he is: a claustrophile, an acrophobe, a compulsive writer."[12]

Finally I wrote to Asimov himself. In my first letter I referred to H. L. Gold, founding editor of the science fiction magazine *Galaxy*, whom Asimov had de-scribed in his autobiography as extremely agoraphobic. I told Asimov I assumed he wasn't as agoraphobic as Gold, but that Elijah Baley certainly had lots of problems with agoraphobia in the robot novels, and so did some of Asimov's other fictional characters. Then I boldly asked:

> Is Baley's agoraphobia in any sense an exaggerated version of your own feelings at being out in the open rather than in an enclosed environ-ment? Have Baley's struggles to overcome or cope with such feelings re-flected your own attempts to come to terms with agoraphobic or acrophobic feelings? If so, have you been successful (or how much have you been successful) in your efforts—either through writing fiction that deals with these issues, or through other means of dealing with them? Or have you simply used your own experiences as a starting-point for

developing a characterization of Baley and others, without making any strong efforts to deal psychologically with feelings that you can deal with more effectively in other ways (such as spending most of your time in a comfortable room without open windows)? Finally . . . somebody told me you had recently taken your first plane ride in many years. If that's true, was that the result of some recent resolution of your agoraphobic or acrophobic feelings, or was it merely a matter of circumstance?

Asimov responded by return mail from his high-rise Manhattan apartment:

Baley's agoraphobia was, perhaps, my way of getting back at Gold for forcing me to do a robot novel, but I do have agoraphobic tendencies myself. Very mild, of course. I prefer enclosed places to open places but only to the extent that I prefer coffee to tea. My typewriter and library are in two rooms in which the blinds are always down. My word-processor, however, is in the living room, where one whole wall, virtually, is glass (and 33 stories up) and where my wife likes to have the sun (or clouds) streaming in. So I work on the word-processor without complaint and without trouble. Again, when I walk through Central Park I prefer to stick to the paths, rather than walk over grass and given my own choice I would prefer to walk around it. I feel comfortable in the canyons of Manhattan, but I will walk across empty spaces if I have to.

My acrophobia is much more severe. I live on the 33rd floor and I don't mind looking out the window horizontally, but I would be very uncomfortable looking *down* and I rarely try it. We have two balconies and I can get out upon them if there is some reason to do it, but I rapidly get uncomfortable and go back in.

However, my writing is certainly not a conscious attempt to deal with this. I feel no need to deal with it. I don't mind being acrophobic since I have no desire whatever to go up in a plane or to climb a mountain or to walk a tightrope.

As for the airplane, that wasn't I. It was Ray Bradbury who finally took an airplane and made the newspapers in so doing. I am made of sterner stuff and feel no urge to go through the kind of traveling that will put me in an airplane. In fact, I have no urge to do *any* kind of traveling. Left to myself, I would be perfectly content to stay on the island of Manhattan for the rest of my life. And when I do leave, it is only for short distances, and I return as soon as I can. . . . [P]lease let me impress upon you the fact that I am happy with myself exactly as I am and I am spending my life *exactly* the way I want to spend it.[13]

So much for my idea that Asimov might have been making his fiction serve a restitutive function. As he presented matters in the letter, he seemed to be ruling out even a defensive function. His agoraphobia was so mild that he could work away while the sun (or clouds!) streamed in; his acrophobia didn't bother him because he had organized his life to avoid dangerous high places; he didn't need to use his writing to deal with anxieties because he was really quite happy. Being a psychologist, I must admit that I felt a little dubious about the latter argument. But I was willing to entertain the possibility that Asimov's writing served mainly an expressive function rather than an anxiety-reducing one. I was also interested in Asimov's intimation that he had modeled Baley's agoraphobia mainly on Horace Gold's severe case rather than on Asimov's own milder version. Here was a psychological function of creative writing that might turn out to be more widespread than I had realized—a passive-aggressive function, a psychology of revenge against obnoxious editors (as well as, in Jack Williamson's case, against obnoxious therapists.)

When I wrote to Asimov again, I asked whether he had consciously made Baley agoraphobic in order to get back at Horace Gold, or whether he only later realized that Baley's character evolved in that direction because Asimov was unconsciously resentful of Gold's editorial demands. I also mentioned the odd combination of agoraphobic and claustrophobic panic in the short story "Nightfall," then said, "You probably don't remember the details of story composition after so long a time (though I've often been impressed by how much you do remember), but I'd be interested to know, for instance, whether you had read any psychological works before writing 'Nightfall' that might have given you some ideas about how to depict the characters' fears." Asimov again responded promptly:

First, about Baley's agoraphobia.

That I was influenced by Gold's agoraphobia is undoubted. That was the thing that was most noticeable about Horace and when I wrote the novel we were at our closest. That I was unconsciously resentful of Horace's demands and took vengeance by making Baley agoraphobic is a later bit of self-analysis. I have no way of proving this was so. There were times when my resentment of Horace became conscious and pronounced but this was not because of his driving me to write specific things but because his rejections were bitterly vituperative. . . .

Secondly, about the reactions in "Nightfall."

That was 44 years ago and it is difficult even for me to reconstruct the situation. . . . I am myself not afraid of the dark (and never was) and am not in the least claustrophobic so it interested me to *pretend* claustrophobia in my own mind and try to imagine what it was like. As for the fear of the stars or the sky, that was a "given" in the story when [*Astounding* editor John W.] Campbell and I discussed it. We had to reverse Emerson's thesis, so I had no choice there. I did *not* read psychological works before "Nightfall, " or after either. I am illiterate in psychology to this day. When any of my stories introduce what seem to be psychological insights, they are either picked up in general reading, or in observation, or in my own very lively imagination.[14]

In addition to my specific inquiries about the robot novels and "Nightfall," my second letter had included a more general paragraph, added hesitantly and phrased tentatively because I was not sure how far I could push Asimov's tolerance of my questions:

I appreciate your feeling that you're happy with yourself and that you're spending your life just the way you want to spend it. . . . But let me raise the question, for the sake of argument—and I think I do need to raise it in my paper, before somebody else raises it for me: May you not be just being defensive, denying your anxieties by avoiding introspection and by writing vast amounts of material that divert your and others' attention away from some kind of underlying uneasiness or self-doubt? I suppose that question represents the stereotypical psychoanalytic assumption, with which I do not necessarily agree, that everybody is neurotic somehow but that not everybody realizes it. Do you have a response to that that satisfies you, if not the psychologists and psychiatrists who might ask it?

Asimov responded:

Finally: Honestly, I am not defensive. I am a genuinely happy person except where the outside world impinges—if I develop clogged coronaries and am threatened with death, if those I love are unhappy for good reason etc. When unthreatened by the outside and left entirely to my own devices, I am openly happy. The fact is I write easily, I receive instant appreciation for my work, I make a good living, my wife and daughter love me, I have good and affectionate friends—I have no *reason* for unhappiness. And in my whole life I have never had self-doubt. I have known exactly what I could do from the very start and I have gone out and done it.[15]

Until those last two sentences, I felt willing to give Asimov the benefit of the doubt. After all, he knew first-hand whether he was happy or not, whether he was anxious or not. He had a lot more information about his psychological state than I did. But never any self-doubt? Asimov himself once wrote that when he made his second *Galaxy* sale to Horace Gold, "a more-than-seven-year agony of self-doubt was relieved."[16] Was it really true, as Asimov asserted in his letter, that he had known exactly what he could do from the very start and had gone out and done it? Not if we can judge from the voluminous evidence of his autobiography. Was he being totally honest with himself, and genuinely undefensive, when he said, "Honestly, I am not defensive. I am a genuinely happy person. . . . I have no reason for unhappiness"? Well, as the narrator of Asimov's mystery novel *Murder at the ABA* puts it, "The super-secure are never secure."[17]

I did realize, of course, that nothing is more likely to put a person on the defensive than a psychologist asking, "Are you being defensive?" So maybe Asimov was just overreacting a bit to my questions when he said he'd never felt any self-doubt and so on. Maybe in less defensive moments he would have admitted to occasional self-doubts, or to intermittent moments of unease amid all the happiness. I was willing to grant in turn that as he now lived his life, mostly indoors and mostly in front of his word-processor keyboard, Isaac Asimov probably was one of the world's happier people. But I decided not to use him as an example of a writer whose work served no significant psychological function.

Indeed, I suspect that his work served all three functions for him. Asimov's case is surely more complicated than I initially assumed, and a detailed functional analysis would require a much more thorough study of his fiction and his autobiographical writings than I or anyone else has yet done. But I think it's safe to say that Asimov's style of life and his writing were simultaneously shaped by a creative engagement between his talents and his fears. His writing clearly served an important expressive function for him; anyone who has read his anthology introductions to other people's stories will know how much Asimov enjoyed being Asimov in print. His writing also served important defensive functions, the dimensions of which are not yet clear. Among other things, his exaggeration of his own phobias in his fictional protagonists may have helped him live more comfortably with his relatively modest anxieties. And his writing probably served significant restitutive functions over the years, though he denied any "conscious attempt" to work in that direction. He may not have mastered all his anxieties, but the self-exploration entailed in his long writing career must have contributed *something* to the evolution of the sensitive, caring individual evident in much of his later work.

In response to further questioning, Asimov might have continued to deny that his writing served any of these functions. I didn't try any further questioning. But as I continued to read Asimov, I found that he had already identified the three functions in his own work. He had used nontechnical language in doing so, and he differentiated among the functions less sharply than I would have liked, but he definitely touched on all of them. He did it in one of his not altogether tongue-in-cheek autobiographical notes:

> The niceness of being a writer, of course, is that you can take all your frustrations and annoyances and spread them out on paper. This pre-
> vents them from building up to dangerous levels and explains why writ-

ers in general are such lovable, normal people and are a joy to all who know them.[18]

There you have it, straight from Isaac Asimov's word-processor: Writing lets you spread parts of your psyche out on paper (expressive function), allows you to let off some steam now and then (defensive function), and ultimately renders you lovable and normal (restitutive function). What more could a writer—or a psychobiographer—ask?

When I finished writing my original paper on Asimov, I thought I had found a piece of common ground to share with him regarding those functions, and I thought he'd be pleased to know it. I sent him a draft of the paper and asked his permission to quote from his correspondence with me. He wrote back to give permission, but he seemed a bit peeved by my paper—especially by my quoting his previously published remark about having gone through "a more-than-seven-year agony of self-doubt" between his first and second sales to Horace Gold at *Galaxy*. Asimov told me,

> I'm not sure if I should say anything about that seven years of self-doubt you quoted from my autobiography. Obviously, when a psychologist thinks you are insecure and asks you if you are, then whether you answer "Yes" or "No," you prove the psychologist correct.
>
> However, I have no self-doubts as to my intelligence or abilities. I know what I can do and what I can't do and I am almost never wrong.
>
> But naturally I have doubts as to whether an editor will like my stuff. Why not? He may be incompetent. So I was concerned about the possibility of being a one-editor writer. I shouldn't have called that *self-doubt*.[19]

As he had more time to think about it, Asimov got more than just a bit peeved. His monthly editorial in the August 1988 issue of *Isaac Asimov's Science Fiction Magazine* was titled "Acrophobia," and it was a direct response to my paper. He acknowledged that he suffered from "severe acrophobia," but he insisted that he was *not* agoraphobic. "I'm not the least bit afraid of open spaces," he said. "I admit that I enjoy enclosed places because I like the feeling of privacy. . . . And although I love the canyons of New York, I also walk freely in Central Park."[20] Compare those statements with his first letter to me or with his autobiography, and you'll find that Asimov was doing some backtracking about his feelings toward open spaces and closed places and Central Park. I didn't mind the backtracking; he had, after all, told me his agoraphobic tendencies were "very mild," and I had chosen to emphasize his acrophobia in my paper. But then, in the last paragraphs of his editorial, Asimov got personal:

Oh, well, the psychologist's thesis is that I write my stories to help me deal with all my various neuroses. In other words, I simply couldn't endure those neuroses unless I defanged them by putting them into stories.

He wrote to ask me questions when he was preparing the article and I told him quite frankly that I was satisfied with my life and that I didn't use my writings as a crutch.

I don't think he believed me.

Psychologists are odd people, though. Once they have worked out a thesis, anything you say—yes, no, maybe, I don't know—can be used by them to support the thesis. That arises from the fact that some aspects of psychology are not yet sciences.

So I'll make up a thesis. I'll suggest that psychologists are driven by neuroses and that the only way they can live with said neuroses is to attempt to prove that other people have them, too, only worse. I am quite confident that anything the psychologist says in an attempt to refute this I can use to support the thesis.[21]

Well, *touché,* Isaac. Not much a psychologist could say in response, is there? I figured Asimov was entitled to diagnose me as I had diagnosed him—though I wished he had done a little psychobiographical research on me first. I also wished his summary of my arguments had been a little more accurate. So I wrote a letter to *Isaac Asimov's Science Fiction Magazine.* I told its readers where they could find my paper on Asimov (somehow he had neglected to mention that), and then added:

I didn't start out to prove the thesis that Dr. Asimov, in his words, "simply couldn't endure [his] neuroses unless [he] defanged them by putting them into stories." At first I assumed that he was "a writer whose work displayed no psychological hangups and served no psychological functions but just told good stories." As I looked more closely at his fiction and learned more about his personality, I decided that "Asimov's case is surely more complicated than I initially assumed." I agree that he's not *simply* defanging neuroses by writing fiction—but as with any writer whose work has a strong impact on a large number of readers, he's not *simply* telling good stories, either.

Dr. Asimov concludes with his own thesis: "that psychologists are driven by neuroses and that the only way they can live with said neuroses is to attempt to prove that other people have them, too, only worse." Could be—I've said something similar in several papers on Sigmund Freud. But Freud's neurotic devotion to cigars, for instance, didn't prevent him from developing remarkable insights about how people build elaborate psychological defenses to protect their self-esteem. Likewise,

Dr. Asimov's acrophobia (plus at least a touch of agoraphobia) hasn't prevented him from becoming a creative and vastly entertaining writer.

I thought that was a pretty good letter. It restated some of the main points from my original paper that Asimov hadn't gotten quite right, but it was friendly and diplomatic and honest in describing my esteem for Asimov's work. Apparently it wasn't diplomatic enough for Asimov—or maybe he was just tired of the whole matter. The magazine never published the letter, and Asimov never responded to it personally. (As Editorial Director of the magazine, his main job was to respond in print to selected letters to the editors.) Maybe that's the final lesson to be learned from this exercise in psychobiography-by-mail: Don't analyze editors if you want something published in their magazine. Writers may be fair game, but editors get the last word. How many psychobiographies of living editors have you read lately?

10

The Mother of Oz:

L. Frank Baum

AT AN AGE when my daughters were old enough for "chapter books" but still young enough to enjoy being read to, I read them the first Oz book: *The Wonderful Wizard of Oz,* by L. Frank Baum. They loved it, so I read them the second Oz book, *The Marvelous Land of Oz.* After that they went on to read Baum's other twelve Oz books by themselves.

I had read *The Wonderful Wizard of Oz* once before, when I was ten. Rereading it as an adult, I found its menaces and delights both fresh and familiar. Though my memories were heavily overlaid with repeated viewings of the film version, the book was still back there somewhere in my brain. The 1939 *Wizard of Oz* with Judy Garland is one of the best movies ever made from a book, but I was pleased to encounter again all the details of character and place and plot that the movie left out.[1]

Rereading *The Marvelous Land of Oz* was a different kind of experience for me. Jack Pumpkinhead and the Saw-Horse and the Woggle-Bug felt like old friends, and General Jinjur's feminist rebellion came back to me as well, though as a ten-year-old I hadn't fully appreciated its satirical intent. But when I encountered the extraordinary events of the book's final paragraphs, culminating in Princess Ozma's restoration to her true form and to her rightful place as ruler of Oz, I drew a total blank. Where had my ten-year-old mind been when I read those remarkable passages—asleep in the poppy fields? Not a trace remained of Ozma's radical transformation—not a conscious trace, anyway.

Obviously, a process of gender-related repression had been at work here. An interesting example of Freudian defense mechanisms, I thought, and I filed it away to use in a class or a paper sometime. I didn't discuss it with my daughters; they were delighted with Princess Ozma's restoration to the throne, and showed no signs of incipient repression. We went on to share other marvels, including the glorious first viewings of the movie *Star Wars.*

Then I ran across an article by a cultural anthropologist in *Psychology Today*, noting the close similarities between two very popular films: *The Wizard of Oz* and *Star Wars*.[2] One film began in dry Kansas, the other on the dry planet Tatooine. Both films featured a young protagonist who was displaced from an aunt and uncle's home. One film had a mysterious Wizard, the other the mysteriously wizard-like Obi-Wan Kenobi; and so on. I didn't often share psychological articles with my daughters, but I thought they might be amused by this one. They were fascinated. Yes, they said, the Wookie looked a lot like the Cowardly Lion. Yes, the Tin Man and C3PO were both tall and made of metal. Yes, Toto and R2D2 were little guys who were always getting into trouble. Yes, Darth Vader was just another black-robed Wicked Witch. "But what about Princess Leia?" my daughters asked. According to the anthropologist, Leia shared certain qualities with the Wizard. But that comparison didn't work very well, and anyway Obi-Wan Kenobi was a better match with the Wizard. Nor did Leia much resemble Dorothy; and besides, Dorothy's role had already been taken by Luke Skywalker. So who *was* the equivalent of Leia in *The Wizard of Oz*?

One daughter soon came up with the answer. (Each daughter now claims to have thought of it first. Once the identification had been made, they both contributed a lot of supporting data.) Nobody in the *Wizard of Oz* film and nobody in the first Oz book was really equivalent to Leia. But somebody in the *second* Oz book certainly was: Princess Ozma. Of course! Both princesses were being held prisoner at the beginning of the story; both were rescued, in part through their own bravery; both regained their rightful throne at story's end.[3] Furthermore, both Ozma and Leia were depicted as psychologically androgynous, displaying behaviors characteristic of both males and females in our society. That particular similarity set me to thinking again about my own repression of the startling conclusion to *The Marvelous Land of Oz*. (If you've never read the book and want to experience its surprise ending for yourself, or if you read it as a child and want to find out how much you repressed before I tell you, go read it now.[4])

The reasons for my repression seemed obvious enough: The androgynous Ozma challenged my own gender identity, at a time when the ten-year-old me still had doubts about my developing masculinity. But I was left wondering: What kind of middle-aged man would have written about a heroine such as Ozma, and especially about her extraordinary physical transformation at the end of *The Marvelous Land of Oz*? I began to gather whatever information I could about L. Frank Baum, but not much was readily available at the time.

Then I learned of the International Wizard of Oz Club, which was soon to hold its annual West Coast convention in Yosemite National Park's Wawona Hotel. My daughters were still very interested in the Oz books; I wanted more information on Baum than the local libraries could provide; and the whole family liked the idea of a summer weekend in one of Yosemite's less populated areas. So we joined the International Wizard of Oz Club and signed up for the Winkie Convention.[5]

Fan clubs and fan conventions can be excellent sources of information about a psychobiographical subject. The people who've been enthusiastically reading and rereading an author's works for many years, who collect the author's books, who read and sometimes write for specialized publications about the author—those people can tell a psychobiographer a lot, not only about the author and the works but about where else to look and who else to ask. I soon found that Fred Meyer, the longtime Secretary of the International Wizard of Oz Club, knew Oz frontward and backward. He also knew who would know the most about L. Frank Baum. I went from Meyer to several other veteran members of the Club, and from them to various obscure publications and little-visited archives. Soon I was in business as a Baum psychobiographer. (I should also note the main disadvantage of working with fans and fan clubs, whether of L. Frank Baum or of Elvis Presley: They're eager to hear the nice things you have to say about their hero, but they don't really want to hear anything they perceive as "negative." At times they act like Defenders of the Faith. Such reactions are understandable, but a psychobiographer needs to be ready for them.)

Psychological and literary interpretations of Oz are plentiful, but they seldom say much about the Oz author.[6] An economic/political/historical interpretation of *The Wonderful Wizard of Oz* has also been going the rounds—the most frequent version being that the Wizard was really William Jennings Bryan, the Yellow Brick Road was the Gold Standard, Dorothy's silver slippers (they're not ruby in the book) were the Silver Standard, etc. But that interpretation displays little knowledge either of L. Frank Baum's actual political position or of his major personal concerns.[7] Time for a psychobiographer, it seemed to me, to take a look at Baum and his world—both his real world and his imaginary world. And my daughters were available for technical consultation.

The World of Oz

L. Frank Baum once described *The Wonderful Wizard of Oz* as his "truest book." It may fairly be described as his wisest, providing the most valuable psychological lesson for the child (and perhaps the adult) reader. This lesson, not explicitly stated but clearly intended by the author, is similar to the moral of various traditional fairy tales as well as Maeterlinck's later play *The Bluebird*: What you seek most fervently is likely to be found within you. The answers to your deepest problems come through self-knowledge and self-acceptance.

The book contains a subtext as well, not consciously intended by Baum and not as psychologically healthy: Males are weak, females are strong. It soon becomes clear that several very powerful females inhabit Oz—the good witches of North and South, the bad witches of East and West, and Dorothy herself, who strikes one witch dead upon arriving in Oz and then begins to reverse the fortunes of various males. It doesn't become evident for some time that all the important male figures in Oz, including the Wizard, suffer from debilitating psychological problems, and that most have serious physical weaknesses as well. The Scarecrow is hung up on a pole, unable to move from the spot until Dorothy frees him. He remains physically uncoordinated and doubts his intellectual powers through most of the book. The Tin Woodman is also immobile until Dorothy oils him. His lack of a heart isn't a serious handicap but he thinks it is, because without it he feels he can't love as other men do. The Lion appears to be in fine shape physically, but he assumes he's a born coward and suspects that he may have heart disease, since "whenever there is danger my heart begins to beat fast."[8] The Wizard himself, who for over half the book appears to be "Great and Terrible," is revealed as "a little old man, with a bald head and a wrinkled face" (p. 263)—a "humbug" who has "lived in deadly fear" of the Wicked Witches for many years (p. 268). He's also afraid to face his subjects, because they "would soon discover I am not a Wizard, and then they would be vexed with me for having deceived them" (p. 285). Even in his attempt to return Dorothy home he proves to be a bumbling balloonist, so Dorothy must use her own powers to attain her goal.

This subtext of male impotence and female power, which might lead us to wonder about the self-image of the man who wrote it, is linked with another subtext, more positive but less remarked upon in previous commentaries: Dorothy's pattern of nurturant feelings and behavior. Her first major act of nurturance (as perceived by the recipients), the release of the Munchkins from years of bondage to the Wicked Witch of the East, is accidental. But her freeing of the Scarecrow and the Tin Woodman comes from her general spirit of helpfulness. After she has killed the Wicked Witch of the West (again unintentionally), she assumes an active maternal role: getting the Woodman and the Scarecrow repaired when necessary, wiping away the Woodman's tears with her apron, making decisions and taking actions that deliver her friends from danger. She is nurturant toward Toto too, often taking the dog in her arms in a maternal or protective way. At two crucial points—just as the "cyclone" approaches and just as the Wizard's balloon is about to leave Oz—Dorothy puts herself at serious risk by rescuing the errant Toto. Finally, her major goal throughout the book is to return to Kansas— not because of the dangers in Oz or the pleasures of the barren Kansas farm, but because she fears that Aunt Em and Uncle Henry will miss her. This concern about the welfare of her guardians could be seen as Dorothy's defensive projection of her own homesickness, and indeed she does often admit to being lonely. But even the all-perceptive Glinda accepts her worries about her aunt and uncle as honest and praiseworthy feelings:

> "My greatest wish now," she [Dorothy] added, "is to get back to Kansas, for Aunt Em will surely think something dreadful has happened to me, and that will make her put on mourning; and unless the crops are

better this year than they were last I am sure Uncle Henry cannot afford it." Glinda leaned forward and kissed the sweet, upturned face of the loving little girl. "Bless your dear heart," she said, "I am sure I can tell you of a way to get back to Kansas."   (p. 334)

It has sometimes been suggested that Baum cast a little girl named Dorothy (or Dot) as the protagonist of this and other stories because he longed for a daughter whom he planned to name Dorothy. Whether or not that's true (and there's no strong evidence for it), Dorothy appears to speak in some sense for Baum himself in *The Wonderful Wizard of Oz*. Her nurturance is his own, as we can see from additional information about him. Other characters in the book—Dorothy's three companions and the Wizard—also express aspects of Baum to some extent. But whereas their principal characteristics are at times made to appear foolish, Dorothy's concern for others, particularly her desire to get home in order to relieve the anxieties of her aunt and uncle, are always treated seriously.

Baum's proclivity for imagining himself in the role of a nurturant female—and perhaps his desire at some level to *become* a nurturant female, a genuine mother figure—is expressed more strongly in his second Oz book, *The Marvelous Land of Oz*. Dorothy doesn't appear in this book, but it's set in the same land, shares several subsidiary characters, and brings to the foreground the implicit themes of *The Wonderful Wizard of Oz*. The theme of weak males and powerful females is stressed to a remarkable degree. A new male character, Jack Pumpkinhead, is depicted mainly in terms of his fear that his wooden limbs will break and his pumpkin head will spoil. His anxieties about his head are expressed in every imaginable form; other characters joke about them cruelly. In one six-page sequence, Jack worries that his head will be spoiled by water, sunshine, stinging bees, and being eaten by his friends; he excuses his cowardice by citing his susceptibility to spoilage; and he is told by his friend the Scarecrow, "All you need fear, my boy, is old age. When your golden youth has decayed we shall quickly part company" (p. 107).

The Scarecrow himself, though now King of the Emerald City, is described as "flimsy, awkward, and unsubstantial" (p. 64), and he proves to be a very weak king. He as well as Jack Pumpkinhead and another new male character, the Saw-Horse, suffer physical damage on several occasions. The Tin Woodman, now referred to as Nick Chopper (the name itself suggests a damaged axe), remains physically intact and often wields his axe to good effect. But he also spends much time getting himself polished and then worrying whether his high polish has been damaged. Still another new male character, the Woggle-Bug, is presented as a pompous pseudo-intellectual and a figure of fun. He tries to be self-important, but he worries about whether he will be made into goulash by a woman.

The book's powerful females include Glinda the Good; a witch named Mombi, who begins as a mere sorceress but soon appears as effectively evil as the first book's Wicked Witches; and an upstart "girl" who calls herself General Jinjur. Much of the book deals with General Jinjur's takeover of the Emerald City, at the head of an all-girl Army of Revolt. Jinjur feels not only that "the Emerald City has been ruled by men long enough"—a good feminist position—but that "Moreover, the City glitters with beautiful gems, which might far better be used for rings, bracelets and necklaces; and there is enough money in the King's treasury to buy every girl in our Army a dozen new gowns" (pp. 78–79).

Jinjur's forces use their knitting needles to conquer the Royal Army of Oz, one "old and feeble" man with an unloaded gun, whose irascible wife has already pulled half his whiskers out by the roots. Jinjur's soldiers then force the men of the Emerald City to take over the housework and to mind the babies, while the women sit around gossiping and eating candy. When one man complains that the housework "is wearing out the strength of every man in the Emerald City," the Scarecrow asks, "If it is such hard work as you say, how did the women manage it so easily?" The man replies "with a deep sigh, 'Perhaps the women are made of cast-iron'" (pp. 159–160). The book's principal male characters manage several limited victories over Jinjur's troops, by capitalizing on such stereotypically feminine characteristics as a fear of mice. But ultimately the feminist revolt is overturned only by the intervention of more disciplined and better armed females.

One male in the book compares with the females in psychological and physical strength. He is Tip, a boy who begins the book as the wicked sorceress Mombi's ward and slave. Tip is first described as being "as strong and rugged as a boy may be" (p. 2). Though Baum later characterizes him as "small and rather delicate in appearance" (p. 33), he continues to be a rather tough, resourceful, and at times powerful boy through most of the book. Tip is not an entirely sympathetic protagonist. In contrast to Dorothy in the first book, he is at times harsh-tongued, "sulky," even mean. He builds the life-sized manikin Jack Pumpkinhead in order to frighten his guardian Mombi, whom he hates: " 'And then,' said Tip to himself, with a laugh, 'she'll squeal louder than the brown pig does when I pull her tail'" (p. 4). Whereas Dorothy typically expresses her nurturance without a thought for herself, Tip assumes the role of father to Jack Pumpkinhead with embarrassment and occasional irritation. He is proud of his creation, and feels obligated not "to leave Jack Pumpkinhead to the tender mercies of old Mombi" (p. 24). But his discomfort with the paternal role continues into the book's final pages: "I shall not be sorry to escape the relationship" (p. 259).

Tip's discomfort may arise partly from the relationship being more maternal than paternal, in terms of traditional concepts. Tip constructs Jack's body and later dresses him, but it's Mombi the witch who quickens Jack with a sperm-like "Powder of Life" (obtained from a "crooked wizard"), which she is testing on Jack's lifeless form to see if the powder is "potent" (p. 13). Jack's insistent attention to Tip, as well as his repeated references to Tip as "dear father" or "noble parent," are more than Tip feels appropriate to a father-son relationship. Only when Tip himself undergoes a radical transformation does the relationship become a truly comfortable one on both sides.

Tip's transformation is surely one of the most startling in any turn-of-the-century children's book. There's little hint of it until the book is four-fifths over. When the Scarecrow attempts to obtain Glinda's help in defeating General Jinjur, Glinda tells him he has no more right to the throne than Jinjur does—that the Wizard of Oz who gave it to him had stolen it from the rightful king, Pastoria, and had magically hidden the now-dead Pastoria's daughter in "some secret place" (p. 228). This disclosure reveals a more sinister and powerful side of the Wizard than anything displayed in the first book. At the same time it draws attention to Mombi the Witch, who had been the Wizard's student in the magic arts, and to Mombi's orphan ward, Tip. Glinda forces Mombi to reveal that Tip is really the enchanted Ozma, Princess of Oz and rightful ruler. Tip cries "in amazement," "I'm no Princess Ozma—I'm not a girl!" (p. 257), and then, "I want to stay a boy . . . I don't want to be a girl!" (p. 259). But he is reassured by his friends that "it don't hurt to be a girl, I'm told. . . . I've always considered girls nicer than boys. . . . They're just as nice, anyway. . . . And they are equally good students" (p. 259). Whereupon Tip "hesitatingly" tells Glinda, "I might try it for awhile,—just to see how it seems, you know." Glinda forces Mombi to dissolve the enchantment. Out of a rose-colored couch draped with curtains of pink gossamer arises

> the form of a young girl, fresh and beautiful as a May morning. . . . All adown her back floated tresses of ruddy gold, with a slender jeweled circlet confining them at the brow. . . . Speaking the words with sweet diffidence, she said: "I hope none of you will care less for me than you did before. I'm just the same Tip, you know; only—only—" "Only you're different!" said the Pumpkinhead; and everyone thought it was the wisest speech he had ever made.   (pp. 263–264)

Glinda's army then captures the Emerald City and sends Jinjur and her girl soldiers home to their mothers. The men cast off their aprons and are welcomed back by their joyous wives, who have grown "so tired of eating their husbands' cooking" (p. 269). The Princess Ozma is formally restored to the throne. This ending is a happy one, but it's also a bit puzzling. Baum has made much fun of General Jinjur's all-girl army and the sex-role reversals of both men and women in Oz. Then suddenly everything is made right by the triumph of another all-girl army and the accession to power of a girl who has just reversed sexes rather than sex roles. What makes one situation wrong and the other right?

Here we see further evidence of the theme of female nurturance, of wanting to be a mother. Jinjur and her girl soldiers have given up all the nurturant activities that in Baum's eyes are appropriate to women, and have seized the Emerald City strictly for self-indulgent, narcissistic reasons. The men are forced to take over the nurturant activities—cooking, housekeeping, caring for children—which, though admirable and demanding, are inappropriate to their gender. As a male, Tip is uncomfortable in a nurturing role; as the female Ozma, she may appropriately assume the role of mother to the entire populace of Oz, as her name indicates: OzMA.[9] (Her father PAstoria was Oz's "pa," its pastor or shepherd—a nurturant figure as well, at least by name, but interestingly enough with a feminine ending to his name!) This transformation of Tip into Ozma and the contrast of Ozma's legitimacy with Jinjur's illegitimate rule are the clearest evidence in the Oz books of Baum's linkage of nurturance and femininity. Being a father is not quite the proper way to be nurturant; being a woman is not by itself the path to happiness and success in life. One must be a *mother*, which means being a nurturant female, even if one must change sexes in order to arrive at that happy state.

Being a mother does not imply being passive or following only the most traditional paths of "feminine" behavior. As *The Marvelous Land of Oz* comes to a close, Ozma has hardly roused herself from her years-long enchantment. But we are told that in later times

> she ruled her people with wisdom and justice. . . . "The Wonderful Wizard was never so wonderful as Queen Ozma," the people said to one another, in whispers; "for he claimed to do many things he could not do; whereas our new Queen does many things no one would ever expect her to accomplish."   (pp. 270–272)

Ozma is physically female; a mother must be that. But she is also, like Dorothy and Glinda, psychologically androgynous, combining important aspects of masculine and feminine sex roles. She remains publicly active, sensible, plain-speaking—qualities popularly perceived in Baum's day as uncharacteristic of females—while at the same time she is profoundly nurturant. She rides to the rescue on numerous occasions, leading a battalion of male soldiers, but she is also "said to be the most beautiful girl the world has ever known," and she supplies her needy subjects with goods "from the great storehouse of the ruler." The essential relationship between ruler and ruled in Oz is simply put: "The people were her children, and she cared for them."[10]

The Life of Baum

What kind of man shaped this world of androgynous women? Lyman Frank Baum was a child of latter-nineteenth-century America, and he was shaped in part by its major social and economic currents. But because of severe physical problems and their effect on his psychological development, he was also partly sheltered from those currents, and was allowed—or forced—to seek his own path to personal fulfillment.

Baum's father Benjamin was an unusually successful entrepreneur, beginning as a cooper (barrel-maker) and then moving rapidly into the oil business when commercial oil wells were first dug in the Eastern United States. Benjamin Baum invested his oil money in real estate, banks, and several other lines of business. He was a wealthy man by the time Frank was old enough to become aware of his father's activities. Less is known about Frank's mother Cynthia. A religious woman, she was never active in the family enterprises, though her husband named an oil refinery for her.

L. Frank Baum was born in 1856 in Chittenango, New York, a small town near Syracuse. Frank was the seventh of nine children, of whom four died young: the first two in infancy, the sixth a month after Frank was born, and the ninth at two years of age, when Frank was around six. Frank himself was thought to have a congenital heart defect, and he was therefore forced into early physical inactivity, according to his son's biography of him:

> Except for games with his brothers and sisters, Frank was a shy and
> sedentary child. Much of his time was spent alone in some favored spot
> in the house or a corner of the yard, where he kept happy for hours
> with the fey playmates his imagination created.[11]

When Frank was 5, the family moved to a fifteen-acre country estate just north of Syracuse. His mother named the estate Rose Lawn because of the hundreds of rose bushes on the ground; she "preferred to bring up her children at Rose Lawn rather than in the city."[12] Frank's father owned an adjacent dairy farm and a commercial grain and livestock farm as well. Frank was schooled at home until he was twelve, as were his siblings. In Frank's case his doctors had initially recommended home schooling because of his weak heart; nonetheless, Frank was sent away to military school at age twelve. His son, without further explanation, says the doctors "decided he was strong enough to attend Peekskill Military Academy."[13]

Frank was intensely unhappy at the military academy. He often complained to his father about the "brutal treatment" he received there, but he was kept in the academy for nearly two years. Finally, after being severely disciplined for looking out a classroom window at a bird, Frank experienced an apparent heart attack and fainted. His father pulled him out of school and his subsequent education was handled at home by private tutors.

Having become fascinated with a print shop at age fourteen, Frank decided he wanted to be a printer or journalist when he grew up. He persuaded his father to buy him a printing press, and began publishing a hand-set monthly newspaper when he was fifteen. After his father acquired a theatre as one of his business holdings, Frank became interested in acting as a career. He first tried to go on stage at age eighteen, over the objections of his father, who was willing to own theatres but who shared the common prejudice of the time against actors. Benjamin relented under pressure from Frank's mother, on the condition that Frank would not use his real name. Frank got a few walk-on roles with a touring company, then realized they were exploiting him because he could afford to buy fancy costumes. He gave up acting temporarily to sell dry goods at one of his father's stores, but within a year or two he joined a theatre company in New York City. He may also have worked on one or two newspapers during this period.

Then Frank's father made him manager, and later owner, of a string of small-town theatres. Frank organized an acting troupe to stage Shakespeare and other productions in the theatre chain. He began to write his own plays—melodramatic pieces designed for popular tastes. His greatest success was *The Maid of Arran* (1882), a pseudo-Irish melodrama in which he also starred. By this time Frank was so busy as an actor, director, and playwright that he couldn't also manage the theatres and the acting company, so his father's brother took over the managing duties. (There may have been additional reasons for this shift in responsibilities; Frank was never noted for his business sense.)

Meanwhile, at age twenty-five, Frank met Maud Gage, who was then twenty. Maud's mother was Matilda Joslyn Gage, a distinguished advocate of women's rights, editor of a national women's suffrage newspaper, and co-author (with Elizabeth Cady Stanton and Susan B. Anthony) of a multivolume *History of Woman Suffrage*.[14] Maud Gage was never as active as her mother in the women's rights movement, but she was described to Frank before he met her as "independent, with a mind and will of her own."[15] So she proved to be. Her mother objected to her becoming an actor's wife, but Maud insisted. She and Frank were married less than a year after they met. They spent the first several months of marriage on tour with Frank's acting company, but Maud wanted to settle down. Frank quit acting, and for a time they lived on the income from his plays and his theatre chain.

After their first son was born, Frank (as that son later wrote) "played with the baby for hours, until Maud protested he was spoiling the child. Nevertheless he spent whole evenings rocking his son in his arms and crooning him to sleep."[16] Frank sang his son the song "Bye, Baby Bunting" so often that the child became known as Bunny. Although the son later recalled his parents' marriage as basically happy, he also referred to "some temperamental difficulties and stresses," which he saw as mainly provoked by Maud and alleviated by Frank:

> Years of living in the shadow of a heart ailment had taught him to avoid upsets that might bring on an attack. . . . In the long years of her widowhood, Maud Baum often mentioned that peace and harmony had always graced her home, but those who knew the family best felt that this was true only because Frank, from the time of their marriage until his death thirty-seven years later, allowed her to have her own way with the household, the children, and the family purse. Only because of his easy nature

and because he remained all those years very much in love with her, was he able philosophically to accept her often unpredictable temper.[17]

It was Maud who spanked the children and sent them to bed without their supper. Frank would then carry food up to their room and tell them stories until they fell asleep. Frank's caretaker role grew even more important when Maud developed peritonitis following the birth of their second son and lay bedridden for several months. During that time, Frank

> spent many hours at home every day so that he would be near if Maud needed him. He whiled away the time playing with their two children, singing to them, rocking them in his arms, keeping them quiet so that Maud would not be disturbed, and finding in them his refuge from anxiety.[18]

During the early years of the marriage, Baum wrote at least two more plays. But the uncle who managed the theatre chain became seriously ill; the bookkeeper disappeared with most of the profits; and one of the theatres burned to the ground along with the acting company's scenery and costumes. At age 28, Frank was forced to sell the entire chain of theatres to pay the bills. Rather than continuing in the theatre world, he became head salesman for Castorine, an axle grease developed by his elder brother. Frank seems to have done well at promoting Castorine on the road. But then both his father and his elder brother became ill and died within a year of each other. The family business faltered without their guidance. It was finished off by another crooked bookkeeper, who gambled away much of the oil firm's money and then shot himself.

Following these two financial failures, Maud persuaded Frank to go West to seek a new fortune. Her sisters and brother were already living in the Dakota Territory. There the Baums moved in 1888, when Frank was 32. Baum opened a variety store in the town of Aberdeen and was briefly successful. But the town's economy had hit its peak and began to slide rapidly. Baum was too generous with credit; in a little over a year his store went bankrupt. With less than a hundred dollars remaining to his name, Baum bought a local newspaper on time payments. This gave him a new opportunity to explore one of his early career choices, journalism, and he proved to be a creative editor. (In one of his columns he described a desperate farmer who put green spectacles on his horses so they'd eat sawdust, thinking it was grass.) But the newspaper also went broke in a year's time. Trying to put behind them a record of four financial failures in less than seven years, the Baums moved part of the way back East, to Chicago. By this time Frank was thirty-five; he and Maud now had four sons.

In Chicago, Frank worked for a few months as a newspaper reporter. He somehow moved from that job into the position of buyer for a department store's crockery department, which led into his becoming a traveling salesman for a crockery company. He was reportedly quite successful at the latter job. But the health problems associated with his heart condition, which he experienced to some degree throughout adulthood, were becoming more serious: "severe nasal hemorrhages and gripping chest pains," according to his son.[19] A heart specialist told him to find a less physically demanding occupation, so after five years on the road, he quit the crockery business forever.

Baum was now 41 years old. After his early success as an actor and playwright, his repeated business reverses must have been profoundly discouraging, even if they were mostly not his fault. Having found a job at which he was a success—the only job he had ever managed to keep for an extended period of time—he was now vividly reminded of his physical inadequacy, indeed of his mortality. His psychological reactions at this point are unknown, but he did not respond by retreating into inactivity. He had a wife and four small children to support. He became, if anything, even more active, though not in a physically strenuous way. He called upon his writing skills, with which he had enjoyed limited and inter-mittent success, and struck out in two radically different directions: the publica-tion of a trade magazine and the writing of children's books.

The trade magazine was *The Show Window*, a monthly that dealt with the trimming of retail store windows. Baum had never held a job as a window trimmer, so he must have drawn upon his retailing experience and his stage background to develop the magazine. *The Show Window* became a rather surpris-ing success. Three years after it began, Baum published a book that drew from the magazine's contents: *The Art of Decorating Dry Goods Windows and Interiors*.

Baum had spent a good deal of time, during his boys' childhood, telling stories to them and their friends. When he was encouraged—some say by his mother-in-law, others by his wife—to put these stories into publishable form, he hit upon the organizing scheme of expanding Mother Goose rhymes into short prose narratives. In 1897, the same year he began the window-dressing magazine, these stories were published as a book under the title *Mother Goose in Prose*. With illustrations by the young artist Maxfield Parrish, the book enjoyed modest sales. Baum began to work on other children's books. In 1899 the second was pub-lished, a series of humorous poems illustrated by W. W. Denslow, titled *Father Goose, His Book*. Its success was astonishing. It became the best-selling juvenile book in America during 1899, and in one version or another its sales continued strong for several years. Its success must have strengthened the self-image that Baum proclaimed in the book's first poem:

> Old Mother Goose became quite new,
>   And joined a Women's Club;
> She left poor Father Goose at home
>   To care for Sis and Bub.

> They called for stories by the score,
>   And laughed and cried to hear
> All of the queer and merry songs
>   That in this book appear.
> When Mother Goose at last returned
>   For her there was no use;
> The goslings much preferred to hear
>   The tales of FATHER GOOSE.

Baum was so delighted by the reception of *Father Goose* that when he bought a summer cottage with his royalties, he called the place "The Sign of the Goose." He decorated it liberally with just such signs: leaded-glass goose windows, a flying-geese frieze on the walls, a life-sized goose sign out front. Baum himself made the cottage's wooden furniture, with carved geese designs and nails bearing goose-shaped nailheads.

But *Father Goose* was only a prelude to the most fantastic success of all: *The Wonderful Wizard of Oz*. According to one estimate, that book in all its editions has sold more copies than any other American children's book ever published.[20] Baum encountered failure at times thereafter, as he attempted other kinds of books, stage productions, and films; but he could hardly doubt his worth as a children's writer. He produced floods of written words, including enough about Oz for him to grow tired of it several times over. Whenever he tried to end the Oz series, he received thousands of demands from children to continue, until he resigned himself to his permanent role as "Royal Historian of Oz." He died in 1919 at age 62, his heart overburdened by a gall-bladder operation. His final thoughts were apparently not of going to Heaven, at least in its traditional sense. Readers of the Oz books know that the Land of Oz is separated from the outside world by a poisonous desert, including an area called the Shifting Sands, across which mortals cannot travel by ordinary means. According to family tradition, L. Frank Baum's last words were, "Now we can cross the Shifting Sands."[21]

Baum and Oz

How may a life history such as Baum's lead to the creation of books such as the Oz series? Any connections we draw must be somewhat tentative, since Baum him-self did not make the links obvious. He wrote no autobiography and left few statements about the books' subjective origins. Furthermore, the major source of biographical information on Baum is not as authoritative as we might wish. It consists largely of recollections by the author's eldest son, written down several decades after Baum's death and supplemented by the research of a conscientious but nonscholarly collaborator.[22] Nonetheless, several of Baum's fictional themes can be traced to elements of his life history with a fair degree of confidence, and other connections can be made with a level of certainty somewhat better than sheer speculation.

Men as weak, women as strong

The influence of personal experience is least arguable for this theme. Baum's history of heart disease from an early age, reinforced by intermittent bouts of poor health and experiences identified as "heart attacks," provides a distinctive source for the physical incompleteness, weakness, or incapacitation of many of his male characters. (Seldom, if ever, is a female character similarly incapacitated.) It's quite possible, given the state of medical diagnostic skills when Baum lived, that his heart condition was not physically all it appeared to be; his heart attacks may at times have been more psychological than physical.[23] What's important for our purposes is that Baum and others *believed* his heart to be seriously defective, and acted in terms of that belief. His parents are likely to have been particularly sensitive to the life-threatening aspects of his heart condition, in view of the early deaths of their first two children and the death of another child shortly after Frank was born.

Baum's damaged male characters can be viewed in other ways than as simple expressions of his concerns about physical health. Baum himself had a broader meaning in mind when he wrote, for instance, about the Tin Woodman's quest for a heart. But the interpreter who sees that quest only as representing a desire for a loving relationship, without also recognizing the contribution of Baum's realistic personal fears about a vital organ, misses an important determinant of Baum's imagery. Baum seems to have felt forced to limit his emotional reactions because of his heart condition, though not to the extent of the Tin Woodman, who felt that he could not love because he had no heart. The Tin Man's reluctance to cry because he might rust and thus become permanently immobilized, as well as the Cowardly Lion's fear of dangerous situations that might set his heart racing, are understandable as expressions of Baum's own concerns.

Other interpreters have seen the Tin Woodman's lack of a heart, and similar physical shortcomings in Baum's male characters, as expressing Baum's castration anxiety.[24] This interpretation is not as outrageous as some Baumian enthusiasts have assumed. The Tin Man did lose each of his limbs before losing his heart—amputation of limbs is a standard symbol for castration in Freudian dreams—and his "heart" was destroyed only when his entire torso was split down the middle. Moreover, a remarkable number of male legs (usually left legs) are broken off and replaced in the Oz books, particularly in *The Marvelous Land of Oz*. Baum may well have felt an inhibition of sexual activity as a result of his heart condition, though he was active enough to sire four sons during his first eight years of marriage. But again, anyone who narrowly interprets the physical damage among Oz's males only in terms of castration anxiety has overlooked a very realistic source of anxiety in Baum's heart condition. Just as Freud is supposed to have said, "A cigar is sometimes only a cigar," so Baum might reasonably have said, "A damaged heart is sometimes only a damaged heart."[25]

The sources of Baum's belief in female strength and power are not as straightforward. We know that his father was an active, energetic, powerful figure well into Frank's adulthood; we do not know how father and mother dealt with each other. Cynthia Baum was reported in later life to be a stern advocate of puritanical religious views, but we know little about her treatment of Baum as a child. We do know that Baum was well acquainted with two very strong women in his adult life: his wife and his feminist mother-in-law, who lived with the Baums for over a decade after her husband died. Maud Baum appears to have ruled the household with an iron hand; she took over the family finances after Frank demonstrated his ineptness in that area.[26] The pervasive tone of female power in the Oz books may have had its origins in Baum's childhood, but it must have received a powerful boost from his adult experiences.

The value of nurturance

The strongly nurturant orientation of Oz's heroines—Dorothy, Ozma, Glinda, and others—is only vaguely anticipated in what we know of Baum's childhood. However, Baum's own nurturant feelings and behavior in adulthood are strongly evident, and we can make educated guesses about how his childhood circumstances led to an unusually nurturant orientation for an adult male of that time (as it would be even now).

The effect of Baum's heart condition was not only to make him anxious about his physical incompleteness and about death, but to influence his treatment by others. He was apparently cut off at least in part from normal male socialization processes, being forbidden the usual rough-and-tumble play of boys outside his immediate family and driven largely to solitary, passive pursuits. Spending much of his time in the house, he was probably exposed more than usual to the feminine play of his sisters and the daily activities of his mother. His father was a very busy man, with far-ranging enterprises that required frequent attention. Benjamin Baum appears to have been indulgent toward Frank, but also—as the military school episode suggests—ambivalent as to how far he should protect Frank from the usual rigors of a masculine upbringing. Frank's recollections about making the rounds of the family businesses with his father (or at least those recollections reported by Frank's son) are largely negative or indifferent: he was frightened by a scarecrow, he was frightened by a snake, he wandered away to become entranced by a print shop, he wandered away again to watch Shakespearean actors at work. As a "delicate" child, Frank may well have felt incapable ever of matching the accomplishments of his self-made father, and therefore made little effort to emulate him. Frank certainly acquired none of the financial sense that enabled his father to amass a fortune in a relatively short time and to continue improving upon it until he was near death.

Baum's protected, largely housebound, and probably mother-oriented child-hood would have presented him with many of the circumstances that appear to instill a nurturant orientation in most girls in our culture.[27] His father's adjacent farm gave him an important opportunity to practice that nurturance. In his late teens, Baum became fascinated with the breeding of poultry, particularly a variety known as Hamburgs (after the port of Hamburg, Germany, from which they were originally imported to America). Baum became an expert on Hamburgs, and at the age of 30 he published his first book, *The Book of the Hamburgs*, which dealt with their care and breeding.[28] Much of the book is taken up with judging points at poultry shows and with the selection of reliable breeders. Baum's nurturant orientation becomes significant only when he describes the birds' behavior. In addition to the usual caretaking tasks required of any show-fowl breeder, the breeder of Hamburgs must take extra precautions, because a key characteristic of Hamburgs is "the absence of the incubating instinct" (p. 6). In the book's one genuinely emotional passage, Baum tells what this means for the breeder:

> To start with, there is one essential point in raising these delicate little creatures—*care*. Give them plenty of care, and they will thrive—*proper* care, we mean. . . . For the first week, perhaps nearly every old hen is faithful to her little brood, and guards them with that maternal tender-ness for which she has been made the symbol of motherly love. But this care soon wearies her, and in a few days she begins to neglect them, marching around in the chill and drenching rains of spring, and drag-ging her little brood with her through the damp grass, entirely oblivious of their sufferings; and one by one they drop off and are left behind, chilled through, or seized with cramp. Only the most persevering are able to keep up, until, perhaps seized with a pang of remorse, she spreads her wings and allows the little ones to find a temporary shelter beneath her warm feathers. Even the strongest often succumb to rheuma-tism and die after this dangerous exposure. The picture is not over-drawn; it is of common occurrence.[29]

Baum's solution to this tragedy of maternal inattention is for the breeder to intervene energetically—Father Goose himself—to keep the chicks warm, dry, clean, and well-fed. Baum was at about this time playing a similar role in his family, taking care of the two small children while Maud lay bedridden. Frank's enjoyment of this nurturant role in the family may have been tempered, however, not only by his wife's illness but by the realization that being a Father Goose or substitute mother hen is usually considered highly inappropriate for men, except as poultry breeders. Maud certainly showed no support for his continuing to play the role, once she got back on her feet. He could not again find a reliably acceptable outlet for his need to nurture until he hit upon the career of writing children's books, eleven years later. Then he made the most of it: in the essential act of creating books for his young audience, in the books' principal themes, and in his subsidiary activities as an author—answering letters from his small fans, giving public readings to them, and designing his summer home. "The Sign of the Goose" seems to have been built more to be enjoyed by visiting children than by anyone else.

The equation of nurturance and female gender

Baum was an extremely nurturant and loving father, according to the testimony of his sons. He was generous and attentive to all the neighborhood children who came his way, male and female. He reached millions of children in his lifetime with messages of warmth and understanding. And yet he continued over the years to be intrigued with the idea of becoming a nurturant female, or at least with temporarily changing sex. He displayed no inclination toward homosexual object choice, nor any strong tendencies toward transvestitism (though he seems to have enjoyed dressing in colorful stage costumes, and was emphatic in his preference for nightshirts over pajamas). Had he been offered the opportunity to undergo a sex change, he probably would have chosen to remain a male, with the attendant perquisites and opportunities. But over and over again in his imaginative activities, Baum displayed a fascination with sex-role reversal, gender ambiguity, and outright sex change. Most often the change was from male to female, or female-male-female.

The most important example of female-male-female sex change has already been mentioned: Ozma's transformations in *The Marvelous Land of Oz*. A similar change takes place in a lesser book, *The Enchanted Island of Yew*, published a year earlier.[30] A female fairy, bored after several centuries of life, persuades a visitor to transform her into a dashing young prince for a year. Accompanied by a masochistic male companion, the fairy enjoys a year's worth of adventures, then is happily transformed back into her female form. Several years later, Baum rewrote parts of this story as a verse play for children, "The Fairy Prince," with the female-male-female transformations constituting an important part of the stage action.[31] Still another temporary transformation occurs in *The Emerald City of Oz*, when a male creature known as a Phanfasm momentarily sheds his "hairy skin" and takes the form of a beautiful woman.[32]

The most explicit and extensive case of sex-role reversal occurs in *The Marvelous Land of Oz*, when General Jinjur's army displaces the males of Oz by force. Less systematic examples are rather frequent, at least in terms of individual females acting like males and males acting like females (e.g., Father Goose taking over the children from the feminist Mother Goose). A particularly vivid example of sex-role reversal involves the hen Billina, in *Ozma of Oz*, who comes with Dorothy to the Land of Ev and is temporarily left in a chicken house. Dorothy returns to find Billina crouching upon the prostrate form of a speckled rooster. . . . "Do you think I'd let that speckled villain of a rooster lord over me, and claim to run this chicken house, as long as I'm able to peck and scratch?"[33]

Billina is also an example of Baum's interest in sexual ambiguity, if not of outright sex reversal. When Billina was first hatched, "no one could tell whether I was going to be a hen or a rooster, so the little boy at the farm where I was born called me Bill" (p. 17). Dorothy prefers to call her Billina in order to make her gender explicit, but the hen finds the name "Bill" quite satisfactory. Earlier instances of sexual ambiguity occur in *The Wonderful Wizard of Oz*, first when Dorothy asks the Witch of the North whether the Wizard is a good man. The Witch replies, "He is a good Wizard. Whether he is a man or not I cannot tell, for I have never seen him" (p. 107). The Wizard later appears to the Scarecrow as "a most lovely lady" (p. 210), though it turns out that he is merely wearing a mask and a gown. The most elaborate case of sexual ambiguity occurs in *John Dough and the Cherub*, where a child named Chick the Cherub goes through the whole book without ever being identified as to gender.[34] With Baum's cooperation, the book's first edition included a coupon for a contest in which readers would try to write "the best answer to the question 'Is the Cherub girl or boy?' "

Baum himself often assumed a feminine persona as a writer. Of the large number of non-Oz children's books he wrote pseudonymously, over two-thirds were published under female names; most of these were intended for female audiences. Baum once participated in a hoax in which a woman played the part of one of his pseudonymous female authors, for the benefit of a publisher who had insisted on meeting her.[35]

Why all this interest in sexual ambiguity and gender transformation? Some attempts at totally innocent explanations have been offered. It has been suggested, for instance, that Tip is transformed into Ozma at the end of *The Marvelous Land of Oz* because Baum was planning to do a stage version and was influenced by "the English pantomime tradition, in which the leading boy is played by a woman, who appears in female clothing at the end."[36] Baum was indeed familiar with the English pantomime tradition, so there may be some truth to this speculation. But it does not explain the sexual ambiguities of such characters as Billina, which had nothing to do with stage productions.

Ozma in particular—a girl forced to live for years in a boy's body, with her problems magically solved when she's transformed physically into a female— sounds very much like the fantasied self-images of many present-day transsexuals. Baum may have felt similarly trapped in a male body, dating back to his early exposure primarily to female socialization patterns because of his heart condition. A more restrained line of speculation would focus on Baum's inability to find acceptable masculine ways to express his powerful feelings of nurturance. Given his personal and cultural circumstances, he may have perceived the only fully nurturant parent to be the mother. In Baum's published fantasies, his children's books, virtually all women are powerful and some women are powerfully nurturant, while men are basically weak and in need of nurturance. Is it so surprising, then, that he sometimes wondered what it might be like to be both a woman and a mother?

Baum exhibited certain stereotypically feminine qualities more than most men of his day, notably his nurturant behavior. But he was by no means lacking in important "masculine" qualities as well. His success as a salesman on the road suggests some degree of positive identification with his entrepreneur father; his financial ineptitude, perhaps a negative identification. His nurturance and general home-bound orientation, as well as his penchant for raising flowers, indicate a positive identification with his mother. His behavior toward the women's movement of the time displays a curious mixture of support and hostility, probably revealing domestic (i.e., household) political pressures as much as a personal mixture of masculine and feminine sympathies. Baum served as secretary of the Equal Suffrage Club in Aberdeen, Dakota Territory, and wrote several pro-suffrage editorials for his newspaper there.[37] But a few years later he wrote a poem that ran in part,

> Then shout Hurrah for the woman new,
> With her rights and her votes and her bloomers too!
> Evolved through bikes and chewing gum,
>   She's come!
> . . . And bid goodbye to the matron sweet,
> To the mother the whole world loves to greet.
> With reverence she's had to quit
>   And flit![38]

According to at least some of the research studies on psychological androgyny, androgynous individuals tend to be more flexible and tolerant than stereotypically masculine or feminine individuals.[39] Baum wasn't very flexible in his attitudes toward women's abandonment of traditional maternal roles. But he was quite open to the idea of women displaying "masculine" initiative and rationality in addition to nurturant feelings. His psychological openness extended broadly to a "democratic tolerance for ways of life alien to his own," as expressed repeatedly in the Oz books.[40]

L. Frank Baum announced at the beginning of *The Wonderful Wizard of Oz* that his "modernized fairy tale" would omit the "fearsome moral" that characterized the old-time fairy tale, while retaining the "wonderment and joy." But the intensely involving personal concerns from which this and Baum's other tales evolved gave them an emotional life and a personal significance for many young readers that ordinary ethical lessons would not have possessed. Over the years, the Oz books appear to have remained more popular with girl readers than with boys. Not only are the books' leading characters mostly female; they also convey the reassuring message that traditionally "masculine" tendencies are tolerable and even valuable in females, as long as feminine nurturance is not abandoned as well. The Oz books tell the receptive girl reader that she can be bright and competent and adventurous and unromantic when she feels like it, and still be the princess she's always wanted to be. But boys may be reassured by the books too, as they are told that their nurturant tendencies are valuable and that they (like the Tin Man and Jack Pumpkinhead and others) will live through their physically oriented self-doubts to become whole people in the end. Baum himself was the best testimonial to the truth of those lessons.

11

Nabokov Contra Freud

IN 1973 I wrote a letter to Vladimir Nabokov. What I wanted, I told him, was "information which may assist me in writing a fairly serious essay, tentatively titled 'Nabokov's Anti-Freudianism.'" I then explained, in what I thought of as a semi-Nabokovian style:

> I have admired your work intensely since my first reading, as a college freshman, of that racy novel *Lolita*. I have admired Sigmund Freud's work intensely since my first reading, at about the same time, of the equally racy *Introductory Lectures on Psychoanalysis*. I am well aware of your extreme distaste for Freud and his followers; and according to the currently popular psychological theory of "cognitive consistency," such an imbalanced situation (Elms admires Nabokov; Elms admires Freud; Nabokov abhors Freud) will not permit me to rest until I somehow convert the perceived inconsistency into consistency. I do not altogether accept cognitive consistency theory, but your insistent rejection of Freudian concepts despite several clear commonalities between your ideas and Freud's does intrigue me. A close reading of your published fiction, critical works, and self-descriptive statements has led me to develop certain hypotheses about your anti-Freudianism; but I have begun to wonder whether these hypotheses are unnecessarily subtle and perhaps even overly Freudian. Therefore, I would appreciate your replies to the following questions. . . .
>
> A. Are your negative comments about Freudians, particularly in the prefaces to the English translations of your Russian novels, directed at anyone in particular (e.g., an obnoxious cousin or an analyst acquaintance), or are your targets broader in scope?
>
> B. Are your objections directed specifically toward Freud's own con-

cepts, as your language sometimes indicates, or only toward the simplified and bastardized versions espoused by some of his followers,
especially semi- or pseudo-Freudian literary critics? One such critic, as I
recall, has suggested that you have never read any of Freud's writings
first-hand, and I myself have suspected this to be the case. Such a possibility offers a tempting resolution to my own feelings of cognitive inconsistency; but I am reluctant to speculate in such a vein without specific
information on your psychoanalytic reading history.

C. If the above questions seem to you impertinent or misdirected, will
you instead give me any other information that might assist in explicat-
ing your anti-Freudianism? You have, I know, occasionally embroidered
upon your basic anti-Freudian stance in interviews; but in more-or-less
Freudian fashion, I am asking not so much how you feel about Freud
now, as how those feelings began or upon what grounds they rest.

I hope that in requesting answers to those questions, I am not unduly
diverting you from your artistic labors. Freud continued writing into his
eighty-third year; in admiration and in grateful expectation, I wish you a
creative life at least as long.

I'd like to report that Nabokov answered my letter in detail by return mail, and
that we then engaged in a clever continuing correspondence until we both tired of
the game. His creative life did continue for four more years, almost until his death
at age 78. But I never heard a peep from him.

I didn't really expect an answer when I wrote the letter, though I included
several flashy little lures designed to elicit a rise from Nabokov (e.g., "One such
critic . . . has suggested that you have never read any of Freud's writings first-
hand"). I knew he had little patience with potential biographers and none with
Freudian sympathizers. I've occasionally wondered, over the past two decades,
whether my letter to Nabokov rests in a locked Nabokovian archive in Washington or New York or Montreux. If it does, it may well bear a Nabokovian scribble:
"Idiotic drivel!" or worse. More likely, it went straight into the nearest waste-
basket.

But let's suppose Nabokov *had* answered my letter, confessing to a personal
grudge against a particularly dogmatic psychoanalyst who had mistreated one of
his close relatives. That still would not have been sufficient explanation for his
extreme and insistent denunciations of Freud through most of his life as a writer.
Nabokov used every opportunity to denounce Freud, Freudians, and psychodynamic interpretations of literary works. He insisted that psychoanalytic theories of personality development were irrelevant to his own life history and to the
lives of his literary characters—although, he said, "the little Freudian who mis-
takes a Pixlok set for the key to a novel will no doubt continue to identify my
characters with his comic-book notion of my parents, sweethearts and serial

selves."[1] For a man who rejected Freud so vehemently, Nabokov was aston-
ishingly preoccupied with him. Gordon Allport told his own story about meeting
Freud over and over again, but it was always the same story, in essentially the
same language. Allport's major responses to Freud, his personality textbook and
his paper on motivational theory, appeared seventeen and thirty-three years after
his fateful encounter with Freud.[2] Nabokov, a year younger than Allport and with
no Freud encounter to stimulate him, began his public attacks on Freud several
years earlier and continued to press them many years longer, in a profusion of
literary forms. Even one of Nabokov's most enthusiastic advocates described his
anti-Freudianism as "obsessive."[3]

Nabokov's Obsession

Nabokov began to make fun of reductionistic psychotherapists as early as his
third novel, *The Defense,* published in 1929. The intensity of his negative feelings
became more evident in a satirical piece published in a Russian émigré newspaper
in 1931:

> Whoever once views the world through the prism of *Freudism for All*
> will not regret it. . . . Gentlemen, you will know nothing of the intricate
> fabric of life if you do not accept one fact: sex governs life. The pen with
> which you write to your beloved or debtor represents the male organ,
> while the mailbox into which we drop the letter is the female organ. . . .
> A little boy energetically whipping his top is a sadist; a ball (preferably
> of large diameter) is attractive to him because it recalls a woman's bo-
> som; playing hide-and-seek is an emiratic [secret, obscure] urge to re-
> turn to the mother's womb. . . . No matter what you are concerned with,
> no matter what you are thinking of, remember that all our acts and ac-
> tions, thoughts and reflections may be explained completely satisfactorily
> in the above manner. Try our patented product *Freudism for All,* and you
> will receive satisfaction.[4]

In other works of the 1930s and 1940s, Nabokov continued to tease the
analysts. In his 1951 autobiography, he really hit his stride:

> It might be rewarding to go into the phylogenetic aspects of the pas-
> sion male children have for things on wheels, particularly railway trains.
> Of course, we know what the Viennese Quack thought of the matter. We
> will leave him and his fellow-travelers to jog on, in their third-class car-
> riage of thought, through the police state of sexual myth (incidentally,
> what a great mistake on the part of dictators to ignore psychoanalysis—a
> whole generation might be so easily corrupted that way!).[5]

By the time *Lolita* came to America in 1958, Nabokov could refer familiarly to "my old feud with Freudian voodooism."[6] *Lolita* itself takes the form of a psychological case history as told by the patient, Humbert Humbert. Humbert makes fun of what he calls "the scholastic rigmarole and standardized symbols of the psychoanalytic racket," and says he owes his "complete restoration" from a "bout with insanity"

> to a discovery I made while being treated at . . . [a] very expensive sanatorium. I discovered there was an endless source of robust enjoyment in trifling with psychiatrists; cunningly leading them on; never letting them see that you know all the tricks of the trade; inventing for them elaborate dreams, pure classics in style (which make *them*, the dream-extortionists, dream and wake up shrieking); teasing them with false "primal scenes"; and never allowing them the slightest glimpse of one's real sexual predicament.[7]

Nabokov insisted that he never shared Humbert's "real sexual predicament," pedophilia; but the pleasure that Humbert gets out of "trifling with psychiatrists" is clearly Nabokov's own.

In his subsequent books, Nabokov rarely resisted taking one or two slaps at Freud and Freudians. As his early Russian novels and stories were translated into English, he used the foreword to each new volume as an occasion to indulge in his obsession. His foreword to *The Eye* asserts, for example, that his books "are not only blessed by a total lack of social significance, but are also mythproof: Freudians flutter around them avidly, approach with itching oviducts, stop, sniff, and recoil."[8] In his foreword to *The Waltz Invention* he continues,

> After the dreadful frustrations Freudians have experienced with my other books, I am sure they will refrain from inflicting upon Waltz a sublimation of the push-button power-feeling such as the manipulation of an elevator, up (erection!) and down (revenge suicide!)[9]

In Nabokov's later years, any half-informed interviewer knew that a question about Freud would elicit a witty denunciation:

> "Have you ever been psychoanalyzed?" "Have I been *what?*" "Subjected to psychoanalytical examination." "Why, good God? . . . The ordeal itself is much too silly and disgusting to be contemplated even as a joke. Freudism and all it has tainted with its grotesque implications and methods appears to me to be one of the vilest deceits practiced by people on themselves and on others. I reject it utterly, along with a few other medieval items still adored by the ignorant, the conventional, or the very sick."[10]

"The parodies of Freud in *Lolita* and *Pale Fire* suggest a wider familiarity with the good doctor than you have ever publicly granted. Would you comment on this?" "Oh, I am not up to discussing again that figure of fun. He is not worthy of more attention than I have granted him in my novels and in *Speak, Memory*. Let the credulous and the vulgar continue to believe that all mental woes can be cured by a daily application of old Greek myths to their private parts. I really do not care."[11]

And so on, even unto Nabokov's final interview:

"Your distaste for the theories of Freud has sometimes sounded to me like the agony of one betrayed, as though the old magus had once fooled you with his famous three-card trick. Were you ever a fan?" "What a bizarre notion! Actually I always loathed the Viennese quack. I used to stalk him down dark alleys of thought, and now we shall never forget the sight of old, flustered Freud seeking to unlock his door with the point of his umbrella."[12]

My personal favorite was from another interview:

Our grandsons no doubt will regard today's psychoanalysts with the same amused contempt as we do astrology and phrenology. One of the greatest pieces of charlatanic, and satanic, nonsense imposed on a gullible public is the Freudian interpretation of dreams. I take gleeful pleasure every morning in refuting the Viennese quack by recalling and explaining the details of my dreams without using one single reference to sexual symbols or mythical complexes.[13]

It may have been that picture of a daily duel with Freud that led me to write my letter to Nabokov. If it wasn't, it should have been.

In Nabokov's Defense

Non-Freudian Nabokovians have offered several explanations for his obsession with Freud. A popular one concerns Nabokov's position as a creative artist. Page Stegner provided the first detailed discussion along such lines, and it remains one of the most comprehensive. Among other things, Stegner described Nabokov as "a believer in the complete freedom of the imagination in art," and especially as a believer "that the artist is the possessor and not the possession of his visionary fancy":[14]

One can understand a strong reaction to the opinion that art is "substitute gratification" and that the artist and the neurotic are not very distinguishable. For Nabokov, structure, composition, precision of language and image are the basis of art: absolute control is primary in the creative process.[15]

Stegner (and others) also suggested that Nabokov had been engaged in a "self-protective bombardment of critics and criticism"—presumably a conscious strategy to forestall Freudian as well as more general criticism.[16] That bombardment was highly effective in fending off psychodynamic interpretations of Nabokov's work for many years. When it didn't fully succeed, Nabokov responded with roaring hostility even to mild and basically friendly attempts by scholars to discuss "Freudian" symbolism in his work.[17] Perhaps even more effective were his repeated warnings that he had planted fake Freudianisms in undisclosed places, ready to make fools of unwary interpreters: "The attractively shaped object or Wienerschnitzel dream that the eager Freudian may think he distinguishes in the remoteness of my wastes will turn out to be on closer inspection a derisive mirage organized by my agents."[18]

Only well after Nabokov's death have a few psychoanalytically oriented literary scholars and literature-oriented psychoanalytic scholars stirred from their bomb shelters.[19] Most critics have remained content to restate Nabokov's own professed reasons for his anti-Freudianism, rather than exploring the issue further. For instance, Vladimir Alexandrov recently wrote that "Nabokov's famous attacks on Freud . . . are authentic instances of repugnance based on a loathing for facile generalizations, which, moreover, are unrelated to his own experiences."[20]

Narcissism and the Preservation of Personal Identity

A "loathing for facile generalizations," a belief in "the complete freedom of the imagination in art," a conscious strategy of "self-protective bombardment"—these all sound like good reasons for a writer to criticize reductive Freudian interpretations of his or her writing. Lots of writers have criticized Freud for just those reasons. But they didn't strike me as *sufficient* reasons for Nabokov's insistent hostility toward Freud. Nabokov's obsession, like Nabokov's writing, was a very special thing, not readily explainable by such "facile generalizations." Few if any other artists have attacked Freud and Freudianism with the frequency, passion, or persistence of Nabokov. What, then, made Nabokov so unusual in this regard?

Let's turn to Freud himself here—not to one of his standard constructs that so angered Nabokov, but to a phenomenon that Freud called the "narcissism of minor differences." He never fully developed this concept, but he returned to it on several occasions over two decades. At times, Freud discussed it in individual terms:

Crawley, in language which differs only slightly from the current terminology of psycho-analysis, declares that each individual is separated from the others by a "taboo of personal isolation," and that it is precisely the minor differences in people who are otherwise alike that form the basis of feelings of strangeness and hostility between them. It would be tempting to pursue this idea and to derive from this "narcissism of minor differences" the hostility which in every human relation we see fighting successfully against feelings of fellowship and overpowering the commandment that all men should love one another.[21]

More often, Freud applied the concept to groups:

[I]t is precisely communities with adjoining territories, and related to each other in other ways as well, who are engaged in constant feuds and in ridiculing each other—like the Spaniards and Portuguese, for instance, the North Germans and South Germans, the English and Scotch, and so on. I gave this phenomenon the name of "the narcissism of minor differences," a name which does not do much to explain it. We can now see that it is a convenient and relatively harmless satisfaction of the inclination to aggression, by means of which cohesion between the members of the community is made easier.[22]

Freud's explanations for the "narcissism of minor differences" appear to have anticipated and then to have drawn upon his concept of the death instinct. But those explanations remain lacking in conceptual clarity: why *should* the Spaniards especially dislike the Portuguese, when they have so many more differences to dislike in the Chinese or the Finns? A vaguely implied but never explicit element in Freud's explanations is the concept of identity—either group identity or personal identity, depending on the level at which the concept is being applied. To maintain your identity, it may prove more useful to draw clear lines between yourself and rather similar individuals than between yourself and very different ones.

By means not explained in his autobiography or elsewhere, the young novelist Vladimir Nabokov developed a theory of personality that was remarkably similar in many ways to Freud's psychoanalytic theory. Even when we omit a considerable number of more-or-less blatant examples of psychoanalytic phenomena in Nabokov's work (presumably put there to trap the unwary Freudian), we can find many instances, important to plot or characterization or both, where he's operating on assumptions much like Freud's. Nabokov's fiction often includes dreams and slips of tongue that express a character's repressed or suppressed motives. Nabokov's characters repeatedly express their sexual desires symbolically. Sometimes they do it intentionally; at other times they appear unaware of what they're doing. Quite separately from Nabokov's burlesques of Freudianism, his fiction incorporates multiple expressions of childhood sexuality, sublimation, oedipal and other incestual urges, desires for a return to the womb, paranoia as an alternative expression of homosexual motives—all familiar stuff to the devoted reader of Nabokov, and even more familiar to the devoted reader of Sigmund Freud.

Neither Nabokov's intellectual understanding of these phenomena nor his emotional reactions to them were identical to Freud's. But given Nabokov's intense desire to be a unique and original creative artist, the similarities were apparently too close for his psychological comfort. According to Jane Grayson, several Russian émigré critics in the 1930s criticized the young novelist "for an overindulgence in psychoanalysis. . . . Nabokov's reaction to this criticism was not to change his approach, but to make his parodies of Freud more telling and more blatant, and set more traps for the unwary reader."[23] Sometimes in his later novels and self-translations from the Russian, Nabokov appears spontaneously to have chosen a sexual symbol or other figure of speech, which at second glance appeared to him too Freudian (for example, gun as penis). He then exaggerated the symbolism or followed it with an anti-Freudian joke. That way he could have his trope and beat it too. I haven't come across any direct evidence of this process, since most of Nabokov's draft manuscripts have been locked away in severely restricted archives. But his continued use of personality constructs similar to Freud's throughout his writing career, in concert with his increasingly vituperative attacks on Freudianism, nicely fits my identity-maintenance version of the narcissism of minor differences. Nabokov didn't hate Freud because their basic concepts of human nature were so radically opposed; he hated Freud because they were so much alike.

Cloud, Castle, Claustrum

But how can we be sure that any apparently Freudian element in Nabokov's writing is not just another of those "traps for the unwary reader"? Obviously we have to step very carefully, not only to avoid the land mines but to catch the authentic flora and fauna of Nabokov's imagination by surprise. In such works as *Lolita* and *Pale Fire,* we are clearly warned that the protagonist is both crazy (i.e., not a reliable narrator) and intent on misleading the psychological observer—so those are probably not the best places to start in finding evidence of Nabokov's genuine perceptions of the human condition.

I decided instead to look at one of my favorite short stories, "Cloud, Castle, Lake." According to Nabokov's most reliable biographer, this story "always remained one of Nabokov's favorites" as well.[24] It was the first story Nabokov translated into English from his Russian work when he moved to America. I wasn't sure what I might find in the story when I began looking at it closely. It seemed to include some deliberately planted Freudiana, but its protagonist wasn't crazy like Humbert Humbert; he was a sympathetic character, and his psychological pain was treated seriously throughout the story. His motives were not altogether clear; they were derided by other characters, but not by the author. Best of all from my perspective as a psychobiographer, the story seemed sufficiently mysterious in certain of its elements to call for a psychological, and maybe even a psychobiographical, interpretation.

Nabokov was particularly contemptuous of Freud's interest in infantile sexuality. Early in his autobiography he derided the "vulgar, shabby, fundamentally medieval world of Freud, with its crankish quest for sexual symbols . . . and its bitter little embryos spying, from their natural nooks, upon the love life of their parents."[25] To my surprise, I found in "Cloud, Castle, Lake" not only more Freudian sexual symbols than Nabokov would ever have been willing to acknowledge, but what seemed to be a symbolic depiction of an embryo's separation from its natural nook. And when I looked at the available information on Nabokov's life at the time he wrote the story, I found good psychobiographical reasons for the presence of that fetal imagery in that particular piece of fiction. Nabokov had undergone several simultaneous life crises that got expressed, projected outward, and placed under esthetic control, all in one ten-page story.

Nabokov wrote "Cloud, Castle, Lake" in 1937 and translated it into English four years later.[26] The story's protagonist is a "modest, mild bachelor" named Vasili Ivanovich, a Russian émigré who lives in Berlin. He wins a "pleasure trip" at an émigré charity ball, and reluctantly embarks on a railway excursion with nine Germans. Though Vasili prefers to read a book of Russian poetry, the Germans insist that he join the group in singing hearty songs and playing games. He suffers their teasing in silence, until they arrive at a lake in a forest. Vasili is overwhelmed by the sight of the lake, which reflects a large cloud, and beyond it "an ancient black castle." He feels that he has suddenly discovered happiness. He goes on alone, finds a "kind of inn" on the lake shore, and decides to stay there for the rest of his life. When he returns to tell the Germans of his decision, they call him a "drunken swine" and insist that he return to Berlin with them. They beat and torture him on the trip back. In Berlin he resigns from his job, telling his employer (the narrator) "that he could not continue, that he had not the strength to belong to mankind any longer." In the story's final words the employer says, "Of course, I let him go."

The meaning of the story has appeared obvious to various commentators. To Andrew Field, it "is quite indisputably a fable or allegory stressing the primacy of memory and individuality over social coercion."[27] Similarly, Douglas Fowler regards it as "Nabokov's essential social parable. . . . There can be no interaction between the individual and the group except on a grossly destructive level; the possibilities that either of them will learn and change are simply nonexistent."[28] Some have read the story more specifically as depicting the destruction of a cultured Russian émigré by crude German Nazis, though Nabokov himself expressed concern about such a narrow interpretation and stated that "really it could have happened in other countries too."[29] Brian Boyd is wisely reluctant to choose among several possibilities:

> The story can be read in many ways: as a damning verdict on the German spirit that could opt for Hitler, as a specific critique of the Nazi program of Strength through Joy, as a study in universal philistinism, as a contrast between the desire to be happy in one's own way and the cruelty of imposing one's conception of unhappiness on others, as a tribute to a world predisposed for happiness and a lament for a world nevertheless condemned by history to so much unhappiness.[30]

The story clearly does involve matters of conflict between a sensitive individual and an insensitive social collective, no matter what the nationality of the characters. But many of the story's details—particularly the central vision of the lake setting, as well as Vasili's powerful reactions to this scene—are only partly accounted for by such interpretations. Some of the scenery and much of the emotional nuance involved in Vasili's placing of "memory and individuality over social coercion" resemble Nabokov's autobiographical descriptions of his longing to return to the remembered Russia of his childhood and adolescence. But why the specific imagery of cloud, castle, and lake, with the associated inn, which don't appear to resemble any part of Nabokov's lost estate in Russia? Why the particular sequence of physical tortures as Vasili is forced to return to Berlin? Why various other peculiar details in the story?

These details make better sense if we consider the story on two levels: first, Nabokov's conscious contrasts between an exiled Russian who yearns to return to his homeland and the brutal Germans who force him to remain in his place of exile; second, Nabokov's apparently unconscious depictions of a maternal figure, a symbolic return to the womb, and a forcible expulsion from the womb. I say "unconscious" because although Nabokov may deliberately have worked two or three exaggerated Freudian symbols into the story, there's no evidence that the story's womb-related imagery was intended as such or that Nabokov recognized it explicitly.

Nabokov does distance himself somewhat from Vasili, both by having a narrator tell the story in an (at times) absent-minded tone and by indicating that not even the narrator directly represents the author. But Vasili's desires, emotions, and experiences are treated sympathetically and seriously. They are not ridiculed, as they would have been had Nabokov intentionally constructed the story to cast aspersions on Freudian or other birth-trauma theories. Furthermore, Nabokov's life at the time was such that fetal and birth imagery would have been quite salient to him, at least partly in anxiety-provoking ways. Finally, other works written by Nabokov during the same period contain similar images, which he neither unmasked later (as he often did with his deliberately planted "Freudian" clues) nor exaggerated to the point of parody.

Claustral Imagery

Sigmund Freud didn't really write much about people wanting to return to the womb. Otto Rank, one of Freud's favorite pupils (for a while), wrote a good deal more about the "trauma of birth." Henry Murray borrowed eclectically from Freud, Rank, and others to suggest a *claustral stage* of personality development before birth. (The word *claustrum* is Latin for an enclosed place, cloister, or womb.) Murray recognized that such a stage, if it existed, would be difficult or impossible to study, but he noted that claustral or womb-related images often appear in dreams and fantasies. These images include enclosures of various sorts as well as representations of the mother, who "furnished the original claustrum. . . . Her embracing arms, her skirts and her protecting peaceful presence may function as a claustrum."[31] Murray thought it possible that such womb-related imagery derives ultimately from actual fetal experiences. But in discussing the psychological significance of such symbols, Murray noted:

> It is not necessary to affirm that the child wants in any literal sense to enter the mother, for if, as supposed, the womb was for him an agreeable place it must have satisfied certain prevailing needs, and after birth there are other places which may just as well or better satisfy these needs when they recur.[32]

Signs of such claustral concerns begin early in the story "Cloud, Castle, Lake." The night before his departure, Vasili begins "to imagine that this trip, thrust upon him by a feminine Fate in a low-cut gown, this trip which he had accepted so reluctantly, would bring him some wonderful, tremulous happiness." The "feminine Fate in a low-cut gown" may refer to the person at the ball who had sold Vasili the prize ticket or awarded him the prize, but the phrase is also suggestive of both maternal and sexual qualities. (Freud on several occasions identified mythic images of Fate as maternal in nature; the "low-cut gown" would reveal breasts with both maternal and sexual significance.) That suggestion is strengthened by Nabokov's description of the "tremulous happiness" Vasili now anticipates, which "would have something in common with his childhood . . . and with that lady, another man's wife, whom he had hopelessly loved for seven years."[33] We learn nothing more about "that lady." But her contiguity to mention of Vasili's childhood would suggest, to the observant Freudian, an oedipal relationship in which the other man's wife is Vasili's mother.

As the train trip commences, Vasili experiences fleeting impressions of the countryside:

The blue dampness of a ravine. A memory of love, disguised as a mead-ow. . . . the anonymity of all the parts of a landscape, so dangerous for the soul, the impossibility of ever finding out where that path you see leads—and look, what a tempting thicket! It happened that on a distant slope or in a gap in the trees there would appear . . . a spot so enchanting—a lawn, a terrace—such perfect expression of tender well-meaning beauty—that it seemed that if one could stop the train and go thither, forever, to you, my love . . . But a thousand beech trunks were already madly leaping by, whirling in a sizzling sun pool, and again the chance for happiness was gone.[34]

This passage so thoroughly blends elements of half-remembered landscape, sensual temptation, and lost love that it could be a textbook example of Freud's pronouncements about landscapes as dream symbols for the female body. For instance, Freud wrote:

It is quite common to dream of a landscape and have the feeling that one has been there before. This landscape is always the maternal genitals, which is undoubtedly the place of which one can say with the greatest certainty that one has been there before, because otherwise one would not be alive.[35]

Nabokov's story proceeds through other imagery that appears more crudely sexual. Vasili contemplates a "configuration of some entirely insignificant objects —a smear on the platform, a cherry stone, a cigarette butt"—a configuration which might be taken to symbolize heterosexual intercourse, but which also prefigures the later pattern of cloud, lake, and castle (in the same sequence as the terms in the original Russian title rather than the English version). The Germans sing, in further phallic and vulval symbolism, "Take a knotted stick and rise. . . . Tramp your country's grass and stubble." They make fun of Vasili's "favorite cucumber" and throw it out the window. After that castrative act, and "In view of the insufficiency of his contribution" to their common provisions, they give him "a smaller portion of sausage." This whole sequence of images and events, espe-cially the cucumber-and-sausage wordplay, may be Nabokov's idea of a Freudian —or anti-Freudian—joke. So may the instance of Vasili being "forced to eat a cigarette butt" after he loses repeatedly at a mildly sexual game.

Then, however, Vasili encounters the moment when "that very happiness of which he had once half dreamed was suddenly discovered." An extraordinary passage describes his first sight of the lake in the woods:

It was a pure, blue lake, with an unusual expression of its water. In the middle, a large cloud was reflected in its entirety. On the other side, on a hill thickly covered with verdure (and the darker the verdure, the more poetic it is), towered, arising from dactyl to dactyl, an ancient black castle. Of course, there are plenty of such views in Central Europe, but just this one—in the inexpressible and unique harmoniousness of its three principal parts, in its smile, in some mysterious innocence it had, my love! my obedient one!—was something so unique, and so familiar, and so long-promised, and it so *understood* the beholder that Vasili Ivanovich even pressed his hand to his heart, as if to see whether his heart was there in order to give it away.[36]

What are we to make of this new blend of familiar landscape, rediscovered love, and "mysterious innocence"? Well, the hill covered with thick dark verdure, the "so familiar, and so long promised" view, and furthermore the landscape that "so understood the beholder," all sound more than ever like Freudian symbolism for aspects of the mother's body. Lakes and other bodies of water, as Freud also suggested, commonly connote "intrauterine life" in dream imagery.[37] Here we even have a lake that contains in its middle a reflection of an entire cloud—neat symbolism for the fetus in the womb. And towering over all is the ancient black castle—what does that represent? An eager Freudian might well espy the paternal phallus. Even those less eager or less Freudian might perceive something phallic, if they knew that in Nabokov's original Russian the story's title and text refer to the castle with the word *bashnya*. *Bashnya* is commonly translated into English as "tower"; it means "castle" mainly in the single-towered (and thus phallic) sense of the chesspiece.

Vasili continues on to the "kind of inn" beside the lake—a building openly anthropomorphized by Nabokov, who describes it as "a piebald two-storied dwelling with a winking window beneath a convex tiled eyelid." The owner, "a tall old man vaguely resembling a Russian war veteran," speaks German so poorly that Vasili switches to Russian, "but the man understood as in a dream and continued in the language of his environment, his family." At the old man's inn— a structure which in Freudian symbolism would also represent a female body, most likely the female parent's body—Vasili feels he has come home. Thus when he enters the upstairs "room for travelers" and immediately says, "You know I shall take it for the rest of my life," his response does not seem inappropriate. The room itself is described as

> most ordinary . . . but from the window one could clearly see the lake
> with its cloud and its castle, in a motionless and perfect correlation of
> happiness. Without reasoning, without considering, only entirely surren-
> dering to an attraction the truth of which consisted in its own strength, a
> strength which he had never experienced before, Vasili Ivanovich in one
> radiant second realized that here in this little room with that view, beau-
> tiful to the verge of tears, life would be at last what he had always
> wished it to be. What exactly it would be like, what would take place

here, that of course he did not know, but all around him were help, promise, and consolation—so that there could not be any doubt that he must live here.[38]

Thus Vasili has found his own consoling womb with a view, and that motionless view—cloud forever reflected in lake, castle forever on guard but *not* joining cloud in lake—perfectly displays the family relationship of fetus, mother, and father that will restore to him what he lost long ago.

Vasili rushes back to tell his unwanted companions, "I shall remain for good in that house over there. We can't travel together any longer. I shall go no farther. I am not going anywhere." But Nabokov knew what must ultimately happen to fetuses, and what always happens to people who try to return to the womb. As the trip leader tells Vasili, there is an "appointed itinerary. . . . There can be no question of anyone—in this case you—refusing to continue this communal journey. . . . Come, children, we are going on." Vasili wails in response as they seize him by the arms, "I have the right to remain where I want. Oh, but this is nothing less than an invitation to a beheading." The phrases "invitation to a beheading" and "they seized him by the arms" suggest that at this point in the story Vasili is beginning to experience a symbolic ejection from the womb. Indeed, a vivid description of that ejection through and out of the birth canal follows:

Swept along a forest road as in a hideous fairy tale, squeezed, twisted, Vasili Ivanovich could not even turn around, and only felt how the radiance behind his back receded, fractured by trees, and then it was no longer there, and all around the dark firs fretted but could not interfere.[39]

He is then beaten for a long time—viciously by the men, who use their "iron heels" like good Nazis, whereas "the women were satisfied to pinch and slap," as if indeed they were dealing with a newborn baby.

The story's final paragraph, in which Vasili begs his Berlin employer to let him go and "insisted that he could not continue, that he had not the strength to belong to mankind any longer," has been read by some as implying an ultimately happy ending. But one temporary return to the womb was all that Nabokov was willing to let Vasili enjoy, even in unacknowledged symbolism. Andrew Field says that "though one assumes he will go back to the perfect and dream-like lake, Nabokov has explained to me: 'He will never find it again.'"[40]

Life Circumstances

Nabokov incorporated additional instances of claustral imagery, further returns to and ejections from the womb, into other works. Those works include his two most important Russian novels, *Invitation to a Beheading* (written two years before

"Cloud, Castle, Lake") and *The Gift* (begun several years before but completed soon after the short story was written). Neither in these novels nor in any other stories, however, is the claustral imagery so concentrated and intense as in "Cloud, Castle, Lake." Why would Nabokov have written such a strongly claustral story at this particular time? And why did its theme apparently take such strong possession of him that neither then nor later did he recognize it for what it was, so that he could have revised it (as he seems to have done with other works) in order to hide or parody its distinctive Freudian symbolism?

"Cloud, Castle, Lake" was written in June 1937, at a crucial juncture in Nabokov's life. He had been living in Berlin since 1922. The Russian Revolution of 1917 had driven him from his homeland at age 19; he had then completed a degree at Oxford before moving to Germany. He had met and married his wife Véra, also a Russian émigré, in Berlin. He had developed his career as a poet and novelist in Berlin, writing in Russian and publishing in the émigré press. He had intentionally avoided mastering conversational German and had made almost no German friends. Instead, he lived in the closed world of Russian émigrés and developed an ever greater mastery of the Russian language and literature. He was fluent in French and had relatives and friends in the large Russian émigré community in Paris, but he avoided moving there for many years. According to his first cousin Nicolas Nabokov, "Moving to Paris would have exposed him to language temptations and contagions. In Germany he could remain a mum observer."[41]

However, it had become increasingly difficult for Nabokov to remain mum in Hitler's Germany. Véra was Jewish, and even if she had not been, the intensely anti-authoritarian Nabokov would have become ever more dismayed by Nazi outrages. An added danger was that one of the assassins of Nabokov's father had recently been appointed to a position in Hitler's government as second-in-command of émigré affairs.[42] Such circumstances led Nabokov later that year to characterize Germany as "a loathsome and terrifying country."[43] Furthermore, the Nabokovs' only child, born in 1934, was no longer a babe in arms and thus had become vulnerable to dangers that the adult Nabokovs might be able to resist. Of this period, Nabokov wrote in his autobiography that he and his wife

> did our best to encompass with vigilant tenderness the trustful tenderness of our child but were inevitably confronted by the fact that the filth left by hoodlums in a sandbox on a playground was the least serious of possible offenses, and that the horrors which former generations had mentally dismissed as anachronisms or things occurring only in remote khanates and mandarinates, were all around us.[44]

Nabokov wrote "Cloud, Castle, Lake" in Marienbad during one of a succession of brief residences outside Germany in 1937. As Russian émigrés, the Nabokovs

held only the problematic Nansen passports, which made it difficult and potentially dangerous to leave Germany except perhaps as tourists. From their month
in Marienbad the Nabokovs went to the French Riviera, after that to Paris, and
they never returned to Germany. But life in Paris was also grim, and the political
situation there deteriorated rapidly. Shortly before German troops entered the
city in 1940, the Nabokovs left for America.

Psychological Circumstances

Several aspects of Nabokov's life in 1937 may have predisposed him to experience
intense fantasies about a return to the womb. He perceived increasing threats to
himself and his loved ones from political circumstances in Germany, while recognizing that his main options for leaving Germany carried their own dangers. He
was particularly concerned with the effects of the situation on his small child,
with whom he strongly identified. Nabokov writes, for instance, of his "almost
couvade-like concern with our baby," then describes his empathic observations of
the child in rather claustral language:

> that swimming, sloping, elusive something about the dark-bluish tint of
> the iris which seemed still to retain the shadows it had absorbed of an-
> cient, fabulous forests . . . where, in some dappled depth, man's mind
> had been born; and, above all, an infant's first journey into the next di-
> mension, the newly established nexus between eye and reachable object
> . . . the mind's birth.[45]

In addition, shortly before their one-month stay in Marienbad, the Nabokovs
went to Prague to visit his mother for the last time before her death. This visit,
made specifically "to show our child to my mother,"[46] is likely to have re-aroused
in Nabokov memories and fantasies of his own early childhood. His son was then
at about the same age as Nabokov recalled having been when he realized that "I
was I and my parents were my parents," an event also described in claustral
terms:

> As if subjected to a second baptism . . . I felt myself plunged abruptly
> into a radiant and mobile medium that was none other than the pure el-
> ement of time. One shared it—just as excited bathers share shining
> seawater—with creatures that were not oneself but that were joined to
> one by time's common flow. . . . I see my diminutive self as celebrating,
> on that August day 1903, the birth of sentient life.[47]

Perhaps most important, Nabokov's departure from Germany under duress
repeated important aspects of his forced exile from Russia at age 19, which had
itself recapitulated in certain ways his loss of an intensely close relationship with
his mother when he was a small child. In leaving Russia, he had simultaneously

left a loved woman, his first sweetheart, whom he called "Tamara" in his auto-biography. "Thenceforth for several years . . . the loss of my country was equated for me with the loss of my love."[48] His homesickness for Russia became inti-mately associated with thoughts not only of Tamara but of his mother and of his lost childhood:

> Tamara, Russia, the wildwood grading into old gardens, my northern
> birches and firs, the sight of my mother getting down on her hands and
> knees to kiss the earth every time we came back to the country from
> town for the summer . . . these are things that fate one day bundled up
> pell-mell and tossed into the sea, completely severing me from my boy-hood.[49]

As he left Germany, Nabokov was not only leaving a long-established home again; he was also preparing again to leave a lover forever. She was a Russian exile named Irina, whom he had recently met in Paris. Nabokov's wife had just learned about the affair. He appears to have been determined to end it, but he did so reluctantly.[50]

"Cloud, Castle, Lake" combines these various elements into Vasili Ivanovich's discovery of a womblike paradise which he associates with memories of his childhood, memories of a longed-for but inaccessible woman, and memories of his lost homeland. Vasili's abrupt expulsion from this paradise suggests that whatever claustral fantasies Nabokov himself entertained at the time he wrote the story, he recognized at some level that even an imagined return to the womb could not last for long.

Furthermore, Nabokov's feelings about the sort of relationship symbolically represented by fetal imagery were not unalloyed. All children feel conflicted at times about issues of oneness with and separation from their parents. As a child Nabokov appears to have experienced such conflict to an unusual degree, partic-ularly with regard to his mother. She encouraged him to feel that she and he were very similar to each other psychologically, for instance in terms of sharing sensa-tions of "colored hearing" (synesthesia) and various kinds of extrasensory experi-ences:

> My numerous childhood illnesses brought my mother and me still closer
> together. . . . [I]n tussles with quinsy or scarlet fever, when I felt enor-mous spheres and huge numbers swell relentlessly in my aching brain
> . . . [b]eneath my delirium, she recognized sensations she had known
> herself, and her understanding would bring my expanding universe back
> to a Newtonian norm. . . . "Oh, yes," she would say as I mentioned this
> or that unusual sensation. "Yes, I know all that. . . ."[51]

Yet much of young Vladimir's contact with adults was not with his mother or with his often-absent father, but with servants. He lists eight tutors and twelve governesses in the index of his autobiography, and the list is incomplete. Nabokov as a child established warm relationships with some of these individuals, but their tenure was usually rather brief.

His conflicted feelings about this alternating closeness to and distance from his mother were expressed in several ways. As a small child, for instance, he developed a game involving a large divan:

> With the help of some grown-up person . . . the divan would be moved several inches away from the wall, so as to form a narrow passage which I would be further helped to roof snugly with the divan's bolsters and close up at the ends with a couple of its cushions. I then had the fantastic pleasure of creeping through that pitch-dark tunnel . . . and then, in a burst of delicious panic, on rapidly thudding hands and knees I would reach the tunnel's far end, push its cushion away, and be welcomed by a mesh of sunshine on the parquet. . . .[52]

This appears to have been a game of mastery over separation anxiety: the child returns to a claustral enclosure, enjoys it for a time, but eventually delights in bursting out into the world of light. Nabokov, anticipating such interpretations, announces, "It was the primordial cave (and not what Freudian mystics might suppose) that lay behind the games I played when I was four." But he provides no more support for his Jungian-mystical-archetypal hypothesis about the "primordial cave" than he does for the explanation presumably favored by "Freudian mystics."

Nabokov's later contemplations of death often involved similar language. He depicted normal existence as a restrictive fetal state that will be ended by bursting into a new and unknowable freedom. In the first paragraphs of his autobiography, he explicitly linked death and pre-birth existence as states to be both sought and feared:

> The cradle rocks above an abyss, and common sense tells us that our existence is but a brief crack of light between two eternities of darkness. . . . I know . . . of a young chronophobiac who experienced something like panic when looking for the first time at homemade movies that had been taken a few weeks before his birth. . . . [W]hat particularly frightened him was the sight of a brand-new baby carriage standing there on the porch, with the smug, encroaching air of a coffin. . . . Over and over again, my mind has made colossal efforts to distinguish the faintest of personal glimmers in the impersonal darkness on both sides of my life. That this darkness is caused merely by the walls of time separating me and my bruised fists from the free world of timelessness is a belief I gladly share with the most gaudily painted savage. I have journeyed back in thought . . . to remote regions where I groped for some

secret outlet only to discover that the prison of time is spherical and without exits. . . . I have doffed my identity in order to pass for a conventional spook and steal into realms that existed before I was conceived.[53]

This is where Nabokov vigorously rejects "the vulgar, shabby, fundamentally medieval world of Freud" with its "bitter little embryos spying, from their natural nooks, upon the love life of their parents." But such an aggressively defensive statement only highlights Nabokov's strong tendency to think and write in claustral terms.

Any mastery over separation anxiety that little Vladimir may have developed through his games of birth appears to have been undermined by later events. One such event was his traumatic departure from Russia (which he describes in active birth terms: "I propelled myself out of Russia so vigorously, with such indignant force, that I have been rolling on and on ever since."[54]) Another such event was the assassination of his father by rightist émigrés when Nabokov was 23. Several passages in his autobiography, as well as similar passages in his fiction, powerfully describe his fear of separation from loved ones and of separation from Earth itself. (Again, in Freudian symbolism as in various mythologies, Earth is equated with the mother's body.) For example:

> Something impels me to measure the consciousness of my love [for a person] against such unimaginable and incalculable things as the behavior of nebulae (whose very remoteness seems a form of insanity), the dreadful pitfalls of eternity, the unknowledgeable beyond the unknown, the helplessness, the cold, the sickening involutions and interpenetrations of space and time. . . . It cannot be helped; I must know where I stand, where you [his wife] and my son stand. When that slow-motion, silent explosion of love takes place in me, unfolding its melting fringes and overwhelming me with the sense of something much vaster, much more enduring and powerful than the accumulation of matter or energy in any imaginable cosmos, then my mind cannot but pinch itself to see if it is really awake. I have to make a rapid inventory of the universe. . . . I have to have all space and all time participate in my emotion, in my mortal love, so that the edge of its mortality is taken off, thus helping me to fight the utter degradation, ridicule, and horror of having developed an infinity of sensation and thought within a finite existence.[55]

Nabokov may well have exaggerated these feelings for literary purposes, especially in his fiction. Nonetheless, it appears that circumstances in his life history led to strong feelings of separation anxiety which continued throughout his life.

Claustral Complexes

At about the time that Nabokov wrote "Cloud, Castle, Lake," Henry Murray was putting the finishing touches on his masterwork, *Explorations in Personality*. Inspired in large part by Freud and Jung, Murray named and first studied empirically a number of psychodynamic constructs, including the *claustral complexes*:

> . . . all complexes that might conceivably be derived from the pre-natal period or from the trauma of birth. The following may be distinguished: 1, a complex constellated about the wish to reinstate the conditions similar to those prevailing before birth; 2, a complex that centers about the anxiety of insupport and helplessness; and 3, a complex that is anxiously directed against suffocation and confinement (anti-claustral tendency).[56]

As Murray further noted, "Various interesting combinations of the three claustral complexes may be found."

Not much use has been made by other psychologists of Murray's characterization of claustral complexes. But Vladimir Nabokov could be presented as a casebook example of all three. First, he displayed many of the characteristics listed for the *simple claustral complex*, which according to Murray "seems to be organized by an unconscious drive to re-experience the state of being that existed before birth." "Cloud, Castle, Lake" provides numerous instances of characteristics associated with the simple claustral complex, especially the key one, "cathection of claustra"—strong emotional investment in claustral enclosures. Murray sounds as though he's describing that particular short story when he lists the sorts of claustra that may be cathected: "a room of one's own . . . a home off the beaten track . . . a castle . . . islands , enclosed valleys, and certain versions of paradise. . . . The subject gets a fixation on his habitation or sanctuary and hates to leave it or to move to another house."[57] Other characteristics described by Murray and exhibited in the story include "Cathection of nurturant objects (mother)," needs for seclusion and for succorance (wanting to be taken care of), cathection of the past, and cathection of death. The simple claustral complex may also include thoughts "that 'death's bright angel' will bring a happy release from the coils of this mortal life."[58] Such thoughts appear to be expressed by the story's final sentences, as well as by many of Nabokov's personal pronouncements about death.

In his autobiography and in fictional works other than "Cloud, Castle, Lake" Nabokov also exhibited certain features of the second claustral complex, the *insupport complex*. This complex "is constituted by a basic insecurity or anxiety of helplessness,"[59] presumably associated with anxieties about leaving the mother's body. In particular, Nabokov described powerful anxieties connected with open space—not *all* open space (as seems to have been the case with Isaac Asimov), but enough to qualify him as suffering from some degree of agoraphobia, one of the main fears in the insupport complex. (It may be noted that in "Cloud, Castle, Lake," the cloud as seen by Vasili was always safely enclosed in the lake rather than floating in the open sky.)

The third claustral complex, named by Murray the *egression complex*, involves feelings associated with active attempts to separate from the mother's body. As Murray suggests, even the presumably ideal environment of the womb becomes a confining space as the fetus develops—a space from which the fetus may eventually yearn to escape. Furthermore, the stresses of the birth process may leave the child with strong desires for autonomy and for "a re-enaction of the birth trauma in order to master the anxiety associated with it."[60] (Lloyd deMause's discussion of "fetal psychology" develops similar ideas in considerably more detail.[61]) Nabokov re-enacted such an escape to freedom in his childhood game with the divan. Repeated fictional re-enactments can be found, for instance, in Nabokov's 1935 novel *Invitation to a Beheading*, which is very much concerned with issues of autonomy.[62]

Nabokov would have regarded as ludicrous his placement in any of these claustral categories. Clearly, they fall far short of encompassing all facets of his highly complex personality and his creative achievements. Moreover, the display of claustral concerns by Nabokov's fictional characters does not necessarily mean that those concerns were consistently or strongly shared by Nabokov himself. Nonetheless, the claustral complexes do provide a basis for looking beyond the simplest Freudian characterizations of unconscious motives, to needs and fears that found frequent expression in Nabokov's fictional and nonfictional writing. He was never incapacitated by these complexes; indeed he used them creatively to fashion works of great intelligence and beauty. But "Cloud, Castle, Lake" and his other fiction suggest that he could not eliminate their influence, particularly during periods of intense personal stress.

Nabokov Contra SF

Nabokov often voiced his hostility not only toward Sigmund Freud but toward science fiction. (Interesting, isn't it, that the initials for both are SF? Who would have made more of that striking coincidence—Nabokov or Freud?) Nabokov enjoyed the science-fictional works of Robert Louis Stevenson and H. G. Wells, but he regarded modern SF as vulgar trash. When he wrote anything resembling SF himself—as he did on a number of occasions, ranging from short stories to plays to entire novels—he made sure to let the reader know that he was either sending up the genre or was really up to something altogether different from SF.

Here again, Nabokov appears to have been displaying the narcissism of minor differences, asserting his own identity by contrasting himself as sharply as possible with apparently similar individuals. "I am *not* that pipsqueak therapist

Freud," he was saying in words that Allport would have approved; "I am *not* one of those writers of lurid juvenile trash!" Indeed, Nabokov *was* a literary genius, as few SF writers are. That's obvious. What's not so obvious is why Nabokov needed to insist on his genius throughout his long life, to anyone who would listen.

There's a world of difference between Nabokov's coruscating literary brilliance and the plain English sentences of his fellow Russian émigré writer Isaac Asimov. But both Nabokov and Asimov used their fiction, their essays, and their encounters with interviewers and others to construct a public persona that asserted a kind of ideal identity. No self-doubts here, both Asimov and Nabokov often proclaimed; I'm an arrogant genius and I'm damned proud of it.

Thus Nabokov's writing served the expressive function well.[63] He also shared with Asimov the use of fiction as a psychological defense. Both men were agoraphobic and both acknowledged other kinds of anxieties in addition. Both wrote fiction in which their protagonists often were much worse off psychologically than they were, or in which the author was clearly in full control. Asimov rejected psychological analyses of his work, wanting to go on believing that he was perfectly happy regardless of what the work might reveal about him. Nabokov rejected Freud and Freudians, wanting to keep unsullied his memories of Mother Russia, Mother and Father Nabokov, and his golden childhood.

But Nabokov used his writing restitutively as well. In his late sixties he took the fractured pieces of his life in Mother Russia and Stepmother America, and blended them into a fantasied Amerussian homeland in which he set his last major novel, *Ada or Ardor*.[64] *Ada* is as much SF as Cordwainer Smith's *Norstrilia* is. Devising the alternative land of Amerussia may have done as much psychologically for Nabokov as devising an alternative life with the catwoman C'mell did for Smith.

Life in *Ada's* Amerussia is by no means perfect. Nabokov was quite aware of the imperfections both of Czarist Russia and of midcentury America. But *Ada* seems in many regards a mellower book than its immediate predecessors. At its end, a semi-fictional version of V. N. and a semi-fictional version of his wife Véra end their lives by fading into the pages of the novel as it is being written. Nabokov's fears of dissolution for himself and his loved ones were surely not at an end; the real end was yet to come. But he seems in *Ada's* final pages to have arrived at some degree of internal peace—a peace that Nabokov achieved without the intervention of that old meddler Sigmund Freud or any of his analytic agents.

PART FOUR

Beneath Politics

12

———————— ■ ————————

Carter and Character

PSYCHOBIOGRAPHY is largely a postdictive enterprise. It looks backward over the course of a person's life and tries to sort out why things happened as they did. That's usually hard enough; predicting the forward course of a single life is a far trickier business. Even predicting the average behavior patterns of a large group of individuals is often more than psychologists can manage. As Sigmund Freud noted at the end of his Leonardo book, the individual's personality constantly intersects with chance occurrences, in ways that set substantial "limits . . . to what psycho-analysis can achieve in the field of biography."[1] These limits apply to psychobiography in general, not just to psychoanalytic biography.

But one kind of psychobiography has been practiced largely as a predictive enterprise: studies of active politicians, especially U.S. presidential candidates. There are several reasons for the predictive focus here. First, the stakes are high. What wouldn't we give to know with greater confidence whether a candidate is likely to be a potential disaster for the country or a potential savior of democracy? Second, the psychobiographer may feel less constrained about doing research on a live subject if that subject is a politician. Politicians keep telling us that their "character" will make them brave and concerned and industrious presidents. Why shouldn't someone research their character to check out such claims? Third, there really is something to predict here. Trying to predict whether a young writer will eventually produce the Great American Novel, or whether a budding psychologist will become another Freud or Skinner, seems pretty silly. But predicting whether a presidential candidate will survive four years in office without committing an impeachable offense appears to be at least within the realm of possibility.

I first began to think about the possibility of predictive political psychobiography when I saw the infamous fifth issue of *Fact* magazine. That's the one that came out shortly before the 1964 Goldwater versus Johnson presidential election, with a cover announcing in big letters that Goldwater was "psychologically unfit to be president."[2] Inside, the magazine quoted at considerable length from individual responses to a mail survey of every psychiatrist in the American Medical Association. Less than twenty percent of the psychiatrists responded at all, and slightly less than half of those who responded agreed that Goldwater was indeed psychologically unfit to be president. But of those psychiatrists who did agree, quite a few were willing to make instant diagnoses on the basis of minimal biographical information about Goldwater: "I believe Goldwater has the same pathological make-up as Hitler, Castro, Stalin and other known schizophrenic leaders"; "I believe Goldwater to be suffering from a chronic psychosis . . . usually in remission but he is maintaining a rather marginal adjustment"; and so forth.

Such assessments were a throwback to the earliest days of psychiatric pathography, and worse. But I was intrigued by the possibility that the sort of thing being tried here might be done much better—not by a sensationalist publication like *Fact* and not by dogmatic diagnosticians like those early psychiatrists, but by serious scholars willing to look at a wide array of potential psychological flaws *and* strengths in major political candidates. It seemed obvious that the personalities of politicians significantly influence their behavior in office. Why not provide voters with expert information on the candidates' personalities before voting day? Why not, in other words, practice a kind of *applied political psychobiography*, usefully calling upon expert psychological and political knowledge at a time when it might count, instead of always doing postdictive analyses of former presidents' personalities?

The 1964 *Fact* magazine poll so tainted any approach resembling applied political psychobiography that nobody tried it in 1968—though voters could have used such information in deciding between Lyndon Johnson and Eugene McCarthy, or between Richard Nixon and Hubert Humphrey. When the first serious psychobiographical studies of an active presidential candidate were attempted in 1972, they were offered cautiously and without much publicity. Bruce Mazlish at first planned to withhold his study of Nixon until Nixon had left office, "in order to prevent misuse of our work for political purposes."[3] James David Barber really did want his work to be used for political purposes—at least for the voters' political purposes.[4] Nevertheless, Barber presented his interpretation of Nixon's personality and his predictions about Nixon's probable second-term behavior only at the end of a long and detailed study of earlier presidents that few voters were likely to read.

Mazlish identified a variety of themes in Nixon's psychological history as potential influences on his presidential behavior—too great a variety to generate any clear predictions. Barber made a fairly simple prediction: that Nixon would display increasing behavioral rigidity during a second term if he found himself backed into a corner with regard to his public presentation of self. The apparent confirmation of this prediction during the Watergate crisis encouraged others to try their hand at psychobiographical analysis in the next presidential campaign, when Jimmy Carter ran against Gerald Ford in 1976. Carter's sheer unfamiliarity to voters and journalists also encouraged such analysis. Ford was a known quantity, while Carter's sudden visibility raised many questions about his personality as well as his politics.

Before the 1976 campaign was over, virtually all the psychobiographical stops had been pulled. Bruce Mazlish and Edwin Diamond published a somewhat sensationalized magazine article on what they called Carter's "thrice-born personality," citing evidence from an incomplete psychobiographical study that they didn't publish in full until Carter's presidential term was nearly over.[5] Doris Kearns Goodwin published side-by-side analyses of Carter's and Ford's personalities in four mass-market women's magazines.[6] She displayed rather less caution and much less information in these brief studies than in her excellent earlier psychobiography of Lyndon Johnson—even though the two presidential candidates could have suffered serious political damage from her analyses, whereas Johnson had been dead for several years by the time her book about him was completed.

Both Mazlish and Goodwin did, however, have substantial previous experience in psychobiographical research, and their contributions to the election debate drew upon serious concepts about the political personality. The same was not the case for numerous journalistic attempts at quickie psychobiography during the 1976 campaign, usually aimed at Jimmy Carter. I began to hope that James David Barber would step in to provide a more thoughtful examination of Carter's personality, or Ford's, or both, since for the past four years Barber had been advocating predictive personality studies of major presidential candidates and telling other people how it should be done. Then I learned that Barber had agreed to refrain from publishing any detailed commentary on either candidate prior to the election, in exchange for permission to study the two campaigns up close.

At that point I began to work on my own small-scale psychobiographical analysis of Jimmy Carter. The election was less than three months away, so I didn't try to reach Carter's friends and relatives or to make an appointment with him on the campaign trail, as I might have if I'd started earlier. Instead, I pulled together the most reliable published sources about his life and personality, along with some less reliable but intriguing sources. I knew the time was too short to do a full-scale psychobiography, but I wanted to correct some of the errors I felt other attempts at psychobiography had fallen into on the basis of weak or inappropriately interpreted data.

Even that limited objective suffered from sheer time pressure. With only a few weeks left in the campaign by the time I wrote my article, I aimed it first at the *New York Times Magazine*, which presumably had a short publication lag. But Norman Mailer got there first, with a long and mystical piece about Carter's personality, Mailer's personality, and Mailer's visit to Plains, Georgia. Then I tried

Newsweek's "My Turn" page; they were booked up too. My article finally appeared in two daily newspapers: the Sacramento (California) *Bee* and the Paducah (Kentucky) *Sun-Democrat*. (My parents live near Paducah.) Oh, well—Carter carried Northern California and Western Kentucky, so maybe I did help to correct a few voters' mistaken impressions of his character.

As the only attempt I've made to do predictive psychobiography, this article is obviously an important historical document. (My parents think so, anyway.) It also illustrates certain problems inherent in applied political psychobiography, as well as certain strategies for dealing with those problems. Here's the article in full, uncorrected by hindsight, exactly as it was published nine days before the election.[7] Afterward I'll discuss the hindsight. The article's title was not mine; somebody at the Sacramento *Bee* supplied it along with a drawing of a bearded and lab-coated psychologist who's peering through a keyhole at Carter on a psychoanalytic couch. The artist seems to have been a bit uncertain about how psychologists do research, but maybe his drawing did capture certain essentials of the psychobiographical enterprise.

Where's the Catch in Carter's Character?

During the 1964 presidential campaign, *Fact* magazine set off a storm of protest by proclaiming, *"1,189 Psychiatrists Say Goldwater Is Psychologically Unfit to Be President!"* Psychiatric journals denounced instant distant diagnoses of nonpatients. Newspapers denounced any psychological diagnosis of active political candidates. Goldwater sued *Fact*, and collected $75,000.

During the 1976 presidential campaign, hundreds of journalists and at least a few behavioral scientists have offered semi-instant psychological diagnoses of Jimmy Carter, but hardly a peep of protest has been heard. Though no one has used terms like "psychologically unfit" or "divorced from reality," the effect of these diagnoses could be as bad for Carter as for Goldwater, seriously damaging his chances for the presidency.

We've come a long way since 1964. We've learned that candidates' personalities may be as serious and valid a voter concern as any policy issue—more valid, perhaps, because issue positions can be so easily abandoned later. We were taught that lesson on a bipartisan basis by Lyndon Johnson and Richard Nixon. We have been shown, by Doris Kearns on Johnson, by Bruce Mazlish on Nixon, and by James David Barber on a broad range of presidents, that careful personality studies may reveal things worth knowing about our leaders. Kearns, Mazlish, and Barber are all studying Carter's personality during this campaign.

Barber and Kearns are, in the interest of fairness, studying Ford as well, but hardly anyone else has paid serious attention to *his* psyche. Most people seem to feel they either know Ford pretty well already or that his personality is too bland to be worth probing.

Carter can't complain much about this unequal examination. From the beginning he has made his campaign primarily one of personality. First against his Democratic rivals and then against Ford, he has pounded away at two broad questions: Who is more worthy of trust? Who has greater qualities of leadership?

Both questions can be answered in part by looking at the candidates' past performances and their plans for future programs, but the questions go much further. Carter is asking us to judge who has the best personality for the presidency.

Carter has answered his own questions by stressing his virtues: High moral character, compassion for the downtrodden, conscientiousness, willingness to work hard in the service of his country. Carter's critics have shifted the ground to his actual or potential faults. Carter is of course more open about his virtues than his faults (though he has said more about the latter than some supporters would prefer, and in the heat of the campaign it's hard to gather honest information on either).

But rather than letting the personality issue go to Ford by default, through allowing speculations about Carter to remain unchallenged while Ford is hardly examined, it is worth reviewing the somewhat limited evidence we already have on the characteristics that worry people about Carter. The objective is not to strip bare his unconscious, but to see whether a strong case exists for the kinds of character flaws that ultimately ruined the Johnson and Nixon—and earlier the Wilson—presidencies. Material for deeper analysis will come later, if Carter wins.

Religiosity   This was probably the first worry that occurred to most people— not whether they agreed with Carter's specific religious beliefs (which differ little from those of many Americans, including several recent presidents), but whether his religious beliefs are so intense that they would bias his political decisions.

Carter is obviously more serious about his religion than most politicians: He prays often, even away from public view; he reads the Bible daily; he has spent considerable volunteer time on church work in ways that could not then have been seen as giving him any political mileage. But these activities do not imply religious fanaticism, as some non-Southerners assume.

Here stands perhaps the widest culture gap in the campaign. In the rural South, the church is still often the focus of one's intellectual, philosophical, and cultural as well as spiritual life. Questions of ultimate meaning and of individual identity are most easily couched in religious terms even when the answers are far from fundamentalist in nature.

Carter's frequent private prayers while in office seem to have functioned much as Jerry Brown's celebrated meditation sessions: As a way to reflect on past and impending decisions, as a means to ease the psychological pressures of public life and to regain some personal perspective. They did not serve state purposes as Nixon's prayer breakfasts did; indeed, Carter ended political prayer breakfasts when he moved into the Georgia governor's mansion.

He may, as he says, use his church's moral tenets as a foundation for his political decisions, but he does so at a rather abstract level. He has been publicly and privately unwilling to impose his specific moral tenets on others with regard to abortion, sex, amnesty. He may thereby gain political advantage in some instances ("Though I personally disapprove of _____, I will support the law upholding it"); but he has taken similar positions even when the net political effect was likely to be negative, as far back as his vote in the Georgia State Senate against the required worship of God.

A similar stance is apparent in his private relationships: For example, he seems never to have held it against Jody Powell, his press secretary, that Powell was expelled from the Air Force Academy for an honor-code violation, though Carter feels the military academies should maintain such codes.

Overcontrol   Carter often is assigned personality characteristics that appear mutually exclusive. For instance, while he is said to be too much bound up in the throes of Christian love, too moralistic, too holy-rollerishly emotional, he also is seen as too cold, calculating, hard, ruthless.

Personality works in curious ways and all these characteristics may be found in the same person, but they don't describe Carter very well. He has consciously stressed self-control in his life, as evidenced in his autobiography and elsewhere. At least one writer has attributed this to Carter's childhood need to navigate between two sharply different parents—much as Mazlish has attributed a similar pattern to Nixon, and Kearns to Johnson. Such a comparison is, at best, over-drawn. Self-control can serve many purposes and is essential to some degree for any rural Southern boy who wants to make his way in the world beyond the farm.

Wherever Carter's self-control comes from, it appears to resemble Johnson's much more than Nixon's in that it is offset to a substantial extent by compassion for the less well-controlled and the less fortunate. Carter may spend a good deal of time talking about his Georgia innovations of government reorganization and zero-based budgets, but his major accomplishments were in improving the state's mental health centers, prisons, day-care facilities, and other people-centered in-stitutions. When he talks about what government reorganization did for Georgia, his emphasis is on improving services, moving employees into useful and satisfy-ing roles, rather than saving money.

Power hunger   Carter has obviously sought power, as have all successful politicians. Some people therefore assume that power is his major motive. But if power were all he wanted, he would probably have stayed in the Navy and worked toward his initial aim, chief of naval operations. When he returned to Plains to run his father's farm, he could not have known he would one day be able to seek the nation's most powerful office.

In terms of the triumvirate of motives most often studied by psychological researchers today, Carter appears to be less concerned with power as such than with achievement and affiliation, which he usually (and often) talks about in terms of "competence" and "compassion."

Here our information on how Carter saw his parents as a child is rather clear: His father was high in competence, middling in compassion (Jimmy's "best friend" but a stern disciplinarian); his mother was high in both, as a nurse and at home. The combined weight of the parental models thus apparently tipped the scales toward competence in young Jimmy's character development. His entry into the Navy, with service under the tremendously competent but dispassionate Hyman Rickover, settled the matter for years.

Then Jimmy returned home to talk to his dying father and to others who knew his father, and discovered that all along his father had been secretly a very compassionate man: Canceling loans to people when they could not pay, buying graduation dresses for poor girls, silently augmenting the standard wage for black farmhands with gifts of food, money, medical care. The balance between competence and compassion was thereby so dramatically equalized for Carter that he quit the competence-oriented world of the submarine service and assumed his father's role in Plains.

Over the years, as Carter sought new outlets for his talents and found them in politics, his emphasis appears to have drifted back again toward achievement, toward competence. This drift may have been helped by his painful discovery that his kind of compassion, particularly when it included blacks, was not always welcome in Plains.

But his renewed stress on competence failed to win him the Georgia governorship on his first try. That defeat, as well as his sister Ruth's message of Christian compassion, once more restored the balance between the contending strains in his character.

Since then, competence and compassion appear to have maintained a creative tension within him. The first and last chapters of his book, *Why Not the Best?* (the title itself proclaiming Rickover's emphasis on competence), highlight the two qualities by expanding them to national concerns: "Can our government be honest, decent, open, fair, and compassionate? Can our government be competent?"

Carter has pointed to the absence of compassion in Ford; yet when asked by reporters about his own stress on love and compassion, he has pointedly reminded them of the importance of competence as well.

Active-negative type Political scientist James David Barber has given us a new term of condemnation for political candidates—three new terms, actually, since only the active-positives in his four-celled categorization of presidents have any likelihood of attaining greatness. Barber classifies presidents and candidates along two character dimensions: Active versus passive and positive versus negative. Nobody seems to doubt that Carter will be an active president, given his performance as governor and his announced intentions.

(Gerald Ford is another matter. Barber tentatively judged him as an active president after a few months in office, but a look at Ford's congressional record and at the rest of his presidency has raised doubts among other observers.)

Carter's position on the positive-negative dimension, however, is more open to debate. This dimension refers to how much a candidate really enjoys himself in office. The active-positive president throws himself into the job with vigor and delight, while the active-negative president compels himself to do unpleasant tasks from a sense of duty or of drivenness, a need to shore up his self-esteem: Wilson, Johnson, Nixon.

Carter's smile and his autobiography suggest he enjoys politics. But some writers contend his smile is mainly for public display, and since he apparently read Barber's book before writing the autobiography, he may have planted clues stressing his positive outlook.

Carter's religious pronouncements about sin and his admiration of Rickover suggest some element of duty-bound compulsion in his personality. But he left Rickover to move toward compassion, trust, love—positive emotions all—and if his religion is much like that of his parents, there's plenty of room for enjoyment of life and plenty of reasons to feel good, not guilty, about himself.

His self-esteem, despite temporary setbacks, seems always to have been far sturdier than Johnson's, Nixon's, or Wilson's. No doubt some competition between joy and duty remains in Carter's personality, paralleling the clash between compassion and competence. But Carter seems determined to give joy the edge— even if he has to work at it.

Indecisiveness   This criticism is now made mainly by opposing partisans and by people who have paid little attention to the Carter campaign. His stands on most major issues have become as firm and explicit as can reasonably be expected of a candidate not yet in office. In several instances they are unlikely to change easily because they derive from important aspects of his own background: His long experience with blacks, his observations of rural poverty, his personal knowledge of the frustrations Hyman Rickover encountered in dealing with military bureaucracy, his encounter with a dangerous nuclear meltdown.

Carter says he may seem ambiguous because his positions are often complex to befit complex issues, and this seems on the whole a fair statement. He does take the sophisticated debater's stance of stressing one facet of his position to one audience, another to another audience; that way he can feel honest while appealing to diverse views.

(Nixon typically used the less complicated and less principled debater's technique of simply switching his position to suit the audience or the times—flip-flopping, as it's known in this campaign.)

In only a few minor instances, some of them involving the temporary omission of qualifying statements, has Carter really presented different positions to different audiences. Wishy-washiness has not been one of his character traits at any time in his political life; from his early clashes with segregationists in Plains to his endorsement of amnesty for draft resisters before veterans' groups, he has held his ground on major issues, regardless of the forces opposing him.

Rigidity   Here again, Carter has been criticized for opposite qualities—some people worrying about his apparent indecisiveness, others concerned that he'll hold too fast to his own positions. The latter seems the more serious cause for worry.

Carter himself says he finds it hard to compromise on issues important to him. That is the principal sin of active-negative presidents. It laid Wilson and LBJ low, and in a peculiar way it was responsible for Nixon's political demise as well—he was never rigid for long on substantive issues, but he stonewalled to the end on Watergate. Carter at times during his governorship resisted compromise with his opponents; but how much must one compromise with Lester Maddox to show a lack of rigidity?

Carter in fact did compromise enough to get his major programs through a somewhat unsympathetic legislature, as he had compromised during his campaign in order to become governor and as he has compromised in other ways to become president. He has never shown the compulsive rigidity that Wilson displayed during his Princeton presidency or the League of Nations charter debate, or that Johnson showed during much of the Vietnam War—rigidity that permits no quarter to be given to one's evil opponents.

Carter appears to possess a realistic view of political necessities; he has shown more concern for getting good programs passed than for maintaining ideological purity or personal freedom from sin. He has lusted after political success, and he knows that God forgives compromise in a worthy cause.

The key consideration about Carter's tendencies toward rigidity or other negative traits is that he is open to improvement. He admits to problems with compromise, but he knows what happened to Wilson, Johnson, Nixon, and why. He has read Barber and Kearns and others on the presidency, and seems to have understood their messages. He devotes a good deal of time—during prayers and otherwise—to self-examination, whereas Nixon and Johnson shrank from it.

Carter has gathered around him in this campaign advisers with many viewpoints; how he responds to their advice is known only to him, but at least he has not limited his staff to yes-men and mindguards.

Carter's personality is well short of being perfect. It is a measure of our lingering fear, born of our having been burned so badly by past presidential imperfections, that we look for perfection and are distressed not to find it.

But Carter's personality does appear solid enough for a fairly safe gamble, and promising enough to be a plus rather than a minus when voters make their final decisions.

That said, we can now turn back to choosing our next president mainly in terms of the problems still facing the nation and the candidates' plans for coping with them.

Problems in Predictive Political Psychobiography

Back to the present. Speaking from the experience of writing "Where's the Catch in Carter's Character?" I can say that studying candidates during a political campaign doesn't present any really new problems. There are lots of problems, but they're just heightened versions of the problems psychobiographers are likely to encounter at any time. They include such matters as obtaining relevant and unbiased data, controlling one's own interpretive biases, avoiding overinterpretation, and developing sufficient context for the understanding of otherwise isolated material. These problems are intensified by the brevity of a presidential campaign and by the size of the political stakes involved, but they aren't different in principle from the difficulties faced by the current-day psychobiographer of Thomas Jefferson or Woodrow Wilson. They do take occasional odd turns, however, as further consideration of the Carter case will illustrate.

Obtaining relevant and unbiased data   As I observed in Chapter 2, it's a lot easier to write a decent psychobiography if one or more good standard biographies of the subject are already available. The psychobiographer will be much better able to pursue major and minor psychological themes if someone else has already taken the trouble to locate and organize a large part of the subject's life record. Here the psychobiographer of Wilson or Jefferson clearly does have a considerable advantage over the psychobiographer of a newly visible political candidate. There'll be multi-volume biographies in print of the earlier figures, along with neatly organized books of letters and other archival materials. Lacking such biographical foundations, a researcher who starts to dig for data only at the time of a candidate's nomination will find the task of winnowing through masses of archival data in any responsible fashion—or even *finding* the right kinds of data, during a hot political campaign—to be nearly overwhelming. Nobody tried during Campaign '76 to review carefully what the Georgia newspapers had said about Carter as governor several years earlier. That information might have provided a good basis for assessing his patterns of interaction with supporters and opponents, as well as his usual modes of approach to controversial issues. It took Betty Glad four years to work through such material, in preparation for a book to be published during Carter's *second* presidential campaign.

Jimmy Carter's own account of his life and his politics, *Why Not the Best?*, was published just before his first campaign for president got into full swing.[8] The book bore certain similarities to Richard Nixon's *Six Crises,* which first appeared during another political campaign—though Nixon's book didn't open with quotations from Reinhold Niebuhr, Bob Dylan, and Dylan Thomas. Books such as these can be quite useful to psychobiographers; indeed, much of the material published on Carter's life and personality during the 1976 campaign was lifted almost verbatim from *Why Not the Best?* But a campaign autobiography must be viewed with even greater caution than an ordinary autobiography. Successful politicians are by definition experts at impression management, and a well-planned autobiography can provide more room for presentation of the right impressions than any other medium available to a candidate. Even a relatively honest autobiographical account (as Carter's seems to be) will be heavily filtered through the candidate's own self-esteem maintenance system.

Similar cautions apply to interviews granted to would-be psychobiographers by the candidates, their relatives, and their friends during the heat of the campaign. Those people know they have a lot riding on the right answers, and it doesn't take much psychological sophistication to figure out what most of the right answers are. By the time Carter had the nomination in hand, his fellow residents in Plains had been so often approached by television and newspaper reporters, magazine writers, and academics that they had developed a set of standard responses, including anecdotes about Carter's early life, that revealed more about the townspeople's desire to see one of their own as president than about Carter's personality. The usual one or two Defenders of the Faith had multiplied; now there were hundreds, if not thousands.

The problem of impression management is compounded when you're dealing with a candidate such as Jimmy Carter, who showed a good deal more psychological sophistication than many of the people studying him. As I indicated in my newspaper article, he had carefully read James David Barber's psychobiographical book *The Presidential Character* before he started his campaign. Therefore Carter knew that an active-positive president is the best of the four types in Barber's conceptual scheme. He also knew that an active-positive candidate is supposed to say certain kinds of things about politics and the presidency, such as that he's going to work hard and be innovative, but also that he's going to enjoy the job a lot. As I suggested in my article, Carter often seemed a mix of positive and negative, of "joy and duty," in his attitudes toward political office. But parts of *Why Not the Best?* sound as though they were deliberately written to impress Barber and other researchers with Carter's credentials as an active-positive candidate. Consider this passage, for instance:

> As Governor of Georgia I had completed the most critical and demand-
> ing portion of my term, but there were hundreds of administrative duties
> which I enjoyed and which I had to perform.[9]

Maybe I'm too suspicious, but I'd like to see the original draft of that sentence. It sounds as though Carter wrote everything else first and then added the phrase "which I enjoyed," to make sure Barber wouldn't stick him in the active-negative pigeonhole along with Richard Nixon.[10]

Psychobiographer bias   In addition to detecting and correcting for the candidate's self-protective efforts, the psychobiographer must remain vigilant about his or her own self-serving impulses. Do you want an inside job at the White House after the election, like historian Arthur Schlesinger, Jr. got from John Kennedy after writing *Kennedy or Nixon: Does It Make Any Difference?* Do you want to save the nation from the historical shame of a Dan Quayle presidency? Or do you just want to nudge your favored candidate a little closer to electoral victory? Whatever the lures, the political psychobiographer may find it hard to resist being overly indulgent toward one candidate or overly harsh toward others. I suggested earlier that psychobiographers should choose subjects about whom they feel considerable ambivalence, a mixture of approval and disapproval strong enough to keep them honest in their examination of data. That rule is especially applicable to work on political candidates, where partisan loyalties or ideological convictions may also be involved.

However, I don't think the psychobiographer's published conclusions about the candidates need be absolutely even-handed. One candidate may after careful consideration appear to be more temperamentally suited for the presidency, or quite unsuited. If that conclusion can be supported by reference to observed behavior and other data, the public should be so informed. A major drawback of Doris Kearns Goodwin's analyses of Ford and Carter during the 1976 campaign was that she seemed to feel obligated to arrive at the same number of merits and demerits for each man—rather like those pseudo-objective television documentaries that spend half the time telling us how the destruction of the ozone layer threatens the survival of humanity, and the other half telling us how less ozone will help us get faster suntans. Goodwin's concluding remarks convey the flavor of her entire analysis:

> The outlines of a Carter Presidency are necessarily vague. We know the limits and strengths of a President Ford. . . . But whether the choice of Carter represents a spirit of adventure or of recklessness, an effort at restoration or toward radical advance, conservative tranquillity or willed turbulence—this we cannot know for sure. The choice on our 200th anniversary is whether we are comfortable with what we already have or whether we are willing to exercise a leap of faith into the unknown, with all the hazards and all the great possibilities such a leap implies.[11]

Perhaps Goodwin wouldn't have gotten her evaluation of the candidates published simultaneously by the *Ladies' Home Journal, Redbook, American Home,* and *womenSports Magazine* if she'd been less wishy-washy. But I'm not sure it was worth publishing that kind of bland, exactly balanced analysis at all.

Psychobiographers can aim for fairness in other ways. First, they should conscientiously gather all the personality-related information they can locate on a candidate before reaching firm conclusions. As in any psychobiographical research, they should attempt to gather the data without prescreening it to support certain favorite hypotheses. Second, they should present to the public the essential data on which they are relying most heavily for their conclusions. If possible, they should publicly identify these data early enough for other researchers to dispute either the data or the conclusions drawn from them. Third, psychobiographers should make clear that the conclusions they are qualified to offer are of a specified degree of tentativeness and deal only with the candidates' personalities, not with substantive policy issues, which for some voters or in some campaigns may remain more important than personalities. In my Sacramento *Bee* article I tried to indicate my level of tentativeness both at the beginning and at the end, with such phrases as "somewhat limited evidence" and "a fairly safe gamble." I felt there was enough evidence to conclude that Carter's personality wasn't the decisive negative issue in the campaign that his opponents were trying to make it out to be. But I also felt there wasn't enough on the record about his positive characteristics to draw any really strong conclusions in his favor, and I felt obligated to let readers know that.

Overinterpretation   This is one of the cardinal psychobiographical sins. Journalists are more often guilty of it than academic researchers, because they've learned the game of looking for deep meanings in trivial clues without learning the appropriate evidential constraints. The academics, however, are not altogether sin-free. It's very tempting for a psychobiographer to play Sigmund Freud now and then—to use odds and ends of evidence about a candidate's current behavior to reach dramatic conclusions about the candidate's early oedipal conflicts or infantile anal hangups. The evidence available on active political candidates is usually far too sketchy to yield firm conclusions of this kind, and psychobiographers should be wary about making such a speculative jump.

The best psychobiographical studies are likely to come from researchers who feel ambivalent not only toward the subject of study, their chosen political candidate, but also ambivalent toward the method of psychobiography itself. Such researchers will continue to worry about the inadequacy of the available data, the flimsiness of the logical and symbolic connections between early experience and adult behavior. They will keep on checking and double-checking their own work to make sure their case is far stronger than it would need to be to convince only the true believers in psychobiography.

Perhaps I shouldn't pick on Bruce Mazlish and Edwin Diamond's study of Jimmy Carter for examples of overinterpretation, when there are much worse examples available. But it distresses me when someone who should know better—someone with the reputation of Bruce Mazlish, who has done several fine psychobiographical books[12]—takes minimal clues and expands them willy-nilly into major psychobiographical conclusions. In 1976, for example, Mazlish and Diamond started with such information as Carter's heavy use of opinion polls, his preference for staying in the homes of supporters rather than in hotels during campaigns, and his statements about feeling a personal relationship with the people in his audience. From there they suddenly arrived at this sweeping conclusion: "Jimmy Carter's identification with the people, we believe, is a mystical union (as was his union with God). There are no intermediaries."[13]

Carter did like to interact directly with ordinary citizens now and then, as his post-1976 presidential "town meetings" continued to indicate. But he was not reluctant to use intermediaries most of the time, and much of his stress on direct contacts with the people was a matter of practical politics, not "mystical union." In *Young Man Luther,* Erik Erikson similarly discussed Martin Luther's desire to achieve a direct mystical relationship with God. But Erikson had a great deal more evidence, including Luther's own reports of various mystical experiences and his public and private stress on a direct relationship with God without intermediaries.[14] Mazlish and Diamond lacked such information on Carter, though they did interview him—more than Erikson was able to do with Martin Luther.

At another point, Mazlish and Diamond say, "In our view, he [Carter] mainly accepted his father's 'authoritarianism'—rather than revolt against it—and internalized it."[15] Their evidence is a set of two successive paragraphs in *Why Not the Best?* In the first paragraph Carter describes how his father once whipped him for not answering when Jimmy was called down from his tree house. That's followed by a paragraph about how Jimmy's father ordered a tailor-made suit that turned out to be much too large, but nobody laughed when he put it on.[16] From these paragraphs Mazlish and Diamond conclude that Carter internalized his father's authoritarianism—though they haven't demonstrated that either Carter or his father *was* authoritarian. They also conclude that Carter's repressed anger at being whipped with little justification by his father "may have become available for resentment against other social injustices—and fueled an identification with victims of such injustices." Such leaps of inference were supposed to help us decide whether Jimmy Carter would make a good president. A preeminent rule of responsible psychobiography is to stay close to your data, to speculate only when the data give you a firm springboard for doing so.[17] That's doubly true during a political campaign, when your overstatements may influence voters in ways that are hard to correct once the votes are in.[18]

Inattention to context   I'm not sure whether the failure to consider the cultural and personal context of behavioral details is a cause or an effect of the psychobiographer's overinterpretive tendencies. Whatever the causal relationship is, however, inattention to context can thoroughly distort psychological interpretations. Such inattention seems especially likely to occur in time-limited campaign studies, when biographers and journalists don't have years to understand how a candidate from a particular background really perceives the world.

Jimmy Carter probably suffered to an unusual degree as a result of this type of psychobiographical error. His cultural background was substantially different from that of much of the voting population and most of the people writing about him, and his natural cultural allies were not necessarily his natural political ones. Thus the people most likely to agree with Carter's liberal political views were on the whole the least likely to understand major aspects of his Southern fundamentalist background, while the people most likely to understand him personally because of their common Southern heritage were often those least likely to agree with him politically on issues of race, pardons for Vietnam War resisters, and so forth. (Bill Clinton has suffered from similar problems.)

Certain instances of inattention to context are simply foolish, if not actually malicious. For instance, *Penthouse* magazine, of all publications, ran a pseudo-psychobiographical article in 1976, which proposed that Jimmy Carter and Richard Nixon had experienced similar childhoods and could thus be assumed to have developed similar personality patterns.[19] Their childhoods were similar in amazing ways: for instance, "Both came from rural backgrounds," and both had a mother who worked as a nurse. However, the article failed to note that the "rural backgrounds" provided by the environs of early-twentieth-century Whittier, California, and Plains, Georgia, differed in several striking ways. Among other things, Whittier during Nixon's boyhood was already a genuine town, on a suburban train route to Los Angeles, while Plains was still a village in rural Georgia. Nixon lived in a semi-rural area where his father tried unsuccessfully to make a living from a grove of lemon trees; Carter not only lived but worked on his father's successful farm. It's true that both mothers sometimes worked as nurses, but nursing as learned and practiced by Hannah Nixon and by Lillian Carter also differed substantially. Hannah Nixon worked as an untrained practical nurse out of sheer desperation, during a period when she was forced to leave her family for three years to care for other tubercular children in order to afford treatment for her own terminally ill child, Richard's older brother. In contrast, Lillian Carter was a hospital-trained registered nurse who served a respected role in Jimmy Carter's own community as she carried out her official duties, and who also often undertook unpaid errands of mercy for poor blacks and whites in the area. The ways in which these mothers' work as nurses influenced their sons' personalities is far from clear, but it's a good bet that the influences were far from identical.

For a more serious example of contextual inattention, let's go back to Mazlish and Diamond. During the 1976 campaign, they wrote of Carter's religious views as though he was a hard-core fundamentalist like Oral Roberts or Jerry Falwell. In so doing, they substantially misrepresented his views, because they were basically unfamiliar with the major varieties of Southern religious language and behavior from which Carter drew his own patterns. Mazlish and Diamond apparently didn't have the time or the inclination during the campaign to develop much familiarity with what was, for them, that strange context for Carter's religiosity. Erik Erikson had encountered an even stranger religious context for the personality development and political behavior of Mohandas Gandhi. But Erikson *realized* the context was strange to him, made few initial assumptions about it, and put a lot of time and effort into trying to understand it before he wrote about Gandhi. (Erikson didn't have to worry about election deadlines, of course; Gandhi was already dead, and had never run for office anyway.) As I observed in my Sacramento *Bee* article, "the church is still often the focus of [a Southerner's] intellectual, philosophical, and cultural as well as spiritual life." Carter used traditional Southern religious language so often that it was easy to get the impression that the Baptist Church was at the very center of his decision-making processes. But when we begin to make allowances for standard Southern uses of such language, the centrality of religion in Carter's political life becomes much less certain, and how we interpret its psychological implications in his case is not at all obvious.

Calculating My Batting Average

Enough knocking of the competition. How did I do in my own 1976 evaluations and predictions regarding Carter's personality? Let's get out the scorecard. On *religiosity,* I'd say I batted one for one. Carter is still "more serious about his religion than most politicians," but he never tried to impose his religious beliefs on others while he was president. On *overcontrol,* I didn't make any very clear predictions in the first place (that's one way professional prophets inflate their scores), but I wasn't too far off. Carter became legendary for trying to control the White House tennis-court schedule, and in certain other regards he veered more toward overcontrol than I suggested he would. But he was if anything not "cold, calculating, hard, ruthless" enough for his own good. He could have cut his losses early on by dropping his friend and budget director Bert Lance like a hot potato; he could have cut other losses much later by ignoring the American hostages in Iran; but he didn't. On *power hunger,* where I emphasized Carter's greater needs for achievement and affiliation than for power, I did pretty well. Maybe in this case his behavior after leaving office makes the case even clearer than his presidential record; as our greatest living ex-President, achievement and affiliation are what he has mainly displayed.

My uneasiness about Carter's *active-negative* potential was well-founded. Even James David Barber, who initially categorized Carter as an active-positive[20] and who regards him as a personal friend, now acknowledges that the categorization "rings too hopeful in history's light."[21] Barber isn't willing to shift Carter entirely from the positive column to the negative one, though. He argues that in the Iranian hostage crisis, "unlike Wilson, Hoover, Johnson, and Nixon [all active-negatives], this President did not freeze onto some disastrous line of policy and ride it to the end."[22] That's not quite accurate, as Barber seems to recognize when he adds that

> one could argue, once it became clear that his leverage over Khomeini had disappeared and that there was nothing left to do until the Iranians decided to free the hostages, Carter should have put the issue aside and moved on to more productive topics.[23]

But I think it's fair to conclude, as I suggested in my own predictions, that Carter's continuing duel with himself on the positive-negative dimension landed him more often on the positive side than the negative. Score one for me (and for Carter).

On the contrasting characteristics of *indecisiveness* and *rigidity,* I said that "The latter seems the more serious cause for worry." I think I was right there too. When we consider later models of indecisiveness, such as Mario Cuomo and early-term Bill Clinton, Carter in retrospect looks pretty good. On rigidity, Barber describes Carter's record accurately: "Throughout his term, Carter again and again returned to his bad negotiating habits, his long-time resistance to playing cooperative politics among independent power brokers."[24] Nonetheless, as Barber also indicates, Carter gradually got better about negotiating with Congress, and "emerged as a negotiating genius" when he brought Sadat of Egypt and Begin of Israel together at Camp David.[25] As I said, presciently, "The key consideration about Carter's tendencies toward rigidity and other negative traits is that he is open to improvement." Score two more for me, for a grand total of somewhere around 5.8 out of a possible 6, or 97 percent. Not bad for two months of research.

Why, then, did Carter lose so disastrously to Reagan in 1980, and why is the Carter presidency still often described in such negative terms? I did say his "personality is well short of perfect," which turned out to be true. But I also said that his "personality does appear solid enough for a fairly safe gamble, and promising enough to be a plus rather than a minus when voters make their final decisions." Given my 97 percent accuracy in individual predictions, where did Carter and I go wrong overall?

That's easy. It was those damned intersections of personality with chance, the ones that Freud warned psychobiographers about. Let's imagine that the Middle Eastern oil sheiks had decided not to be greedy about their profits, so we wouldn't have experienced an energy crisis in the middle of Carter's term. Let's imagine that the Iranian students had found a more creative way to express their displeasure toward America than taking hostages. Or let's imagine that a couple of those military helicopters hadn't been disabled by a sandstorm, but instead went in there and pulled those hostages out, as Carter was praying they would. Let's imagine, in other words, that chance had tilted a little in Carter's direction instead of a little against. My score would still be 97 percent, or maybe a little less (since his location on Barber's positive-negative dimension wouldn't have slipped as much toward the negative end), but Carter would have ended up looking a lot better in the history books. Indeed, he might have been president for four more years, and that would have given him time to learn even more about being a flexible, positive president—though it would also have given him more time to be the target for who knows what assaults by chance.[26]

Have I tried to improve my record as a presidential prophet in the years since Carter? Not yet. After all, how much better could I expect to get? I did look forward to Alexander Haig's presidential campaign in 1988, since I felt I had already figured out some significant things about his personality (see Chapter 14). But fortunately for the country if not for my role as prophet, Haig dropped out of the race early. I've considered making more predictions in 1996, but if I tried to analyze Dan Quayle, I'd violate one of Freud's clearest proscriptive guidelines ("Don't pathographize!"), and I'm not sure who else is a likely enough candidate to work on. Bill Clinton could still use some serious psychobiographical analysis, but I grew up in Arkansas and my middle name is Clinton, so I might be seen as having a conflict of interest. So instead of doing the work myself, I'm planning to give lots of advice to other people who want to get into this field of applied political psychobiography. Here are the introductory installments:

First, don't abandon the field to journalists and sensationalists. I still think the American populace needs information on the personalities as well as the ideologies of the major presidential candidates. In the key position of the U.S. presidency more than anywhere else, personality does count, even if chance also plays an important role. Psychologists, psychiatrists, political scientists, and historians may not be the perfect analysts of our politicians' personalities, but they bring skills and ideas to the job that journalists generally do not.[27]

Second, get in there and go to work on a candidate even if other people are already studying him or her. Some of the most troublesome aspects of psychobiography —in terms of theoretical biases, researcher countertransference, and so on—can be at least partially remedied if several researchers independently produce analyses of the same candidate. When their judgments converge (as has happened to some degree, for instance, with the various retrospective analyses of Woodrow Wilson), we as voters can feel more confidence in their conclusions. When their judgments diverge, that's a signal for caution and for further study.

Third, get started early. Just think what my predictive percentage might have been if I'd begun studying Jimmy Carter's character in 1973 or 1974 instead of August 1976. Somebody could have deduced in 1984 that Vice President George Bush was a likely candidate for president in 1988, and could have prepared a thorough psychobiography in time for the 1988 campaign season—but nobody did that, including me. Somebody should be able to do an in-depth study of Al Gore, a psychologically fascinating character, before he runs for president in the year 2000—or maybe earlier. Other nominees for 2000 and beyond can be identified with enough confidence to make them worth studying, far enough in advance for thorough data-collection and thoughtful conclusion-drawing. Even if your chosen candidate doesn't make it into the final contest, a detailed psychological study of a politician like Mario Cuomo or Newt Gingrich or Ross Perot would hardly be a waste of time. Indeed, when we consider again not only the personal but the national and international stakes involved in wise versus foolish choices of the person who'll fill the U.S. presidency, whatever we can do to improve the art and science of applied political psychobiography should be well worth doing.

13

The Counterplayers:

George Bush and Saddam Hussein

"C OUNTERPLAYER" is a key term in Erik Erikson's magnificent psychobiography of Mahatma Gandhi. An early chapter is titled "The Counterplayer"; a later one is "Companions and Counterplayers."[1] Erikson says his host on his first visit to India had been "Gandhi's prime counterplayer" during a crucial campaign of *satyagraha* (nonviolent resistance). Yet the term "counterplayer" is not listed in the book's extensive index, and it is not defined by Erikson. When I asked him where he had gotten the term, he seemed surprised that the question should even arise. He thought of it as a standard English word.[2]

"Counterplayer" is not a standard English word. It does not appear in the *Oxford English Dictionary* or the *American Heritage Dictionary* or *Webster's Third New International*. I don't know of anyone who used it in psychobiography before Erikson. But it's a word that should be used more often. It reflects Erikson's strong sense that each human life is lived out in a thoroughly social context—a perspective that psychobiographers often seem to forget as they focus on *one* life at a time. In order to understand the course taken by one life, we need to develop some understanding of the other lives that intersect with it in important ways or at crucial moments.

Certain intersecting individuals may be so consistently helpful that they deserve to be called co-players in our game of life. Other people function as chance variables in our life history, unintentionally furthering our goals or getting in our way, as random as a thundershower or a sunny day. (I don't have a term for them yet.) Still others become occupied for a time with what they see as our role in *their* game, and they play to beat us. They are the people Erikson seems to have in mind when he uses the term "counterplayer."

Counterplayers are not necessarily intent on destroying us; their motivations may not be malicious at all. Gandhi's principal counterplayer was a respectful and even admiring friend who had chosen the other side in a labor dispute. But counterplayers do work to oppose certain of our goals in a sustained fashion. At times, the psychobiographer can understand crucial events in a subject's life only by looking at a counterplayer's activities as well.

That's why this chapter deals with two lives rather than one. I first began to think seriously about George Bush's life not while he was campaigning for president but toward the end of his term, when he was orchestrating the Persian Gulf War. It takes at least two sides to fight a war, so after a while I found myself looking not only at President George Bush but at his principal counterplayer, President Saddam Hussein of Iraq. I haven't been to Iraq recently—never, actually—and I don't know Hussein's cultural context nearly as well as Jimmy Carter's South. I've tried to find the best secondary sources available on Hussein's life history, but I wish he'd written an autobiography. I have been to Washington recently, and I was living in Texas when George Bush first tried to become a Senator there. But I found *his* autobiography more informative than anything I could collect firsthand.

A course of events like the Gulf War is determined by many factors beyond the decisions of individual national leaders. At the same time, it's clear that George Bush's personality made its mark on U.S. foreign policy, especially with regard to the Middle East, and that Saddam Hussein's personality has made its mark on the entire nation of Iraq. International politics is not only a matter of vast impersonal forces; the actions of national leaders have always made a difference, and they'll continue to do so. If we want to increase our understanding of how such politically polarizing and life-destroying phenomena as the Gulf War evolve, one place to look is the personalities of Bush and Hussein and how those personalities interacted.

Saddam Hussein and How He Got That Way

George Bush has described Saddam Hussein as "Hitler revisited."[3] Is that a fair description of Bush's main international counterplayer? Is Hussein an inhuman monster or a perverted psychopath, as others have described him? Or is he just a typical Iraqi politician, mouthing the same public clichés as any other Iraqi who attains high office? In any case, how did he become the Saddam Hussein we know and hate?

Hussein's personality development began with a harsh childhood. His father died or disappeared before Saddam's birth in 1937.[4] Saddam's mother turned her small child over to her brother's family, where he remained until the brother was imprisoned for taking part in an uprising against the Iraqi monarchy and its British military backers.[5] At that point the four-year-old Saddam was returned to his mother. She had married her late husband's brother, who evidently was not happy to gain a stepson. According to one account, Saddam's new stepfather "was a brutish man who used to amuse himself by humiliating Saddam."[6] He beat

Saddam often, forced him to steal chickens and sheep, called him "son of a whore" and "son of a dog," and refused to let him go to school.

Saddam endured this treatment until he was 10 years old. At that time he went back to live with his maternal uncle, Khairallah Tulfah, who had recently been let out of prison after serving five years for his part in the uprising. Uncle Khairallah was not the most admirable of role models, at least from a liberal Western perspective. He later wrote a notorious pamphlet titled *Three Whom God Should Not Have Created: Persians, Jews, and Flies,*[7] and he became so corrupt as Mayor of Baghdad that Saddam Hussein (who was by then President of Iraq) felt obligated to remove him from office. But Khairallah was helpful to the young Saddam, encouraging him to get an education and providing a home for him until Saddam was 20 years old.[8]

What can we say about Saddam Hussein's personality at age 20? We need to be more than usually cautious in our assessment, because Hussein developed within a very different culture than the American and European settings in which most personality research has been done—and very different as well from the Indian setting in which Erikson looked at Gandhi and his counterplayer. Furthermore, there's little reliable information on Hussein's early years. But we do know from extensive research in our society that if a child is subjected to prolonged physical abuse, the child may well grow up to be a physically abusive or violent adult. There are reports of Saddam torturing animals with a red-hot iron bar when he was still a boy; but such reports come from Iraqi exiles, enemies of Saddam, so they may be exaggerations or inventions. On the other hand there's a report that the young Saddam loved his horse so much that, when it died, "he experienced paralysis of his hand for over a week."[9] That story derives from his semi-official biography, so we can't trust its benevolent picture of the young Saddam either. (If we were good Freudians we might ask, "Why was it specifically his hand that showed a hysterical paralysis? Had he been beating the horse before its death?")

We *can* safely assume certain other things about Saddam's personality development. Here's a boy whose father abandoned him—by death or otherwise—before he was born; a boy whose mother left him with another family in his earliest years; a boy whose stepfather beat him, called him names, and treated him as something close to a slave. Such a boy would, at the least, be likely to grow up with a negative or profoundly uncertain sense of self-worth. Here's a boy who is exposed to consistently inconsistent parenting almost from birth, a boy whose principal role model—Uncle Khairallah—himself appears rather deficient in the area of moral development. Such a boy would, at the least, be likely to grow up with a severely impaired conscience or superego.

In these regards Saddam Hussein may not have been much different from many other deprived and abused Iraqis of his generation. But Saddam possessed, in addition, a strong ambition to rise above his lowly origins. Perhaps he got that ambition from his maternal uncle, who had been a military officer before he was imprisoned. When Saddam pursued his ambition by applying to the Baghdad Military Academy from which Uncle Khairallah had graduated, he was rejected, apparently because of poor grades in school or on the entrance exams. He soon found another way to emulate his uncle—by becoming involved in political violence. While he was still in high school he joined the Baath Party, which at the time was a small and fairly radical group that advocated pan-Arab nationalism. At age 21, Saddam was accused of murdering a political rival, who was also his brother-in-law.[10] As a result, he and Uncle Khairallah were both imprisoned. They were released six months later for lack of evidence.

Saddam promptly plunged into a much more serious case of political violence: an attempt to assassinate the ruler of Iraq, General Abd al-Karim Qassem. In the crossfire, the General and Saddam were both wounded but survived. Hussein's wound was reportedly inflicted by one of his own comrades, though it was later treated more heroically by his propagandists. Hussein escaped across the border to Syria, where he was welcomed by the Syrian branch of the Baath Party. He was similarly received by the Egyptian branch when he moved on to Cairo. He remained in Egypt for three years, where he moved up in the hierarchy of the Baath Party, finished high school, got married to Uncle Khairallah's daughter, and started law school—a busy man! He never finished law school, but as one biography reports,

> Nine years after abandoning his studies in Egypt, having enrolled in law studies at the University of Baghdad, he appeared at the University with a pistol in his belt and accompanied by four bodyguards to receive his [law] certificate.[11]

I won't go into detail on Hussein's adult political career. When he finally returned to Iraq following the successful assassination of General Qassem, he used his connections with relatives and friends to advance himself in the Baath Party. He was involved in various plots to take over the government by force; he was again thrown into prison, this time for two years; he escaped to do further plotting. He participated in several unsuccessful and successful coup attempts over the next decade, eventually becoming the second most powerful man in Iraq—a status that must have given the most powerful man in Iraq, President Ahmad Hasan al-Bakr, many sleepless nights. With good reason: after Saddam managed to eliminate several other rivals, he forced the resignation of President Bakr (who was his cousin and in-law as well as his closest ally) and became president himself, at age 42. There Saddam has remained, through wars and plots and counterplots, for a decade and a half.

Saddam the Narcissist

What can we say about Saddam Hussein's personality as an adult? A number of psychologists, psychoanalysts, political scientists, and journalists have attempted to reach a diagnosis.[12] The most widely publicized diagnosis was made by Jerrold Post, whose official title is Professor of Psychiatry, Political Psychology, and International Affairs at George Washington University.[13] Before he became a full-time academic, Post did psychobiographical studies for the CIA.[14] Whatever his political biases may be, he has probably written more personality profiles of foreign leaders than anyone else in the business, so he comes to his study of Saddam Hussein with a good deal of expertise. His description of Hussein sounds awfully pathographic, and I approached it initially with serious reservations. But given what I've been able to learn about Hussein from other sources, it fits.

In diagnosing Hussein, Post refers to a personality syndrome called *malignant narcissism*. This syndrome was originally formulated without reference to Hussein by one of the best contemporary psychoanalytic theorists, Otto Kernberg.[15] Malignant narcissism is not technically a psychosis, but it is a serious personality disorder. The malignant narcissist is so thoroughly self-absorbed that he ignores the feelings of other people, and readily harms or destroys others in order to gain his own ends. More formally, the malignant narcissism syndrome includes four major components:

1. An "extreme sense of grandiosity," according to Kernberg; or as Jerrold Post puts it, a "messianic ambition for unlimited power."[16] This certainly sounds like Hussein. He often describes himself as the descendant or heir of the great figures of Iraqi history, and he has promoted a personality cult that identifies him as the savior not only of Iraq but of the entire Arab world. A visible expression of this grandiosity is the Victory Arch in Baghdad, erected on the basis of Saddam's own design in 1989. Two huge arms, representing "the arm[s] of the Leader-President, Saddam Hussein himself . . . enlarged forty times" (according to the opening-day invitation), hold crossed 24-ton swords. The monument's arms were developed "from plaster casts of the President's arms taken from just above the elbow, with a sword inserted into each fist."[17] The pathological element of this grandiose display is indicated by the fact that the "Victory" thus celebrated was at best an extremely expensive and bloody draw, at the end of a long war with Iran.

2. "Sadistic cruelty" (Kernberg) or "unconstrained aggression" (Post). We can find many examples of this in Hussein's history. A particularly vivid one is described by Post:

> In 1982, when the war with Iran was going very badly for Iraq and Saddam wished to terminate hostilities, Khomeini [the Ayatollah of Iran] . . . insisted there could be no peace until Saddam was removed from power. At a cabinet meeting, Saddam asked his ministers to candidly give their advice, and the Minister of Health suggested Saddam temporarily step down, to resume the presidency after peace had been established. Saddam reportedly thanked him for his candor and ordered his arrest. His wife pleaded for her husband's return. The next day, Saddam re-

turned her husband's body to her in a black canvas bag, chopped into
pieces.[18]

In another version of this story, Saddam suggested that he and the Health Minister "'go into the other room and discuss the matter further.' . . . The minister
agreed and the two left the room. A moment later, a shot was heard, and Hussein
returned alone to the cabinet as though nothing had happened."[19] Either way, the
Health Minister's good health had come to an end.

3. "Suspiciousness to the point of paranoia" (Kernberg). Hussein seems to see
plots everywhere. He has often demanded the execution of, or has himself reportedly executed, the presumed plotters.[20] As Jerrold Post notes, Hussein may well
have reason to see himself "as surrounded by enemies. But he ignores his role in
creating those enemies."[21] Or as Kernberg says about malignant narcissists in
general, "They project their own cruelty onto their enemies."[22] A striking example is a Hussein speech broadcast by Radio Baghdad on February 24, 1991, just
after U.N. forces began their ground assault in response to Iraq's invasion of
Kuwait. Here's part of the Associated Press translation; the rest of Saddam's
speech contains more of the same:

> At the time when the United Nations Security Council decided to dis-
> cuss the Soviet peace initiative, which we endorsed, the treacherous com-
> mitted treachery. The despicable Bush and his treasonous agent Fahd
> [King of Saudi Arabia], and all those who supported them in committing
> crimes, shame, and aggression, committed the treachery. Those cowards
> who have perfected the acts of treachery, treason, and vileness, commit-
> ted treachery after they departed from every path of virtue, goodness,
> and humanity. They have committed treachery and launched their
> ground offensive on a wide scale Sunday morning at our armed forces.
> They even betrayed those who along with them signed the infamous res-
> olutions which were adopted at the United Nations Security Council pri-
> or to the military aggression against our country. . . . They betrayed
> everyone. God, however, is above everyone. . . . He will strike back their
> treachery on their necks and shame them until their ranks and their fail-
> ing horde are repulsed.[23]

Under such circumstances, of course, we shouldn't expect Hussein to present a
thoughtful discussion of the international scene. It's also true that Iraqi rhetorical
traditions are somewhat different from ours. Nonetheless, an air of paranoia does
appear to pervade the whole speech. On this point in particular (but in combination with points 1 and 2), Bush's characterization of Saddam as "Hitler revisited"
appears more on the mark than the usual demonizing of international opponents.

4. "An utter lack of remorse" (Kernberg) or an "absence of conscience" (Post).
As Kernberg adds, malignant narcissists "lie, cheat, exploit people without any

remorse, though they can be loyal to people they feel they need."[24] This lack of remorse is the one feature of malignant narcissism that I'm not sure we can pin on Hussein, since we really don't know how he feels inside. He has been seen wiping tears from his eyes as he ordered close associates to be taken away for execution, but we don't know whether those were real or crocodile tears. As I suggested earlier, Hussein's childhood was the sort of childhood that often leaves people with an impaired conscience. But we don't know *how* impaired Hussein's conscience is. In any event, he seems able to overcome whatever pangs of remorse he experiences as he destroys those who interfere with his ambitions. Not surprisingly, Hussein's favorite movie has been reported to be *The Godfather*.[25]

George Bush and How He Got That Way

Saddam Hussein has described George Bush as displaying a "deep-rooted evil."[26] Is Bush indeed nothing more than a running-dog capitalist, motivated only by money and oil? Is he basically a devious schemer, wearing a public mask of civility? Or is George just a nice fellow who happened to get elected President of the United States of America?

A childhood more different from Hussein's is hard to imagine. Rather than being born into abject poverty, George Herbert Walker Bush was born into comfort and wealth. Rather than being abandoned by both parents at an early age, Bush grew up in a traditional American nuclear family, all of whose members participated actively in family life and in the life of Greenwich, Connecticut, a wealthy suburb. George Bush remembers his childhood through a golden haze:

> [Our parents] were our biggest boosters, always there when we needed
> them. They believed in an old-fashioned way of bringing up a family—
> generous measures of both love and discipline. Religious teaching was
> also part of our home life. Each morning, as we gathered at the breakfast
> table, Mother or Dad read a Bible lesson to us. Our family is Episco-
> palian, and we regularly attended Sunday services at Christ Church in
> Greenwich.
>
> We were a close, happy family, and never closer or happier than when
> we crammed into the station wagon each summer—five kids, two dogs,
> with Mother driving—to visit Walker's Point in Kennebunkport, Maine.
> It was named after my [maternal] grandfather, George Herbert Walker,
> and his father, David, who had bought it jointly as a family vacation
> home.[27]

Grandfather Walker, after whom George had been named, was a formidable figure: head of his own investment firm, a champion polo player, a skilled sailor and fisherman, president of the U.S. Golf Association for several years. When George was four years old, Grandfather Walker established the Walker Cup, "a trophy still awarded each year, with America's best amateur golfers competing against Great Britain's best."[28]

George's father, Prescott Bush, was equally formidable. George describes him as "an imposing presence, six feet four, with deep-set blue-gray eyes and a resonant voice."[29] Prescott Bush made his money as "a business administrator whose forte was reorganizing failing companies, turning money losers into profit makers."[30] He was quite successful at that ultimate capitalist occupation, and eventually became a partner in an investment banking firm. He also became active in politics, in Greenwich and beyond.

George remembers that when he was a child, "Dad was really scary."[31] He didn't usually discipline George physically, but that was always a possibility. George told interviewer David Frost, "Remember Teddy Roosevelt's 'Speak softly and carry a big stick'? My dad spoke *loudly* and carried the same big stick. He got our attention pretty quick."[32]

George's mother Dorothy was an impressive figure too. George remembers her as "a first rate athlete" (like her father), and says, "I don't recall a footrace Mother was ever in that she didn't come in first."[33] Her main role in disciplining the children was to demand that they be modest about themselves and their accomplishments. George seems to have taken her demands more to heart than anyone else in the family. In grade school and junior high, he was the smallest kid in his class, and he learned to be submissive and ingratiating. Among his siblings he acquired the nickname "Have Half," because whenever he got a treat he'd quickly say to anyone around, "Have half." The family also joked that the best grade on his report card was always in one deportment category: "Claims no more than his fair share of time and attention."

That was what his mother had taught George as a child, and that was a lesson she continued to emphasize. According to one biographical sketch,

> If a Bush child burst into the house to say he'd hit a home run that day, Dorothy Bush would sweetly reply, "How did the *team* do, dear?" . . . Talking about yourself—your accomplishments or deepest feelings—was frowned upon as self-absorption and poor taste and drew from Dorothy Bush the admonishment, "I don't want to hear any more about the Great I Am."[34]

Bush reports a similar story in his autobiography:

> Fifty years later Mother still stays on the alert for anything that sounds like "braggadocio" coming from one of her children. "You're talking about yourself too much, George," she told me after reading a news report covering one of my campaign speeches. I pointed out that as a candidate, I was expected to tell voters something about my qualifications. She thought about that a moment, then reluctantly conceded. "Well, I understand that," she said, "but try to restrain yourself."[35]

This combination of family influences—being intimidated by his powerful father and grandfather, and being admonished by his mother to be modest and emotionally restrained—left George Bush in his late teens with a rather uninteresting personality. His major motive appears to have been what Henry Murray called *n Aff*, the need for affiliation: wanting to be friends with as many people as possible, under as many circumstances as possible.[36] Bush's major strategy for doing this was ingratiation: being quietly nice and friendly and modest toward those he wanted as his friends, and never claiming more than his fair share of time and attention.

However, other motives and strategies were contending with those primary ones. George had been taught that on the playing field, it's okay to be competitive and tough. He had also begun to realize that to be really happy with himself, he needed to get out from under the thumbs of his domineering parents and grandfather. He joined the U.S. Navy on his eighteenth birthday, seven months after the attack on Pearl Harbor, and soon began to train as a fighter pilot. George Bush may have been affiliative and ingratiating in his personal relationships, but he didn't lack physical courage, and in a clearly defined competitive situation he was ready to fight hard. He flew 58 combat missions against Japanese forces in the Pacific, was shot down once, and returned to active duty as soon as he could.[37]

After the war George went to Yale, the obvious college choice for a wealthy Connecticut boy whose father was a Yale alumnus. George captained the baseball team there, majored in economics, and earned a Phi Beta Kappa key. His baseball idol at the time was Lou Gehrig: "Nothing flashy, no hotdogging, the ideal sportsman. He could field, hit, hit-with-power, and come through in a clutch. A great athlete and team leader."[38] That's what George hoped to become on the Yale baseball team, but his talents lay more in being a team leader than a great athlete. He says he progressed, over his years there, from "Good field, no hit" to "Good field, fair hit."[39]

After graduation, George could have taken his Yale degree in economics and moved right into the investment banking business like his father and grandfather. But again, he made a move that kept him relatively independent of them: he accepted a family friend's offer of a job in the West Texas oilfields. He learned the oil business for two and a half years, mainly as an equipment clerk and salesman; then he and a friend set up their own independent oil company. Bush borrowed a good deal of money from his father's friends and acquaintances; he made a good deal of money for himself and his investors; and for over a decade he worked as a Texas oil man.

Not long after George moved to Texas, his father ran for the U.S. Senate. On his second try, Prescott Bush became the junior Senator from Connecticut. George himself began to get interested in politics, Texas-style. He started off slowly, with a successful run for the elective office of Republican County Chairman. Bush says that during that race

I found out that jugular politics—going for the opposition's throat—wasn't my style. It was a lesson carried over from my experience in business. When competition gets cutthroat, everybody loses. Sometimes confrontation is the only way to resolve problems—but only as a last resort, after all other avenues have been explored.[40]

That statement is certainly congruent with George's previous personality development: go for affiliation and ingratiation before you try anything else. It's in considerable contrast to some of his later political behavior, as in the 1988 presidential campaign with those mean-sounding anti-Dukakis "Willie Horton" commercials. We might also contrast it with Saddam Hussein's political philosophy and behavior, where "going for the opposition's throat" is not just a metaphor. But George Bush in 1962, beginning his political career, wanted to be a nice candidate—and he won that election.

Being nice, however, didn't always work. Maybe that's one reason Bush's strategy had changed by 1988. He got soundly defeated in his first run for the U.S. Senate in 1964, and he promptly issued a public statement: "I have been trying to think whom we could blame for this and regretfully conclude that the only one I can blame is myself."[41] In 1966 he ran for the House of Representatives and won, with a lot of help from Richard Nixon. He ran again for the Senate in 1970, and lost again. But in part as a reward for his willingness to give the Senate races a shot, Bush started being appointed to various nonelective offices: Ambassador to the United Nations, Chairman of the Republican National Committee, Chief of the U.S. Liaison Office in mainland China, Director of the CIA. While Saddam Hussein was moving up in the hierarchy of the Baath Party through intrigues and coups and occasional executions, George Bush was moving up in the hierarchy of the Republican Party—partly through some intrigues of his own, partly through looking politically clean at a time when Nixon and crew were becoming increasingly tainted by Watergate, but most of all (as Bush suggests in his biography) by being a nice guy and making lots of friends.

Being a nice guy and having lots of friends didn't help Bush enough during his first try for the presidential nomination, in 1980. Ronald Reagan put on a show of being an even nicer guy, with more friends and more backbone than Bush. But there was the vice-presidency—an ideal position for somebody who's ingratiating and modest and very affiliative. So for eight years, that's what George Bush did as vice president: he acted ingratiating toward the president, he never claimed more than his fair share of time and attention, and he made lots more friends.

When Bush ran for president again in 1988, this pattern of behavior became a serious problem for him. That was the year many journalists rediscovered what they called the "Character Issue." In the primaries, they called into question Gary Hart's womanizing, Joe Biden's plagiarizing, and various other presumably fatal flaws in candidate character. In the presidential campaign that followed the primaries, the major "character issues" were: Is Michael Dukakis too rigid and humorless to be president? Is George Bush too much of a wimp?

The wimp issue had emerged in the primaries, especially when *Newsweek* ran a cover story titled "George Bush: Fighting the 'Wimp Factor.'" *Newsweek* described the "wimp factor" as "a perception that he [Bush] isn't strong enough or tough enough for the challenges of the Oval Office."[42] According to *Newsweek*, Bush was even then taking steps to prove definitively that he was not a wimp—jogging with high school kids, talking tough to the Communist leaders of Poland, posing for *Newsweek*'s cover with a macho frown as he piloted his speedboat. But the label continued to dog him, even after he won the election. The political cartoonist Oliphant, for instance, went on drawing Bush as carrying a purse—not to show he was effeminate, but to underline his wimpishness. (After Bush threw up on the Japanese Prime Minister at a state dinner, Oliphant drew Bush carrying a barf bag. Same idea.)

What can we say overall about George Bush's adult personality profile? First, no pathological syndrome or psychiatric label applies to Bush. In clinical terms, he qualifies as a psychologically healthy individual. Second, he appears to have retained to a large extent the principal motivational patterns of his childhood and youth. Like almost any politician who succeeds at a national level, he has some degree of power motivation. And even though he tends to dismiss what he calls "the vision thing," he probably wouldn't have bothered to run three times for the presidency if he didn't also possess a substantial amount of achievement motivation, a desire to attain a high standard of excellence in his public performance. But of those three motives most often studied by political psychologists, Bush appears to have remained unusually high in affiliation motivation—wanting to make friend after friend and to keep those friends he has already made.[43] One of his advisers in the 1980 campaign referred, not altogether jokingly, to "George Bush's 2,000 closest friends"[44]—and George doubtless made a lot more friends as he attained higher office. Some critics complained that as president, Bush was slow to respond to the needs of people he didn't know personally, such as the Kurdish refugees or the homeless in America. But for those people he did know as friends, he remained eager to please.

Are there any major flaws in Bush's personality? Well, that high affiliation motive can sometimes create problems, as I'll explain further in the next section. I don't think being a wimp is necessarily a problem, even if we could prove that Bush *is* a wimp. More problematic were Bush's efforts to prove he wasn't a wimp. I suspect he still feels serious self-doubts about his masculinity, dating back to when he was the smallest boy in his class and his father was a big powerful man. Those self-doubts were surely not helped by journalists and cartoonists raising the wimp question at every opportunity. Nor were the self-doubts relieved by Barbara Bush telling journalists at one time or another, "George is a sissy."

Under those circumstances, Bush had to keep finding new ways of proving his masculinity to himself. At the same time, he seemed afraid to do any genuine self-exploration, for fear of what he might find in there. At the beginning of his autobiography, he quotes Edward Everett Hale, a popular turn-of-the-century writer and U.S. Senate Chaplain: "Look up and not down; look out and not in; look forward and not back; and lend a hand." I'm glad George wants to lend a hand. But perhaps he'd understand more about his own motives for lending a hand, and more about who most needs a helping hand, if he'd look down and in and back as well as up and out and forward.

Counterplaying: Bush vs. Hussein

What can these analyses of Hussein's and Bush's personality development tell us about the origins of the Persian Gulf War? In Saddam Hussein's case, I think the answer is fairly clear. His malignant narcissism, at first directed toward those closest to him, gradually became extended outward toward such neighbors as Kuwait, and eventually toward the whole world. His outward redirection of his paranoid tendencies may well have made him a more popular and powerful leader within his own country. According to one study of paranoia in politics,

> [I]n order to be an effective charismatic leader it is useful to be at least somewhat paranoid. To genuinely believe that the source of the problems is "out there" and effectively communicate this is very persuasive to the followers seeking a strong leader with clear answers. It is comforting to hear that the problem is not with "us" but with "them" and that therefore the solution is to get rid of "them."[45]

Add to that paranoia a grandiose ambition for unlimited power, a tendency toward uncontrolled aggression, and "the absence of an ordinary sense of morality"[46]—all characteristic of Hussein's malignant narcissism—and you get a national leader who's quite willing to invade his neighbors and commit his troops to war after war.

In George Bush's case, the connection between his personality and his willingness (perhaps even eagerness) to go to war in Kuwait may not be quite so obvious. After all, George is *such* a nice guy. Why would a highly affiliative president like him lead the country into war?

One reason is that such presidents are prime candidates for the phenomenon Irving Janis called "groupthink." According to Janis, groupthink contributed significantly to our involvement in such wars as the Vietnam conflict—and I suspect it did the same with the Persian Gulf War.

Janis defined groupthink as

> a mode of thinking that people engage in when they are deeply involved in a cohesive in-group, when the members' strivings for unanimity over-

ride their motivation to realistically appraise alternative courses of action. . . . Groupthink refers to a deterioration of mental efficiency, reality testing, and moral judgment that results from in-group pressures. . . . *The more amiability and esprit de corps among the members of a policy-making in-group, the greater is the danger that independent critical thinking will be replaced by groupthink, which is likely to result in irrational and dehumanizing actions directed against outgroups.*[47]

How did groupthink influence George Bush's decision to go to war over Kuwait? As Bob Woodward described the White House decision-making process under Bush, the question of whether to emphasize the economic containment of Iraq or to take strong military action against its invasion of Kuwait was mainly handled by a small in-group. The group consisted of Bush plus his hard-line advisers John Sununu and Brent Scowcroft, with other cabinet members and advisers occasionally sitting in on the meetings. General Colin Powell, Chairman of the Joint Chiefs of Staff, became "concerned that no one was laying out the alternatives [especially on containment] to the President. Bush might not be hearing everything he needed to hear. A full slate of options should be presented."[48] So Powell went to meet with Bush and the top cabinet officers in the Oval Office. As Woodward describes the meeting (apparently from Powell's account):

> The sun was streaming in. For some reason the atmosphere wasn't right. There were interruptions; it was the President's office, the wrong place for this kind of discussion, Powell felt. He preferred the formality of the [military] Situation Room, where Bush could stay focused. The mood in the Oval Office was too relaxed, too convivial—the boys sitting around shooting the shit before the weekend. It was a general problem with these meetings, Powell felt. Often they had no beginning, middle or end. They would kick the ball around. Feet would be up on the table, cowboy boots gleaming.[49]

General Powell tried to get his case across anyway, to persuade the president that economic containment should be given a chance to work before a military invasion was attempted. But Bush said, "I don't think there's time politically for that strategy."[50]

Bob Woodward doesn't use the term "groupthink," but those informal Oval Office meetings sound like fertile ground for the growth of groupthink. The scene was much like the White House meetings of 30 years earlier, when John Kennedy and his small in-group were planning the Bay of Pigs invasion of Cuba. As Theodore Sorensen described those meetings, "[D]oubts were entertained but never pressed, partly out of fear of being labeled 'soft' or undaring in the eyes of . . . colleagues."[51] In early 1991, George Bush surely did not want to be labeled as soft or undaring in the eyes of *his* tough-minded colleagues. He wanted to keep their friendship and at the same time to show them, to show the world, that he was not a wimp. So the decision was made to march into Kuwait and Iraq.[52]

Bush's invasion of Iraq turned out rather better than Kennedy's semi-invasion of Cuba. But that wasn't because of Bush's brilliant decision making. In retrospect, Operation Desert Storm appears to have been successful largely because the United States and other U.N. forces were able to deploy massive firepower, and because the Iraqi forces had already been seriously weakened by their long war with Iran. The next time an American president makes a major military decision under the influence of groupthink, he—and we—may not be nearly so lucky.[53]

Would the war have happened anyway, with other counterplayers besides Bush or Hussein in the leadership roles? Little information is available on the personalities of other potential leaders in Iraq. But several exiled Iraqi politicians have criticized Hussein's tendencies toward paranoia and violence. Perhaps if they had been in office, they would not have resorted to force so quickly. In the United States, we probably would have seen a decision similar to Bush's if somebody like Dan Quayle or Jesse Helms had been president instead. Helms's personality appears more aggressive than Bush's, and Quayle is at least as affiliative.

But consider other possibilities. What if Michael Dukakis had been president, for instance? Whatever Dukakis's personality problems, he's not a groupthink kind of guy. What if Jimmy Carter had been in office, with his self-image as a peacemaker and his history of successful mediation between Sadat and Begin? He probably would have pursued economic sanctions all the way. His record with the Iran hostage crisis suggests that he might not have known when to stop. How about a Republican with a firmer sense of self and a less affiliative orientation than George Bush—Bob Dole, for instance? I'd need to do a full-scale study to make even a decent guess.

Perhaps with Saddam Hussein as the counterplayer, we needed George Bush to make our moves. Perhaps military action was the best response after all. We'll never know. But I have a lingering suspicion that with a different personality on one side or both, another resolution would have been reached well short of war, many fewer combatants and noncombatants would have died, and the people of Iraq *and* Kuwait would be in no worse shape than they are today.

14

From Colonel House to General Haig

EMBOLDENED by my two-lives-at-a-time comparison of counterplayers Bush and Hussein, I'll move on to even larger numbers in this chapter. I'm not ready to adopt the research strategy of my office neighbor, Dean Simonton, who often analyzes data on hundreds or even thousands of lives at a time.[1] But I do recognize that even in psychobiographical research it's sometimes useful to do multiple comparisons. So let's pick a number somewhere between one and 5,000. How about four?

Actually, I have a good reason for choosing that number. I looked at three lives in Chapter 7, one each for the three main psychological functions of creative writing. Here I want to look at three styles of political behavior that have been widely studied, so again I need at least three biographical examples. But I also want to show how one of those styles can be expressed in different ways. So with one example each for two styles, and two examples for the third, we arrive at a grand total of four. That's the most complex statistical analysis I'll undertake in this book.

Most psychobiographical research on political figures has been directed at U.S. presidents or presidential candidates. But a variety of other important actors populate the political stage, including appointed officials as well as elected ones. The most influential appointed official in our national government is often the president's principal foreign-policy adviser—usually but not always called the Secretary of State. As high-level diplomats and presidential representatives, these foreign-policy advisers tend not to drift very far from the political mainstream in their ideological positions. But their *personal styles* of expressing such mainstream positions may differ sharply, and may lead to ultimate success or failure in their governmental roles. Excessively flexible and excessively rigid diplomatic styles, for instance, may be equally disastrous when they're applied to international negotiations that require both compromise and trust.

Three stylistic patterns seem especially relevant to the behavior of foreign policy advisers: Machiavellianism, ego-idealism, and authoritarianism. Each has its own characteristically extreme form of expression. Highly Machiavellian individuals tend toward extreme flexibility, with style triumphing over substance. Highly ego-idealistic individuals tend toward extreme rigidity, with a stern adherence to a specific position regardless of diplomatic effectiveness. Highly authoritarian individuals focus their concerns on displays of power, regardless of the substantive issues involved. Other stylistic patterns can also be found in senior foreign-policy advisers, but these three have gained prominent expression in the American diplomatic history of this century.

Machiavellianism is, as its name indicates, a psychological pattern that largely (but in most cases unintentionally) recapitulates the teachings of that master foreign-policy adviser, Niccolo Machiavelli.[2] In laboratory studies, several qualities have been identified as major components of the Machiavellian personality: "(1) belief that people are manipulatable; (2) willingness to practice or attempt manipulation; (3) skill or ability in manipulation."[3] Furthermore, "In attending to the explicit, cognitive cues relevant to winning [in a social transaction], high Machs do not allow ethical, ideological, or interpersonal concerns to distract them from task-relevant strategy."[4] Highly Machiavellian individuals may profess to believe in a specific ideology, but they are typically willing to compromise or even to abandon their ideological position in order to gain a competitive advantage in the exercise of their manipulative skills.

Ego-idealism involves the opposite pattern: defending one's ideological position without compromise, even when external criteria strongly indicate that the cause will thereby be lost. For the ego-idealist, the important questions are: Does my position on public issues square with my conscience? Will my internalized moral standards be satisfied, or will my ego-ideal validate my worth, if I staunchly pursue a particular path regardless of the practical outcome?

As I noted in Chapter 1, I arrived at this construct only after first identifying a pattern I called "superego-tripping."[5] The late-sixties slang term "ego-tripping" referred to behaving in certain ways primarily to pump up your ego. I thought of superego-tripping as a process of pumping up your superego so much that you think you can change the world—or, more formally defined, as a pattern of "acting on the assumption that whatever behavior best satisfies the demands of one's superego will be most effective in attaining one's realistic goals."[6] I still think the concept is useful; superego-tripping didn't disappear along with the heyday of the student left. But some leftist activists eventually realized that thinking righteous thoughts doesn't necessarily lead to dramatic changes in the real world, and they *still* stuck with their righteous thoughts. Come hell or high water, they insisted on judging their own beliefs and actions, as well as those of others, principally in terms of their highest standards of moral perfection. That's what I call ego-idealism.

As Freud usually used the terms, the *superego* includes both the *conscience*, which tells us what's sinful or morally wrong and punishes us for doing it anyway, and the *ego ideal*, which tells us what's morally right and makes us feel virtuous if we do that instead. I'm sure many politicians derive whatever ethical standards they have mainly from their childhood fears of punishment for doing wrong.[7] But I suspect that ego-idealistic concerns are more prominent at the higher reaches of political life.

Authoritarianism, our third stylistic pattern, has long been familiar to social and personality psychologists. But it's probably less frequent among international diplomats than in the general populace. A key characteristic of authoritarianism in the original research was a "hierarchical conception of human relationships."[8] This hierarchical conception includes a preoccupation "with social mobility, with the dichotomy of the 'weak and the strong,' 'the bottom and the top,' and with the idea of moving upwards through the help of the powerful and the influential."[9] Authoritarianism also includes such interconnected characteristics as self-glorification, "pseudo-masculinity" (what we now call "machismo"), and conventional moralism.[10] Other standard features are the moralistic condemnation of outgroups (based on a punitive superego or conscience rather than a demanding ego ideal), extrapunitiveness ("a tendency to blame other people rather than oneself"), distrust and suspicion of others, and "exploitive-manipulative opportunism."[11] That final item may sound like basic Machiavellianism, but there's one real difference: the Machiavellian has fun manipulating others and delights in doing it with finesse, while the authoritarian's manipulative efforts are characteristically crude and joyless.

To compare and contrast Machiavellianism, ego-idealism, and authoritarianism in foreign-policy advisers, I've chosen four examples. John Foster Dulles, secretary of state under President Eisenhower, appears to have been high in ego-idealism, and was so regarded during his term in office. (Of course, the specific term was not in use then.) Both "Colonel" Edward House, who was Woodrow Wilson's principal foreign-policy adviser, and Henry Kissinger, secretary of state under Presidents Nixon and Ford, displayed a substantial degree of Machiavellianism. Their different versions of this general stylistic pattern are as instructive as their similarities. Finally, Alexander Haig, secretary of state during Ronald Reagan's first years in office, displayed aspects of both ego-idealism and Machiavellianism —but he turns out to be a better example of authoritarianism.

John Foster Dulles

John Foster Dulles's early environment nourished his development of a strong ego ideal. His father was a Presbyterian minister; his paternal grandfather and great-grandmother had been Christian missionaries.[12] Foster Dulles's father was theologically rather liberal, but that didn't mean he allowed any religious laxity at home. The family began each day with hymns and prayers, and joined in daily Bible study. The children were expected to take notes on their father's sermons, to discuss them at Sunday dinner,[13] and to memorize long passages from *The Pilgrim's Progress*.[14] Even as a small child, Foster gave evidence of having strongly internalized the standards of his parents and grandparents. When he was two, his mother noted that he "always says Amen very heartily" at morning prayers and the blessing of meals.[15] When Foster was five, she noted that "he is reverential to a striking degree. Whenever he sees . . . his father or mother in the attitude of prayer, he will instantly assume the same attitude and so remain until they rise." In his teens, according to one biographer, "he was such a fervent Christian and so generously strong of purpose that he often made the other two [siblings Allen and Eleanor] feel sinful and guilty in their weaknesses. He already had adopted a rigid code by which he had decided to direct his life."[17]

But Foster Dulles's personal standards of judgment were shaped by more than his early religious influences. His parents were more cosmopolitan than most small-town ministers and their spouses. Allen Macy Dulles had done postgraduate studies at Leipzig and Göttingen, and had met his future wife in Paris. Edith Foster Dulles was the daughter of John Watson Foster, a prominent diplomat who became Benjamin Harrison's secretary of state in 1892. Secretary Foster's grandson and namesake, John Foster Dulles, was then four years old. Edith Dulles's brother-in-law, Robert Lansing, became Woodrow Wilson's secretary of state when Foster Dulles was in his twenties. Foster Dulles "greatly admired his grandfather," "bent an avid ear" toward "Uncle Bert" Lansing's stories of Washington politics, and shaped his own ambitions accordingly.[18] When the time came for Dulles to choose a career, toward the end of his senior year at Princeton, he told his family that instead of becoming a minister as they had expected, he "could make a greater contribution as a Christian lawyer."[19] Dulles's ego ideal seems to have been prodding him even then, if we can judge by his sister's later account:

> When he meditated on his father's life, he came to a conclusion—which
> he did not often discuss but which I knew was a genuine feeling—that
> he could not follow adequately in his father's footsteps. He said he didn't
> think he was "good enough." He was not sure that he could serve in the
> same spirit as my father had.[20]

Dulles thus became a lawyer, though whether he was a consistently Christian one is open to question. After law school his grandfather's intervention enabled him to join a prominent Wall Street law firm. Through family connections and his own brilliance he rose rapidly in the firm, as he "combined law with international finance and diplomacy."[21] He did well by his clients, including several German corporations and government bodies. At age 38, he became the law firm's senior partner.

Dulles was regarded by his law partners as a pragmatist, quite willing to exploit in business the international contacts he made in his occasional diplomatic missions. He was also deeply involved for a time in the stock manipulations that contributed to the great market crash of 1929. According to one biographer, "His statements and writings took on a hard-headed, pragmatic thrust in which [his previous] Wilsonian 'idealism' was buried too deeply for most to see."[22] Indeed, Dulles's Christian orientation was so little in evidence during this period that a later political ally, Thomas E. Dewey, received the impression that "he spent some years as an atheist."[23]

In his late forties, however, John Foster Dulles reverted to the ego-idealism of his childhood and youth. His sister felt the change was initiated by their father's death in 1930, when Dulles "lost the man to whom he had always looked for guiding principles, for an unswerving sense of direction—a man he loved."[24] But his brother and law partner, Allen, recalled Foster as continuing to defend his German corporations from criticism well into the 1930s. Matters reached the point where Allen—later CIA director and not usually the family moralizer—shouted at Foster, "How can you call yourself a Christian and ignore what is happening in Germany?"[25] In 1935 the entire law firm rebelled at Foster Dulles's "cold-bloodedness in allowing business with his German (now Nazi) clients to go on as usual, simply because they were highly profitable."[26] His partners threatened to resign en masse if he continued as before. "Foster Dulles was at first bewildered, then adamant. . . . [F]inally, however, he capitulated in tears."[27]

This confrontation may only have accelerated changes already well advanced in Dulles's psyche. A few months earlier he had written a high-minded but rather abstract article for the *Atlantic Monthly,* titled "The Road to Peace." The article's more emotional passages could have been describing the repressed conflicts and psychological changes of a man's midlife crisis, rather than the processes of world politics:

> The true explanation of the imminence of war lies in the inevitability of change and the fact that peace efforts have been misdirected toward the prevention of change. Thereby forces which are in the long run irresistible are temporarily dammed up. When they finally break through, they do so with violence.[28]

Dulles's internal changes, progressing in conjunction with change in the international scene, appear to have been consolidated by his experiences at two peace conferences held in successive weeks in 1937. The first, a secular meeting sponsored by the League of Nations, struck him as "absolutely futile." The second, sponsored by the Federal Council of Churches, impressed him with its "spirit of unity and fellowship." The contrast led him to conclude (according to a later council publication, probably drafted by Dulles himself) that "peace must have a spiritual basis. . . . [D]iplomacy had failed. His search for a successful method led to the conclusion that the qualities taught by the great religions were needed for the practical solution of world problems."[29] Thereafter Dulles became increasingly active as a Christian layman and indeed as a Christian lawyer, his original career goal. Dulles identified his religious awakening as marking the end of a long period of secular uncertainty: "For many years it never occurred to me that the Christian Gospel had any practical bearing on the solution of international problems. So I came to my present views only after 30 years of experience with futility."[30]

This return to the childhood religious basis for his ego-idealism led in turn to the heavily moralistic stance that characterized Dulles as secretary of state in the 1950s. Ole Holsti has made an extensive analysis of Secretary Dulles's ideological system, his "operational code."[31] The picture that emerges is one of almost unremitting ego-idealism. The mature Dulles's key beliefs, according to Holsti's analysis, included such precepts as "The nature of foreign policy is determined by the spiritual quality of those who formulate it" and "The cold war is fundamentally a moral rather than a political conflict."[32] As Holsti summarized Dulles's views on the Soviets:

> Dulles selected two aspects of Marxist theory—materialism and atheism—for special emphasis. In *War or Peace*, for example, he had written, "Soviet Communism starts with an atheistic Godless premise. Everything else flows from that premise." After pointing out that the free world had such high moral standards as to preclude the use of immoral methods, Dulles concluded that "atheists can hardly be expected to conform to an ideal so high." He argued that the anti-spiritual rather than the political aspects of the communist creed were most important, ascribing the evils of the latter to the former. He attributed the characteristics of the Soviet leaders—insincerity, immorality, brutality, and deceitfulness—primarily to their atheism.[33]

Dulles's specific beliefs about the causes of war, about policies for dealing with its aftermath, and about other international issues changed in various ways over the course of his diplomatic career. Often those changes in beliefs cannot be clearly related to the course of his life history outside his direct experiences in international politics.[34] But Dulles's general stylistic approach of intense moralism in international affairs can be traced to his childhood history of ego-idealism, renewed in later adulthood. The problems arising from his tendency to judge international politics strictly by his own internalized moral criteria, rather than by more flexible or pragmatic standards, were perceptively identified by theologian Reinhold Niebuhr:

> Mr. Dulles' moral universe makes everything quite clear, too clear. Yet it does not illuminate any of the problems created by the Russian economic advances both at home and in Asia and Africa. And it does complicate

our relations with our allies, who find our self-righteousness very vex-
atious. For self-righteousness is the inevitable fruit of simple moral judgments, placed in the service of moral complacency.[35]

Colonel House

Edward M. House's father was not a minister but an entrepreneur. A self-made
man, Thomas House earned his riches initially in sugar cane, cotton, and banking. During the Civil War his ships ran the Union blockade of Galveston, Texas, to
sell military necessities to the Confederate Army. Thomas House's Confederate
sympathies did not overcome his business sense: "Since he believed that the
Confederacy must fail ultimately, he avoided accumulating its currency and added
to his gold reserves in England whenever possible. Thus at the end of the war, he
had $300,000 in gold laid away in England."[36]

You might guess from this brief history that the senior House was more Machiavellian than moralistic. His son Edward admired and identified with him:

[H]e seemed to me then, as he seems to me now, among the ablest men
I have ever known. . . . I owe more to my father than to any person, living or dead. He not only made it possible for me to pursue the bent of
my inclinations by leaving me a fortune sufficient for all moderate wants,
but he gave me an insight into the philosophy of life that has been of in-
calculable value.[37]

Edward House's childhood memories emphasized the violence and danger of
early Texas and the Civil War years. He played in a gang that fought pitched gun
battles with other gangs of boys; several times real casualties resulted. The young
Edward established himself among his peers by displays of physical prowess,
until at age twelve he fell from a swing and hit his head. "Brain fever ensued, and
for a long time I hovered between life and death. Upon my recovery, malaria
fastened upon me, and I have never been strong since."[38] Thereafter he found
himself unable to triumph physically over his peers, responded poorly to the heat
of Texas (and Washington) summers, and periodically experienced malarial fe-
vers.

In adolescence, House turned from the physical pursuit of power to more
psychological strategies. Indeed, such tendencies may have begun earlier. In their
classic psychobiographical study, *Woodrow Wilson and Colonel House,* Alexander
and Juliette George suggest that "it was feelings of inadequacy as youngest son in
a large family and as the small boy among bigger playmates, as well as the fall
from the swing when he was twelve, that made him so eager a manipulator of
others."[39] House told an early biographer, "I used to like to set boys at each other
to see what they would do, and then try to bring them around again."[40] A Cornell
classmate remembered him as "a quiet peacemaker in college rows. . . . When-

ever there was a disturbance Ed would silently appear, and in a few minutes—you wouldn't know exactly how it happened—the trouble would be over."[41] House himself recalled less benevolent examples of his manipulativeness:

> It was always a joy to play such pranks and appear an innocent by-stander. I used to ask questions and get minute instructions about how to do this or that thing, or how to play games in which I was already more proficient than those who sought to teach me. In some instances I would gradually show my skill. In others I would do so at once much to the chagrin of my would-be teachers.[42]

At eighteen, House became intrigued by presidential politics. But he decided, according to his memoirs, that he lacked the physical stamina and the oratorical skills to become a national political leader. A biographer paraphrased his thoughts at the time: "Better far, he reasoned with uncanny shrewdness for a boy of eighteen, to shape his life so that he might become one of those policy-makers and counselors who sit behind the scenes and inspire the course of events."[43] However much House may have later exaggerated his adolescent insights, this was in fact the course his life took.

When House was twenty-four, his father died and left him a modest fortune. House's brief description of subsequent events conceals as much as it reveals: "I applied myself assiduously for a few years to business, but was unable to keep my health and I left Houston, the place of my nativity, for the hills of Austin."[44] House at this time was working to expand his inherited fortune, but he was also eager to become active politically. In Austin, the state capitol, he moved quietly but quickly into a position of power. He became a close friend of the state attorney general, James Hogg, who was subsequently elected governor. When Hogg ran for a second term, against heavy opposition from the railroads and other corporate interests, the thirty-four-year-old Edward House volunteered to run his campaign. Hogg won resoundingly, and conferred upon House the honorary title of Colonel. It was as Colonel House that he became known to the larger public and to history.

House exercised his organizing skills to win the next several Texas gubernatorial campaigns for a succession of candidates. According to Alexander and Juliette George, he displayed "a genius for political strategy, a rare ability to detach himself from the heat of political battle, coolly to appraise the essential elements of a situation and then, quietly and without waste motion, to address himself to the tasks which most tellingly advanced his patron's interests."[45] In return, House asked for nothing except the opportunity to give his elected candidates useful advice on how to run the government. Machiavelli would have been proud of him.

During the early years of the twentieth century, House's eye turned increasingly toward the national scene. He was a Democrat, but he correctly judged the

Democratic candidates for president during this period to be unelectable. Furthermore, House had reservations of a characterological nature concerning the Democrats' favorite standard-bearer, William Jennings Bryan: "I do not believe that any one ever succeeded in changing his mind upon any subject that he had determined upon. . . . I believe he feels that his ideas are God-given and are not susceptible to the mutability of those of the ordinary human being."[46] As a true Machiavellian, House wanted a candidate whom he could not only help get elected but whom, once elected, he could influence.

House found his man in Woodrow Wilson. A thoroughgoing ego-idealist (and a minister's son), Wilson could at times be as dogmatic as Bryan. But Wilson could also be influenced by the right appeals, as House recognized immediately. The day after their first meeting in 1911, House wrote of Wilson, "He is not the biggest man I have ever met, but he is one of the pleasantest and I would rather play with him than any prospective candidate I have seen." Two days later House wrote, "The more I see of Governor Wilson the better I like him, and I think he is going to be a man one can advise with some degree of satisfaction. This, you know, you could never do with Mr. Bryan."[47]

House was the ideal match for Wilson. First, he was able, convincingly, to tell Wilson what Wilson wanted to hear about himself. Second, he did not openly dispute Wilson's judgments even when he privately disagreed with them. Third, House was as flexible as Wilson was dogmatic, as skilled diplomatically as Wilson was unskilled. Wilson needed such a person to save his own programs from defeat by the hostility his uncompromising moralism often aroused in his opponents. This was especially true with regard to foreign relations.

Wilson came to regard House as his most trusted confidant, so similar to the president in basic views that he could be counted on to act as an extension of Wilson's self. According to Alexander and Juliette George, "On numerous occasions when he placed House in charge of complex negotiations, he told the Colonel that the need for giving him instructions was obviated by the fact that their thoughts and purposes were as one."[48] This closeness became particularly important to Wilson during the difficult diplomatic moves required by World War I.

House's basic views on domestic and world politics were in fact substantially congruent with Wilson's. But he worked hard to underline their congruence and to promote Wilson's trust in him, even when House himself realized that the congruence was not perfect. George and George note that some of Wilson's other associates disliked House for what they perceived as his "Machiavellian scheming" in his approaches to Wilson. While attempting to dispute this perception, the Georges actually inventory House's Machiavellian qualities:

It is true that House consciously tried to manipulate Wilson. The Colonel's conduct was studied, unspontaneous, and detached. . . . If he

coated his recommendations with skillful flattery and assurances of affection, which were at least partially simulated, doubtless he felt justified by
the fact that he could not otherwise hope to gain Wilson's acceptance of
his advice. If he deliberately exploited his insights into Wilson's personality to augment his own influence, doubtless he felt justified by the
hope that he was creating a possibility to serve the President and their
shared ideals.[49]

Richard Christie and Florence Geis, in their laboratory studies of Machiavellians, did not argue that such people lack beliefs, ideals, or honest emotions.
Rather, the Machiavellian's emphasis is differently placed: on the manipulation of
others' emotions, on utilitarianism over conventional morality, on "getting things
done" rather than on holding uncompromisingly to "long-range ideological
goals."[50] Colonel House would have surely ranked high on all these criteria of
Machiavellianism. In *Philip Dru: Administrator*, his utopian fantasy published
anonymously in 1912, House had his would-be benevolent dictator Philip speak
in classically Machiavellian terms: "If we would convince and convert, we must
veil our thoughts and curb our enthusiasm, so that those we would influence will
think us reasonable."[51]

The friendship between House and Wilson finally ran aground precisely on the
conflict between compromising to get things done and upholding ideological
goals. Other matters were involved as well: specific disagreements on certain
complex issues involved in the settling of World War I; House's increasing tendency to act on his own rather than to remain the faceless power behind the
throne; the second Mrs. Wilson's strong personal dislike of House. But the ultimate incompatibility involved Wilson's belief in the virtuousness of his own
positions on the settlement of the war, and thus his unwillingness to engage in
significant compromise, versus House's feeling that multiple compromises both
international and domestic must be made to ensure a lasting peace. The ego-
idealist and the Machiavellian, though still close in terms of basic ideological
positions, were unable to reconcile the differences in their personal styles. Late in
1919, the "fruitful collaboration" of seven years came to an abrupt end.

Henry Kissinger

Henry Kissinger was the first Machiavellian foreign-policy adviser I looked at,
nearly twenty years ago.[52] Since then, a good deal of new material on Kissinger
has become available to support my analysis. Here I'll review my earlier arguments and add to them. In some regards the Machiavellian characteristics that
Colonel House displayed in the early 1900s remain on display in Kissinger in the
late 1900s. But there are enough differences between Kissinger and Colonel

House to show that similar personal styles may express strongly contrasting ideological positions.

Whereas House had an admired, successful, and probably Machiavellian father, Kissinger's father was unable to cope effectively with the dangers of being a Jew in Nazi Germany or an immigrant in America. Kissinger's own description of his father suggests a failed non-Machiavellian: "a man of great goodness in a world where goodness has no meaning."[53] Kissinger's mother may have provided a more Machiavellian model; at least she took the steps necessary to get the family to America and to survive there. Like House, Kissinger showed no strong signs of Machiavellian traits as a child but apparently developed or intensified such traits as an adolescent. For House, a loss of physical power was the crucial experience. For Kissinger, it seems to have been his observation of his father's loss of prestige and self-esteem.

As a young American soldier in Germany at the end of World War II, Kissinger began to impress people as a man "high on energy, low on passion," someone who "always talked in manipulative terms."[54] When he moved into academia, Kissinger wrote admiringly about the manipulative talents of both Metternich and Bismarck.[55] When he became a foreign-policy adviser himself, Kissinger displayed the essential qualities of the Machiavellian personality. He strongly emphasized utility over morality in the conduct of foreign policy. He easily overcame his own emotional investments when he switched political and personal allegiance from his political mentor, Nelson Rockefeller, to the previously despised Richard Nixon. He displayed (at least privately) great pleasure in manipulating others, from White House reporters to heads of state. William Safire has described, on the basis of extensive personal acquaintance in the White House, the range of Kissinger's mind: "from the creation of grand geopolitical concepts to the manipulation of minute bargaining levers . . . from niggling little bureaucratic intrigues and tricks to a profound concern for 'moral authority.'"[56] Bruce Mazlish, in a psychobiographical study, has commented on Kissinger's

> gift of flattery, including the flattery of seeing his opponent's side. . . . In many of his negotiating situations Kissinger is able to invoke an almost sexual note. He woos and courts the people whom he hopes to win over. Like a lover, he tells those with whom he negotiates what they want to hear. He is not blatantly duplicitous, for that would be self-defeating . . . but he so phrases things as to say them in the way the other person wishes to hear them. In this he is like a good confidence man playing the role of lover.[57]

Kissinger and House would have understood each other. They probably would have admired each other's diplomatic skills. But they might well have been on different sides of the political fence had they faced the same issues. Though

House was raised in a violent time and developed the Texas youth's legendary skill with a six-shooter, his efforts on the international scene were directed consistently toward compromise and away from the forceful imposition of national might. Kissinger has reportedly fantasized himself as the lone cowboy who keeps order "without even a pistol, maybe, because he doesn't go in for shooting."[58] But he has often argued for a combination of negotiation and force in international affairs.[59] He seems to have felt little compunction in promoting two of the most deadly aerial bombardments of the Vietnam War, the 1969 secret bombing of Cambodia and the 1972 Christmas bombing of Hanoi.[60]

There's a further difference. House placed the Machiavellian skills of his fictional hero Philip Dru at the service of a radical overhaul of the nation's social and economic structure—anticipating in significant ways not only Woodrow Wilson's major domestic reforms but Roosevelt's New Deal of two decades later. House always emphasized moderation, but he applied that moderation to achieve progressive goals. In contrast, Kissinger's basic goals have been conservative, stressing "order, restraint, and the general maintenance of the status quo against the revolutionary."[61]

Kissinger's personality has intrigued several biographers and psychobiographers. Dana Ward has diagnosed him as neurotically depressive, reacting against feelings of worthlessness.[62] Bruce Mazlish proposes instead that Kissinger displays a strong fear of being dependent, as well as various kinds of sexual sublimation, displacement of hostility from the Nazis onto the Communists, and other psychodynamic patterns.[63] Starr finds room in Kissinger's personality for traits identified both by Ward and by Mazlish, as well as for Machiavellianism, a strong power motive, and other characteristics.[64] Kissinger's most recent and most thorough biographer, Walter Isaacson, never refers to Machiavelli or Machiavellianism in discussing Kissinger, but characterizes his personality in what sound like high-Mach terms: "brilliant, conspiratorial, furtive, sensitive to linkages and nuances, prone to rivalries and power struggles, charming yet at times deceitful."[65]

With these personological assessments of Kissinger in mind, this is a good place to emphasize that descriptions of foreign-policy advisers as Machiavellians, ego-idealists, etc., should not be regarded as complete characterizations. Machiavellianism appears to be an important dimension for the understanding of Kissinger's behavior as a foreign-policy adviser, as it was for Colonel House. But other personality dimensions, as well as any of a number of ideological patterns, may fit comfortably with Machiavellianism, especially in an individual as complex as Henry Kissinger.

Alexander Haig

Alexander Haig may appear to combine aspects of ego-idealism and Machiavellianism. His anti-Communist views have typically been stated in hard-line "God-on-our-side" tones reminiscent of Dulles at his most moralistic. At the same time, Haig has acquired a reputation for deviousness, especially in connection with the circumstances leading to Richard Nixon's resignation and subsequent pardon.[66] As I understand them, ego-idealism and Machiavellianism are at opposite ends of a continuum, at least in terms of their occurrence as significant personality patterns. Moderate amounts of each tendency may co-exist in one personality, but (at least in theory) not high levels of both. So it's worth considering, to clarify the constructs as well as to improve our understanding of a prominent politician, whether Alexander Haig was in fact dominated by both patterns simultaneously, or whether his predominant personal style is better characterized in other ways.

Haig was born into what he has described as a "well-to-do, upper-middle-class family" living in a Main Line suburb of Philadelphia. His lawyer father died at age thirty-eight when Haig was nine, leaving a widow with three children and (in Haig's words) a "minimum estate, just enough to carry us five years."[67] He told another interviewer, "I had pretty much to fend for myself in terms of economics. I had newspaper routes, worked for the Post Office, the Atlantic Refining Company. I even worked as a floorwalker in the ladies' department of John Wanamaker's to support myself."[68]

Haig's mother, seven years older than his father, turned her ambitions toward her children when her husband died. Haig describes her as "a strong, exceptional woman. . . . She was lace-curtain Philadelphia Irish. Her brothers were all doctors and lawyers."[69] She later recalled that her son Alec "always had a housefull of boys around. Alec was the leader. I wanted him to be an attorney like his father. But he always wanted West Point. . . . If he had followed my advice years ago, he'd be a Senator by now. I wanted him to be a lawyer. The Army is such a slow procedure, and you can't make any money. Money is the thing you want as you get older."[70]

Haig once said he had decided to go to West Point because of "financial necessity."[71] But financial issues were probably less important than personal motives. The first page of Haig's 1992 memoir concerns his childhood fascination with his father's military uniform and equipment, discovered in his grandparents' attic:

> Alexander Meigs Haig was an aloof father who neither punished nor
> conversed with his children, and although his death was, and remains,
> the critical event of my life, I remember the uniform I never saw him
> wear better than I remember him.[72]

Haig failed at his first attempts to enter West Point, but "the magnetic pull of military life" stayed with him until an uncle got him in through a congressional appointment.[73] Even then, West Point's strong appeal to Haig did not guarantee him unusual success there. In 1947 he graduated 214th out of a class of 310. He did impress his classmates, however; his yearbook photograph was captioned, "Strong convictions and even stronger ambitions."[74]

Haig was able to hold his convictions in check as he began to move up the Army chain of command. After being assigned to U.S. occupation headquarters in postwar Japan, he met and married the daughter of General Alonzo Fox, chief of staff of the Far East Command. Haig became Fox's aide de camp and thus joined the elite staff of General Douglas MacArthur, de facto ruler of Japan. Haig came to admire MacArthur as being "highly independent, self-assured, competent . . . the focal point of policy in that part of the world."[75]

Haig served as aide to another of MacArthur's generals during the Korean War. After President Truman removed MacArthur from command for insubordination, Haig's own career languished for a decade, until he earned a master's degree in international affairs at Georgetown University. His master's thesis called for "a 'new breed of military professional' who could 'continually appraise military policy in terms of its political implications,' and who should occupy 'a seat at the pinnacle' among presidential advisers."[76]

Haig moved a little closer to the pinnacle with a staff job at the Pentagon. He soon became an assistant to Army Secretary Cyrus Vance, and followed him up the ladder when Vance became secretary of defense. As the Vietnam War escalated, Haig put in six months on active duty there. He was wounded once and received several medals for bravery. This service was followed by a year and a half at West Point, as a regimental commander and then as deputy commandant. One of Haig's more outspoken cadets at West Point later described Haig's insistence that cadets

> march even more rigidly than regulations required, with elbows locked, fingers cocked at the second knuckle and thumb, and index finger "pointed like an arrow" to the ground. . . . Haig told his cadet officers, "If they can get that hand straight, that elbow stuff, then all the rest falls into place. Every directive becomes second nature," adding, "It's my way of putting my signature on a unit."[77]

But Haig was soon needed for more important work than straightening out the index fingers of West Point cadets. In the new Nixon administration, Henry Kissinger had been appointed as Assistant to the President for National Security Affairs, and he wanted a military aide to organize the operations of the National Security Council. Haig, who had carried out similar functions for Cyrus Vance in the Kennedy administration, was recommended for the job. Kissinger hired him after one interview. Kissinger's later description of Haig is an interesting and perhaps Machiavellian mixture of praise and insinuation:

> He disciplined my anarchic tendencies and established coherence and procedure in an NSC staff of talented prima donnas. . . . Over the course

of Nixon's first term he acted as my partner, strong in crises, decisive in judgment, skillful in bureaucratic infighting, indefatigable in his labors.

To be sure, nobody survives in the rough-and-tumble of White House politics—especially of the Nixon White House—without a good measure of ruthlessness. I could not help noticing that Haig was implacable in squeezing to the sidelines potential competitors for my attention.[78]

Haig was probably better informed about world affairs than most military men, but he had not been trained as a diplomat. He lacked the political sophistication of a House or a Kissinger, as much as he lacked the lofty aims and virtually lifelong diplomatic experience of a Dulles. According to William Safire, "Kissinger's Haig was a military staff man who would lay out options for a commander, offer his opinion when asked for it, and then put his complete loyalty and penchant for orderliness behind whatever decision his superior made."[79]

There was, however, a superior even higher than Kissinger. When H. R. ("Bob") Haldeman was forced to resign at the height of the Watergate furor, President Nixon asked Haig to assume his position as White House chief of staff. Haig accepted.

Kissinger admired Haig's performance in the Watergate White House, even though he remained ambivalent about Haig's character:

> By sheer willpower, dedication, and self-discipline, he held the government together. He more than anyone succeeded in conveying the impression of a functioning White House. He saw to it that decisions emerged from predictable processes. He served his President loyally but he never forgot his duty to his country. To be sure, only a man of colossal self-confidence could have sustained such a role. His methods were sometimes rough; his insistence on formal status could be grating. But the role assigned to Haig was not one that could be filled by choirboys.[80]

Haig managed to escape from Watergate's "White House Horrors" with his reputation intact—indeed, with increased prestige. For several months he served as chief of staff for President Ford. But a man who had been a sort of acting president during Nixon's final months did not mesh comfortably with the staff of a new president. Haig was kicked upstairs (and out of the country) to become Supreme Allied Commander of NATO. He continued in that role during the early years of the Carter administration. He eventually resigned in order to test the waters for a possible race for the presidency, but never formally announced his candidacy.[81] Ronald Reagan was nominated instead. When Reagan was elected president, he chose Alexander Haig as his secretary of state.

Secretary of State Haig quickly focused his attention not upon the actual conduct of foreign affairs but upon the question of where he stood in the White House hierarchy. Haig's 1984 memoir of his term in office displays an obsession with this question of hierarchical position. According to Haig, "[T]he essential point, the very first order of business, was the structure of the foreign policy establishment. The President had to decide who was going to do what, and put his decision into writing."[82] To Haig's vast frustration, Reagan never dealt with that "very first order of business." While Haig tried to persuade him to do so over many months, other members of the president's staff repeatedly undercut Haig or got between him and Reagan. From the beginning they saw Haig as excessively ambitious. The more he insisted on a clear line of command in the White House, with himself just under the president, the more they resisted his ambitions. Their suspicions were confirmed only three months into the presidency, during the confusion after Reagan was shot. Haig proclaimed (incorrectly) that he was constitutionally third in line to exercise presidential power, and that in the vice president's absence, "As of now, I am in control here, in the White House."[83]

Though Haig later claimed he had been misunderstood, this apparent revelation of naked ambition dogged him during his remaining 15 months as secretary of state. Much of his time and energy continued to be spent in bureaucratic infighting with other members of the president's staff, sometimes on specific policy issues, often simply on arguments about who was speaking for the president or who should be. When Haig finally made another clear hierarchical error (he gave an order about foreign policy that he had not previously cleared with Reagan), the president "accepted his resignation."

How can Haig's personal style best be described? As I've already indicated, his rhetoric has sometimes sounded so like Dulles's, in proclaiming a moral war between the virtuous West and the evil Soviet Empire, that he might be mistaken for an ego-idealist. But no moral rigidity was evident when Haig testified at his confirmation hearing with regard to the Watergate cover-up, the secret bombing of Cambodia, and the Christmas bombing of Hanoi:

> I cannot bring myself to render judgment on Richard Nixon, or, for that matter, Henry Kissinger. I worked intimately for both men. It is not for me, it is not in me, to render moral judgments on them. I must leave that to others, to history, and to God.[84]

This statement may have helped Haig get the favorable vote of a Senate committee. It did not signal the presence of an energetic ego ideal.

Was Haig, then, primarily a Machiavellian personality? He certainly learned a lot from Henry Kissinger about how to survive in government. Even before he met Kissinger, he had occasionally made rather Machiavellian moves to advance his own career. But Haig was never the Machiavellian that Kissinger was. Much of Haig's energies were expended not on courtly intrigues but on grinding away at getting the office organized, putting the data in the right order to present to the president, setting up and maintaining the rules of procedure. A true Machiavellian such as Kissinger plays between the rules. A Haig may try to establish rules that give him an advantage, but once they're established, he wants them kept. Kissinger would never have spent a year and a half, as Haig did, trying to get the president and his men to agree in writing to a particular organizational schema. Kissinger would have instead used the ambiguity to his advantage. Kissinger never let the mask over his own ambition slip as badly as Haig did during the crisis of the Reagan assassination attempt. Haig may have wanted to be a true Machiavellian, but he came to the Kissinger school too late. He is, at best, a failed Machiavellian.

Haig's fascination with hierarchy suggests that he is better characterized in terms of another stylistic dimension: authoritarianism. He has displayed not only an overriding concern with moving upward through military and government hierarchies with "the help of the powerful and the influential,"[85] but also many of the other authoritarian characteristics listed earlier: self-glorification, macho pseudo-masculinity, extrapunitiveness, and so on. Haig's memoir *Caveat* could be analyzed as a case document in authoritarianism. His account of his prolonged battle with other White House staffers exemplifies the following passage from the classic work on the topic, *The Authoritarian Personality*:

> The high [authoritarian] scorer's feeling of really belonging to the privi-
> leged group is highly tenuous. Due to his real or imagined social and
> psychological marginality he feels persistently threatened of being de-
> graded in one way or another. It is as a defense against the possibility of
> being grouped with the outcast and underdog that he rigidly has to as-
> sert his identification with the privileged groups. This loud and explicit
> assertion of being on top seems to ensue from his silent and implicit
> conviction that he really is, or belongs, at the bottom.[86]

The final sentence in that paragraph suggests a developmental source for Haig's authoritarianism. The authoritarian syndrome was conceptualized as deriving from parental behaviors that force the child to repress his ordinary feelings of hostility toward his parents, and later to displace such feelings onto outgroups and those lower in the social hierarchy. We don't know enough about Haig's relationships with his parents, either the "aloof" and "impeccably dressed" father[87] or the ambitious older mother, to apply this derivation to Haig's own early history. But the abrupt drop in the family's economic status after his father's death, forcing Haig to work at such (to him) demeaning jobs as floor walker in a women's clothing department, appears to have left him unusually sensitive about his own hierarchical position and about new threats to that position. He may well have acquired much of the detail of his hierarchical approach to life from his long experience in the Army. But from his early yearning for a West Point education to his insistence on hierarchy at the White House, Alexander Haig has carried his own authoritarian agenda within him.

Variations on Several Styles

For each of these four men, the influence of personal life history on the development of a public political style is evident from the record. We don't have the kinds of early biographical detail for any of them that would support deep probing of unconscious motivational patterns. But Dulles's stress on moralistic concerns emerged from his family religious context at a remarkably early age. Though he wandered astray in young and middle adulthood, his early ego-idealism had returned in strength by the time he became secretary of state. House and Kissinger developed Machiavellian patterns for different reasons in adolescence, but both then exercised their Machiavellian skills with zeal in domestic and international politics. Haig seems to have recognized the Army as an appropriate place for his incipient authoritarianism well before anyone else did. He probably would have done better to remain in the Army, but his successes as well as his failures in national and international politics clearly owe much to his authoritarian style.

The stylistic variations possible among American secretaries of state and other high-level foreign policy advisers are not exhausted by this limited consideration of four men and three expressive styles. Jeane Kirkpatrick, in her pre-governmental role as an academic researcher, identified certain women legislators as "moralizers," especially concerned with "questions of right and wrong, good and bad and [a] tendency to emphasize the moral dimension."[88] I wonder whether Kirkpatrick is herself a "moralizer" of the ego-idealistic type, or whether she exemplifies another kind of moralizer with strongly punitive superego concerns. I wonder, too, whether some of the personality syndromes identified among domestic politicians by Lloyd Etheredge—including Robert Tucker's concept of "warfare personality," Friedlander and Cohen's "compensatory masculinity," and Iremonger's "Phaeton complex"—may be equally plentiful among prominent actors on the international scene.[89]

Our most recent secretaries of state have been distinguished more by their undistinguished personalities than by anything as clear as the stylistic patterns of House, Dulles, Kissinger, and Haig. These four men provide fascinating fodder for political psychobiographers. But perhaps we're better off in the long run with senior foreign policy advisers who merely do a competent job, without any dramatic public displays of their underlying psychodynamics.

PART FIVE

Other Methods, Other Lives

15

Going Beyond Scratch

ONE OF MY friends in Davis, California, is a science fiction writer named Kim Stanley Robinson. Stan got his doctorate in English literature and has taught at the University of California, but he prefers to make his living as a writer. He is an inspired and effective writer. He has won several important science fiction awards, and he's rapidly becoming a Major Figure in the Field. I occasionally pat myself on the back for having recognized early just how good a writer he is.

Some science fiction writers know a lot more about science than about writing fiction, and some know a lot more about literature than about science. Stan is a triple threat. He's intimately familiar with the history and tradition of science fiction, he knows a great deal about contemporary science, and he has a literary scholar's understanding of postmodernism and other current critical approaches. It was probably the latter talent that got us into an extended discussion of a question he asked me one day: When I'm preparing my psychobiographical studies, am I really doing anything that different from what Stan does when he writes science fiction?

At first, I thought the answer was obvious: My studies are factual and Stan's fiction is, well, fictional. But Stan didn't see it as that obvious, and he made a case that set me to thinking seriously about the philosophy of psychobiography. I do put together a story about somebody's life, or at least about key incidents in a life, don't I? Yes, and so does he. I do make inferences about what that person thought or felt during those key incidents, and I speculate about why the person did what he or she did, don't I? Yes; and so does Stan. I try to write all this down in pleasing language and give it a narrative shape, don't I? Yes—like Stan. So what's different?

Well, I said, I write about real people. But so does Stan—identifiably so at times, as in his story about the pilot of the plane that was sent to A-bomb

Hiroshima;[1] at other times in disguise, but still as real as he can make them. Well, I do lots of research, I said. But so does Stan—as I already knew, having given him a quick orientation to the Library of Congress stacks one memorable day. Stan's novel *Red Mars* is as thorough and accurate an account of the human colonization of Mars as you're likely to find before the planet is actually colonized.[2] His utopian novel *Pacific Edge* is a more honest and thoughtful and *human* utopia than anything else in print.[3]

Well, I told Stan in desperation, my work is different from yours because I keep trying to increase the accuracy of my life histories and to reduce my level of speculation. I do that iteratively and by any means necessary—through research not only in the library stacks but in archives and personal interviews and wherever else I can think of. I keep trying to tie my life narratives and my interpretations of lives as closely as possible to the factual record. Fiction writers may do some of that too, but they don't feel *obligated* to do it, or they wouldn't be writing fiction.

Stan was willing to allow that I might have something there. Even though we often use similar methods (including close observations of behavior as well as the standard scholarly research techniques), and though we share certain similar aims (including depictions of the psychological essence of a life), he doesn't always aim for literal accuracy. He acknowledged that even though I won't ever completely achieve that aim, it makes sense for me to keep trying. In that regard, he recognized, there is a difference between science and science fiction, and what I'm doing is more science than fiction.

Much the same issue came up several years ago in my own psychology department, though it began on the other side of the fence from Stan's questions. When Stan initially suggested that he and I are both writing a kind of psychologically insightful speculative fiction, he wasn't trying to insult me; he was welcoming me to the fold. When several of my psychologist colleagues argued that I'm writing some sort of "humanistic" or "journalistic" or "literary" stuff, they never quite called it "fiction." But they were clearly saying that they didn't consider it science and that I wasn't in *their* fold.

The issue got serious when two of my graduate students proposed to do psychobiographical studies as their doctoral dissertations. Departmental rules, from the early days of our Ph.D. program, had stipulated one primary methodological requirement: that a doctoral dissertation must be based on empirical research. When my students submitted their dissertation proposals, those argumentative faculty members suddenly announced that they'd always taken the word *empirical* in our program description to mean only "quantifiable" or "nomothetic" research—even though the issue had never been addressed publicly, and though dictionaries inside and outside psychology commonly define *empirical* in the broadest terms, such as "related to facts or experiences . . . based on factual investigation."[4] The rules are clear, these earnestly nomothetic professors said: no Ph.D.'s granted for psychobiographical dissertations in *our* department.

Perceiving not only my students but my own professional identity under attack, I responded as vigorously as I could. Serious psychobiography involves "factual investigation" of the most painstaking kinds, I said. There is no inherent difference between the many items of biographical fact collected about one individual in a life-historical study and the few facts collected about each of many individuals in the standard sort of "empirical" psychological research. My students would be using rigorous methods of data collection and interpretation in their research, and they would be dealing with important psychological issues.

When the votes were counted, most of my departmental colleagues proved tolerant enough to permit the formation of two dissertation committees, each one appropriate to supervise a psychobiographical study. But to a few psychologists there and to many psychologists elsewhere, the idea that a biographical study of one individual can be genuinely "empirical" remains a sore point of considerable dimensions. I hope the still-troubled members of my own department, at least, feel somewhat reassured by the firmly factual but methodologically and theoretically creative dissertations that evolved out of my students' work.[5]

In response to continuing pressures from both directions—from those who see psychobiography as a kind of fiction and like it that way, and from those who see it as a non-science and don't like it that way—psychobiographers must keep up their own pressure. They must go beyond the "starting-from-scratch" methodological guidelines that I reviewed in Chapter 2 and those I've illustrated elsewhere in this book, to increase the scientific sophistication of their research and the accuracy of their case histories. They must insist that although psychobiography is not a totally perfectible enterprise, it is like other scientific approaches an *improvable* enterprise. Its chosen phenomena may be more intractable (individual lives rather than group averages) and its developmental history is briefer than in the more well-established sciences, including certain of the psychological sciences. But as W. M. Runyan has pointed out, there are ways to assess the progress of psychobiography as a scientific enterprise, and by his assessment, it has indeed progressed measurably from Freud's time to ours.[6]

I don't expect ever to convince all my psychological colleagues (or other kinds of scientists) that psychobiography is a scientific approach. In at least some cases, their own personal histories have produced a cognitive style or a defensive structure that doesn't mesh well with ambiguity or lack of closure. By its very nature, psychobiography deals with higher levels of ambiguity in its data and its interpretations than fields where the usual measures generate specific numbers that can be plugged into standard formulas. Whether the latter approaches are more efficient at generating useful "truths" is itself a question for debate, and I'm not going to debate it here. Instead, I'll go on advocating greater methodological precision in psychobiography, and trying to collect so much data on my own psychobiographical subjects that my conclusions will persuade even reluctant audiences. But I need to keep reminding myself that some ambiguity-intolerant psychologists will remain unable to accept any conclusions derived from individual life-history data.

Going "beyond scratch" means a good deal more than considering such philosophical questions about the scientific nature of psychobiographical knowledge, or adopting increasingly sophisticated methodological guidelines. For one thing, it means looking beyond the usual array of famous white male achievers to see whether psychobiographical approaches to women or to members of non-white ethnic groups introduce any new questions (or answers) to the field. It also means looking more closely at the ethics of psychobiographical research. We must often deal with ethical issues that seldom arise in psychology's more impersonal subfields, so we need to begin developing ethical standards that are specific to the collection and use of life-historical data. I'll deal with each of these topics only briefly here; they obviously deserve more than a book apiece.

Scientific Methods

So if psychobiography is a scientific approach, why don't I use the scientific method?

That's a trick question. A long time ago, when I first began to read widely in the philosophy of science, I learned to my surprise that there's no such thing as *the* scientific method. Instead, as Nobel Prize-winning physicist Percy W. Bridgman liked to say, "The scientific method, as far as it is a method, is doing one's damnedest with one's mind, no holds barred."[7] Actually, that definition may be a little too broad even for my taste—it would include Stan Robinson's writing of science fiction, for instance.[8] But it does properly imply that there are many sciences and many scientific approaches (with more to come), not just one set-in-concrete way to collect truly scientific data. That being the case, the trick question can be converted into real ones: Can we do psychobiography scientifically, and if so, how?

Freud began to suggest some of the ways in his Leonardo book, though he didn't stick closely to them. Erik Erikson suggested more ways, as he looked with a fine eye at the available biographical data on Luther, Gandhi, and others. In organizing and interpreting those data so that they cohered into meaningful patterns, he did his damnedest with *his* extraordinary mind. Erikson wrote few strictly methodological papers, but his ideas of scientific method as applied to biography permeate his full-scale psychobiographies and often inform his shorter works.[9] More recently, other psychoanalytic scholars have published thoughtful volumes about the theory and method of psychobiography or psychohistory, though they haven't been striving to be distinctively scientific.[10]

As I suggested in Chapter 1, psychologists are more likely than psychiatrists or historians to be interested in improving the scientific methodology of psychobiography. Among the small number of psychologists active in psychobiography, William McKinley Runyan and Irving Alexander have devised especially helpful lists of methodological essentials. As we move "beyond scratch," it's worth taking a quick look at the sorts of criteria they've proposed for assessing psycho-biographical data and hypotheses.

Mac Runyan published the first substantial book on psychobiographical theory and method, and he has continued to express that interest in other papers and book chapters. Runyan is especially good at clearing away the undergrowth of alternative hypotheses: how do you decide among thirteen different (published) explanations of why Van Gogh cut off his ear, or four explanations of why King George III sometimes acted really crazy? Runyan offers a quick summary of major criteria for comparing and evaluating such explanations:

> (1) their logical soundness, (2) their comprehensiveness in accounting for a number of puzzling aspects of the events in question, (3) their survival of tests of attempted falsification, such as tests of derived predictions or retrodictions, (4) their consistency with the full range of available relevant evidence, (5) their support from above, or their consistency with more general knowledge about human functioning or about the person in question, and (6) their credibility relative to other explanatory hypotheses.[11]

Runyan presents his own examples and expanded discussions of these criteria. All the criteria are sound guidelines, and I've silently applied each of them in one chapter or another throughout this book.

Irv Alexander's psychobiographical research has largely focused on three psychological theorists: Freud, Jung, and Harry Stack Sullivan. Alexander's most useful contribution to psychobiographical methodology has been his inventory of the "principal identifiers of salience"[12]—specific criteria for deciding which data are most important out of the vast profusion of information that may be available on a biographical subject. Alexander drew not only upon the methodological traditions of psychoanalysis but upon the academic research literature about learning and perception as he formulated these criteria. They include:

Primacy   People tend to speak or write first about what is most on their minds, though they may do so in somewhat disguised form. Early memories, first experiences (as with James David Barber's use of a politician's first independent political success as a predictor of later behavior patterns[13]), an autobiography's introductory remarks (as with Alexander Haig's first paragraph[14])—all these are likely to be worth special attention by the psychobiographer.

Frequency   As Alexander says, "When someone tells us the same message about himself repeatedly but short of monotony we are likely to assign importance to that message."[15] Gordon Allport's frequent retelling of the story about his meeting with Freud did get monotonous to some people, but its frequency certainly suggests that it was of high salience to Allport.

Uniqueness   This criterion is the flip side of the previous one: If you have many biographical data that say one thing and you suddenly come across something that says another, it's worth a closer look. That's part of what caught Freud's eye with regard to Leonardo's "vulture" fantasy; Leonardo was not in the habit of telling stories about his childhood, so this one really stood out. And it was just so *odd*—a bird's tail in little Leo's mouth? (As I noted in Chapter 3, Freud had his own personal reasons for being sensitive to the particular content of this fantasy, but that's another story.)

Negation   When a biographical subject tells you who he or she *is*—as Jung does repeatedly in his biography, for example—you obviously should pay attention. But when the subject tells you who she or he *isn't*, you should pay at least as much attention, and sometimes even more. "I am not that little boy," Allport kept saying, and he could have been right; but his emphasis on that negation was a red flag. "I have no problems," Isaac Asimov told me in several different ways, apparently hoping I'd believe him and wanting to believe it himself. "No crises," B. F. Skinner told me, the last time we met. Maybe he was just tired of my raising questions about those identity crises from earlier in his life—but should I have taken "No" for an answer, or did that particular "No" point to further questions?

Emphasis   It seems reasonable that when a biographical subject places heavy stress on an experience, we should pay attention. Alexander, however, subdivides this criterion in interesting ways: over-, under-, and misplaced emphasis. When the subject is unusually emphatic about "something considered to be commonplace"; when the subject hardly mentions something that most people would see as a major life experience; when the subject emphasizes an apparently irrelevant aspect of a crucial event—when any of these happens, the psychobiographer should be on the alert. When Nabokov said he considered Freud a fraud, that was already a tired pun and it revealed little about Nabokov. When Nabokov said it over and over again in the most extreme terms, that was overemphasis and it meant something.

Omission   This is the Sherlock Holmes rule: Sometimes we should ask more questions when a dog doesn't bark than when it does. Why didn't Jung's autobiography discuss his close collaborator, Toni Wolff? Why did it hardly even mention his wife? Maybe we can safely ignore the fact that Jung's favorite dog Joggi doesn't bark anywhere in *Memories, Dreams, Reflections*—but Emma Jung's autobiographical absence is a signal that we need to begin searching below the book's surface.

Error or distortion   This was one of Freud's favorite sources of psychological revelation. He used it repeatedly in the Leonardo book, as well as in that famous case of motivated misquotation which revealed to Freud that his brother had made an Italian woman pregnant.[16] Freudian slips may not always mean as much as Freud said they did, but when they happen they tell us something is worth our closer attention. When Elvis garbled the words of the song "Are You Lonesome Tonight?" at almost every performance, it meant more than just that he was stoned.[17] When a U.S. Senator recently announced his retirement from politics, he said there was no dramatic reason for his deciding not to run for reelection; he still had his health, his family, and his "love for the bottle—battle." I won't follow that slip into a psychobiographical investigation, but doesn't it make you wonder?

Isolation   As Alexander explains this, "If in reading or listening, one finds oneself asking the question, 'Where did that come from?' or 'That doesn't seem to follow?,' it is highly likely that important personal material is contained in the communication."[18] Maybe this should be titled the "Come again?" criterion. One example I've already cited (in Chapter 9) is Isaac Asimov's story "Nightfall," about a planet whose inhabitants have never seen the night sky. When they finally do see it, Asimov tells us they go mad from claustrophobia—but the story actually describes them as overwhelmed by their vision of the limitless universe. Come again, Isaac? Then there's that oddly constructed sentence I quoted from Jimmy Carter's autobiography in Chapter 12: "[T]here were hundreds of administrative duties which I *enjoyed* and which I *had to perform*."[19] Come again, Jimmy?

Incompletion   The person you're studying starts a story but stops in the middle. The person starts a story and then changes the subject, subtly or not. The person starts a story and finishes it, but omits something important from the middle. Freud tells us he had a dream about his patient Irma; he explains a lot about it, but he avoids commenting on its obviously sexual elements. Jung tells us about the young Englishwoman he met in Nairobi, and about how the Governor of the Sudan asked him to escort her to Cairo. But what went on between Jung and Miss Bailey between Nairobi and the Sudan? Jung doesn't say.

When I first saw Irv Alexander's list of criteria, it made immediate sense to me, in terms of its individual items and as a whole list. Virtually every example I've noted had already arisen in my own work. Most of Alexander's criteria could be quantified and computerized—indeed, that's already started—but just having the list as a reminder of what to look for may be enough. When you've been working with biographical data long enough, you can hear the bells going off in your head without needing a computer to amplify them. A non sequitur in the middle of a subject's chapter on his childhood—*bing!* A dirty joke from a subject who never tells dirty jokes—*brrring!* "But I didn't inhale"—*bong! bong! bong!*

At least one attempted computerization of psychobiography is already available, though unfortunately it doesn't incorporate Irv Alexander's criteria. I was recently asked to try out a piece of Russian software called LifeLine, developed by Alexander Kronick in collaboration with Alexei Pajitnov (creator of the famous computer game Tetris) and Boris Levin.[20] The program accepts various kinds of psychological and biographical data, analyzes the data by means that neither the Russian-language manual nor the English translation made altogether clear to me, and emits a psychobiographical assessment. You can enter data for a selected psychobiographical subject, or you can enter data on yourself to get your own life-historical analysis. I tried the latter, but the program turned out to demand some rather odd kinds of data (what color *was* my first sexual experience?), and the results had to be expressed in terms of the software authors' own idiosyncratic personality theory. So I never finished my self-analysis, and I think I'll wait for a more theoretically flexible version of LifeLine before I try it on another subject.

Yes, psychobiography is an improvable scientific approach. But we've got a long way to go before a software program can tell us whether a specific case is better understood through a Slavic color analysis, or an Eriksonian look at identity issues, or a Horneyan stress on the neurotic need for love.

Psychobiographical Diversity

When a physicist studies subatomic particles, nobody says, "Hey, you've been spending your research time exclusively on quarks; it's time to give tachyons a little attention." But on several occasions, I've been confronted by women students who tell me I should pay more attention to the lives of famous women. If I hadn't already included Freud on Moses and Erikson on Gandhi in my undergraduate psychobiography course, other students might have been demanding that I say more about ethnically diverse lives.

In my own research I've covered a greater range of subjects than most psychobiographers—from a secularized Austrian Jew and a mystical Swiss Protestant to several varieties of American personality theorists; from a small-town Texas fantasist to a world-traveling polyglot science fiction writer; from Elvis Presley to Vladimir Nabokov; from Carter to Bush and from House to Haig. But neither I nor most of those other psychobiographers have gone out of our way to study important and intriguing lives from nonwhite ethnic groups. Surely Martin Luther King, Jr. and Malcolm X would be fascinating subjects. So would one of my ethnic heroes, the great Cherokee scholar Sequoyah, if I could find enough information about him. Prominent women, especially in the arts, are being given increasing amounts of psychobiographical attention, but rarely from male psychobiographers.

Maybe I'm just rationalizing, but I think there's a legitimate reason for that white male reluctance to look at subjects of the other gender or of other ethnic origins. As I indicated in earlier chapters, the psychobiographer's empathy for the subject—an important research tool—is often helped along if he or she has experienced similarities in life history or at least comes from a similar cultural background. Psychobiographers don't always stay culturally close to home, as witness Freud looking at Leonardo. But Freud didn't need to defer to any fifteenth-century Florentine psychobiographers who might have empathized more effectively with Leonardo. For contemporary women subjects, there are plenty of women scholars around who could potentially exercise such empathy. Though few practicing psychobiographers have come from nonwhite minorities, they too have an obvious empathic edge when it comes to studying subjects of similar ethnicity. Thus white male psychobiographers are likely to feel damned if they don't look beyond their fellow white males for subjects, and equally or even more damned if they do—because they appear to lack the right psychological equipment, the correct qualities of soul.

We've been told most emphatically, in recent years, that women biographers have special qualities which uniquely qualify them to study female subjects. Blanche Weisen Cook, the distinguished biographer of Eleanor Roosevelt, phrases such claims as bluntly as I've seen:

> Feminist women have revolutionized biography. We ask different questions, perceive different issues, look for secrets, and take seriously issues of lust and passion. . . . We are sensitive to nuance—the sigh, the frown, the unspoken; and we respect the lives, voices, and struggles of women.[21]

I'm sure some of those characteristics do make certain female biographers the best matches for certain female subjects. And I assume that women biographers in general are likely to do a better job than men when they deal with certain aspects of women's lives. For example, when Doris Kearns Goodwin wrote about the Fitzgerald and Kennedy clans, she devoted an unusual amount of attention to Rose Fitzgerald Kennedy (in comparison to the various elected and male Fitzgeralds and Kennedys.) In so doing, Goodwin displayed a special empathy for Rose Kennedy's disappointments with father and husband, for her blighted career, for her efforts to raise the large Kennedy family while trying to hold onto some sort of life of her own.[22] When Nigel Hamilton later addressed the same material, his Rose Kennedy emerged as a resentful shrew and a harshly cold taskmaster to the children—characterizations that may have accurately described certain aspects of Rose's behavior, but did not persuasively capture her inner life in the way Goodwin was able to do.[23] Hamilton appears to hold animosities toward the whole Kennedy clan that may have little to do with his being male. However, I suspect that his failure to entertain certain kinds of biographical questions had a good deal to do with his never having been a busy mother like Goodwin.

On the other hand (or perhaps I should say *another* hand, for there's surely more than one side to this issue), I think it's reasonable for a psychobiographer to make the following assumptions: 1.) In some regards humans are humans regardless of gender or race or nationality, and any psychobiographer can—with care—develop useful ideas about any individual for whom sufficient life-history data are available. 2.) In certain cases a male white (or other-colored) psychobiographer may have more basis for empathic understanding of a female or different-ethnic-group subject than does another psychobiographer with the race-correct and gender-correct credentials. One science fiction writer high on my list of future subjects is James Tiptree, Jr., who fooled a lot of people into thinking he was a distinctively masculine writer with surprising insights into feminine psychology. Tiptree was really a woman named Alice Sheldon, who also wrote vigorously feminist stories under the pseudonym Raccoona Sheldon. Alice Sheldon had a Ph.D. in experimental psychology, and I can relate to that. She worked in military intelligence and later for the CIA; through my work on Cordwainer Smith/Paul Linebarger, I can relate to that too. Alice Sheldon ended her life by first shooting her beloved but Alzheimer's-afflicted husband and then herself; I have a harder time relating to that. But her decision to take such actions seems to me to have been more relevant to her basic humanness in the face of harsh realities than to her being female. When I get around to writing about Alice Sheldon, I won't try to say everything that needs to be said about her. But I think I can add a few useful insights to what has already been written, or may yet be written, by women psychobiographers.[24]

So much for a defense of me and the other white males in the business. I'd rather be proactive than reactive. I've already supervised the initial training of two female psychobiographers, both of whom have gone on to do impressive work on their own, and I'm currently encouraging several more women in the same direction. The field needs more women, more African-Americans and Asian-Americans and Hispanic-Americans and Native Americans, more Republicans, more Russians and Mississippians and whoever. I'd like to see a Russian psychobiography of Vladimir Nabokov, for example. I doubt that it would displace or "disprove" my own understanding of Nabokov, but it should add insights that I and other American psychobiographers wouldn't think of. I'd like to see a black Mississippian's psychological take on Elvis, and a female psychobiographer's response to my discussion of L. Frank Baum's nurturant yearnings and transsexual fantasies.

Psychobiography as a still-developing field will not benefit from being divided into preserves where certain subjects are studied only by like-gendered or like-cultured or like-minded psychobiographers. Instead, we should be encouraging the efforts of anyone who can make important additions to our understanding of the subjects chosen for study. As Henry Murray often said about personality, psychobiography is a complex topic and we're still exploring its frontiers. We need the contributions of as many explorers as we can send out, with as many ways to look at the terrain as they can bring to bear.

Psychobiographical Ethics

At various points during the preparation of a psychobiography, the psychobiographer will need to meet and resolve certain ethical issues—to his or her own satisfaction, if not that of others. The first issues arise at the time a subject is chosen: Do I do research on live people or only on dead ones? Recently dead or long dead? Then there are questions about what kinds of data it's permissible to use: anything I can get my hands on, or only officially archived materials, or only what the subject's family wants me to see? And what do I say in print: only what the subject or the family wants to hear, or a diplomatically but honestly phrased presentation of my major data and conclusions—or do I try to meet the competition of the mass-market biographers by stripping naked every hint of sex and selfishness in my subject's life?

On such ethical questions, my own major professional organization doesn't offer much guidance. The American Psychological Association has given a lot of attention to ethical issues in psychological research, from animal care to human boredom. But its ethical guidelines say nothing specifically about psychobiography. With so few psychologists doing psychobiography, that's not surprising. The American Psychiatric Association (to which I don't belong) has had a good deal to say about the ethics of psychobiography, but its pronouncements have obfuscated certain issues rather than clarified them.

The leadership of the American Psychiatric Association appears to have been traumatized by the *Fact* magazine poll of psychiatrists on Goldwater's fitness to become the U.S. president. After denouncing the poll editorially, the APA leadership set up a task force to devise appropriate ethical guidelines for psychobiography and psychohistory. These guidelines were issued in 1976 and presumably are still taken seriously by American Psychiatric Association members.[25] Basically the guidelines say it's okay to do a psychobiography of a dead person—preferably a long-dead person, who has no surviving relatives close enough to be embarrassed by unsavory revelations. It's not okay to do a psychobiography of a living person, unless he or she has freely consented to be studied, interviewed, and written up for publication. The one interesting exception to the latter guideline might be called the Jerrold Post Proviso, in honor of the most prominent ex-CIA psychobiographer, though I don't know that he had anything directly to do with it. This proviso says a psychiatrist may ethically prepare "for the confidential use of government officials psychobiographies or profiles of significant international figures whose personality formation needs to be understood to carry out national policy more effectively."[26] So watch out, Saddam Hussein—Tomahawk missiles and APA-approved psychobiographies incoming!

Actually, even Jerrold Post's work on Hussein appears to fall outside the APA guidelines, since he didn't limit its circulation to "the confidential use of government officials" but got it into the *Congressional Record,* major and minor news media, and eventually the professional journal *Political Psychology.* Post has, however, criticized other professionals (nonpsychiatrists) for ignoring the APA guidelines by doing psychobiographical studies of people like Ronald Reagan and George Bush without obtaining informed consent. The finer distinctions escape me here. Reagan and Bush are certainly "significant international figures." Furthermore, in the elections of 1980, 1984, and 1988, there were a lot of people out there—registered voters—who needed to understand their personality formation in order "to carry out national policy more effectively." I still think politicians are fair game for psychobiographers, as long as the psychobiographers play the game fairly as suggested in Chapter 12.

What would I consider playing the game unfairly? Dishonest use of biographical data, obviously. Emphasizing aspects of life history and personality that display no clear connections to significant components of political performance (aspects that might include, in specific cases, such matters as infantile toilet training patterns or consenting-adult sexual preferences). Speculating well beyond the bounds of the available data and then presenting your speculations as conclusive. Pretending you know more than you do about how this theory applies to that candidate, or how this personality pattern is necessarily going to produce that unfortunate pattern of behavior once the candidate gets into office. I don't see how any professional organization can draw up a set of rules that would clearly and comprehensively define such violations of elementary fairness and responsibility. But I do think serious psychobiographers need to police themselves and others, even in the absence of official rules, by pointing out both privately and publicly those instances where somebody crosses such ethical boundaries.

In choosing subjects for my own research, I apply one ethical rule-of-thumb to nonpoliticians but ignore it for politicians. Throughout their vote-seeking careers, politicians regularly hold themselves up for public inspection, and I think professional psychobiographers have as much right and responsibility to inspect their qualifications for office as journalists and competing politicians do. But consider the hard-working novelist or rock singer or psychological theorist or nuclear physicist, who offers certain products of his or her work to the public for inspection but doesn't offer his or her personality and life history as a central part of the public package. As an informed critic, I have a right to offer my assessment of the person's public achievements. But do I have any right to present a psychobiographical assessment as well? Whereas I'd say "Definitely yes" for the politician, I'd say "Yes and No" for these other subjects.

Yes, I should be allowed to be a psychobiographer. I should be allowed to put together biographical data that are already in the public domain, or that the subject and the subject's friends and relatives have given to me. I should be allowed to draw conclusions about how these data relate to the subject's public productions, about how they enable us to understand better the processes by which the subject created those productions. As long as I'm not breaking into the subject's confidential files or blackmailing his or her former lovers to get information, I have a legal right to practice my psychobiographical profession.[27]

However—and for nonpolitical subjects this is a big however—I don't think I have a right to do things that might significantly interfere with the subject's own profession. Being voted on by a presumably informed public is an essential aspect of a politician's professional career, and being voted on may involve losing elections as well as winning them. Therefore I don't feel I'd be unethically interfering with a politician's career by presenting relevant evidence about the politician's personality; instead, I'm helping the electoral process function more effectively. But let's say we've got a creative writer working away over here, and a psychologist appears out of the blue to identify the writer's major fictional themes as defensive fantasies protecting the writer against overwhelming anti-parental rage. Or let's say, to put the best light on it, that the psychologist pronounces the writer to have successfully transformed his or her work into a restitutive masterpiece that has freed the writer from long-standing infantile conflicts. Writers learn to deal with, to tolerate or to ignore, all sorts of irritating commentary from editors and reviewers and literary scholars. But I think that kind of judgment by a psychologist, linking the writer's personality, past history, and current work, would be in most instances an unwarranted intrusion into the writer's own business. It could make a writer terribly sensitive to the kinds of issues and images pinpointed by the psychologist, and could thereby derail or at least temporarily block the writer's normal pattern of work. Maybe I'm exaggerating the psychobiographer's power to affect the subject's thinking, but I wouldn't want that possibility of serious disruption of a creative individual's life on my conscience.

I do sometimes study live writers and theorists, as several chapters of this book have shown. Evidently, I make some kind of exception to the rule implicit in the above paragraph—an Alan Elms Proviso, as it were. The Alan Elms Proviso is this: Whereas I generally refrain from psychobiographical pronouncements on living nonpolitical subjects, I am willing to study such individuals late in their careers. I haven't arrived at a precise definition of "late," but in practice I seem to have been thinking in terms of age 75 or older—B. F. Skinner, Henry Murray, Jack Williamson, Isaac Asimov. At that age the creative individual is likely to have completed the bulk of his or her life's work. He or she may still be producing (as indeed all these people were when I studied them), but is probably beyond the point of producing anything dramatically innovative. Perhaps most important from the standpoint of my own profession's ethical code, such people are probably well able to fend off any interference with their thinking by (relatively) young whippersnappers like me.

Erik Erikson, it's true, told me he was uneasy about my subjecting him to the kind of psychobiographical analysis he had directed toward many other people. But I doubt that Erikson was distracted for more than a few hours by my questions about his life and psychological development. Jack Williamson told me that hearing my psychobiographical commentary on him and his classic work, before a room full of fellow Science Fiction Research Association members, was like being back in psychoanalysis for one more hour. But Jack has produced three or four novels and several short stories since then, and they don't appear to avoid the issues I identified. Isaac Asimov fended off my interpretations very efficiently with his armor of confident egotism. When Harry Murray read the first draft of my paper on "The Personalities of Henry A. Murray," he had no problems dealing with this Inquiring Psychobiographer: "I think it's very good the way it is. There were just one or two things that I think are really wrong. Maybe it's a good idea to get some wrong things in, then you start a discussion and pretty soon you get some better things than you had before."[28]

Though I've been dealing mainly with the ethics of research on living individuals, certain problems do remain with regard to the dead. You can't libel a dead person, according to U.S. law and legal tradition. But that doesn't lessen a psychobiographer's responsibility to treat a dead person's life history fairly. In many instances, biographers and psychobiographers sooner or later gain access to the dead person's most intimate documents (unless those documents have been shredded or burned). I think there's an obligation to treat that intimate knowledge respectfully. But as Freud and others in his tradition have shown us, it may be the intimate details of love and sex and personal hatreds that reveal a person's psychology most clearly. I usually say little about such matters when I write about a living subject, but for a dead subject, I'm not going to ignore those intimacies out of misguided politeness.

One source of intimate knowledge has recently generated considerable controversy: a psychotherapist's records of therapy sessions with a client who later becomes a psychobiographical subject. The specific controversy involved the poet Anne Sexton, whose therapist gave his tape recordings of her therapy sessions to psychobiographer Diane Middlebrook, eleven or twelve years after Sexton killed herself.[29] The contents of the tapes radically altered (and presumably improved) Middlebrook's understanding of Sexton, but a number of therapists and others objected to her use of them.

A therapist's obligation to confidentiality concerning a long-deceased patient is less clear than such obligations toward living patients. But it's not in the best interest of therapists generally for patients to assume that their private remarks in therapy sessions may be shared with a biographer hardly more than a decade after the patient's death. On the other hand—well, the other hand was neatly described by one prominent psychotherapist/psychobiographer, who said that as a therapist he was appalled by Middlebrook's use of the therapy tapes; as a biographer he couldn't have resisted using them himself.

In the case of Anne Sexton, as Middlebrook has pointed out, exceptional circumstances supported the use of the tapes. Sexton was herself extremely self-revealing in public (and in her poetry) during her lifetime. Sexton told her therapist, by his account, that he should keep the tapes "to use as I saw fit to help others."[30] Sexton's daughter (who was also her literary executor) permitted and indeed encouraged Middlebrook's use of the tapes. Under other circumstances I might personally have rejected the psychobiographical use of therapy notes or tapes. In this case I think the right decision was made.

That phrase from Sexton's therapist, "to use as I saw fit to help others," identifies a significant element of ethical decision-making in psychological research. In almost any research on human beings, there's a potential degree of harm to subjects, if only the minor harm of boredom or loss of time. Federally mandated Institutional Review Boards require research psychologists to justify any potential harm by comparing it with the research's potential benefits. If the potential harm is substantial, the potential benefits must be even more so—up to a point where the potential harm is so likely and long-lasting that no benefit could ethically be cited to outweigh it. In the case of Anne Sexton's psychobiography, Diane Middlebrook argues that important lessons can be learned from reading about this life, and that they outweigh the ethical ambiguities involved in using the tapes:

> If suffering like hers had any use, she [Sexton] reasoned, it was not to the sufferer. The only way that an individual's pain gained meaning was through its communication to others. I have tried to honor that attitude of Sexton's in writing about her life.[31]

In like manner, I think every psychobiography needs to be justified ethically to some degree. Are we just having voyeuristic fun here, rummaging through the intriguing intimacies of somebody's life and spreading them out for public consumption? Are we acting, as biographer Janet Malcolm sees us, "like the professional burglar, breaking into a house, rifling through certain drawers that he has good reason to think contain the jewelry and money, and triumphantly bearing his loot away"?[32] Or are we contributing meaningfully to a clearer picture of this person's life and, beyond that, adding another strand to the whole warp and woof of psychological explanation? Ethical psychobiography doesn't just avoid the unethical; it adds to our human understanding of ourselves and other human beings.

Coming Home

I'll end with one last personal note. When I entered the field of psychology, I was fascinated by basic human nature and by its varied expression in a multitude of individual personalities. I wanted to understand why people live their lives as they do, and if possible to help them live better or at least more self-directed lives. I assumed that psychology would provide me with a set of already well-established insights into such matters, or that it would help me develop my own insights into them.

I hardly had time to become disappointed. I soon learned that most of the time psychology deals with other matters entirely. I began to study those other matters with interest, trying to become as hard a hard scientist as a psychologist could be. But I found myself moving from one crisscrossing path to another. Initially, I went from running solitary rats in a Skinner box to observing howler monkeys' social behavior in the Panamanian jungle. For a while, I did tightly controlled laboratory studies of attitude change via role-playing, and even more tightly controlled research on obedience to authority. Then I moved on to questionnaire research on authoritarianism and moral development, and from there to open-ended interview research on life-history variables as they affect current political behavior.

As I moved still further, tentatively and then wholeheartedly into outright psychobiography, some of my colleagues began to express concern that I had gone astray. Undoubtedly some still think so. But I feel instead that I've come home. Far from abandoning the field of psychology, I think I've found a route to its very center, to the understanding of human beings in their full complexity. I know there are many routes to that center, including the various paths I abandoned as unsuited to my own skills and my own personality. But I look for increasing numbers of psychologists to join me along the path of psychobiography, until it becomes a well-traveled avenue.

NOTES

Chapter One *The Psychologist as Biographer*

1. George Will. (1992). "The 'Truman Paradigm.'" *Newsweek*, September 7, p. 70.

2. Psychohistory is historical analysis that makes substantial use of psychological concepts. When psychohistory focuses on the life of a prominent historical figure, it becomes psychobiography. David Stannard's *Shrinking History: On Freud and the Failure of Psychohistory* (New York: Oxford University Press, 1980) gleefully attacks Freudian psychobiography as the worst kind of psychohistory.

3. Nancy Gager Clinch. (1973). *The Kennedy Neurosis* (New York: Grosset & Dunlap).

4. Fawn M. Brodie. (1981). *Richard Nixon: The Shaping of His Character* (New York: Norton).

5. Albert Goldman. (1981). *Elvis* (New York: McGraw-Hill), pp. 65, 494.

6. Erik H. Erikson. (1969). *Gandhi's Truth* (New York: Norton), p. 98.

7. Marie Balmary. (1982). *Psychoanalyzing Psychoanalysis: Freud and the Hidden Fault of the Father,* trans. Ned Lukacher (Baltimore: Johns Hopkins Press). The punch line was "Rebecca, you can take off your wedding-gown, you're not a bride any longer." Freud included it in a letter to his friend Wilhelm Fliess, who apparently didn't need to be told why it was funny. Balmary mistranslated the punch line and misunderstood the joke, then built on that tottering foundation a whole book of speculations about Freud and his family.

8. Peter Swales. (1982). "Freud, Minna Bernays, and the Conquest of Rome." *New American Review*, Spring/Summer.

9. This book, published a decade ago by a small Southern California press, is so appallingly inept that it doesn't deserve a more specific citation. A similar book by another author (or under a different pseudonym?) was recently published by a small press in Durham, N.C.

10. William McGuire, ed. (1974). *The Freud/Jung Letters* (Princeton: Princeton University Press), p. 255.

11. Interview with Henry A. Murray, Cambridge, Mass., August 10, 1977.

12. Interview with Murray, August 10, 1977.

13. In his biography of Murray, *Love's Story Told* (Cambridge, Mass.: Harvard University Press, 1992), Forrest Robinson describes a somewhat different sequence of events; in either instance Murray was greatly discouraged by Aiken's responses. In his long old age, Murray gave mildly inconsistent accounts of his early life history to various interviewers.

14. Henry A. Murray, ed. (1949). *Pierre, or, the Ambiguities,* by Herman Melville

(New York: Hendricks House). Murray's introduction may also be found in his volume of collected papers, *Endeavors in Psychology*, ed. E. S. Shneidman (New York: Harper & Row, 1981).

15. Henry A. Murray. (1951). "In Nomine Diaboli." *New England Quarterly, 24*.

16. Shneidman, introduction to *Endeavors in Psychology*, p. 5.

17. See Robinson, *Love's Story Told*.

18. Murray spent six months on a secret study of Adolf Hitler, prepared for the Office of Strategic Services during World War II. Much of its content was incorporated into another report by Murray's boss at OSS, psychoanalyst Walter Langer. The latter report was eventually published under Langer's name, without crediting Murray, as *The Mind of Adolf Hitler* (New York: Basic Books, 1972). See Robinson, *Love's Story Told*, pp. 276–278.

19. Henry A. Murray. (1938). *Explorations in Personality* (New York: Oxford University Press), pp. 39 and 43; his italics.

20. Gordon W. Allport. (1929). "The Study of Personality by the Intuitive Method: An Experiment in Teaching from *The Locomotive God*." *Journal of Abnormal and Social Psychology, 24*.

21. Abraham H. Maslow. (1972). *The Farther Reaches of Human Nature* (New York: Viking; Penguin Books reprint, 1976), pp. 40–41.

22. B. F. Skinner. (1979). *The Shaping of a Behaviorist* (New York: Knopf), pp. 208 and 245.

23. Gordon W. Allport, ed. (1965). *Letters from Jenny* (New York: Harcourt, Brace).

24. See, for example: Erik H. Erikson. (1975). *Life History and the Historical Moment* (New York: Norton). Leon Edel. (1984). *Writing Lives: Principia Biographica* (New York: Norton).

25. Prominent among them have been William McKinley Runyan, especially with his pioneering textbook/handbook, *Life Histories and Psychobiography* (New York: Oxford, 1982); Irving E. Alexander, whose main methodological lessons in *Personology: Method and Content in Personality Assessment and Psychobiography* (Durham, N.C.: Duke University Press, 1990) are reviewed in the final chapter of the present book; and James W. Anderson, whose methodological papers and psychobiographical studies have not yet been collected into a book. Anderson's major methodological papers are "The Methodology of Psychological Biography," *Journal of Interdisciplinary History, 11*, 1981, and "Psychobiographical Methodology: The Case of William James," *Review of Personality and Social Psychology, 2*, 1981.

26. David McCullough. (1992). *Truman* (New York: Simon & Schuster).

27. See especially his *Young Man Luther* (New York: Norton, 1958), as well as *Gandhi's Truth*.

28. See, for example, the several essays from a Kohutian perspective in Charles B. Strozier and Daniel Offer, eds., *The Leader: Psychohistorical Essays* (New York: Plenum, 1985).

29. For instance, George E. Atwood and Robert D. Stolorow have made good use of transitional objects in discussing C. G. Jung's personality development; see their *Faces in a Cloud: Intersubjectivity in Personality Theory*, rev. ed. (Northvale, N. J.: Aronson, 1993), pp. 89–92, 98–100.

30. Murray, *Explorations in Personality*.

31. David C. McClelland, W. N. Davis, R. Kalin, and E. Wanner. (1972). *The Drinking Man* (New York: Free Press). David G. Winter. (1973). *The Power Motive* (New York: Free Press).

32. Theodore Millon. (1981). *Disorders of Personality: DSM-III: Axis II* (New York: Wiley).

33. Silvan S. Tomkins. (1987). "Script Theory." In J. Aronoff, A. I. Rabin, and R. Zucker, eds., *The Emergence of Personality* (New York: Springer).

34. Rae Carlson. (1981). "Studies in Script Theory: I. Adult Analogs of a Childhood Nuclear Scene." *Journal of Personality and Social Psychology, 40*. Rae Carlson. (1982). "Studies in Script Theory: II. Altruistic Nuclear Scripts." *Perceptual and Motor Skills, 55*.

35. Further examples of nonpsychoanalytic theories applicable to psychobiography can be found in Runyan, *Life Histories and Psychobiography*, pp. 222–230, as well as in his later book *Psychology and Historical Interpretation* (New York: Oxford University Press, 1988), pp. 225–236.

36. Sigmund Freud. (1957). *Leonardo da Vinci and a Memory of His Childhood*. In J. Strachey, ed. and trans., *The Standard Edition of the Complete Psychological Works of Sigmund Freud*, vol. 11 (London: Hogarth Press). Original work published in 1910.

37. Silvan S. Tomkins. (1988). "What Personology Needs as a Science." Paper presented at the Personology Society's annual conference, Durham, N.C., June 18.

38. Donald Spence. (1982). *Narrative Truth and Historical Truth: Meaning and Interpretation in Psychoanalysis* (New York: Norton). Adolf Grünbaum. (1984). *The Foundations of Psychoanalysis: A Philosophical Critique* (Berkeley: University of California Press).

39. Alan C. Elms. (1976). *Personality in Politics* (New York: Harcourt Brace Jovanovich), pp. 48–57.

40. Freeman Dyson. (1988). *Infinite in All Directions* (New York: Harper & Row), pp. 44–45. Dyson's version of the French "saying," sometimes attributed to Flaubert, can be translated as "The good God loves details"; it is more often heard in English as "God is in the details," though I've also seen it rendered as "The Devil is in the details"!

41. Gordon W. Allport. (1937). *Personality: A Psychological Interpretation* (New York: Henry Holt).

42. Robert R. Holt. (1962). "Individuality and Generalization in the Psychology of Personality." *Journal of Personality, 30*.

43. Holt, pp. 377, 389, 390.

44. Gordon W. Allport. (1962). "The General and the Unique in Psychological Science." *Journal of Personality, 30*.

45. Leon Edel. (1985). *Henry James: A Life* (New York: Harper & Row), p. xiv.

46. A partial account of our work is contained in B. Heller and A. Elms, "Seven Versions of Lonesome: Control and Loss in the Music of Elvis Presley," paper presented to the Bay Area Psychobiography Study Group, July 9, 1992.

47. Allport, *Letters from Jenny*.

48. Runyan has noted recent institutional developments that suggest the field's growing strength; *Psychology and Historical Interpretation,* pp. 19–33.

49. Henry D. Thoreau. (1993). *Faith in a Seed* (Washington, D.C.: Island Press).

Chapter Two Starting from Scratch

1. Alan C. Elms. (1972). *Social Psychology and Social Relevance* (Boston: Little, Brown), pp. 328–329.

2. Freud, *Leonardo da Vinci.*

3. Brodie, *Richard Nixon.*

4. Ernest Jones. (1953–57). *The Life and Work of Sigmund Freud* (New York: Basic Books).

5. Samuel H. Baron and Carl Pletsch. (1985). *Introspection in Biography: The Biographer's Quest for Self-Awareness* (Hillsdale, N.J.: Analytic Press). Also see Eva Schepeler, "The Biographer's Transference: A Chapter in Psychobiographical Epistemology," *Biography, 13,* 1990.

6. Peter Gay. (1988). *Freud: A Life for Our Time* (New York: W. W. Norton). Elisabeth Young-Bruehl. (1988). *Anna Freud* (New York: Summit Books).

7. Sigmund Freud. (1964). *Moses and Monotheism.* In J. Strachey, ed. and trans., *The Standard Edition of the Complete Psychological Works of Sigmund Freud,* vol. 23 (London: Hogarth Press). Original work published in 1939.

8. For example, Rae Carlson. (1988). "Exemplary Lives: The Uses of Psychobiography for Theory Development." *Journal of Personality, 56.*

9. See James W. Anderson's discussion of this point in "Psychobiographical Methodology: The Case of William James."

10. Elena S. Danielson. (1989). "The Ethics of Access." *American Archivist, 52,* p. 59.

11. See especially Jacqueline Rose, *The Haunting of Sylvia Plath* (Cambridge, Mass.: Harvard University Press, 1992), pp. 65–113, and Janet Malcolm, *The Silent Woman: Sylvia Plath & Ted Hughes* (New York: Knopf, 1994).

12. Few publications have dealt with the strategy and practice of biographical interviewing. One that resonates strongly with my own experience and adds to it is Horace Freeland Judson's account of interviewing prominent molecular biologists, "Reweaving the Web of Discovery," *The Sciences, 23* (6), 1983.

13. CD-ROM disks are now available that combine the white pages of virtually every telephone directory in the country. The CompuServe Information Service provides similar information online, for a reasonable price; if you're a subscriber, type "GO PHONEFILE."

14. Sue Grafton. (1985). *B Is for Burglar* (New York: Holt, Rinehart & Winston; Bantam reprint, 1986), p. 33.

Chapter Three Freud as Leonardo

1. Erik H. Erikson. (1954). "The Dream Specimen of Psychoanalysis." *Journal of the American Psychoanalytic Association, 2.*

2. Freud, *Leonardo da Vinci.*

3. Kenneth M. Clark. (1967). *Leonardo da Vinci,* rev. ed. (Harmondsworth, England: Penguin), pp. 20 and 137.

4. Ladislao Reti, ed. (1974). *The Unknown Leonardo* (New York: McGraw-Hill), p. 6.

5. Serge Bramly. (1991). *Leonardo: Discovering the Life of Leonardo da Vinci* (New York: HarperCollins), p. 49.

6. Stannard, *Shrinking History,* p. 3.

7. McGuire, *Freud-Jung Letters,* p. 256.

8. McGuire, p. 261.

9. McGuire, p. 255.

10. Joyce Carol Oates has often been credited with inventing the word "pathography" (e.g., by Arthur M. Schlesinger Jr., "The Perils of Pathography," *New Republic,* May 3, 1993, p. 36). But it was already being used by several writers in the early 1900s, in both German and English. It meant more or less the same thing then as in Oates's usage: a biographical study with an emphasis on pathological tendencies.

11. H. Nunberg and E. Federn, eds. (1962). *Minutes of the Vienna Psychoanalytic Society,* vol. 1 (New York: International Universities Press), p. 257.

12. H. C. Abraham and E. L. Freud, eds. (1965). *A Psycho-analytic Dialogue: The Letters of Sigmund Freud and Karl Abraham 1907–1926* (New York: Basic Books), p. 71.

13. Abraham and Freud, p. 83.

14. McGuire, *Freud-Jung Letters,* p. 271.

15. McGuire, p. 296.

16. Gerhard Fichtner, ed. (1992). *Sigmund Freud/Ludwig Binswanger: Briefwechsel 1908–1938* (Frankfurt, Germany: S. Fischer), p. 36. My thanks to Eva Schepeler for providing a translation of this letter.

17. McGuire, *Freud-Jung Letters,* p. 301.

18. See K. R. Eissler, *Leonardo da Vinci: Psychoanalytic Notes on the Enigma* (New York: International Universities Press, 1961), for a thorough review of the factual issues involved.

19. Various points of identification between Freud and Leonardo have been discussed by Jones, *Life and Work of Sigmund Freud,* vol. 2, p. 432; J. D. Lichtenberg, "Freud's Leonardo: Psychobiography and Autobiography of Genius," *Journal of the American Psychoanalytic Association,* 26 (1978); E. R. Wallace, "Freud and Leonardo," *Psychiatric Forum,* 8 (1978–79); and Harry Trosman, *Freud and the Imaginative World* (Hillsdale, NJ: Analytic Press, 1985), pp. 170–171. Stannard, *Shrinking History,* pp. 20–21, lists ten such points, though some are doubtful or definitely inapplicable.

20. Frank Hartman, personal communication.

21. Freud, *Leonardo,* p. 93.

22. David H. Fischer. (1970). *Historians' Fallacies* (New York: Harper & Row), p. 305.

23. Freud, *Leonardo,* p. 107.

24. Sigmund Freud. (1958). *The Interpretation of Dreams.* In James Strachey, ed. and trans., *The Standard Edition of the Complete Psychological Works of Sigmund Freud,*

vols. 4–5, (London: Hogarth Press), p. 583; Freud's italics. Original work published in 1900.

25. Freud, *Interpretation of Dreams*, p. 584.

26. Freud, *Leonardo*, p. 117.

27. Jeffrey M. Masson, ed. (1985). *The Complete Letters of Sigmund Freud to Wilhelm Fliess* (Cambridge, Mass.: Harvard University Press), p. 269.

28. Ruth Abraham. (1982–83). "Freud's Mother Conflict and the Formulation of the Oedipal Father." *Psychoanalytic Review, 69*.

29. Freud, *Leonardo*, p. 63.

30. Freud, *Leonardo*, p. 130.

31. Freud, *Leonardo*, p. 117.

32. Ernst L. Freud, ed. (1960). *Letters of Sigmund Freud* (New York: Basic Books), p. 306.

33. Freud, *Leonardo*, p. 63.

34. Freud, *Leonardo*, p. 77.

35. Freud, *Leonardo*, p. 80.

36. Freud, *Leonardo*, pp. 80–81.

37. Freud, *Leonardo*, p. 131; my italics. Abulia is a neurotic indecision or lack of will.

38. Freud, *Leonardo*, p. 135.

39. Erik H. Erikson. (1963). *Childhood and Society,* rev. ed. (New York: Norton), p. 265.

40. For example, in F. B. Davis, "Three Letters from Sigmund Freud to Andre Breton." *Journal of the American Psychoanalytic Association, 21* (1973), p. 130.

41. Sigmund Freud. (1959). "'Civilized' Sexual Morality and Modern Nervous Illness." *Standard Edition*, vol. 9, pp. 194–195. Original work published in 1908.

42. For example, Marise Choisy, *Sigmund Freud: A New Appraisal* (New York: Philosophical Library, 1963); Erich Fromm, *Sigmund Freud's Mission* (New York: Harper & Row, 1959).

43. See, for example, his letter of August 20, 1893, in Masson, *Complete Letters of Freud to Fliess,* p. 54.

44. Alan C. Elms. (1980). "Freud, Irma, Martha: Sex and Marriage in the 'Dream of Irma's Injection.'" *Psychoanalytic Review, 67*.

45. See letter of December 17, 1896, in Masson, *Complete Letters of Freud to Fliess,* p. 217.

46. As Frank Sulloway has indicated in *Freud, Biologist of the Mind* (New York: Basic Books, 1979, pp. 176–177), Freud was by no means the first to think of sublimation in some form, and his specific conception of it was clearly influenced by the ideas of his friend Fliess. Freud's personal situation, however, is likely to have made him more receptive to ideas from others concerning sublimation, as well as more sensitive to the co-occurrence of low sexual activity and high creativity in various cases, including his own.

47. For example, Sigmund Freud, "Sexuality in the Aetiology of the Neuroses." *Standard Edition*, vol. 3 (1962), p. 281. Original work published in 1898.

48. Sigmund Freud. (1953). *Three Essays on the Theory of Sexuality. Standard Edition*, vol. 7, p. 178. Original work published in 1905.

49. McGuire, *Freud-Jung Letters*, p. 82.

50. Freud, "'Civilized' Sexual Morality," p. 197.

51. McGuire, *Freud-Jung Letters*, p. 292.

52. The unreliability of Jung's gossip about Freud and Minna is discussed in Alan C. Elms, "Freud and Minna," *Psychology Today* (December 1982). The gossip continues to be repeated, most recently by John Kerr in *A Most Dangerous Method: The Story of Jung, Freud, and Sabina Spielrein* (New York: Knopf, 1993, pp. 135–140)—but with no better evidence than before.

53. McGuire, *Freud-Jung Letters*, p. 255.

54. H. Nunberg and E. Federn, eds. (1967). *Minutes of the Vienna Psychoanalytic Society*, vol. 2 (New York: International Universities Press), pp. 342–343.

55. In his conclusion to the *Five Lectures on Psychoanalysis* (*Standard Edition*, vol. 11, 1910/1957), written at about the same time, Freud referred to sublimation as the probable origin of "our highest cultural successes." However, he devoted more space to the limitations than to the contributions of sexual abstinence as a source of energies for creative sublimation.

56. Freud, *Leonardo*, pp. 133–134.

57. For milder comments, see Sigmund Freud, "On the Grounds for Detaching a Particular Syndrome from Neurasthenia under the Description 'Anxiety Neurosis'" (*Standard Edition*, vol. 3, 1895/1962), p. 102, and "Psycho-analytic Notes on an Autobiographical Account of a Case of Paranoia" (*Standard Edition*, vol. 12, 1911/1958), pp. 45–46.

58. Max Schur. (1972). *Freud: Living and Dying* (New York: International Universities Press), pp. 256–257.

59. Freud, *Moses and Monotheism*.

60. See Marthe Robert, *From Oedipus to Moses: Freud's Jewish Identity* (New York: Doubleday, 1976); Emanuel Rice, *Freud and Moses: The Long Journey Home* (Albany: State University of New York Press, 1992); and Yosef Hayim Yerushalmi, *Freud's Moses: Judaism Terminable and Interminable* (New Haven: Yale University Press, 1992).

Chapter Four The Auntification of C. G. Jung

1. André Maurois. (1929). *Aspects of Biography* (Cambridge: Cambridge University Press), p. 111.

2. B. F. Skinner's three volumes of autobiography are a notable example—especially volume one, *Particulars of My Life* (New York: Knopf, 1976). But see Chapter 6 of the present book for an account of the subjective Skinner.

3. C. G. Jung. (1963). *Memories, Dreams, Reflections*, recorded and edited by Aniela Jaffé; trans. Richard and Clara Winston (New York: Pantheon Books).

4. Jung, *Memories, Dreams, Reflections*, pp. viii–ix.

5. See, for example, Vincent Brome, *Jung: Man and Myth* (New York: Atheneum, 1978); Barbara Hannah, *Jung: His Life and Work* (New York: Putnam, 1976); Gerhard

Wehr, *Jung: A Biography* (Boston: Shambhala, 1987); Gerhard Wehr, *An Illustrated Biography of C. G. Jung* (Boston: Shambhala, 1989).

6. Jung, *Memories, Dreams, Reflections,* p. 3.

7. The Frances G. Wickes Foundation. Frances Wickes was a Jungian analyst and writer. The oral history project was proposed to the Foundation by two members of its Board of Directors, Henry Murray and William McGuire. Murray, a friend of both Wickes and Jung, recommended Nameche as the interviewer.

8. I am grateful to Eugene Taylor for directing my attention to the Countway manuscript, and to Richard Wolfe, Curator of Manuscripts and Archives at the Countway Library, for letting me consult it at length. Sonu Shamdasani has independently studied the Countway manuscript and other evidence on the evolution of Jung's published autobiography. His discussion of *MDR,* complementary in various ways to mine, will be published as "Memories, Dreams, Omissions" in *Spring: A Journal of Archetype and Culture, 56,* 1994.

9. The seminar notes containing this material were for many years available only in a few mimeographed copies whose circulation or duplication was forbidden. They have now been published under William McGuire's editorship; see C. G. Jung, *Analytical Psychology: Notes of the Seminar Given in 1925* (Princeton: Princeton University Press, 1989).

10. Jolande Jacobi, interview by Gene Nameche, C. G. Jung Biographical Archive, Countway Library.

11. Jaffé later wrote several substantial works of her own, especially *The Myth of Meaning* (New York: Putnam, 1971) and *From the Life and Work of C. G. Jung* (New York: Harper & Row, 1971).

12. Letter from C. G. Jung to Aniela Jaffé, October 21, 1957; copy in Bollingen Foundation Collection, Library of Congress.

13. See William McGuire letter to Vaun Gillmore, May 5, 1957, and R.F.C. Hull memo, July 27, 1960, both in the Bollingen Foundation Collection, Library of Congress.

14. See Hull, July 27, 1960, third paragraph.

15. Hull, July 27, 1960, pp. 2–4. I am grateful to Birte-Lene Hull for permission to quote from her late husband's unpublished letters.

16. C. G. Jung. (1975). *Letters* (ed. Gerhard Adler with Aniela Jaffé; Princeton, N.J.: Princeton University Press), vol. 2, pp. 451–453, letter of June 17, 1958.

17. Aniela Jaffé, ed. (1979). *C. G. Jung: Word and Image* (Princeton: Princeton University Press). See also Jaffé, *From the Life and Work of C. G. Jung.*

18. According to Barbara Hannah (*Jung: His Life and Work,* p. 7), Jung's children "thoroughly disapproved" of her biography of their father.

19. R.F.C. Hull, interview by Gene Nameche, C. G. Jung Biographical Archive, Countway Library.

20. Aniela Jaffé. (1984). "Details about C. G. Jung's Family." *Spring: An Annual of Archetypal Psychology and Jungian Thought.*

21. Hull interview by Nameche.

22. R.F.C. Hull to John D. Barrett, December 17, 1961; Bollingen Foundation Papers, Library of Congress.

23. Hull to Aniela Jaffé, September 9, 1961; copy in the Bollingen Foundation Papers, Library of Congress.

24. Jung, *Memories, Dreams, Reflections,* p. 39.

25. Hull interview by Nameche.

26. Hull to Jaffé, September 9, 1961.

27. William B. Goodheart. (1984). "C. G. Jung's First 'Patient': On the Seminal Emergence of Jung's Thought." *Journal of Analytical Psychology,* 29, p. 3.

28. Jung, *Memories, Dreams, Reflections,* p. x.

29. Hull, interview by Nameche.

30. Aniela Jaffé, interview by Gene Nameche, C. G. Jung Biographical Archive, Countway Library.

31. Jung, *Memories, Dreams, Reflections,* pp. 185–186.

32. Jung, *Memories, Dreams, Reflections,* p. 195. Curiously, in the proto-Urtext materials at the Library of Congress, Jung describes this patient as Dutch, whereas Sabina Spielrein was Russian. Jung first discussed Spielrein's case publicly at a conference in Amsterdam, so he may later have chose that associative detail to disguise Spielrein's identity, even in his interviews with Aniela Jaffé. It's also possible that another woman contributed to the evolution of the anima archetype, along with Sabina Spielrein and Toni Wolff. William McGuire has suggested to me that Maria Moltzer is a likely candidate. Moltzer was Dutch by birth and was, according to Jung, displaying "a loving jealousy" concerning him in 1910 (McGuire, ed., *Freud-Jung Letters,* pp. 351–352.) In 1912, Freud told a friend that Jung was "having an affair" with Moltzer (Eva Brabant et al., eds., *The Correspondence of Sigmund Freud and Sándor Ferenczi,* vol. 1, trans. Peter T. Hoffer [Cambridge, Mass.: Belknap Press of Harvard University Press, 1993], p. 446). Except for the Dutch background, however, what we know of Spielrein strikes me as fitting Jung's description of his anima figure much better than what we know of Moltzer. See also Shamdasani, "Memories, Dreams, Omissions," for further evidence in favor of Moltzer as the anima voice, and Kerr, *A Most Dangerous Method,* pp. 502–507, for further evidence in favor of Spielrein.

33. In the proto-Urtext material at the Library of Congress, Jung does mention Spielrein as contributing to Freud's concept of the death instinct; he does not discuss her contributions to his own ideas or his close personal relationship with her. Saul Rosenzweig has argued persuasively that Jung's oldest daughter, Agathe, went through a period of intensified sexual curiosity, anxiety, and distrust of her father at age four, at the same time that "the scandal about Jung's relationship to Sabina had reached its climax" (Rosenzweig, *Freud, Jung and Hall the King-Maker* [Seattle, Wash.: Hogrefe & Huber, 1992], p. 147). Of course Agathe had no direct knowledge of the relationship with Sabina; Rosenzweig suggests that she was reacting to her mother's anxiety about the affair.

34. Aldo Carotenuto. (1982). *A Secret Symmetry: Sabina Spielrein between Jung and Freud* (New York: Pantheon). The 1984 reprint edition includes additional material. Kerr's *A Most Dangerous Method* adds a great deal of background and detail, but Carotenuto's book more effectively conveys the personal relationship between Jung and Spielrein.

35. Carotenuto, *A Secret Symmetry, p.* 190; Jung's emphasis.

36. Jung, *Memories, Dreams, Reflections*, p. 187.

37. Jung, *Memories, Dreams, Reflections*, p. 185.

38. McGuire, *Freud-Jung Letters*, p. 95.

39. Jacobi interview by Nameche.

40. Jung, *Memories, Dreams, Reflections*, pp. 12–13.

41. Atwood and Stolorow, *Faces in a Cloud,* chapter 3.

Chapter Five *Allport Meets Freud and the Clean Little Boy*

1. Gordon W. Allport. (1967). "Autobiography." In E. G. Boring and G. Lindzey, eds., *A History of Psychology in Autobiography,* vol. 5 (Boston: Appleton). Allport, *Letters from Jenny.* Gordon W. Allport. (1942). *The Use of Personal Documents in Psychological Science* (New York: Social Science Research Council Bulletin No. 49). Allport, "The Study of Personality by the Intuitive Method." Gordon W. Allport. (1922). *An Experimental Study of the Traits of Personality* (unpublished doctoral dissertation, Harvard University).

2. Alan C. Elms. (1972). "Allport, Freud, and the Clean Little Boy." *Psychoanalytic Review, 59.*

3. *New York Times,* October 10, 1967.

4. Gordon W. Allport. (1962). "My Encounters with Personality Theory." Unpublished manuscript, recorded and edited by W.G.T. Douglas, Boston University School of Theology, October 29, p. 2. Gordon W. Allport Papers, Harvard University Archives, Cambridge, Mass. Extracts in this chapter from the unpublished papers of Gordon W. Allport are quoted by permission of Robert B. Allport, the Harvard University Archives, the Archives of the History of American Psychology, and the Library of Congress.

5. The 1958 version is in an unpublished manuscript, "G. W. Allport Recalls a Visit to Sigmund Freud," in the Sigmund Freud Archives, Library of Congress, Washington, D.C. The 1962 version is in "My Encounters with Personality Theory." The 1967 version is in Allport's "Autobiography." The 1970 version derives from a 1964 filmed interview with Richard Evans, who transcribed the interview for his book, *Gordon Allport: The Man and His Ideas* (New York: Dutton, 1970).

6. 1964 filmed interview, somewhat reworded in Evans, *Gordon Allport,* pp. 4–5.

7. Allport, "Autobiography," p. 8. The paper he cites here, "The Trend in Motivational Theory," was published in the *American Journal of Orthopsychiatry, 25* (1953).

8. For example, M. D. Faber, "Allport's Visit with Freud," *Psychoanalytic Review, 57* (1970); L. C. Morey, "Observations on the Meeting between Allport and Freud," *Psychoanalytic Review, 74* (1987).

9. Allport, "Autobiography," pp. 4–5.

10. Gordon W. Allport. (1937). *Personality: A Psychological Interpretation* (New York: Holt), p. 466.

11. Elms, "Allport, Freud, and the Clean Little Boy," pp. 629–631.

12. Elms, "Allport, Freud, and the Clean Little Boy," p. 631.

13. Henry A. Murray, letter to Ada L. Allport, September 22, 1972. Gordon W.

Allport Papers, Harvard University Archives, Cambridge, Mass. Quoted by permission of Nina Murray and the Harvard University Archives.

14. Daniel M. Ogilvie. (1984). "Personality and Paradox: Gordon Allport's Final Contribution." *Personality Forum, 2*, p. 13.

15. Thomas Pettigrew, interview, August 11, 1977.

16. Thomas Pettigrew, personal communication, September 30, 1988; Robert Allport, personal communication, October 26, 1988.

17. Allport, "G. W. Allport Recalls a Visit to Sigmund Freud," p. 3.

18. Gordon W. Allport, letter to W. S. Taylor, July 25, 1922. William S. Taylor Papers, Archives of the History of American Psychology, University of Akron, Akron, Ohio.

19. Gordon W. Allport, letter to W. S. Taylor, December 18, 1922. William S. Taylor Papers, Archives of the History of American Psychology, University of Akron, Akron, Ohio.

20. Gordon W. Allport, letter to W. S. Taylor, March 21, 1923. William S. Taylor Papers, Archives of the History of American Psychology, University of Akron, Akron, Ohio.

21. Salvatore R. Maddi and P. T. Costa. (1972). *Humanism in Personology: Allport, Maslow, Murray* (Chicago: Aldine), p. 139. Technically, Allport's book may have tied for earliest publication of a personality text; Ross Stagner came out with one the same month. But Allport's became much more influential.

22. Allport, "Autobiography," p. 15.

23. Allport, "My Encounters with Personality Theory," p. 5; his emphases.

24. To be clear, the term "Clean Personality" is mine; the theory it describes is Allport's.

25. Allport, *Personality,* p. 181, n. 27.

26. Allport, "Autobiography," pp. 7, 12.

27. Gordon W. Allport. (No date). "Personal Experience with Racial and Religious Attitudes," unpublished manuscript. Gordon W. Allport Papers, Harvard University Archives, Cambridge, Mass.

28. Gordon W. Allport, letter to W. E. Leonard, April 5, 1928. Gordon W. Allport Papers, Harvard University Archives, Cambridge, Mass.

29. Allport, *Personality,* p. vii.

30. Allport, *Personality,* pp. 565–566.

31. Floyd H. Allport. (1924). *Social Psychology* (Boston: Houghton Mifflin), pp. 8–9.

32. Allport, *Personality,* p. 549.

33. Erikson, *Young Man Luther,* pp. 23, 36.

34. Allport, *Personality,* p. 213.

35. Allport, *Personality,* pp. 213–214, 217.

36. Allport, *Personality,* p. 223.

37. Allport, *Personality,* p. 214.

38. Allport, *Personality,* p. 226; his emphasis.

39. Floyd H. Allport. (1933). *Institutional Behavior* (Chapel Hill: University of North Carolina Press), p. 458.

40. Allport, *Personality,* p. 227.
41. Allport, *Personality,* p. 216; his emphasis.
42. Allport, *Personality,* p. 352, n. 8.

Chapter Six Skinner's Dark Year and Walden Two

1. Indications of Skinner's continuing eminence and influence can be found in a special issue of the *American Psychologist,* 47 (November 1992), "Reflections on B. F. Skinner and Psychology."
2. B. F. Skinner. (1948). *Walden Two* (New York: Macmillan). Page numbers cited are from the 1976 edition.
3. B. F. Skinner. (1967). "Autobiography." In E. G. Boring and G. Lindzey, eds., *A History of Psychology in Autobiography,* vol. 5 (New York: Appleton-Century-Crofts), p. 408.
4. Skinner, "Autobiography," p. 403.
5. Skinner, *Shaping of a Behaviorist,* p. 298.
6. Skinner, *Shaping of a Behaviorist,* p. 298.
7. Skinner, *Shaping of a Behaviorist,* p. 297.
8. Skinner, *Shaping of a Behaviorist,* p. 292.
9. Skinner, "Autobiography," p. 403.
10. Skinner, *Shaping of a Behaviorist,* p. 292.
11. Skinner, *Shaping of a Behaviorist,* p. 293.
12. B. F. Skinner. (1976). "Walden Two Revisited." In *Walden Two,* 2nd ed. (New York: Macmillan), p. v.
13. Skinner, "Autobiography," p. 403.
14. Skinner, *Shaping of a Behaviorist,* p. 296.
15. Daniel J. Levinson. (1978). *The Seasons of a Man's Life* (New York: Knopf), p. 192.
16. Levinson, p. 199.
17. Skinner, *Particulars of My Life,* p. 134.
18. Erikson discusses identity crises most extensively in *Childhood and Society, Young Man Luther,* and *Identity: Youth and Crisis* (New York: Norton, 1968).
19. Erikson, *Childhood and Society,* p. 262.
20. Skinner, "Autobiography," p. 394.
21. Skinner, *Particulars of My Life,* p. 264.
22. Skinner, *Particulars of My Life,* pp. 264–265.
23. Skinner, *Particulars of My Life,* p. 265.
24. Skinner, *Particulars of My Life,* pp. 266–267.
25. Skinner, *Particulars of My Life,* p. 265.
26. Skinner, *Particulars of My Life,* p. 271.
27. Skinner, *Particulars of My Life,* pp. 279–280.
28. Skinner, *Particulars of My Life,* p. 287.
29. Skinner, *Particulars of My Life,* pp. 282–283.
30. Skinner, *Particulars of My Life,* pp. 264–265.
31. Skinner, "Autobiography," p. 394.

32. Skinner, *Particulars of My Life*, p. 285.

33. Skinner, *Particulars of My Life*, p. 286.

34. Erikson, *Identity: Youth and Crisis*, p. 163.

35. The italics are Erikson's.

36. Skinner, *Particulars of My Life*, p. 298.

37. Skinner, *Shaping of a Behaviorist*, p. 48.

38. Skinner, *Shaping of a Behaviorist*, pp. 114–115.

39. Skinner, *Shaping of a Behaviorist*, p. 117. Methodological behaviorists say we should study overt behavior because research on internal psychological processes is impractical. Radical behaviorists say we should study overt behavior because our internal psychological processes are unimportant; environment rules.

40. Skinner, *Shaping of a Behaviorist*, p. 119.

41. Skinner, *Shaping of a Behaviorist*, p. 226.

42. Skinner, *Shaping of a Behaviorist*, p. 243.

43. Skinner, *Shaping of a Behaviorist*, p. 245.

44. Skinner, *Shaping of a Behaviorist*, p. 274.

45. Skinner, *Shaping of a Behaviorist*, p. 284.

46. Skinner, *Shaping of a Behaviorist*, p. 286.

47. Skinner, *Shaping of a Behaviorist*, p. 285.

48. Skinner, *Shaping of a Behaviorist*, p. 285.

49. Skinner, *Particulars of My Life*, p. v.

50. Skinner, *Shaping of a Behaviorist*, p. 296.

51. Levinson, *Seasons of a Man's Life*, pp. 192–194.

52. Levinson, pp. 199–200.

53. Interview with B. F. Skinner, Cambridge, Mass., August 9, 1977.

54. Interview, August 9, 1977.

55. Skinner, *Particulars of My Life*, pp. 216–217.

56. Skinner, *Particulars of My Life*, p. 264.

57. Skinner, *Particulars of My Life*, p. 265.

58. Skinner, *Particulars of My Life*, p. 283.

59. Interview, August 9, 1977.

60. Skinner, *Shaping of a Behaviorist*, p. 299.

61. Skinner, *Walden Two*, p. 296.

Chapter Seven   The Thing from Inner Space

1. John W. Campbell, Jr. (1938). "Who Goes There?" *Astounding Science Fiction*, August. Reprinted in Ben Bova, ed., *The Science Fiction Hall of Fame*, vol. 2A (Garden City, N.Y.: Doubleday, 1973).

2. Campbell, "Who Goes There?" in Bova, pp. 41–42.

3. David Hartwell, ed. (1992). *Foundations of Fear* (New York: Tor).

4. Or at least he didn't intend it to be. As Campbell the editor often told his writers, using much the same words each time, "[Y]ou should know that you-the-conscious-intellect don't write stories, and you-the-conscious-intellect can't determine what comes out of the typewriter. Writing is done by a subconscious set of

circuits in the mind . . . . Those circuits even think in ways you dislike and resent, and force you to tell a somewhat different story than the one you had all planned." From Perry A. Chapdelaine, Sr., T. Chapdelaine, and G. Hay, eds., *The John W. Campbell Letters,* vol. 1 (Franklin, Tenn.: AC Projects, 1985), p. 587 (letter of September 8, 1970).

5. Bova, *Science Fiction Hall of Fame,* p. x.

6. Sam Moskowitz. (1967). *Seekers of Tomorrow: Masters of Modern Science Fiction* (New York: Ballantine), p. 36.

7. Moskowitz, pp. 36–37.

8. Moskowitz, pp. 51–52.

9. After Campbell's death, Moskowitz was initially given permission to use his personal papers as the basis for a full-scale biography. That permission was subsequently withdrawn, according to Moskowitz, because the Campbell family's lawyer feared that the papers might contain libelous material. Sam Moskowitz, personal communication, June 10, 1983.

10. Chapdelaine, Chapdelaine, and Hay, eds., *John W. Campbell Letters,* p. 208.

11. Lester Del Rey, ed. (1976). *The Best of John W. Campbell* (Garden City, N.Y.: Nelson Doubleday), pp. 164–245. The stories are "Out of Night," originally published in *Astounding Stories,* October 1937, and "Cloak of Aesir," originally published in *Astounding Science Fiction,* March 1939.

12. This categorization derives from social-psychological theories of attitude functions and clinical theories of personality processes. For a summary of the social-psychological approach, see Alan C. Elms, *Attitudes* (Milton Keynes, England: Open University Press, 1976), pp. 28–41, and Gregory M. Herek, "The Instrumentality of Attitudes: Toward a Neofunctional Theory," *Journal of Social Issues,* 42 (2), 1986. For a discussion of the clinical distinction between defensive and restitutive processes, see Robert D. Stolorow and George E. Atwood, *Faces in a Cloud: Subjectivity in Personality Theory* (New York: Aronson, 1979), pp. 184–185.

13. For example, Daniel Katz, "The Functional Approach to the Study of Attitudes," *Public Opinion Quarterly,* 24, 1960; Abraham H. Maslow, *Toward a Psychology of Being* (Princeton, N.J.: Van Nostrand, 1968).

14. Erik Erikson is again the major source for concepts about identity; see Chapter 6. The self-concept, in one form or another, has become central to psychoanalytic theory (as in Heinz Kohut's *Analysis of the Self,* New York: International Universities Press, 1971) and to social psychology (as in Barry Schlenker's edited volume, *The Self and Social Life,* New York: McGraw-Hill, 1985).

15. Stanley G. Weinbaum. (1934). "A Martian Odyssey." *Wonder Stories,* July. Reprinted in Tom Shippey, ed., *The Oxford Book of Science Fiction Stories* (Oxford and New York: Oxford University Press, 1992), and many other places. In the Shippey volume, the quoted passage is on p. 86.

16. Weinbaum, p. 86.

17. Isaac Asimov, ed. (1974). *Before the Golden Age: A Science Fiction Anthology of the 1930s* (Garden City, N.Y.: Doubleday), p. 795. Asimov reprints Campbell's story, which was originally published in *Thrilling Wonder Stories,* December 1936.

18. Freud, *Interpretation of Dreams*, pp. 264–266.

19. Freud, *Interpretation of Dreams*, p. 266.

20. The Conan stories have appeared in several versions, some heavily rewritten by others. The most accurate texts available are those edited by Karl Edward Wagner: *The Hour of the Dragon, The People of the Black Circle,* and *Red Nails,* all published by Berkley Publishing Co., New York, in 1977.

21. Reprinted in *The People of the Black Circle,* pp. 52–55.

22. The most extensive biography of Howard is *Dark Valley Destiny: The Life of Robert E. Howard,* by L. Sprague de Camp, Catherine Crook de Camp, and Jane Whittington Griffin (New York: Bluejay Books, 1983). The book makes some effort to be a psychobiography, but a good deal remains to be said about Howard's psychology.

23. Chapdelaine, Chapdelaine, and Hay, eds., *John W. Campbell Letters,* pp. 34, 75, 220, among others.

24. The most complete collection of Smith's stories is *The Rediscovery of Man,* edited by James A. Mann (Framingham, Mass.: NESFA Press, 1993). A good selection is contained in J. J. Pierce, ed., *The Best of Cordwainer Smith* (New York: Ballantine/Del Rey, 1975).

25. Ursula K. Le Guin. (1993). Introduction to *The Norton Book of Science Fiction,* Ursula K. Le Guin and Brian Attebery, eds., with Karen Joy Fowler (New York: Norton), p. 38.

26. Smith, *Rediscovery of Man,* p. 97. Originally published in *Galaxy,* April 1960.

27. Letter of October 1943, quoted by permission of Rosana [Linebarger] Hart.

28. It can be found in, among other places, *The Science Fiction Hall of Fame,* vol. 1, Robert Silverberg, ed. (Garden City, N.Y.: Doubleday, 1970). Originally published in *Fantasy Book,* 1950.

29. This story, too, has been often anthologized; it is included both in *The Best of Cordwainer Smith* and in *The Rediscovery of Man.*

30. Smith, *Rediscovery of Man,* p. 165; his italics.

31. In addition to his academic career and his writing, Linebarger continued to work for Army Intelligence on active reserve status, and occasionally consulted for the CIA.

32. Cordwainer Smith. (1975). *Norstrilia* (New York: Ballantine). This is the complete edition of the novel; it was published earlier in two truncated pieces as *The Planet Buyer* and *The Underpeople.*

33. Cordwainer Smith, *Norstrilia,* pp. 250–251; his italics.

34. Cordwainer Smith, *Norstrilia,* p. 262.

35. For more on Cordwainer Smith, see Alan C. Elms, "The Creation of Cordwainer Smith," *Science-Fiction Studies, 11,* 1984, and Alan C. Elms, "Origins of the Underpeople: Cats, Kuomintang and Cordwainer Smith," in Tom Shippey, ed., *Fictional Space: Essays on Contemporary Science Fiction* (Atlantic Highlands, N.J.: Humanities Press, 1991).

Chapter Eight Darker Than He Thought

1. Jack Williamson. (1984). *Wonder's Child: My Life in Science Fiction* (New York: Bluejay Books).

2. Both of these examples are thoughtfully discussed in Jeffrey Berman's *The Talking Cure: Literary Representations of Psychoanalysis* (New York: New York University Press, 1985), along with other literary uses of psychotherapy.

3. See Eusebio L. Rodrigues, "Reichianism in *Henderson the Rain King,*" *Criticism,* 15, 1973, and Ruth Miller, *Saul Bellow: A Biography of the Imagination* (New York: St. Martin's Press, 1991), pp. 87–89, 122–126.

4. Jack Williamson. (1948). *Darker Than You Think* (Reading, Pa.: Fantasy Press).

5. Alfred D. Stewart. (1981). "Jack Williamson." In David Cowart and Thomas L. Wymer, eds., *Dictionary of Literary Biography, vol. 8: Twentieth Century American Science-Fiction Writers, Part 2* (Detroit: Gale), p. 205.

6. Martin M. Wooster. (1986). "Jack Williamson." In Curtis C. Smith, ed., *Twentieth-Century Science-Fiction Writers,* 2nd ed. (Chicago: St. James Press), p. 799.

7. Jack Williamson. (1940). "Darker Than You Think." *Unknown, 4* (4), December.

8. Williamson, *Wonder's Child,* pp. 125, 178.

9. Jack Williamson, personal communication, November 16, 1987.

10. Williamson, *Wonder's Child,* p. 23.

11. Williamson, *Wonder's Child,* p. 26.

12. Williamson, *Wonder's Child,* p. 38.

13. Williamson, *Wonder's Child,* p. 11.

14. Williamson, *Wonder's Child,* p. 8.

15. Williamson, *Wonder's Child,* p. 50.

16. Williamson, *Wonder's Child,* pp. 19, 22.

17. Jack Williamson. (1975). *The Early Williamson* (Garden City, N.Y.: Doubleday; page numbers from London: Sphere Books reprint, 1978), pp. 11–12.

18. Williamson, *Early Williamson,* p. 12.

19. Williamson, *Wonder's Child,* p. 57.

20. Williamson, *Wonder's Child,* p. 94.

21. Williamson, *Wonder's Child,* p. 98.

22. Charles W. Tidd. (1936). "Increasing Reality Acceptance by a Schizoid Personality during Analysis." *Bulletin of the Menninger Clinic, 1.*

23. Jack Williamson. (1937). "Under Psychoanalysis: A Patient Reviews the First Year." Unpublished manuscript, Williamson Collection, Golden Library, Eastern New Mexico University. I am grateful to Jack Williamson for providing a copy of this manuscript and for giving me permission to quote from it, as well as for helping in other ways during the preparation of this chapter in its original form. He is, of course, not responsible for my conclusions.

24. Williamson, *Wonder's Child,* pp. 101–107.

25. Tidd, p. 182.

26. Williamson, "Under Psychoanalysis," p. 2.

27. Tidd, p. 177.

28. Williamson, "Under Psychoanalysis," pp. 12–13.

29. Tidd, p. 176.

30. Robert L. Spitzer, Andrew E. Shodol, Miriam Gibbon, and Janet B. W. Williams. (1981). *DSM-III Case Book* (Washington, D.C.: American Psychiatric Association), p. 176.

31. Millon, *Disorders of Personality: DSM-III: Axis II*, p. 304. Personality psychologists have identified similar patterns in nonclinical populations of adults: "dismissive avoidants," who like schizoid patients unambivalently dismiss or reject social relationships, and "fearful avoidants," who like Williamson and other DSM-III avoidants simultaneously desire and fear close relationships. See K. Bartholomew and L. M. Horowitz, "Attachment Styles among Young Adults: A Test of a Four-Category Model," *Journal of Personality and Social Psychology, 61*, 1991, and Phillip R. Shaver and Cindy Hazan, "Adult Romantic Attachment: Theory and Evidence," in D. Perlman and W. Jones, eds., *Advances in Personal Relationships, 4*, 1992.

32. Personal communication, November 16, 1987.

33. Millon, p. 323.

34. Millon, p. 323.

35. Tidd, p. 177.

36. Tidd, p. 178.

37. Williamson, "Under Psychoanalysis," pp. 2, 4, 6, 8, 10, 14.

38. Williamson, "Under Psychoanalysis," p. 15.

39. Williamson, "Under Psychoanalysis," pp. 4, 5.

40. Williamson, *Wonder's Child,* p. 100.

41. Williamson, *Wonder's Child,* p. 101.

42. Tidd, p. 178.

43. Tidd, p. 180.

44. Tidd, p. 181.

45. According to Erikson, the normal adolescent identity crisis is usually resolved by choices of career and ideology. But it will persist or reappear if the individual fails to "detect some meaningful resemblance between what he has come to see in himself and what his sharpened awareness tells him others judge and expect him to be" (*Young Man Luther,* p. 14).

46. Williamson, *Wonder's Child,* p. 107.

47. Williamson, *Wonder's Child,* p. 107.

48. Williamson, *Wonder's Child,* p. 115.

49. Williamson, *Wonder's Child,* p. 113.

50. Williamson, *Wonder's Child,* p. 123.

51. Williamson, *Wonder's Child,* p. 125.

52. Page numbers in this section are from *Darker Than You Think,* Bluejay Books reprint, New York, 1984.

53. Williamson, *Wonder's Child,* p. 125.

54. Williamson, *Early Williamson,* p. 78.

55. The name "Will" might be seen as referring to "will power," but it probably came directly from "Williamson." Williamson used the same first name as part of his major professional pseudonym, Will Stewart.

56. Williamson, *Wonder's Child,* p. 125.

57. Sigmund Freud. (1964). *New Introductory Lectures on Psychoanalysis*. In James Strachey, ed. and trans., *The Standard Edition of the Complete Psychological Works of Sigmund Freud*, vol. 22 (London: Hogarth Press), p. 80. Original work published in 1932.

58. Tidd, p. 183.

59. Williamson, *Wonder's Child*, p. 125.

60. Jack Williamson. (1949). *The Humanoids* (New York: Simon & Schuster). Jack Williamson. (1951). *Dragon's Island* (Simon & Schuster).

61. And he's still publishing it, over 65 years after that first story appeared in the December 1928 issue of *Amazing Stories!* A new story by Jack was published in the Winter 1994 issue of *Amazing Stories;* his latest novel is *Demon Moon* (New York: Tor, 1994); and as we go to press, he's working on another novel, tentatively titled *The Black Sun* (Jack Williamson, personal communication, March 12, 1994.)

Chapter Nine Asimov as Acrophobe

1. Isaac Asimov. (1983). *The Robots of Dawn* (Garden City, N.Y.: Doubleday).

2. Isaac Asimov. (1983). *The Robot Collection* (Garden City, N.Y.: Doubleday). Includes texts of *The Caves of Steel*, 1954, and *The Naked Sun*, 1957.

3. Asimov, *Robots of Dawn*, pp. 58–59.

4. Asimov, *Caves of Steel*, p. 123; Asimov, *Naked Sun*, pp. 209–211.

5. Isaac Asimov. (1969). *Asimov's Mysteries* (New York: Dell), p. 47.

6. Originally published in *Astounding Science Fiction*, September 1941; widely reprinted, for example, in Isaac Asimov, *Nightfall and Other Stories* (New York: Fawcett, 1971).

7. Isaac Asimov. (1979). *In Memory yet Green* (Garden City, N.Y.: Doubleday), p. 267.

8. Asimov, *Robots of Dawn*, p. 111.

9. Asimov, *In Memory Yet Green*, pp. 124–125. Asimov amplifies on his "liking for enclosed places" in his posthumously published memoir, *I. Asimov* (New York: Doubleday, 1994, pp. 129–131); the chapter is titled "Claustrophilia." Asimov's second wife, incidentally, was a psychiatrist.

10. Asimov, *In Memory Yet Green*, p. 149. In his later memoir, Asimov speculates that he might have been "born with the phobia": *I. Asimov*, p. 127.

11. James Gunn. (1982). *Isaac Asimov: The Foundations of Science Fiction* (New York: Oxford University Press), p. 17.

12. Gunn, pp. 130, 25.

13. Isaac Asimov, personal communication, March 9, 1985; his emphases. I very much appreciate Asimov's willingness to answer my questions and to let me quote from his letters to me.

14. Isaac Asimov, personal communication, June 4, 1985; his emphases.

15. Isaac Asimov, personal communication, June 4, 1985; his emphasis.

16. Isaac Asimov. (1970). *Nightfall and Other Stories* (New York: Fawcett), p. 45.

17. Isaac Asimov. (1976). *Murder at the ABA* (Garden City, N.Y.: Doubleday), p. 51.

18. Asimov, *Nightfall and Other Stories*, pp. 249–250.

19. Isaac Asimov, personal communication, August 2, 1985; emphasis his.

20. Isaac Asimov. (1988). "Acrophobia." *Isaac Asimov's Science Fiction Magazine,* 12 (8), August, p. 6. He was similarly insistent in his posthumously published memoir: "I don't have any touch of agoraphobia (the morbid fear of open places), though I would rather walk the canyons of Manhattan with tall buildings hemming me in than in Central Park, which is open" (*I. Asimov*, p. 130).

21. Asimov, "Acrophobia," p. 7.

Chapter Ten *The Mother of Oz*

1. *The Wonderful Wizard of Oz* was first published in 1900 (Chicago: George M. Hill). Page numbers cited later in this chapter refer to Michael Patrick Hearn, ed., *The Annotated Wizard of Oz* (New York: Clarkson N. Potter, 1973).

2. Conrad Phillip Kottak. (1978). "Social-Science Fiction." *Psychology Today, 11* (9), February.

3. Further discussion of these similarities and others—including Ozma's and Leia's strikingly similar hairdos—can be found in Alan C. Elms, "Oz in Science Fiction Film," *The Baum Bugle: A Journal of Oz,* Winter 1983.

4. L. Frank Baum. (1904). *The Marvelous Land of Oz* (Chicago: Reilly & Britton). This book is most readily available in the paperback edition titled *The Land of Oz* (New York: Del Rey/Ballantine, 1979); page numbers are taken from that edition. Careful reproductions of the first editions of both *The Wonderful Wizard of Oz* and *The Marvelous Land of Oz* have been published by Books of Wonder, New York.

5. The Winkies live in the western part of the Land of Oz, so the West Coast conventions are Winkie Conventions. The Munchkins live in the East, so the East Coast conventions are Munchkin conventions. And so on.

6. One of the better thematic interpretations is Sheldon Kopp's paper, "The Wizard of Oz Behind the Couch" (*Voices, 4, 1968*; reprinted in *Psychology Today, 3* [10], 1970). Copp argues that the Wizard's interactions with Dorothy and her friends proceed very much in the manner of a good psychotherapist working with a patient.

7. In the original version of the economic "interpretation," published by Henry M. Littlefield in 1964, it was the Cowardly Lion who stood in for William Jennings Bryan; the Wizard was any of several U.S. Presidents. The further history of Littlefield's interpretation and its ambiguous relevance to Baum's own political views are discussed in Michael Gessel's "Tale of a Parable" and Henry M. Littlefield's "The Wizard of Allegory," both in *The Baum Bugle, 36* (1), Spring 1992.

8. Baum, *Wonderful Wizard of Oz*, p. 149.

9. Some writers have suggested that the MA in Ozma's name came from the name of Baum's wife MAud. Maybe that's what Frank told Maud, but she was never known for being nurturant.

10. L. Frank Baum. (1910). *The Emerald City of Oz* (Chicago: Reilly & Britton), pp. 30–33.

11. Frank J. Baum and Russell P. MacFall. (1961). *To Please a Child* (Chicago: Reilly & Lee), p. 20.

12. Baum and MacFall, p. 1.

13. Baum and MacFall, p. 23.

14. E. T. James, ed. (1971). *Notable American Women 1607–1950*, vol. 2 (Cambridge, Mass: The Belknap Press of Harvard University Press), pp. 4–6.

15. Baum and MacFall, p. 43.

16. Baum and MacFall, p. 46.

17. Baum and MacFall, pp. 47–48.

18. Baum and MacFall, p. 56.

19. Baum and MacFall, p. 93.

20. David L. Greene and Dick Martin. (1977). *The Oz Scrapbook* (New York: Random House), p. v.

21. Baum and MacFall, p. 275.

22. Baum and MacFall, p. 275. Frank J. Baum's original manuscript of *To Please a Child* (located in the Syracuse University Library) is even more biased in favor of his father and against his mother than the published version. Russell MacFall told me that one of his important roles in rewriting the manuscript for publication was to tone down the son's excesses in the original draft. Michael Patrick Hearn's forthcoming biography of L. Frank Baum should be a much more reliable source.

23. Daniel Mannix has described the attack that ended Baum's stay in military school as a "nervous breakdown," but with no more evidence than for a genuine heart attack. See p. 38 of Mannix, "The Father of the Wizard of Oz," *American Heritage, 16* (1), December 1964.

24. See, for instance, Osmond Beckwith, "The Oddness of Oz", *Kulchur, 1* (4), 1961, which is partially reprinted in L. Frank Baum, *The Wizard of Oz*, Michael Patrick Hearn, ed. (New York: Schocken Books, 1983).

25. Indeed, Baum may have been a good deal more likely to make that remark than Freud was to have made the now-famous remark about the cigar. See Alan C. Elms, "Freud's Greatest Hits," forthcoming.

26. Peter Hanff. (1977). "Frank Baum: Success and Frustration." *Baum Bugle, 21* (3), Winter, p. 30.

27. See Nancy Chodorow's account of this process in *The Reproduction of Mothering* (Berkeley: University of California Press, 1978).

28. L. Frank Baum. (1886). *The Book of the Hamburgs* (Hartford, Conn: H. H. Stoddard).

29. Baum, *Book of the Hamburgs,* pp. 58–59. The italics are Baum's.

30. L. Frank Baum. (1903). *The Enchanted Island of Yew* (Indianapolis: Bobbs-Merrill).

31. L. Frank Baum. (1909). "The Fairy Prince." *Entertaining,* December; reprinted in *Baum Bugle, 11* (3), Christmas 1967.

32. Baum, *Emerald City of Oz*, pp. 123–124.

33. L. Frank Baum. (1907). *Ozma of Oz* (Chicago: Reilly & Britton; reprinted by Ballantine/Del Rey, New York, 1979), pp. 106–107.

34. L. Frank Baum. (1906). *John Dough and the Cherub* (Chicago: Reilly & Britton; reprinted by Dover, New York, 1974).

35. Martin Gardner and R. B. Nye. (1957). *The Wizard of Oz and Who He Was* (East Lansing, Mich.: Michigan State University Press), p. 33.

36. Greene and Martin, p. 19.

37. M. J. Gage. (1966). "The Dakota Days of L. Frank Baum," part 3. *Baum Bugle,* 10 (3), Christmas.

38. L. Frank Baum. "La Reine Est Mort—Vive La Reine!" Chicago *Times-Herald,* June 23; reprinted in *Baum Bugle,* 22 (3), Winter 1978.

39. Janet T. Spence and Robert L. Helmreich. (1978). *Masculinity and Femininity* (Austin: University of Texas Press). This line of research has remained among the more contentious in social psychology.

40. Gardner and Nye, p. 29.

Chapter Eleven *Nabokov Contra Freud*

1. Vladimir Nabokov. (1964). *The Defense* (New York: Putnam), p. 11.

2. Allport, *Personality: A Psychological Interpretation,* 1937; Allport, "The Trend in Motivational Theory," 1953.

3. Page Stegner. (1966). *Escape into Aesthetics: The Art of Vladimir Nabokov* (New York: William Morrow). Apollo edition, 1969, p. 43.

4. Quoted in translation by Andrew Field, *Nabokov: His Life in Art* (Boston: Little, Brown, 1967), pp. 263–264.

5. Vladimir Nabokov. (1951). *Conclusive Evidence* (New York: Harper), p. 230.

6. Vladimir Nabokov. (1958.) *Lolita* (New York: Putnam), p. 316.

7. Nabokov, *Lolita,* p. 36.

8. Vladimir Nabokov. (1965). *The Eye* (New York: Phaedra), p. 9.

9. Vladimir Nabokov. (1966). *The Waltz Invention* (New York: Phaedra), p. iii.

10. Vladimir Nabokov. (1973). *Strong Opinions* (New York: McGraw-Hill), pp. 23–24.

11. Nabokov, *Strong Opinions,* p. 66.

12. Robert Robinson. (1981). "The Last Interview." In Peter Quennell, ed., *Vladimir Nabokov: A Tribute* (New York: William Morrow), p. 124.

13. Nabokov, *Strong Opinions,* p. 47.

14. Stegner, p. 36.

15. Stegner, p. 41.

16. Stegner, p. 43. Jenefer Shute has provided a considerably more complex discussion of Nabokov's artistic "struggle against an encroaching hermeneutics," in "Nabokov and Freud: The Play of Power," *Modern Fiction Studies, 30,* 1984, p. 641.

17. William W. Rowe. (1971). *Nabokov's Deceptive World* (New York: New York University Press). Vladimir Nabokov. (1971). "Rowe's Symbols." *New York Review of Books,* October 7.

18. Vladimir Nabokov. (1966). *Despair* (New York: Putnam), p. 8.

19. See, for instance, Phyllis Roth, "Toward the Man Behind the Mystification," in J. E. Rivers and C. Nicol, eds., *Nabokov's Fifth Arc* (Austin: University of Texas Press, 1982); Jeffrey Berman, *The Talking Cure,* ch. 8; and Geoffrey Green, *Freud and Nabokov* (Lincoln: University of Nebraska Press, 1988.)

20. Vladimir E. Alexandrov. (1991). *Nabokov's Otherworld* (Princeton, N.J.: Princeton University Press), p. 52. Actually, Freud took much the same position as Nabokov on the general-versus-specific issue in the creative arts. When Marie Bonaparte asked

him whether any writers inspired by his work had written great works of art, Freud replied with a firm no. Books directly inspired by psychoanalytic theory may be interesting, he said, but their external inspiration makes them too schematic. Truly creative writing, Freud insisted, must originate from within the individual writer. (My thanks to Frank Hartman, who is editing Marie Bonaparte's journals, for showing me the relevant passage.)

21. Sigmund Freud. (1963). "The Taboo of Virginity." In J. Strachey, ed. and trans., *Standard Edition of the Complete Psychological Works of Sigmund Freud,* vol. 16 (London: Hogarth), p. 199. Original edition published in 1918.

22. Sigmund Freud. (1961). *Civilization and Its Discontents.* In J. Strachey, ed. and trans., *Standard Edition of the Complete Psychological Works of Sigmund Freud,* vol. 21 (London: Hogarth), p. 114. Original edition published in 1930.

23. Jane Grayson. (1977). *Nabokov Translated* (Oxford: Oxford University Press), p. 116.

24. Brian Boyd. (1990). *Vladimir Nabokov: The Russian Years* (Princeton, N.J.: Princeton University Press), p. 439.

25. Vladimir Nabokov. (1966). *Speak, Memory* (New York: Putnam), p. 20.

26. The English translation is in *Nabokov's Dozen* (Garden City, N.Y.: Doubleday, 1958). The Russian version, "Oblako, Ozero, Bashnya," is available in Nabokov's *Vesna v Fial'te* (New York: Chekhov, 1956).

27. Field, *Nabokov: His Life in Art*, p. 197.

28. Douglas Fowler. (1974). *Reading Nabokov* (Ithaca, N.Y.: Cornell University Press), p. 66.

29. Simon Karlinsky, ed. (1980). *The Nabokov-Wilson Letters* (New York: Harper Colophon), p. 39.

30. Boyd, p. 439.

31. Murray, *Explorations in Personality*, p. 364.

32. Murray, *Explorations in Personality,* p. 363.

33. Eight years in the original Russian version. One might speculate on the psychological significance of the different numbers, but I won't.

34. Nabokov, *Nabokov's Dozen*, p. 116.

35. Sigmund Freud and Oskar Pfister. (1963). *Psychoanalysis and Faith: The Letters of Sigmund Freud and Oskar Pfister* (London: Hogarth Press), pp. 20–21.

36. Nabokov, *Nabokov's Dozen*, p. 120; Nabokov's italics.

37. Freud, *Interpretation of Dreams*, p. 399.

38. Nabokov, *Nabokov's Dozen*, p. 121.

39. Nabokov, *Nabokov's Dozen*, p. 123.

40. Field, *Nabokov: His Life in Art*, p. 197.

41. Nicolas Nabokov. (1975). *Bagazh* (New York: Atheneum), p. 112.

42. Andrew Field. (1986). *VN: The Life and Art of Vladimir Nabokov* (New York: Crown), p. 175. Boyd, pp. 427–428.

43. Andrew Field. (1977). *Nabokov: His Life in Part* (New York: Viking), p. 201.

44. Nabokov, *Speak, Memory*, p. 306.

45. Nabokov, *Speak, Memory*, pp. 297–298.

46. Nabokov, *Speak, Memory,* p. 306.

47. Nabokov, *Speak, Memory,* pp. 21–22.

48. Nabokov, *Speak, Memory,* p. 245.

49. Nabokov, *Speak, Memory,* pp. 249–250.

50. Boyd, pp. 438–439.

51. Nabokov, *Speak, Memory*, pp. 36–39.

52. Nabokov, *Speak, Memory,* p. 23.

53. Nabokov, *Speak, Memory,* pp. 19–20.

54. Alfred Appel, Jr., ed. (1970). *The Annotated Lolita* by Vladimir Nabokov (New York: McGraw-Hill), p. xlv.

55. Nabokov, *Speak, Memory,* pp. 296–297.

56. Murray, *Explorations in Personality*, p. 363.

57. Murray, *Explorations in Personality*, pp. 363–364.

58. Murray, *Explorations in Personality*, p. 365.

59. Murray, *Explorations in Personality*, p. 366.

60. Murray, *Explorations in Personality*, p. 368.

61. Lloyd deMause. (1981). "The Fetal Origins of History." *Journal of Psychohistory, 9.*

62. Vladimir Nabokov. (1959). *Invitation to a Beheading* (New York: Putnam). Original edition published in 1935.

63. Nabokov himself was insistent on that. In *Strong Opinions,* p. 179, he says, "My purpose is not to be facetiously flashy or grotesquely obscure but to express what I feel and think with the utmost truthfulness and perception."

64. Vladimir Nabokov. (1969). *Ada or Ardor: A Family Chronicle* (New York: McGraw-Hill).

Chapter Twelve Carter and Character

1. Freud, *Leonardo da Vinci,* p. 97.

2. *Fact, 1* (5), September-October 1964, "The Unconscious of a Conservative: A Special Issue on the Mind of Barry Goldwater." See also Elms, *Personality in Politics,* pp. 88–90.

3. Bruce Mazlish. (1972). *In Search of Nixon: A Psychohistorical Inquiry* (New York: Basic Books; Pelican reprint, 1973), p. vi.

4. James David Barber. (1972). *The Presidential Character: Predicting Performance in the White House* (Englewood Cliffs, N.J.: Prentice-Hall.)

5. Bruce Mazlish and Edwin Diamond. (1976). "Thrice-Born: A Psychohistory of Jimmy Carter's 'Rebirth.'" *New York,* August 30.

6. Doris Kearns Goodwin. (1976). "Ford and Carter: The Character of the Candidates." *Ladies' Home Journal,* November.

7. Sacramento *Bee,* Sunday, October 24, 1976, Forum Section, p. 1.

8. Jimmy Carter. (1975). *Why Not the Best?* (Nashville: Broadman Press; page citations from Bantam Books 1976 reprint).

9. Carter, 161.

10. In her 1980 psychobiography of Carter, Betty Glad presented evidence that Carter talked to reporters and relatives during the 1976 campaign about how he would strive to be "active and positive in approach as president," and that he often referred to the Barber volume in that context. See Betty Glad, *Jimmy Carter: In Search of the Great White House* (New York: Norton, 1980), pp. 486–487.

11. Goodwin, p. C-8.

12. See, for instance, his *James and John Stuart Mill: Father and Son in the Nineteenth Century* (New York: Basic Books, 1975).

13. Mazlish and Diamond, "Thrice-Born," p. 30.

14. Erikson, *Young Man Luther.*

15. Mazlish and Diamond, "Thrice-Born," p. 31.

16. Carter, pp. 9–10.

17. It's the fourth of Freud's proscriptive guidelines, discussed in Chapter 3.

18. I should note in fairness that by the time Mazlish and Diamond finally produced their full-scale psychobiography of Carter in late 1979, they had considerably softened or qualified most of the positions they took in their 1976 article. By that time, however, it was too late for their analysis to interest many voters. The book is still useful as a complement to Barber's chapter on Carter in the fourth edition of *Presidential Character,* and especially as an alternative perspective to Betty Glad's more detailed but less sympathetic psychobiography of Carter. See Bruce Mazlish and Edwin Diamond, *Jimmy Carter: An Interpretive Biography* (New York: Simon & Schuster, 1979).

19. Benjamin Stein. (1976). "If You Liked Richard Nixon, You'll Love Jimmy Carter." *Penthouse,* November.

20. James David Barber. (1992). *The Presidential Character,* 4th ed. (Englewood Cliffs, N.J.: Prentice-Hall), p. 431.

21. Barber, *Presidential Character,* 4th ed., p. 446.

22. Barber, *Presidential Character,* 4th ed., p. 446.

23. Barber, *Presidential Character,* 4th ed., p. 453.

24. Barber, *Presidential Character,* 4th ed., p. 439.

25. Barber, *Presidential Character,* 4th ed., p. 441.

26. I sent a draft of this chapter to Jimmy Carter, asking for comments. He wrote back to compliment me on my use of humor and to say he appreciated my being "fairly positive." He added that he's planning to publish a book of poetry soon, which he says might be the best basis for psychoanalyzing him. Will he still appreciate my sense of humor if I suggest that he title it *Why Not the Verse?*

27. My office neighbor Dean Simonton has brought strong quantitative skills to the analysis of biographical data on past U.S. Presidents, in his *Why Presidents Succeed: A Political Psychology of Leadership* (New Haven: Yale University Press, 1987). Dean hasn't made any official predictions yet about who'd make a good future president, but he's already thinking (or fantasizing) about a computer program that would do the predicting for him. See his papers, "Putting the Best Leaders in the White House" and "Further Details on VOTER HELPER™ 1.0," both in *Political Psychology, 14,* 1993.

Chapter Thirteen The Counterplayers

1. Erikson, *Gandhi's Truth*, pp. 68 and 296.

2. Interview with Erik Erikson, Cotuit, Mass., August 10, 1982.

3. "Frontline: The Mind of Hussein," Public Broadcasting System, February 26, 1991.

4. Hussein himself says his "father died months before his birth" (John Bullock and Harvey Morris, *Saddam's War* [London: Faber & Faber, 1991], p. 45). But in another account, "a private secretary of Saddam's, who later broke with him, has suggested that Saddam's father abandoned his wife and young children" (Judith Miller and Laurie Mylroie, *Saddam Hussein and the Crisis in the Gulf* [New York: Times Books, 1990], p. 26.)

5. Efraim Karsh and Inari Rautsi. (1991). *Saddam Hussein: A Political Biography* (New York: Free Press), pp. 7–8.

6. Karsh and Rautsi, p. 10.

7. Samir al-Khalil. (1989). *Republic of Fear: The Inside Story of Saddam's Iraq* (Berkeley: University of California Press; Pantheon Books reprint, New York, 1990), p. 17.

8. Karsh and Rautsi, p. 10.

9. Karsh and Rautsi, p. 10.

10. Elaine Sciolino. (1991). *The Outlaw State: Saddam Hussein's Quest for Power and the Gulf Crisis* (New York: Wiley), p. 59.

11. Sciolino, p. 20.

12. It has been reported that "the U.S. intelligence community" produced three different psychological profiles of Hussein in 1990, and that Israeli military intelligence produced its own 200-page psychological profile (U.S. News & World Report, *Triumph without Victory: The Unreported History of the Persian Gulf War* [New York: Times Books, 1992], pp. 151–152). An impartial comparison of these still largely secret assessments might prove interesting.

13. Jerrold M. Post. (1991). "Saddam Hussein of Iraq: A Political Psychology Profile." *Political Psychology,* 12 (2). Post presented his findings at hearings of two U.S. House of Representatives committees, and was interviewed many times on the topic by broadcast and print journalists. See also Jerrold M. Post, "Current Concepts of the Narcissistic Personality: Implications for Political Psychology," *Political Psychology,* 14 (1), 1993, and Jerrold M. Post, "The Defining Moment of Saddam's Life," in Stanley A. Renshon, ed., *The Political Psychology of the Gulf War* (Pittsburgh, Pa.: University of Pittsburgh Press, 1993).

14. Bob Woodward. (1987). *Veil: The Secret Wars of the CIA 1981–1987* (New York: Simon & Schuster; Pocket Books reprint, 1988), p. 275.

15. Otto Kernberg. (1984). *Severe Personality Disorders: Psychotherapeutic Strategies* (New Haven: Yale University Press), pp. 290–311. Kernberg summarized the major elements of malignant narcissism in an interview by Daniel Goleman, excerpted in the *New York Times,* January 29, 1991; subsequent quotations and paraphrases of Kernberg are from that interview unless otherwise noted.

16. Post, "Saddam Hussein of Iraq," p. 285.

17. Samir al-Khalil. (1991). *The Monument: Art, Vulgarity and Responsibility in Iraq* (Berkeley: University of California Press), p. 3.

18. Post, "Saddam Hussein of Iraq," p. 284.

19. Karsh and Rautsi, p. 166.

20. When ABC Television's Diane Sawyer interviewed Saddam in June 1990, she asked about the Health Minister incident; Saddam evaded her questions. She asked directly, "Have you ever personally killed someone who opposed you?" Saddam replied, "Never. It has never happened. I have never killed anybody." So now you know. The interview is quoted in Sciolino, *The Outlaw State,* p. 91.

21. Post, "Saddam Hussein of Iraq," p. 284.

22. Kernberg interview in *New York Times.*

23. Associated Press. (1991). "Excerpts from Address by Saddam Hussein." *New York Times,* February 25.

24. Kernberg interview in *New York Times.*

25. Miller and Mylroie, p. 24.

26. "Frontline: The Mind of Hussein."

27. George Bush. (1987). *Looking Forward: An Autobiography* (New York: Doubleday), p. 27.

28. Bush, p. 28.

29. Bush, p. 30.

30. Bush, p. 24.

31. Gail Sheehy. (1988). *Character: America's Search for Leadership* (New York: William Morrow), p. 161.

32. Quoted in Sheehy, p. 162.

33. Bush, p. 26.

34. *Newsweek,* October 19, 1987, p. 32.

35. Bush, pp. 26–27.

36. Murray, *Explorations in Personality,* p. 174.

37. Sidney Blumenthal has raised the psychobiographically interesting possibility that Bush's later attitudes toward war were shaped in part by his unresolved guilt over the deaths of his crew members when his plane was shot down. Fifty years after the event, however, the data appear too vague and contradictory to make much of such connections. See Sidney Blumenthal, "War Story," *New Republic,* October 12, 1992.

38. Bush, p. 44.

39. Bush, p. 42.

40. Bush, p. 86.

41. Bush, p. 88.

42. *Newsweek,* October 19, 1987, p. 29.

43. In a quantitative analysis of Bush's major public speeches, he was found to be high in both affiliative and achievement motivation, but only about average (for a national politician) on power needs (David G. Winter, Margaret G. Hermann, Walter Weintraub, and Stephen G. Walker, "The Personalities of Bush and Gorbachev Measured at a Distance," *Political Psychology, 12,* 1991.) James David Barber identified Bush as an active-positive President, a pattern that overlaps partially but not com-

pletely with the high-achievement and high-affiliation pattern (Barber, *The Presidential Character,* 4th ed., pp. 457 ff.).

44. *Newsweek,* October 19, 1987, p. 32.

45. Robert S. Robins and Jerrold Post. (1987). "The Paranoid Political Actor." *Biography, 10,* p. 4.

46. This is one of Kernberg's phrases that describe the malignant narcissist; he doesn't specifically apply it to Saddam. See Kernberg, *Severe Personality Disorders,* p. 247.

47. Irving L. Janis. (1983). *Groupthink: Psychological Studies of Policy Decisions and Fiascoes,* 2nd ed., rev. (Boston: Houghton Mifflin), pp. 9, 13; his italics.

48. Bob Woodward. (1991). *The Commanders* (New York: Simon & Schuster; Pocket Books reprint, 1992), p. 284.

49. Woodward, *The Commanders,* pp. 7–8.

50. Woodward, *The Commanders,* p. 9.

51. Theodore C. Sorensen. (1965). *Kennedy* (New York: Harper & Row), p. 306.

52. Winter et al., in "The Personalities of Bush and Gorbachev Measured at a Distance," had made their assessment of Bush's motivational pattern before the Gulf War. In a followup paper written after the Gulf War, they point out that in laboratory studies, *"affiliation-motivated people are the least cooperative and the most suspicious and defensive bargainers. . . . [L]eaders with Bush's motive profile are likely to be 'peaceful' only when they are comfortable—that is, when they interact with similar people whom they like. . . . With dissimilar people, in contrast, affiliation-motivated people distance themselves and respond with dislike"* (Winter, Hermann, Weintraub, and Walker, "The Personalities of Bush and Gorbachev at a Distance: Follow-up on Predictions," *Political Psychology, 12,* 1991, pp. 459–460 [their italics]). Shortly before he signed the attack authorization, Bush told members of his White House staff, "I have resolved all moral questions in my mind. This is black and white, good vs. evil" (Sciolino, p. 244).

53. In a paper that I didn't see until after this chapter was completed, Stephen J. Wayne presents a rather similar account of the pressures toward groupthink associated with Bush's decision-making during the Persian Gulf crisis, though Wayne doesn't use the term "groupthink." The paper is "President Bush Goes to War: A Psychological Interpretation from a Distance," in Renshon, ed., *The Political Psychology of the Gulf War,* especially pp. 43–46.

Chapter Fourteen *From Colonel House to General Haig*

1. See his *Psychology, Science, and History* (New Haven: Yale University Press, 1990) and *Greatness* (New York: Guilford, 1994), as well as the numerically more limited *Why Presidents Succeed* (only 39 lives to study there!).

2. Richard Christie and Florence Geis. (1970). *Studies in Machiavellianism* (New York: Academic Press).

3. Florence L. Geis. (1978). "Machiavellianism." In H. London and J. Exner, eds., *Dimensions of Personality* (New York: Wiley), p. 309.

4. Geis, p. 354.

5. Elms, *Social Psychology and Social Relevance,* pp. 95–97; Elms, *Personality in Politics,* pp. 48–57.

6. Elms, *Personality in Politics,* p. 50.

7. Robert Lane, for instance, provides an interesting discussion of how certain political positions assist the people who adopt them in "the control of forbidden impulses": *Political Thinking and Consciousness* (Chicago: Markham, 1969), pp. 211–212.

8. Theodor W. Adorno, Else Frenkel-Brunswik, Daniel J. Levinson, and R. Nevitt Sanford. (1950). *The Authoritarian Personality* (New York: Harper & Row), p. 413.

9. Adorno et al., p. 414.

10. Adorno et al., pp. 422 ff.

11. Adorno et al., pp. 406 ff.

12. Adorno et al., p. 61.

13. R. W. Pruessen. (1982). *John Foster Dulles: The Road to Power* (New York: Free Press), p. 4.

14. Townsend Hoopes. (1973). *The Devil and John Foster Dulles* (Boston: Little, Brown), p. 13.

15. Pruessen, p. 4.

16. Quoted by Hoopes, p. 11.

17. Leonard Mosley. (1978). *Dulles* (New York: Dial Press/James Wade), p. 23.

18. Mosley, pp. 19–20.

19. Pruessen, p. 10.

20. Eleanor Lansing Dulles. (1963). *John Foster Dulles: The Last Year* (New York: Harcourt, Brace, World), p. 127.

21. Hoopes, p. 33.

22. Pruessen, p. 102.

23. Quoted by Hoopes, p. 35.

24. E. L. Dulles, p. 129.

25. Quoted by Mosley, p. 96.

26. Mosley, p. 91.

27. Hoopes, p. 47.

28. John Foster Dulles. (1935). "The Road to Peace." *Atlantic Monthly,* October, pp. 154–155.

29. Quoted by Hoopes, p. 50.

30. Quoted by Hoopes, p. 51.

31. Ole Holsti. (1962). "The Belief System and National Images: A Case Study." *Journal of Conflict Resolution, 6.* Ole Holsti. (1970). "The 'Operational Code' Approach to the Study of Political Leaders: John Foster Dulles' Philosophical and Instrumental Beliefs." *Canadian Journal of Political Science, 3.*

32. Holsti, " 'Operational Code' Approach," p. 129.

33. Holsti, " 'Operational Code' Approach," p. 130.

34. See Holsti, "'Operational Code' Approach," especially pp. 155–157, for a discussion of such changes.

35. Reinhold Niebuhr. (1958). "The Moral World of John Foster Dulles." *New Republic,* December 1, p. 8.

36. R. N. Richardson. (1964). *Colonel Edward M. House: The Texas Years* (Abilene, Tex.: Hardin-Simmons University), p. 6.

37. Edward M. House. (1926). *The Intimate Papers of Colonel House* (Boston: Houghton Mifflin), pp. 17–18.

38. House, *Intimate Papers,* p. 16.

39. Alexander L. George and Juliette L. George. (1964). *Woodrow Wilson and Colonel House* (New York: Dover), p. 329.

40. Quoted by Arthur D. Howden Smith. (1940). *Mr. House of Texas* (New York: Funk & Wagnalls), p. 11.

41. Smith, pp. 15–16.

42. Quoted by George and George, p. 81.

43. Smith, p. 15.

44. Quoted by Richardson, p. 33.

45. George and George, p. 84.

46. Quoted by George and George, p. 85.

47. House, *Intimate Papers,* p. 46.

48. George and George, p. 128.

49. George and George, pp. 127–128.

50. Christie and Geis, p. 4.

51. Edward M. House. (1912). *Philip Dru: Administrator* (New York: B. W. Huebsch). Reprinted in 1969 (Upper Saddle River, N. J.: Literature House/Gregg Press), p. 64.

52. Elms, *Personality in Politics,* pp. 136–148.

53. Quoted by Joseph Kraft. (1971). "In Search of Kissinger." *Harper's,* January, p. 57.

54. Ralph Blumenfeld. (1974). *Henry Kissinger: The Private and Public Story* (New York: New American Library), pp. 66, 85.

55. Henry Kissinger. (1957). *A World Restored* (Boston: Houghton Mifflin). Henry Kissinger. (1968). "The White Revolutionary: Reflections on Bismarck." *Daedalus, 97.* Kissinger's admiration for Metternich and Bismarck is further expressed in his latest book, *Diplomacy* (New York: Simon & Schuster, 1994).

56. William Safire. (1975). *Before the Fall* (New York: Doubleday; Belmont Tower Books reprint, New York, 1975), p. 169.

57. Bruce Mazlish. (1976). *Kissinger: The European Mind in American Policy* (New York: Basic Books), p. 206.

58. Quoted by Oriana Fallaci. (1972). "An Interview with Oriana Fallaci: Kissinger." *New Republic,* December 16.

59. Harvey Starr. (1984.) *Henry Kissinger: Perceptions of International Politics* (Lexington, Ky.: University Press of Kentucky), pp. 70–71.

60. Seymour Hersh. (1983). *The Price of Power: Kissinger in the Nixon White House* (New York: Summit Books).

61. Starr, p. 73.

62. Dana Ward. (1975). "Kissinger: A Psychohistory." *History of Childhood Quarterly, 2.* A revised version is in D. Caldwell, ed., *Henry Kissinger: His Personality and Policies* (Durham, N.C.: Duke University Press, 1983).

63. Mazlish, *Kissinger.*

64. Starr, *Henry Kissinger.*

65. Walter Isaacson. (1992). *Kissinger: A Biography* (New York: Simon & Schuster), p. 15.

66. Seymour Hersh. (1983). "The Pardon." *Atlantic Monthly,* August.

67. Quoted by Nick Thimmesch. (1973). "Chief of Staff." *Potomac Magazine* section of *Washington Post,* November 25, p. 13. Haig's most recent memoir indicates that after his father's death, the family survived mainly through the financial assistance of relatives (Alexander M. Haig, Jr. and Charles McCarry, *Inner Circles: How America Changed the World* [New York: Warner Books, 1992], pp. 7–8).

68. Quoted by Lloyd Shearer. (1972). "Keep Your Eye on Al." *Parade,* August 20, p. 4.

69. Thimmesch, p. 13.

70. Quoted by Thimmesch, pp. 13, 46.

71. Shearer, p. 4.

72. Haig and McCarry, p. 4.

73. Haig and McCarry, p. 12.

74. Roger Morris. (1982). *Haig: The General's Progress* (New York: Playboy Press), p. 16.

75. Quoted by Thimmesch, p. 15.

76. Morris, p. 54.

77. Lucian Truscott IV, paraphrased by Morris, p. 91.

78. Henry Kissinger. (1982). *Years of Upheaval* (Boston: Little Brown), p. 107.

79. Safire, p. 165.

80. Kissinger, *Years of Upheaval,* p. 1197.

81. He was, briefly, a declared candidate 8 years later.

82. Alexander M. Haig, Jr. (1984). *Caveat: Realism, Reagan, and Foreign Policy* (New York: Macmillan), p. 57.

83. Haig, p. 160.

84. Haig, p. 52.

85. Adorno et al., p. 414.

86. Adorno et al., p. 485.

87. Haig and McCarry, p. 4.

88. Jeane J. Kirkpatrick. (1974). *Political Woman* (New York: Basic Books), p. 175.

89. Lloyd Etheredge. (1979.) "Hardball Politics: A Model." *Political Psychology, 1.*

Chapter Fifteen *Going Beyond Scratch*

1. Kim Stanley Robinson. (1986). "The Lucky Strike." Reprinted in *The Planet on the Table* (New York: Tor Books). See also his meditation on historical processes, "A Sensitive Dependence on Initial Conditions," in *Remaking History* (New York: Tor, 1991).

2. Kim Stanley Robinson. (1993). *Red Mars* (New York: Bantam). *Red Mars* is the first volume of a massively detailed trilogy, which continues with *Green Mars* (New York: Bantam, 1994) and will conclude with *Blue Mars.*

3. Kim Stanley Robinson. (1990). *Pacific Edge* (New York: Tor Books).

4. Horace B. English and Ava C. English. (1958). *A Comprehensive Dictionary of Psychological and Psychoanalytical Terms* (New York: Longmans Green).

5. Eva Schepeler has published a portion of her dissertation as "Jean Piaget's Experiences on the Couch: Some Clues to a Mystery," in the *International Journal of Psycho-Analysis, 74*, 1993. William T. Schultz's dissertation, *A Psychobiographical Inquiry into the Life, Mind, and Creative Work of James Agee*, is being revised for publication.

6. William McKinley Runyan. (1988). "Progress in Psychobiography." In Dan P. McAdams and Richard L. Ochberg, eds., *Psychobiography and Life Narratives* (Durham, N.C.: Duke University Press).

7. P. W. Bridgman. (1950). *Reflections of a Physicist* (New York: Philosophical Library), p. 351. In another essay collected in the same volume, Bridgman wrote, "I like to say that there is no scientific method as such, but that the most vital feature of the scientist's procedure has been merely to do his utmost with his mind, *no holds barred*" (p. 370; his emphasis).

8. But maybe it should. For instance, Stan's extrapolation of data about Mars and space travel and human psychology into his closely reasoned picture of Martian terraforming in *Green Mars* strikes me as a genuine contribution to scientific planning for the exploration and settlement of Mars.

9. One strongly methodological paper by Erikson is "On the Nature of Psychohistorical Evidence: In Search of Gandhi," *Daedalus, 97*, Summer 1968.

10. Among these are Peter Loewenberg, *Decoding the Past: The Psychohistorical Approach* (New York: Knopf, 1983); Peter Gay, *Freud for Historians* (New York: Oxford University Press, 1985); and Edwin R. Wallace IV, *Historiography and Causation in Psychoanalysis* (Hillsdale, N.J.: Analytic Press, 1985).

11. Runyan, *Life Histories and Psychobiography*, p. 47.

12. Alexander, *Personology*, p. 13.

13. Barber, *Presidential Character*.

14. Haig and McCarry, p. 3.

15. Alexander, *Personology*, p. 15.

16. Freud, *Psychopathology of Everyday Life;* Elms, "Freud and Minna."

17. Heller and Elms, "Seven Versions of Lonesome."

18. Alexander, *Personology*, p. 21.

19. Carter, *Why Not the Best?*, p. 161; my italics.

20. Alexander Kronick, Alexei Pajitnov, and Boris Levin. (1991). *LifeLine* (Moscow: ParaGraph).

21. Blanche Weisen Cook. (1991). "The Womanly Art of Biography." *Ms.,* January-February, p. 60. See also Carolyn G. Heilbrun, *Writing a Woman's Life* (New York: Norton, 1988), and Sara Alpern, Joyce Antler, Elisabeth Israels Perry, and Ingrid Winther Scobie, eds., *The Challenge of Feminist Biography* (Urbana: University of Illinois Press, 1992).

22. Doris Kearns Goodwin. (1987). *The Fitzgeralds and the Kennedys* (New York: Simon & Schuster).

23. Nigel Hamilton. (1992). *JFK: Reckless Youth* (New York: Random House).

24. Like Cordwainer Smith, James Tiptree, Jr. did her best work in fiction shorter

than novel-length. The most complete collection of her stories is *Her Smoke Rose Up Forever* (Sauk City, Wisc.: Arkham House, 1990.)

25. American Psychiatric Association, Report of the Task Force on Psychohistory. (1976). *The Psychiatrist as Psychohistorian* (Washington, D.C.: American Psychiatric Association).

26. American Psychiatric Association, p. 12.

27. It has recently become fashionable for public figures to respond aggressively to "unauthorized" biographers, threatening them with unspecified legal actions and sending nasty letters to friends and relatives who might be interviewed by them. The courts have been properly unsympathetic to such threats. Any biographer worth his or her salt would not write a legally "authorized" biography under the usual restrictive terms anyway.

28. Henry A. Murray, personal communication, July 29, 1983.

29. Diane Wood Middlebrook. (1991). *Anne Sexton: A Biography* (Boston: Houghton Mifflin). Reprinted in 1992 with a "Coda" discussing the controversy (New York: Vintage Books.)

30. Middlebrook, 1992, p. 403.

31. Middlebrook, 1992, p. xxiii.

32. Malcolm, *The Silent Woman,* p. 9.

BIBLIOGRAPHY

Abraham, H. C., and Freud, E. L., eds. (1965). *A Psycho-analytic Dialogue: The Letters of Sigmund Freud and Karl Abraham 1907–1926.* New York: Basic Books.

Abraham, Ruth. (1982–83). "Freud's Mother Conflict and the Formulation of the Oedipal Father." *Psychoanalytic Review, 69.*

Adorno, Theodor W.; Frenkel-Brunswik, Else; Levinson, Daniel J.; and Sanford, R. Nevitt. (1950). *The Authoritarian Personality.* New York: Harper & Row.

Al-Khalil, Samir. (1989). *Republic of Fear: The Inside Story of Saddam's Iraq.* Berkeley: University of California Press. Pantheon Books reprint, New York, 1990.

Al-Khalil, Samir. (1991). *The Monument: Art, Vulgarity and Responsibility in Iraq.* Berkeley: University of California Press.

Alexander, Irving E. (1990). *Personology: Method and Content in Personality Assessment and Psychobiography.* Durham, N.C.: Duke University Press.

Alexandrov, Vladimir E. (1991). *Nabokov's Otherworld.* Princeton, N.J.: Princeton University Press.

Allport, Floyd H. (1924). *Social Psychology.* Boston: Houghton Mifflin.

Allport, Floyd H. (1933). *Institutional Behavior.* Chapel Hill, N.C.: University of North Carolina Press.

Allport, Gordon W. (1922). *An Experimental Study of the Traits of Personality.* Cambridge, Mass.: Harvard University, unpublished doctoral dissertation.

Allport, Gordon W. (1929). "The Study of Personality by the Intuitive Method: An Experiment in Teaching from *The Locomotive God.*" *Journal of Abnormal and Social Psychology, 24.*

Allport, Gordon W. (1937). *Personality: A Psychological Interpretation.* New York: Holt.

Allport, Gordon W. (1942). *The Use of Personal Documents in Psychological Science.* New York: Social Science Research Council Bulletin No. 49.

Allport, Gordon W. (1953). "The Trend in Motivational Theory." *American Journal of Orthopsychiatry, 25.*

Allport, Gordon W. (1958). "G. W. Allport Recalls a Visit to Sigmund Freud." Unpublished manuscript, Sigmund Freud Archives, Library of Congress, Washington, D.C.

Allport, Gordon W. (1962). "The General and the Unique in Psychological Science." *Journal of Personality, 30.*

Allport, Gordon W. (1962). "My Encounters with Personality Theory." Unpublished manuscript, recorded and edited by W.G.T. Douglas, Boston University School of

Theology, October 29. Gordon W. Allport Papers, Harvard University Archives, Cambridge, Mass.

Allport, Gordon W. (1967). "Autobiography." In E. G. Boring and G. Lindzey, eds., *A History of Psychology in Autobiography,* vol. 5. Boston: Appleton-Century-Crofts.

Allport, Gordon W. (No date). "Personal Experience with Racial and Religious Attitudes." Unpublished manuscript. Gordon W. Allport Papers, Harvard University Archives, Cambridge, Mass.

Allport, Gordon W., ed. (1965). *Letters from Jenny.* New York: Harcourt, Brace.

Alpern, Sara; Antler, Joyce; Perry, Elisabeth Israels; and Scobie, Ingrid Winther, eds. (1992). *The Challenge of Feminist Biography.* Urbana: University of Illinois Press.

American Psychiatric Association, Report of the Task Force of Psychohistory. (1976). *The Psychiatrist as Psychohistorian.* Washington, D.C.: American Psychiatric Association.

American Psychologist, 47, November 1992. Special issue, "Reflections on B. F. Skinner and Psychology."

Anderson, James W., III. (1981). "Psychobiographical Methodology: The Case of William James." *Review of Personality and Social Psychology, 2.*

Anderson, James W., III. (1981). "The Methodology of Psychological Biography." *Journal of Interdisciplinary History, 11.*

Appel, Alfred, Jr., ed. (1970). *The Annotated Lolita* by Vladimir Nabokov. New York: McGraw-Hill.

Asimov, Isaac, ed. (1974). *Before the Golden Age: A Science Fiction Anthology of the 1930s.* Garden City, N.Y.: Doubleday.

Asimov, Isaac. (1941). "Nightfall." *Astounding Science Fiction,* September.

Asimov, Isaac. (1969). *Asimov's Mysteries.* New York: Dell.

Asimov, Isaac. (1971). *Nightfall and Other Stories.* New York: Fawcett.

Asimov, Isaac, (1976). *Murder at the ABA.* Garden City, N.Y.: Doubleday.

Asimov, Isaac. (1979). *In Memory yet Green.* Garden City, N.Y.: Doubleday.

Asimov, Isaac. (1983). *The Robot Collection.* Garden City, N.Y.: Doubleday.

Asimov, Isaac. (1983). *The Robots of Dawn.* Garden City, N.Y.: Doubleday.

Asimov, Isaac. (1988). "Acrophobia." *Isaac Asimov's Science Fiction Magazine, 12* (8), August.

Asimov, Isaac. (1994). *I. Asimov.* New York: Doubleday.

Associated Press. (1991). "Excerpts from Address by Saddam Hussein." New York *Times,* February 25.

Atwood, George E., and Stolorow, Robert D. (1993). *Faces in a Cloud: Intersubjectivity in Personality Theory,* rev. ed. Northvale, N.J.: Aronson.

Balmary, Marie. (1982). *Psychoanalyzing Psychoanalysis: Freud and the Hidden Fault of the Father,* trans. Ned Lukacher. Baltimore: Johns Hopkins Press.

Barber, James David. (1972). *The Presidential Character: Predicting Performance in the White House.* Englewood Cliffs, N.J.: Prentice-Hall.

Barber, James David. (1992). *The Presidential Character,* 4th ed. Englewood Cliffs, N.J.: Prentice-Hall.

Baron, Samuel H., and Pletsch, Carl. (1985). *Introspection in Biography: The Biographer's Quest for Self-Awareness.* Hillsdale, N.J.: Analytic Press.

Bartholomew, K., and Horowitz, L. M. (1991). "Attachment Styles among Young Adults: A Test of a Four-Category Model." *Journal of Personality and Social Psychology, 61.*

Baum, Frank J., and MacFall, Russell P. (1961). *To Please a Child.* Chicago: Reilly & Lee.

Baum, L. Frank. (1886). *The Book of the Hamburgs.* Hartford, Conn.: H. H. Stoddard.

Baum, L. Frank. (1895). "La Reine Est Mort—Vive La Reine!" Chicago *Times-Herald,* June 23; reprinted in *Baum Bugle,* 22 (3), Winter 1978.

Baum, L. Frank. (1900). *The Wonderful Wizard of Oz.* Chicago: George M. Hill.

Baum, L. Frank. (1903). *The Enchanted Island of Yew.* Indianapolis: Bobbs-Merrill.

Baum, L. Frank. (1904). *The Marvelous Land of Oz.* Chicago: Reilly & Britton. Reprint edition titled *The Land of Oz,* New York: Del Rey/Ballantine, 1979.

Baum, L. Frank. (1906). *John Dough and the Cherub.* Chicago: Reilly & Britton; reprinted by Dover, New York, 1974.

Baum, L. Frank. (1907). *Ozma of Oz.* Chicago: Reilly & Britton; reprinted by Ballantine/Del Rey, New York, 1979.

Baum, L. Frank. (1909). "The Fairy Prince." *Entertaining,* December; reprinted in *Baum Bugle,* 11 (3), Christmas 1967.

Baum, L. Frank. (1910). *The Emerald City of Oz.* Chicago: Reilly & Britton.

Baum, L. Frank. (1983). *The Wizard of Oz,* ed. Michael Patrick Hearn. New York: Schocken Books.

Beckwith, Osmond. (1961). "The Oddness of Oz." *Kulchur, 1* (4).

Berman, Jeffrey. (1985). *The Talking Cure: Literary Representations of Psychoanalysis.* New York: New York University Press.

Blumenfeld, Ralph. (1974). *Henry Kissinger: The Private and Public Story.* New York: New American Library.

Bova, Ben, ed.. (1973). *The Science Fiction Hall of Fame,* vol. 2A. Garden City, N.Y.: Doubleday.

Boyd, Brian. (1990). *Vladimir Nabokov: The Russian Years.* Princeton, N.J.: Princeton University Press.

Brabant, Eva; Falzeder, Ernst; and Giampieri-Deutsch, Patrizia, eds. (1993). *The Correspondence of Sigmund Freud and Sándor Ferenczi,* vol. 1, trans. Peter T. Hoffer. Cambridge, Mass.: Belknap Press of Harvard University Press.

Bramly, Serge. (1991). *Leonardo: Discovering the Life of Leonardo da Vinci.* New York: HarperCollins.

Bridgman, P. W. (1950). *Reflections of a Physicist.* New York: Philosophical Library.

Brodie, Fawn M. (1981). *Richard Nixon: The Shaping of His Character.* New York: Norton.

Brome, Vincent. (1978). *Jung: Man and Myth.* New York: Atheneum.

Bullock, John, and Morris, Harvey. (1991). *Saddam's War.* London: Faber & Faber.

Bush, George. (1987). *Looking Forward: An Autobiography.* New York: Doubleday.

Campbell, John W., Jr. (1938). "Who Goes There?" *Astounding Science Fiction,* August.

Carlson, Rae. (1981). "Studies in Script Theory: I. Adult Analogs of a Childhood Nuclear Scene." *Journal of Personality and Social Psychology, 40.*

Carlson, Rae. (1982). "Studies in Script Theory: II. Altruistic Nuclear Scripts." *Perceptual and Motor Skills, 55.*

Carlson, Rae. (1988). "Exemplary Lives: The Uses of Psychobiography for Theory Development." *Journal of Personality, 56.*

Carotenuto, Aldo. (1982). *A Secret Symmetry: Sabina Spielrein between Jung and Freud.* New York: Pantheon.

Carter, Jimmy. (1975). *Why Not the Best?* Nashville: Broadman Press. Bantam Books reprint, New York, 1976.

Chapdelaine, Perry A., Sr.; Chapdelaine, T.; and Hay, G., eds. (1985). *The John W. Campbell Letters,* vol. 1. Franklin, Tenn.: AC Projects.

Chodorow, Nancy. (1978). *The Reproduction of Mothering.* Berkeley: University of California Press.

Choisy, Marise. (1963). *Sigmund Freud: A New Appraisal.* New York: Philosophical Library.

Christie, Richard, and Geis, Florence. (1970). *Studies in Machiavellianism.* New York: Academic Press.

Clark, Kenneth M. (1967). *Leonardo da Vinci,* revised edition. Harmondsworth, England: Penguin.

Clinch, Nancy Gager. (1973). *The Kennedy Neurosis.* New York: Grosset & Dunlap.

Cook, Blanche Weisen. (1991). "The Womanly Art of Biography." *Ms.,* January-February.

Danielson, Elena S. (1989). "The Ethics of Access." *American Archivist, 52.*

Davis, F. B. (1973). "Three Letters from Sigmund Freud to Andre Breton." *Journal of the American Psychoanalytic Association, 21.*

De Camp, L. Sprague; de Camp, Cathryn Crook; and Griffin, Jane Whittington. (1983). *Dark Valley Destiny: The Life of Robert E. Howard.* New York: Bluejay Books.

Del Rey, Lester, ed. (1976). *The Best of John W. Campbell.* Garden City, N.Y.: Nelson Doubleday.

DeMause, Lloyd. (1981). "The Fetal Origins of History." *Journal of Psychohistory, 9.*

Dulles, Eleanor Lansing. (1963). *John Foster Dulles: The Last Year.* New York: Harcourt, Brace, World.

Dulles, John Foster. (1935). "The Road to Peace." *Atlantic Monthly,* October.

Dyson, Freeman. (1988). *Infinite in All Directions.* New York: Harper & Row.

Edel, Leon. (1984). *Writing Lives: Principia Biographica.* New York: Norton.

Edel, Leon. (1985). *Henry James: A Life.* New York: Harper & Row.

Eissler, K. R. (1961). *Leonardo da Vinci: Psychoanalytic Notes on the Enigma.* New York: International Universities Press.

Elms, Alan C. (1972). "Allport, Freud, and the Clean Little Boy." *Psychoanalytic Review, 59.*

Elms, Alan C. (1972). *Social Psychology and Social Relevance.* Boston: Little, Brown.

Elms, Alan C. (1976). "Where's the Catch in Carter's Character?" Sacramento *Bee,* October 24.

Elms, Alan C. (1976). *Attitudes.* Milton Keynes, England: Open University Press.

Elms, Alan C. (1976). *Personality in Politics.* New York: Harcourt Brace Jovanovich.

Elms, Alan C. (1980). "Freud, Irma, Martha: Sex and Marriage in the 'Dream of Irma's Injection.'" *Psychoanalytic Review, 67.*

Elms, Alan C. (1982). "Freud and Minna." *Psychology Today,* December.

Elms, Alan C. (1983). "Oz in Science Fiction Film." *The Baum Bugle: A Journal of Oz,* Winter.

Elms, Alan C. (1984). "The Creation of Cordwainer Smith." *Science-Fiction Studies, 11.*

Elms, Alan C. (1991). "Origins of the Underpeople: Cats, Kuomintang and Cordwainer Smith." In Tom Shippey, ed., *Fictional Space: Essays on Contemporary Science Fiction.* Atlantic Highlands, N.J.: Humanities Press.

English, Horace B., and English, Ava C. (1958). *A Comprehensive Dictionary of Psychological and Psychoanalytical Terms.* New York: Longmans Green.

Erikson, Erik H. (1954). "The Dream Specimen of Psychoanalysis." *Journal of the American Psychoanalytic Association, 2.*

Erikson, Erik H. (1958). *Young Man Luther.* New York: Norton.

Erikson, Erik H. (1963). *Childhood and Society,* revised edition. New York: Norton.

Erikson, Erik H. (1968). "On the Nature of Psychohistorical Evidence: In Search of Gandhi." *Daedalus, 97,* Summer.

Erikson, Erik H. (1968). *Identity: Youth and Crisis.* New York: Norton.

Erikson, Erik H. (1969). *Gandhi's Truth.* New York: Norton.

Erikson, Erik H. (1975). *Life History and the Historical Moment.* New York: Norton.

Etheredge, Lloyd. (1979). "Hardball Politics: A Model." *Political Psychology, 1.*

Evans, Richard. (1970). *Gordon Allport: The Man and His Ideas.* New York: Dutton.

Faber, M. D. (1970). "Allport's Visit with Freud." *Psychoanalytic Review, 57.*

Fact, 1 (5), September-October 1964. "The Unconscious of a Conservative: A Special Issue on the Mind of Barry Goldwater."

Fallaci, Oriana. (1972). "An Interview with Oriana Fallaci: Kissinger." *New Republic,* December 16.

Fichtner, Gerhard, ed. (1992). *Sigmund Freud/Ludwig Binswanger: Briefwechsel 1908–1938.* Frankfurt, Germany: S. Fischer.

Field, Andrew. (1967). *Nabokov: His Life in Art.* Boston: Little, Brown.

Field, Andrew. (1977). *Nabokov: His Life in Part.* New York: Viking.

Field, Andrew. (1986). *VN: The Life and Art of Vladimir Nabokov.* New York: Crown.

Fischer, David Hackett. (1970). *Historians' Fallacies.* New York: Harper & Row.

Fowler, Douglas. (1974). *Reading Nabokov.* Ithaca, N.Y.: Cornell University Press.

Freud, Ernst L., ed. (1960). *Letters of Sigmund Freud.* New York: Basic Books.

Freud, Sigmund, and Pfister, Oskar. (1963). *Psychoanalysis and Faith: The Letters of Sigmund Freud and Oskar Pfister.* London: Hogarth Press.

Freud, Sigmund. (1953). *The Interpretation of Dreams*. In James Strachey, ed. and trans., *The Standard Edition of the Complete Psychological Works of Sigmund Freud*, vols. 4 and 5. London: Hogarth. Original work published in 1900.

Freud, Sigmund. (1953). *Three Essays on the Theory of Sexuality*. In James Strachey, ed. and trans., *The Standard Edition of the Complete Psychological Works of Sigmund Freud*, vol. 7. Original work published in 1905.

Freud, Sigmund. (1957). *Five Lectures on Psychoanalysis*. In James Strachey, ed. and trans., *The Standard Edition of the Complete Psychological Works of Sigmund Freud*, vol. 11. Original work published in 1910.

Freud, Sigmund. (1957). *Leonardo da Vinci and a Memory of His Childhood*. In James Strachey, ed. and trans., *The Standard Edition of the Complete Psychological Works of Sigmund Freud*, vol. 11. London: Hogarth Press. Original work published in 1910.

Freud, Sigmund. (1958). "Psycho-analytic Notes on an Autobiographical Account of a Case of Paranoia." In James Strachey, ed. and trans., *The Standard Edition of the Complete Psychological Works of Sigmund Freud*, vol. 12. Original work published in 1911.

Freud, Sigmund. (1959). "'Civilized' Sexual Morality and Modern Nervous Illness." In James Strachey, ed. and trans., *The Standard Edition of the Complete Psychological Works of Sigmund Freud*, vol. 9. Original work published in 1908.

Freud, Sigmund. (1961). *Civilization and Its Discontents*. In James Strachey, ed. and trans., *The Standard Edition of the Complete Psychological Works of Sigmund Freud*, vol. 21. London: Hogarth. Original work published in 1930.

Freud, Sigmund. (1962). "On the Grounds for Detaching a Particular Syndrome from Neurasthenia under the Description 'Anxiety Neurosis.'" In James Strachey, ed. and trans., *The Standard Edition of the Complete Psychological Works of Sigmund Freud*, vol. 3. Original work published in 1895.

Freud, Sigmund. (1962). "Sexuality in the Aetiology of the Neuroses." In James Strachey, ed. and trans., *The Standard Edition of the Complete Psychological Works of Sigmund Freud*, vol. 3. Original work published in 1898.

Freud, Sigmund. (1963). "The Taboo of Virginity." In James Strachey, ed. and trans., *The Standard Edition of the Complete Psychological Works of Sigmund Freud*, vol. 16. London: Hogarth. Original edition published in 1918.

Freud, Sigmund. (1964). *Moses and Monotheism*. In James Strachey, ed. and trans., *The Standard Edition of the Complete Psychological Works of Sigmund Freud*, vol. 23. London: Hogarth Press. Original work published in 1939.

Freud, Sigmund. (1964). *New Introductory Lectures on Psychoanalysis*. In James Strachey, ed. and trans., *The Standard Edition of the Complete Psychological Works of Sigmund Freud*, vol. 22. London: Hogarth Press. Original work published in 1932.

Fromm, Erich. (1959). *Sigmund Freud's Mission*. New York: Harper & Row.

Gage, M. J. (1966). "The Dakota Days of L. Frank Baum," part 3. *Baum Bugle, 10* (3), Christmas.

Gardner, Martin, and Nye, R. B. (1957). *The Wizard of Oz and Who He Was*. East Lansing, Mich.: Michigan State University Press.

Gay, Peter. (1985). *Freud for Historians*. New York: Oxford University Press.

Gay, Peter. (1988). *Freud: A Life for Our Time*. New York: Norton.

Geis, Florence L. (1978). "Machiavellianism." In H. London and J. Exner, eds., *Dimensions of Personality*. New York: Wiley.

George, Alexander L., and George, Juliette L. (1964). *Woodrow Wilson and Colonel House*. New York: Dover.

Gessel, Michael. (1992). "Tale of a Parable." *Baum Bugle, 36* (1), Spring.

Glad, Betty. (1980). *Jimmy Carter: In Search of the Great White House*. New York: Norton.

Goldman, Albert. (1981). *Elvis*. New York: McGraw-Hill.

Goleman, Daniel. (1991). "The Experts Differ on Dissecting Psyches." *New York Times,* January 29.

Goodheart, William B. (1984). "C. G. Jung's First 'Patient': On the Seminal Emergence of Jung's Thought." *Journal of Analytical Psychology, 29.*

Goodwin, Doris Kearns. (1976). "Ford and Carter: The Character of the Candidates." *Ladies' Home Journal,* November.

Goodwin, Doris Kearns. (1987). *The Fitzgeralds and the Kennedys*. New York: Simon & Schuster.

Grafton, Sue. (1985). *B Is for Burglar*. New York: Holt, Rinehart & Winston. Bantam reprint, New York, 1986.

Grayson, Jane. (1977). *Nabokov Translated*. Oxford: Oxford University Press.

Green, Geoffrey. (1988). *Freud and Nabokov*. Lincoln: University of Nebraska Press.

Greene, David L., and Martin, Dick. (1977). *The Oz Scrapbook*. New York: Random House.

Grünbaum, Adolf. (1984). *The Foundations of Psychoanalysis: A Philosophical Critique*. Berkeley: University of California Press.

Gunn, James. (1982). *Isaac Asimov: The Foundations of Science Fiction*. New York: Oxford University Press.

Haig, Alexander M., Jr. (1984). *Caveat: Realism, Reagan, and Foreign Policy*. New York: Macmillan.

Haig, Alexander M., Jr., and McCarry, Charles. (1992). *Inner Circles: How America Changed the World*. New York: Warner Books.

Hamilton, Nigel. (1992). *JFK: Reckless Youth*. New York: Random House.

Hanff, Peter. (1977). "Frank Baum: Success and Frustration." *Baum Bugle, 21* (3), Winter.

Hannah, Barbara. (1976). *Jung: His Life and Work*. New York: Putnam.

Hartwell, David, ed. (1992). *Foundations of Fear*. New York: Tor.

Hearn, Michael Patrick, ed. (1973). *The Annotated Wizard of Oz*. New York: Clarkson N. Potter.

Heilbrun, Carolyn G. (1988). *Writing a Woman's Life*. New York: Norton.

Heller, Bruce, and Elms, Alan C. (1992). "Seven Versions of Lonesome: Control and Loss in the Music of Elvis Presley." Paper presented to the Bay Area Psychobiography Study Group, July 9.

Herik, Gregory. (1986). "The Instrumentality of Attitudes: Toward a Neofunctional Theory." *Journal of Social Issues, 42* (2).

Hersh, Seymour. (1983). "The Pardon." *Atlantic Monthly,* August.

Hersh, Seymour. (1983). *The Price of Power: Kissinger in the Nixon White House.* New York: Summit Books.

Holsti, Ole. (1962). "The Belief System and National Images: A Case Study." *Journal of Conflict Resolution, 6.*

Holsti, Ole. (1970). "The 'Operational Code' Approach to the Study of Political Leaders: John Foster Dulles' Philosophical and Instrumental Beliefs." *Canadian Journal of Political Science, 3.*

Holt, Robert R. (1962). "Individuality and Generalization in the Psychology of Personality." *Journal of Personality, 30.*

Hoopes, Townsend. (1973). *The Devil and John Foster Dulles.* Boston: Little, Brown.

House, Edward M. (1912). *Philip Dru: Administrator.* New York: B. W. Huebsch. Reprinted by Literature House/Gregg Press, Upper Saddle River, N.J., 1969.

House, Edward M. (1926). *The Intimate Papers of Colonel House.* Boston: Houghton Mifflin.

Howard, Robert E. (1977). *Red Nails,* ed. Karl Edward Wagner. New York: Berkley.

Howard, Robert E. (1977). *The Hour of the Dragon,* ed. Karl Edward Wagner. New York: Berkley.

Howard, Robert E. (1977). *The People of the Black Circle,* ed. Karl Edward Wagner. New York: Berkley.

Isaacson, Walter. (1992). *Kissinger: A Biography.* New York: Simon & Schuster.

Jaffé, Aniela, ed. (1979). *C. G. Jung: Word and Image.* Princeton: Princeton University Press.

Jaffé, Aniela. (1971). *From the Life and Work of C. G. Jung.* New York: Harper & Row.

Jaffé, Aniela. (1971). *The Myth of Meaning.* New York: Putnam.

Jaffé, Aniela. (1984). "Details about C. G. Jung's Family." *Spring: An Annual of Archetypal Psychology and Jungian Thought.*

James, E. T., ed. (1971). *Notable American Women 1607–1950,* vol. 2. Cambridge, Mass.: The Belknap Press of Harvard University Press.

Janis, Irving L. (1983). *Groupthink: Psychological Studies of Policy Decisions and Fiascoes,* 2nd ed., rev. Boston: Houghton Mifflin.

Jones, Ernest. (1953–57). *The Life and Work of Sigmund Freud.* New York: Basic Books.

Judson, Horace Freeland. (1983). "Reweaving the Web of Discovery." *The Sciences, 23* (6).

Jung, C. G. (1975). *Letters,* ed. Gerhard Adler with Aniela Jaffé. Princeton, N.J.: Princeton University Press.

Jung, C. G. (1989). *Analytical Psychology: Notes of the Seminar Given in 1925,* ed. William McGuire. Princeton: Princeton University Press.

Jung, C. G. (1963). *Memories, Dreams, Reflections,* recorded and edited by Aniela Jaffé; trans. Richard and Clara Winston. New York: Pantheon Books.

Karlinsky, Simon, ed. (1980). *The Nabokov-Wilson Letters.* New York: Harper Colophon.

Karsh, Efraim, and Rautsi, Inari. (1991). *Saddam Hussein: A Political Biography.* New York: Free Press.

Katz, Daniel. (1960). "The Functional Approach to the Study of Attitudes." *Public Opinion Quarterly, 24.*

Kernberg, Otto. (1984). *Severe Personality Disorders: Psychotherapeutic Strategies.* New Haven: Yale University Press.

Kerr, John. (1993). *A Most Dangerous Method: The Story of Jung, Freud, and Sabina Spielrein.* New York: Knopf.

Kirkpatrick, Jeane J. (1974). *Political Women.* New York: Basic Books.

Kissinger, Henry. (1957). *A World Restored.* Boston: Houghton Mifflin.

Kissinger, Henry. (1968). "The White Revolutionary: Reflections on Bismarck." *Daedalus, 97.*

Kissinger, Henry. (1982). *Years of Upheaval.* Boston: Little Brown.

Kissinger, Henry. (1994). *Diplomacy.* New York: Simon & Schuster.

Kohut, Heinz. (1971). *Analysis of the Self.* New York: International Universities Press.

Kopp, Sheldon. (1968). "The Wizard of Oz Behind the Couch." *Voices, 4.* Reprinted in *Psychology Today, 3* (10), 1970.

Kottak, Conrad Phillip. (1978). "Social-Science Fiction." *Psychology Today, 11* (9), February.

Kraft, Joseph. (1971). "In Search of Kissinger." *Harper's,* January.

Kronick, Alexander; Pajitnov, Alexei; and Levin, Boris. (1991). *LifeLine.* Moscow: ParaGraph.

Lane, Robert E. (1969). *Political Thinking and Consciousness.* Chicago: Markham.

Langer, Walter. (1972). *The Mind of Adolf Hitler.* New York: Basic Books.

Le Guin, Ursula K. (1993). Introduction to *The Norton Book of Science Fiction,* ed. Ursula K. Le Guin and Brian Attebery with Karen Joy Fowler. New York: Norton.

Levinson, Daniel J. (1978). *The Seasons of a Man's Life.* New York: Knopf.

Lichtenberg, J. D. (1978). "Freud's Leonardo: Psychobiography and Autobiography of Genius." *Journal of the American Psychoanalytic Association, 26.*

Littlefield, Henry M. (1992). "The Wizard of Allegory." *Baum Bugle, 36* (1), Spring.

Loewenberg, Peter. (1983). *Decoding the Past: The Psychohistorical Approach.* New York: Knopf.

Maddi, Salvatore, and Costa, P. T. (1972). *Humanism in Personology: Allport, Maslow, Murray.* Chicago: Aldine.

Malcolm, Janet. (1994). *The Silent Woman: Sylvia Plath & Ted Hughes.* New York: Knopf.

Mannix, Daniel. (1964). "The Father of the Wizard of Oz." *American Heritage, 16* (1), December.

Masson, Jeffrey M., ed. (1985). *The Complete Letters of Sigmund Freud to Wilhelm Fliess.* Cambridge, Mass.: Harvard University Press.

Maslow, Abraham H. (1968). *Toward a Psychology of Being.* Princeton, N.J.: Van Nostrand.

Maslow, Abraham H. (1972). *The Farther Reaches of Human Nature.* New York: Viking. Penguin Books reprint, New York, 1976.

Maurois, André. (1929). *Aspects of Biography.* Cambridge: Cambridge University Press.

Mazlish, Bruce, and Diamond, Edwin. (1976). "Thrice-Born: A Psychohistory of Jimmy Carter's 'Rebirth.'" *New York,* August 30.

Mazlish, Bruce, and Diamond, Edwin. (1979). *Jimmy Carter: An Interpretive Biography.* New York: Simon & Schuster.

Mazlish, Bruce. (1972). *In Search of Nixon: A Psychohistorical Inquiry.* New York: Basic Books. Pelican reprint, 1973.

Mazlish, Bruce. (1975). *James and John Stuart Mill: Father and Son in the Nineteenth Century.* New York: Basic Books.

Mazlish, Bruce. (1976). *Kissinger: The European Mind in American Policy.* New York: Basic Books.

McClelland, David C.; Davis, W. N.; Kalin, R.; and Wanner, E. (1972). *The Drinking Man.* New York: Free Press.

McCullough, David. (1992). *Truman.* New York: Simon & Schuster.

McGuire, William, ed. (1974). *The Freud/Jung Letters.* Princeton: Princeton University Press.

Middlebrook, Diane Wood. (1991). *Anne Sexton: A Biography.* Boston: Houghton Mifflin. Reprinted with "Coda," Vintage Books, New York, 1992.

Miller, Judith, and Mylroie, Laurie. (1990). *Saddam Hussein and the Crisis in the Gulf.* New York: Times Books.

Miller, Ruth. (1991). *Saul Bellow: A Biography of the Imagination.* New York: St. Martin's Press.

Millon, Theodore. (1981). *Disorders of Personality: DSM-III: Axis II.* New York: Wiley.

Morey, L. C. (1987). "Observations on the Meeting between Allport and Freud." *Psychoanalytic Review,* 74.

Morris, Roger. (1982). *Haig: The General's Progress.* New York: Playboy Press.

Moskowitz, Sam. (1967). *Seekers of Tomorrow: Masters of Modern Science Fiction.* New York: Ballantine.

Mosley, Leonard. (1978). *Dulles.* New York: Dial Press/James Wade.

Murray, Henry A. (1938). *Explorations in Personality.* New York: Oxford University Press.

Murray, Henry A. (1951). "In Nomine Diaboli." *New England Quarterly,* 24.

Murray, Henry A. (1981). *Endeavors in Psychology,* ed. E. S. Shneidman. New York: Harper & Row, 1981.

Murray, Henry A., ed. (1949). *Pierre, or, the Ambiguities,* by Herman Melville. New York: Hendricks House.

Nabokov, Nicolas. (1975). *Bagazh.* New York: Atheneum.

Nabokov, Vladimir. (1951). *Conclusive Evidence.* New York: Harper.

Nabokov, Vladimir. (1956). *Vesna v Fial'te.* New York: Chekhov.

Nabokov, Vladimir. (1958). *Lolita.* New York: Putnam.

Nabokov, Vladimir. (1958). *Nabokov's Dozen*. Garden City, N.Y.: Doubleday.

Nabokov, Vladimir. (1959). *Invitation to a Beheading*. New York: Putnam.

Nabokov, Vladimir. (1964). *The Defense*. New York: Putnam.

Nabokov, Vladimir. (1965). *The Eye*. New York: Phaedra.

Nabokov, Vladimir. (1966). *Despair*. New York: Putnam.

Nabokov, Vladimir. (1966). *Speak, Memory*. New York: Putnam.

Nabokov, Vladimir. (1966). *The Waltz Invention*. New York: Phaedra.

Nabokov, Vladimir. (1969). *Ada or Ardor: A Family Chronicle*. New York: McGraw-Hill.

Nabokov, Vladimir. (1971). "Rowe's Symbols." *New York Review of Books,* October 7.

Nabokov, Vladimir. (1973). *Strong Opinions*. New York: McGraw-Hill.

Niebuhr, Reinhold. (1958). "The Moral World of John Foster Dulles." *New Republic,* December 1.

Nunberg, H., and Federn, E., eds. (1962). *Minutes of the Vienna Psychoanalytic Society,* vol. 1. New York: International Universities Press.

Numberg, H., and Federn, E., eds. (1967). *Minutes of the Vienna Psychoanalytic Society,* vol. 2. New York: International Universities Press.

Ogilvie, Daniel M. (1984). "Personality and Paradox: Gordon Allport's Final Contribution." *Personality Forum, 2.*

Post, Jerrold M. (1991). "Saddam Hussein of Iraq: A Political Psychology Profile." *Political Psychology, 12.*

Post, Jerrold M. (1993). "The Defining Moment of Saddam's Life." In Stanley A. Renshon, ed., *The Political Psychology of the Gulf War*. Pittsburgh, Pa.: University of Pittsburgh Press.

Post, Jerrold M. (1993). "Current Concepts of the Narcissistic Personality: Implications for Political Psychology." *Political Psychology, 14.*

Pruessen, R. W. (1982). *John Foster Dulles: The Road to Power*. New York: Free Press.

Reti, Ladislao, ed. (1974). *The Unknown Leonardo*. New York: McGraw-Hill.

Rice, Emanuel. (1992). *Freud and Moses: The Long Journey Home*. Albany: State University of New York Press.

Richardson, R. N. (1964). *Colonel Edward M. House: The Texas Years*. Abilene, Tex.: Hardin-Simmons University.

Robert, Marthe. (1976). *From Oedipus to Moses: Freud's Jewish Identity*. New York: Doubleday.

Robins, Robert S., and Post, Jerrold. (1987). "The Paranoid Political Actor." *Biography, 10.*

Robinson, Forrest. (1992). *Love's Story Told*. Cambridge, Mass.: Harvard University Press.

Robinson, Kim Stanley. (1986). *The Planet on the Table*. New York: Tor.

Robinson, Kim Stanley. (1990). *Pacific Edge*. New York: Tor.

Robinson, Kim Stanley. (1991). *Remaking History*. New York: Tor.

Robinson, Kim Stanley. (1993). *Red Mars*. New York: Bantam.

Robinson, Kim Stanley. (1994). *Green Mars*. New York: Bantam.

Robinson, Robert. (1981). "The Last Interview." In Peter Quennell, ed., *Vladimir Nabokov: A Tribute*. New York: William Morrow.

Rodrigues, Eusebio L. (1973). "Reichianism in *Henderson the Rain King*." *Criticism, 15*.

Rose, Jacqueline. (1992). *The Haunting of Sylvia Plath*. Cambridge, Mass.: Harvard University Press.

Roth, Phyllis. (1982). "Toward the Man Behind the Mystification." In J. E. Rivers and C. Nicol, eds. *Nabokov's Fifth Arc*. Austin: University of Texas Press.

Rowe, William W. (1971). *Nabokov's Deceptive World*. New York: New York University Press.

Runyan, William McKinley. (1982). *Life Histories and Psychobiography: Explorations in Theory and Method*. New York: Oxford.

Runyan, William McKinley. (1988). "Progress in Psychobiography." In Dan P. McAdams and Richard L. Ochberg, eds., *Psychobiography and Life Narratives*. Durham, N.C.: Duke University Press.

Runyan, William McKinley. (1988). *Psychology and Historical Interpretation*. New York: Oxford University Press.

Safire, William. (1975). *Before the Fall*. New York: Doubleday. Belmont Tower Books reprint, New York, 1975.

Schepeler, Eva. (1990). "The Biographer's Transference: A Chapter in Psycho-biographical Epistemology." *Biography, 13*.

Schepeler, Eva. (1993). "Jean Piaget's Experiences on the Couch: Some Clues to a Mystery." *International Journal of Psycho-Analysis, 74*.

Schlenker, Barry, ed. (1985). *The Self and Social Life*. New York: McGraw-Hill.

Schlesinger, Arthur M., Jr. (1993). "The Perils of Pathography." *New Republic*, May 3.

Schultz, William T. (1993). *A Psychobiographical Inquiry into the Life, Mind, and Creative Work of James Agee*. Unpublished doctoral dissertation, University Of California, Davis.

Schur, Max. (1972). *Freud: Living and Dying*. New York: International Universities Press.

Sciolino, Elaine. (1991). *The Outlaw State: Saddam Hussein's Quest for Power and the Gulf Crisis*. New York: Wiley.

Shaver, Phillip R., and Hazan, Cindy. (1992). "Adult Romantic Attachment: Theory and Evidence." In D. Perlman and W. Jones, eds., *Advances in Personal Relationships, 4*.

Shearer, Lloyd. (1972). "Keep Your Eye on Al." *Parade,* August 20.

Sheehy, Gail. (1988). *Character: America's Search for Leadership*. New York: William Morrow.

Shute, Jenefer. (1984). "Nabokov and Freud: The Play of Power." *Modern Fiction Studies, 30*.

Silverberg, Robert, ed. (1970). *The Science Fiction Hall of Fame*, vol. 1. Garden City, N.Y.: Doubleday.

Simonton, Dean Keith. (1987). *Why Presidents Succeed: A Political Psychology of Leadership*. New Haven: Yale University Press.

Simonton, Dean Keith. (1990). *Psychology, Science, and History: An Introduction to Historiometry*. New Haven: Yale University Press.

Simonton, Dean Keith. (1993). "Putting the Best Leaders in the White House." *Political Psychology, 14*.

Simonton, Dean Keith. (1993). "Further Details on VOTER HELPER™ 1.0." *Political Psychology, 14*.

Simonton, Dean. (1994). *Greatness: Who Makes History and Why*. New York: Guilford.

Skinner, B. F. (1948). *Walden Two*. New York: Macmillan.

Skinner, B. F. (1967). "Autobiography." In E. G. Boring and G. Lindzey, eds., *A History of Psychology in Autobiography*, vol. 5. New York: Appleton-Century-Crofts.

Skinner, B. F. (1976). "Walden Two Revisited." In *Walden Two*, 2nd ed. New York: Macmillan.

Skinner, B. F. (1976). *Particulars of My Life*. New York: Knopf.

Skinner, B. F. (1979). *The Shaping of a Behaviorist*. New York: Knopf.

Smith, Arthur D. Howden. (1940). *Mr. House of Texas*. New York: Funk & Wagnalls.

Smith, Cordwainer. (1975). *Norstrilia*. New York: Ballantine/Del Rey.

Smith, Cordwainer. (1975). *The Best of Cordwainer Smith*. New York: Ballantine/Del Rey.

Smith, Cordwainer. (1993). *The Rediscovery of Man*, ed. James A. Mann. Framingham, Mass.: NESFA Press.

Sorensen, Theodore C. (1965). *Kennedy*. New York: Harper & Row.

Spence, Donald. (1982). *Narrative Truth and Historical Truth: Meaning and Interpretation in Psychoanalysis*. New York: Norton.

Spence, Janet T., and Helmreich, Robert L. (1978). *Masculinity and Femininity*. Austin: University of Texas Press.

Spitzer, Robert L.; Shodol, Andrew E.; Gibbon, Miriam; and Williams, Janet B. W. (1981). *DSM-III Case Book*. Washington, D.C.: American Psychiatric Association.

Stannard, David. (1980). *Shrinking History: On Freud and the Failure of Psychohistory*. New York: Oxford University Press.

Starr, Harvey. (1984). *Henry Kissinger: Perceptions of International Politics*. Lexington, Ky.: University Press of Kentucky.

Stegner, Page. (1966). *Escape into Aesthetics: The Art of Vladimir Nabokov*. New York: William Morrow. Apollo reprint, New York, 1969.

Stein, Benjamin. (1976). "If You Liked Richard Nixon, You'll Love Jimmy Carter." *Penthouse*, November.

Stewart, Alfred D. (1981). "Jack Williamson." In David Cowart and Thomas L. Wymer, eds., *Dictionary of Literary Biography*, vol. 8: *Twentieth Century American Science-Fiction Writers, Part 2*. Detroit: Gale.

Stolorow, Robert D., and Atwood, George E. (1979). *Faces in a Cloud: Subjectivity in Personality Theory*. New York: Aronson.

Strozier, Charles B., and Offer, Daniel, eds. (1985). *The Leader: Psychohistorical Essays*. New York: Plenum.

Sulloway, Frank. (1979). *Freud, Biologist of the Mind.* New York: Basic Books.

Swales, Peter. (1982). "Freud, Minna Bernays, and the Conquest of Rome." *New American Review,* Spring/Summer.

Thimmesch, Nick. (1973). "Chief of Staff." *Washington Post, Potomac Magazine* section, November 25.

Thoreau, Henry D. (1993). *Faith in a Seed.* Washington, D.C.: Island Press.

Tidd, Charles W. (1936). "Increasing Reality Acceptance by a Schizoid Personality during Analysis." *Bulletin of the Menninger Clinic, 1.*

Tiptree, James, Jr. (1990). *Her Smoke Rose Up Forever.* Sauk City, Wisc.: Arkham House.

Tomkins, Silvan S. (1987). "Script Theory." In J. Aronoff, A. I. Rabin, and R. Zucker, eds., *The Emergence of Personality.* New York: Springer.

Tomkins, Silvan S. (1988). "What Personology Needs as a Science." Paper presented at the Personology Society annual conference, Durham, N.C., June 18.

Trosman, Harry. (1985). *Freud and the Imaginative World.* Hillsdale, N.J.: Analytic Press.

U.S. News & World Report. (1992). *Triumph without Victory: The Unreported History of the Persian Gulf War.* New York: Times Books, 1992.

Wallace, Edwin R., IV. (1978–79). "Freud and Leonardo." *Psychiatric Forum, 8.*

Wallace, Edwin R., IV. (1985). *Historiography and Causation in Psychoanalysis.* Hillsdale, N.J.: Analytic Press.

Ward, Dana. (1975). "Kissinger: A Psychohistory." *History of Childhood Quarterly, 2.* Revised version in D. Caldwell, ed. (1983). *Henry Kissinger: His Personality and Policies.* Durham, N.C.: Duke University Press.

Wayne, Stephen J. (1993). "President Bush Goes to War: A Psychological Interpretation from a Distance." In Stanley A. Renshon, ed., *The Political Psychology of the Gulf War.* Pittsburgh, Pa.: University of Pittsburgh Press.

Wehr, Gerhard. (1987). *Jung: A Biography.* Boston: Shambhala.

Wehr, Gerhard. (1989). *An Illustrated Biography of C. G. Jung.* Boston: Shambhala.

Weinbaum, Stanley G. (1934). "A Martian Odyssey." *Wonder Stories,* July. Reprinted in Tom Shippey, ed. (1992). *The Oxford Book of Science Fiction Stories.* Oxford and New York: Oxford University Press.

Will, George. (1992). "The 'Truman Paradigm.'" *Newsweek,* September 7.

Williamson, Jack. (1937). "Under Psychoanalysis: A Patient Reviews the First Year." Unpublished manuscript, Williamson Collection, Golden Library, Eastern New Mexico University.

Williamson, Jack. (1940). "Darker Than You Think." *Unknown,* 4 (4), December.

Williamson, Jack. (1948). *Darker Than You Think.* Reading, Pa.: Fantasy Press.

Williamson, Jack. (1949). *The Humanoids.* New York: Simon & Schuster.

Williamson, Jack. (1951). *Dragon's Island.* New York: Simon & Schuster.

Williamson, Jack. (1975). *The Early Williamson.* Garden City, N.Y.: Doubleday. Sphere Books reprint, London, 1978.

Williamson, Jack. (1984). *Wonder's Child: My Life in Science Fiction.* New York: Bluejay Books.

Williamson, Jack. (1994). *Demon Moon*. New York: Tor.

Winter, David G. (1973). *The Power Motive*. New York: Free Press.

Winter, David G.; Hermann, Margaret G.; Weintraub, Walter; and Walker, Stephen G. (1991). "The Personalities of Bush and Gorbachev Measured at a Distance." *Political Psychology, 12.*

Winter, David G.; Hermann, Margaret G.; Weintraub, Walter; and Walker, Stephen G. (1991). "The Personalities of Bush and Gorbachev at a Distance: Follow-up on Predictions." *Political Psychology, 12.*

Woodward, Bob. (1987). *Veil: The Secret Wars of the CIA 1981–1987*. New York: Simon & Schuster. Pocket Books reprint, New York, 1988

Woodward, Bob. (1991). *The Commanders*. New York: Simon & Schuster. Pocket Books reprint, New York, 1992.

Wooster, Martin M. (1986). "Jack Williamson." In Curtis C. Smith, ed., *Twentieth-Century Science-Fiction Writers,* 2nd ed. Chicago: St. James Press.

Yerushalmi, Yosef Hayim. (1992). *Freud's Moses: Judaism Terminable and Interminable*. New Haven: Yale University Press.

Young-Bruehl, Elisabeth. (1988). *Anna Freud*. New York: Summit Books.

INDEX